Fruits Basket™

Volume 12

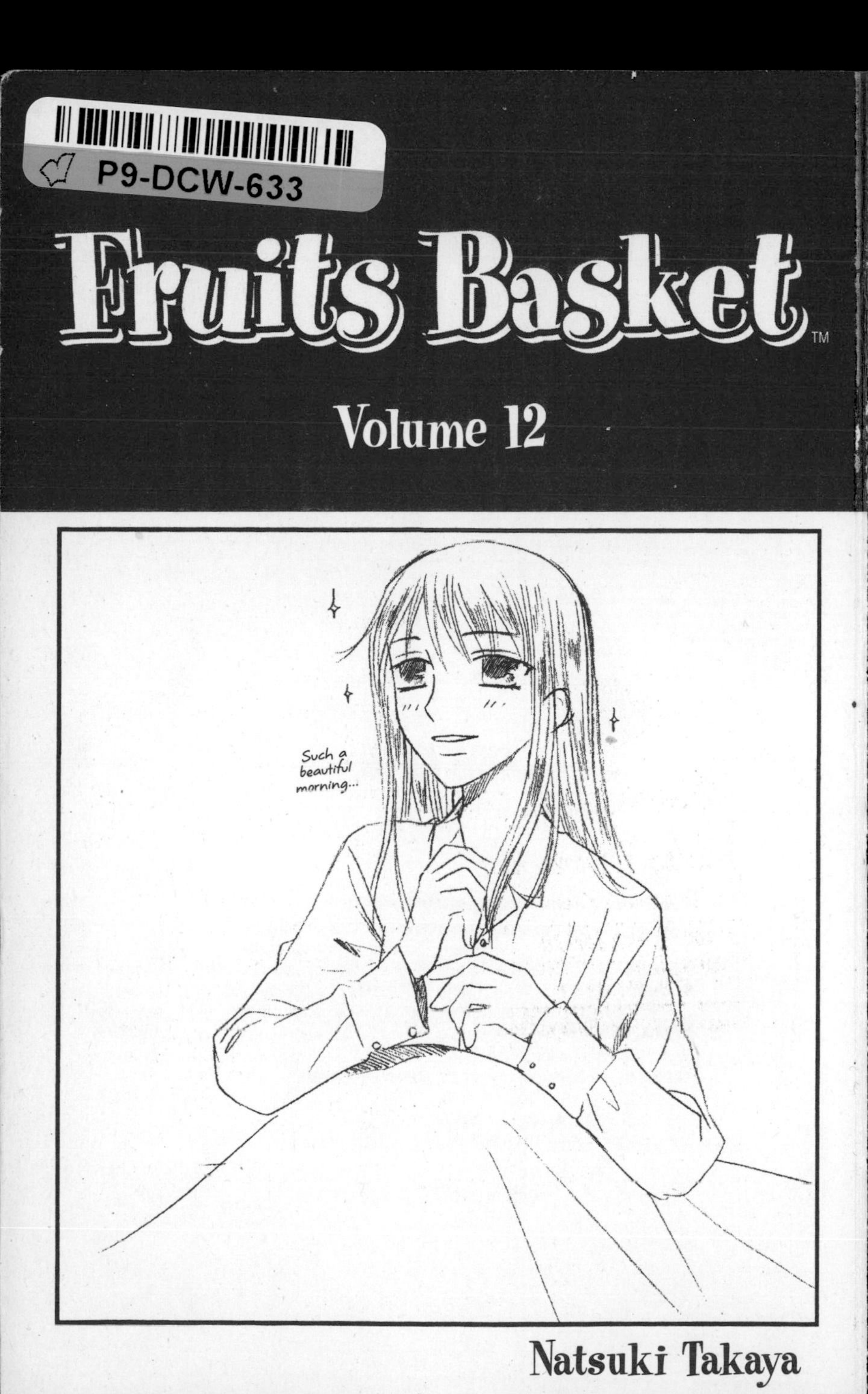
Such a beautiful morning...

Natsuki Takaya

Fruits Basket Vol. 12
Created by Natsuki Takaya

Translation - Alethea Nibley and Athena Nibley
English Adaptation - Jake Forbes
Contributing Writer - Adam Arnold
Associate Editor - Peter Ahlstrom
Retouch and Lettering - Deron Bennett
Production Artist - Jason Milligan
Cover Design - Christian Lownds

Editor - Paul Morrissey
Digital Imaging Manager - Chris Buford
Production Managers - Jennifer Miller and Mutsumi Miyazaki
Managing Editor - Lindsey Johnston
VP of Production - Ron Klamert
Publisher and E.I.C. - Mike Kiley
President and C.O.O. - John Parker
C.E.O. - Stuart Levy

A **TOKYOPOP**® Manga

TOKYOPOP Inc.
5900 Wilshire Blvd. Suite 2000
Los Angeles, CA 90036

E-mail: info@TOKYOPOP.com
Come visit us online at www.TOKYOPOP.com

ISBN: 1-59532-407-0

First TOKYOPOP printing: December 2005
10 9 8 7 6 5 4
Printed in the USA

Fruits Basket™

Volume 12

By
Natsuki Takaya

HAMBURG // LONDON // LOS ANGELES // TOKYO

Fruits Basket™

Table of Contents

STORY SO FAR...

Hello, I'm Tohru Honda and I have come to know a terrible secret. After the death of my mother, I was living by myself in a tent, when the Sohma family took me in. I soon learned that the Sohma family lives with a curse! Each family member is possessed by the vengeful spirit of an animal from the Chinese Zodiac. Whenever one of them becomes weak or is hugged by a member of the opposite sex, they change into their Zodiac animal!

TODAY I LEARNED A TERRIBLE THING! ONCE OUR SENIOR YEAR OF HIGH SCHOOL IS OVER, YUKI-KUN WILL HAVE TO RETURN TO THE SOHMA ESTATE AND KYO-KUN WILL BE CONFINED FOR LIFE! IT'S ALL PART OF THE SOHMA CURSE.
I KNOW I HAVE NO RIGHT TO INTERFERE WITH THE SOHMA FAMILY'S AFFAIRS, BUT I WANT TO HELP THEM WITH ALL OF MY HEART SO THAT THEY CAN KEEP SMILING...EVEN IF IT MEANS I'LL BE PUNISHED BY AKITO-SAN!
NOW, I WONDER WHAT I CAN DO TO BREAK THE SOHMA CURSE...?

Tohru Honda

The ever-optimistic hero of our story. An orphan, she now lives in Shigure's house, along with Yuki and Kyo, and is the only person outside of the family who knows the Sohma family's curse.

Yuki Sohma, the Rat

Soft-spoken. Self-esteem issues. At school he's called "Prince Yuki."

Kyo Sohma, the Cat

The Cat who was left out of the Zodiac. Hates Yuki, leeks and miso. But mostly Yuki.

Kagura Sohma, the Boar

Bashful, yet headstrong. Determined to marry Kyo, even if it kills him.

Fruits Basket Characters

Mabudachi Trio

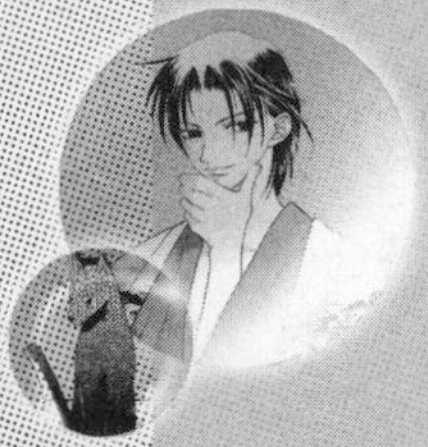

Shigure Sohma, the Dog

Enigmatic, mischievous and a little perverted. A popular novelist.

Hatori Sohma, the Dragon

Family doctor to the Sohmas. Only thing he can't cure is his broken heart.

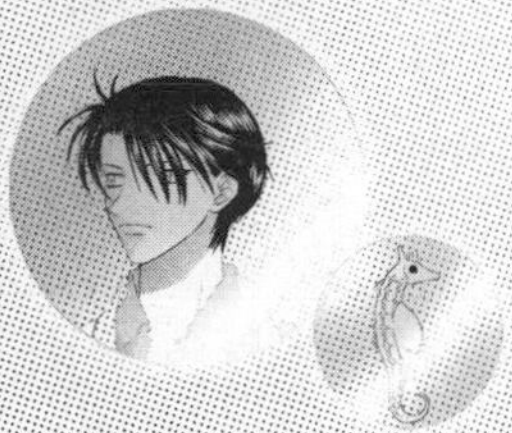

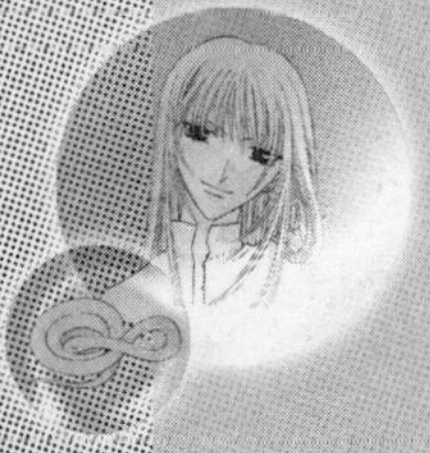

Ayame Sohma, the Snake

Yuki's older brother. A proud and playful drama queen…er, king. Runs a costume shop.

Saki Hanajima

"Hana-chan." Can sense people's "waves." Goth demeanor scares her classmates.

Arisa Uotani

"Uo-chan." A tough-talking "Yankee" who looks out for her friends.

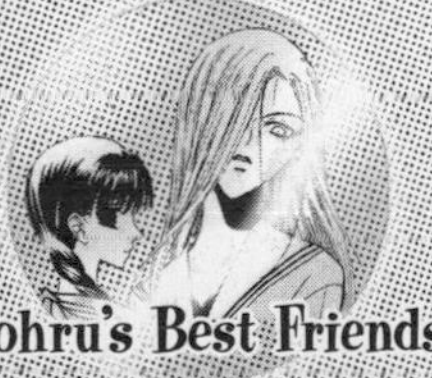

Tohru's Best Friends

Hiro Sohma, the Ram (or sheep)

This caustic tyke is skilled at throwing verbal barbs, but he has a soft spot for Kisa.

Momiji Sohma, the Rabbit

Half-German. He's older than he looks. Mother rejected him because of the Sohma curse.

Hatsuharu Sohma, the Ox

The nicest of guys, except when he goes "Black." Then you'd better watch out.

Kisa Sohma, the Tiger

Kisa became shy and self-conscious due to constant teasing by her classmates. Yuki, who has similar insecurities, feels particularly close to Kisa.

Fruits Basket Characters

Isuzu "Rin" Sohma, the Horse

She has the hots for Shigure...and Tohru leaves her rather cold. Rin is full of pride, and she can't stand the amount of deference the other Sohma family members give Akito.

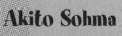

Ritsu Sohma, the Monkey

This shy kimono-wearing member of the Sohma family is gorgeous. But this "she" is really a he!! Crossdressing calms his nerves.

Akito Sohma

The head of the Sohma clan. A dark figure of many secrets. Treated with fear and reverence.

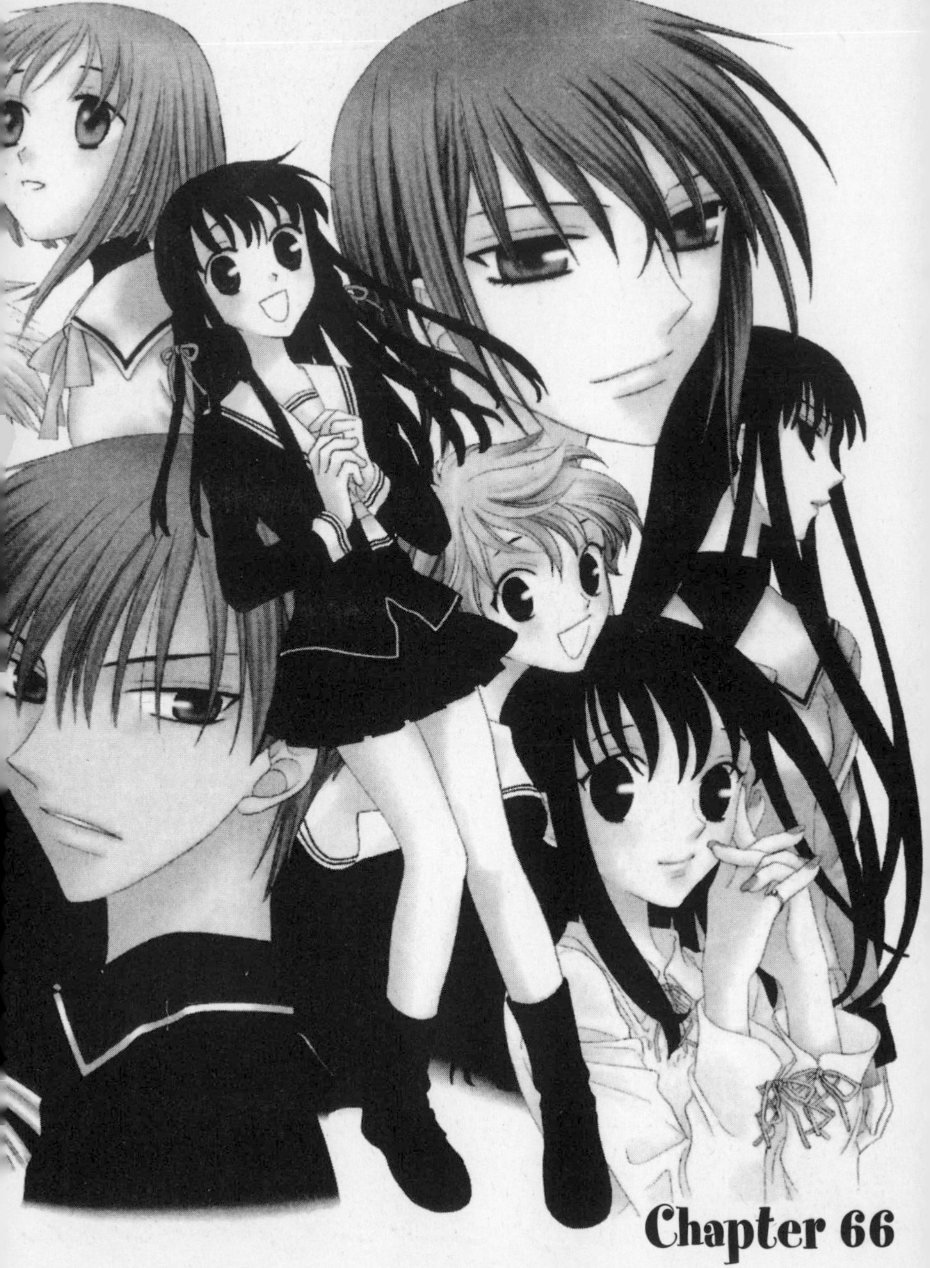

Chapter 66

Fruits Basket™

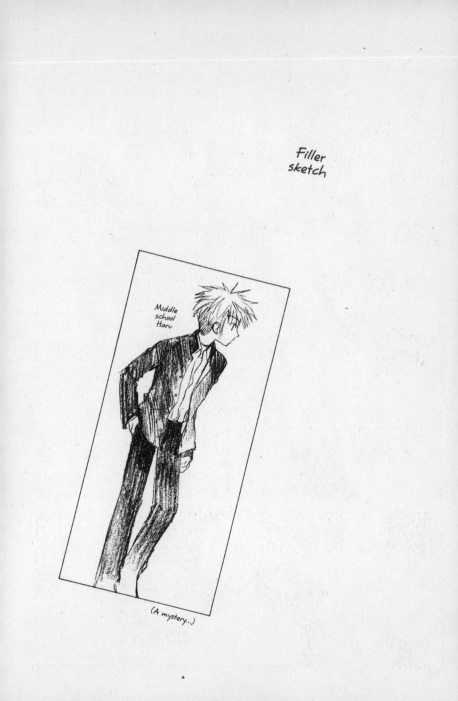

Filler sketch

Middle school Haru

(A mystery...)

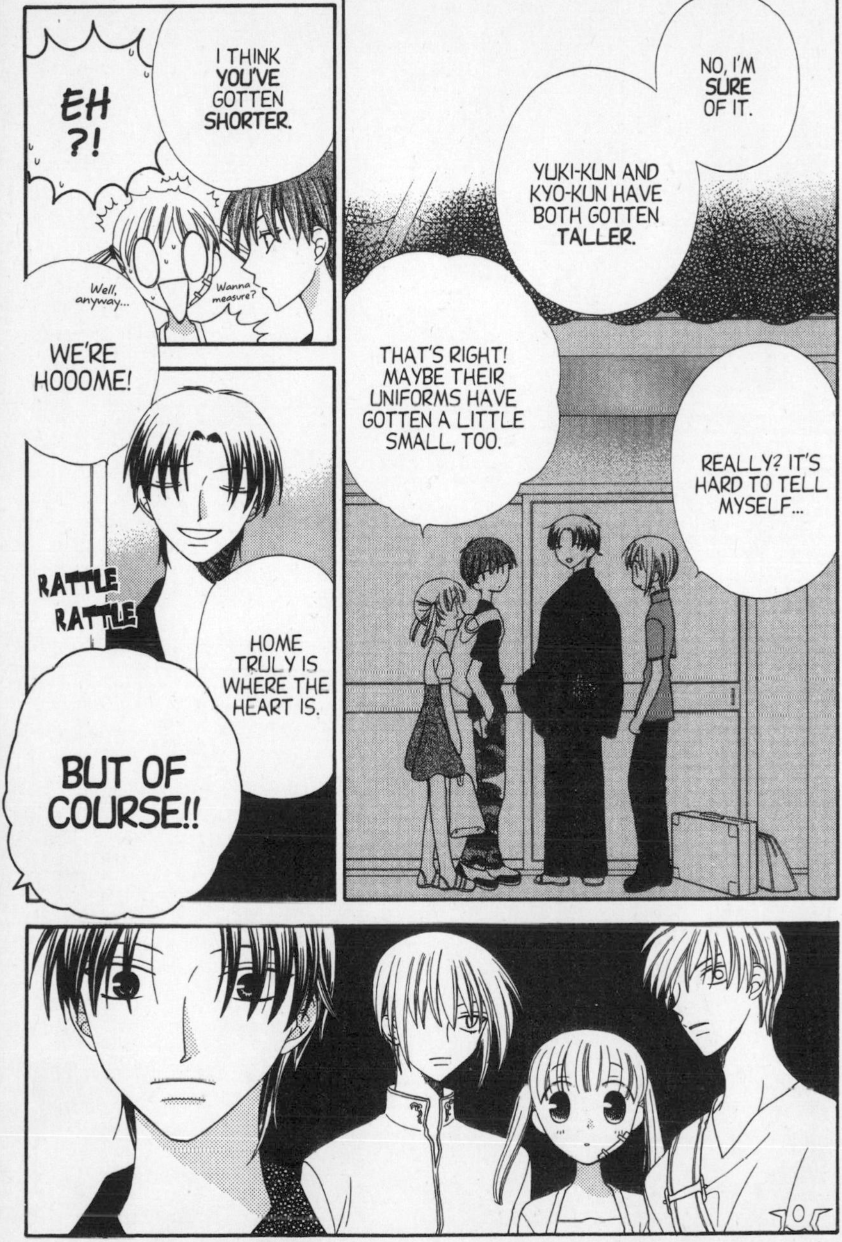

NO, I'M SURE OF IT.
YUKI-KUN AND KYO-KUN HAVE BOTH GOTTEN TALLER.
REALLY? IT'S HARD TO TELL MYSELF...
THAT'S RIGHT! MAYBE THEIR UNIFORMS HAVE GOTTEN A LITTLE SMALL, TOO.
I THINK YOU'VE GOTTEN SHORTER.
EH ?!
Wanna measure?
Well, anyway...
WE'RE HOOOME!
HOME TRULY IS WHERE THE HEART IS.
RATTLE RATTLE
BUT OF COURSE!!

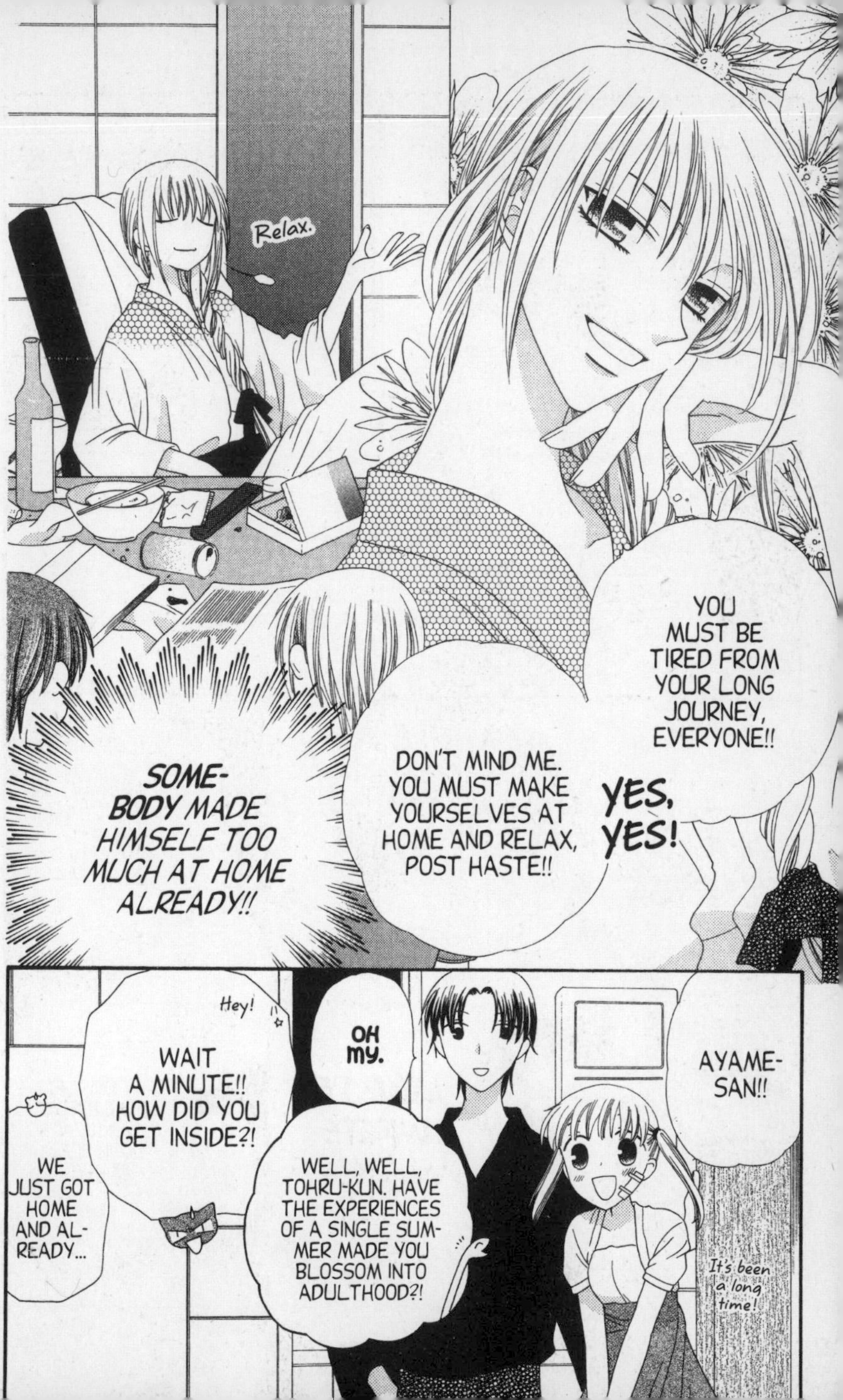
YOU MUST BE TIRED FROM YOUR LONG JOURNEY, EVERYONE!!
YES, YES!
DON'T MIND ME. YOU MUST MAKE YOURSELVES AT HOME AND RELAX, POST HASTE!!
Relax.
SOME-BODY MADE HIMSELF TOO MUCH AT HOME ALREADY!!
AYAME-SAN!!
It's been a long time!
OH my.
WELL, WELL, TOHRU-KUN. HAVE THE EXPERIENCES OF A SINGLE SUM-MER MADE YOU BLOSSOM INTO ADULTHOOD?!
Hey!
WAIT A MINUTE!! HOW DID YOU GET INSIDE?!
WE JUST GOT HOME AND AL-READY...

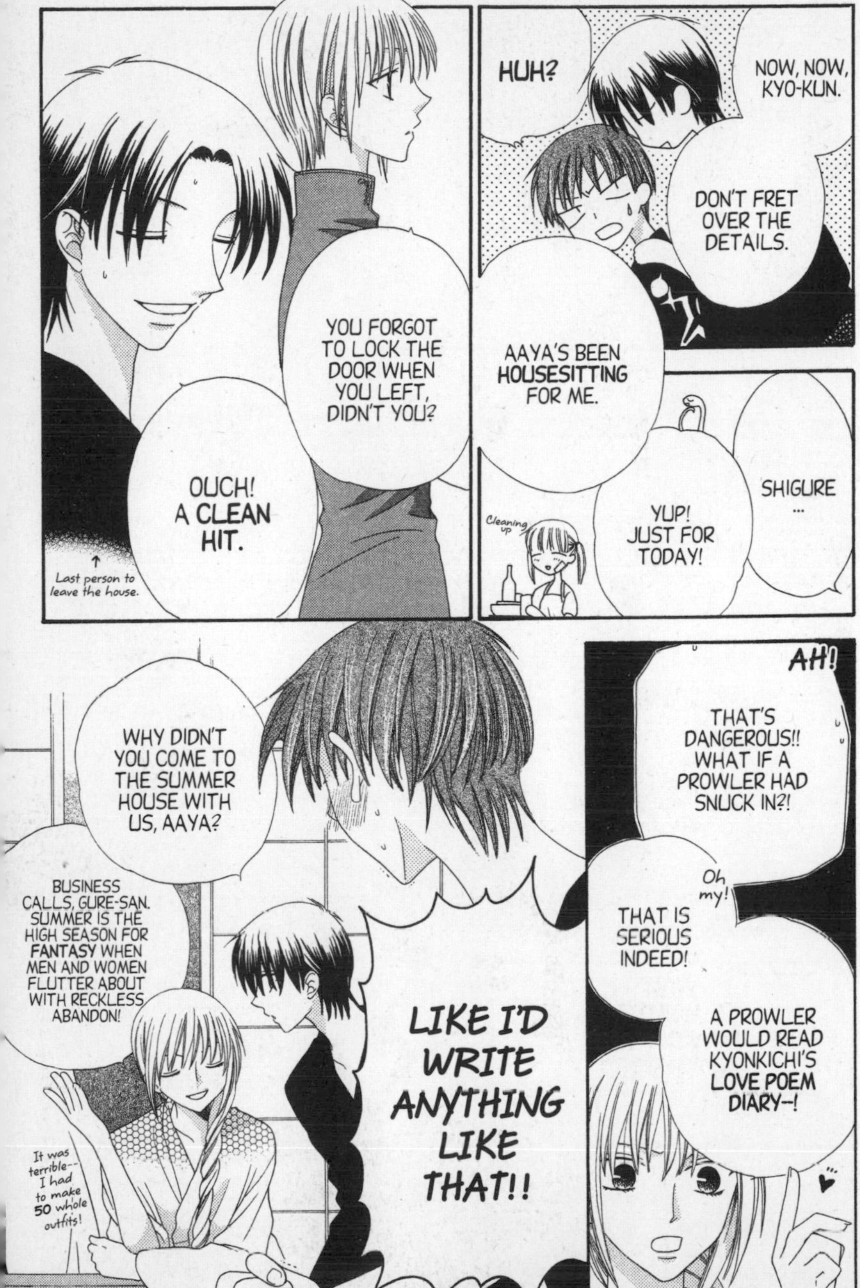
NOW, NOW, KYO-KUN.
HUH?
DON'T FRET OVER THE DETAILS.
AAYA'S BEEN HOUSESITTING FOR ME.
SHIGURE...
YUP! JUST FOR TODAY!
Cleaning up
YOU FORGOT TO LOCK THE DOOR WHEN YOU LEFT, DIDN'T YOU?
OUCH! A CLEAN HIT.
Last person to leave the house.
AH!
THAT'S DANGEROUS!! WHAT IF A PROWLER HAD SNUCK IN?!
Oh my!
THAT IS SERIOUS INDEED!
A PROWLER WOULD READ KYONKICHI'S LOVE POEM DIARY--!
LIKE I'D WRITE ANYTHING LIKE THAT!!
WHY DIDN'T YOU COME TO THE SUMMER HOUSE WITH US, AAYA?
BUSINESS CALLS, GURE-SAN. SUMMER IS THE HIGH SEASON FOR FANTASY WHEN MEN AND WOMEN FLUTTER ABOUT WITH RECKLESS ABANDON!
It was terrible-- I had to make 50 whole outfits!

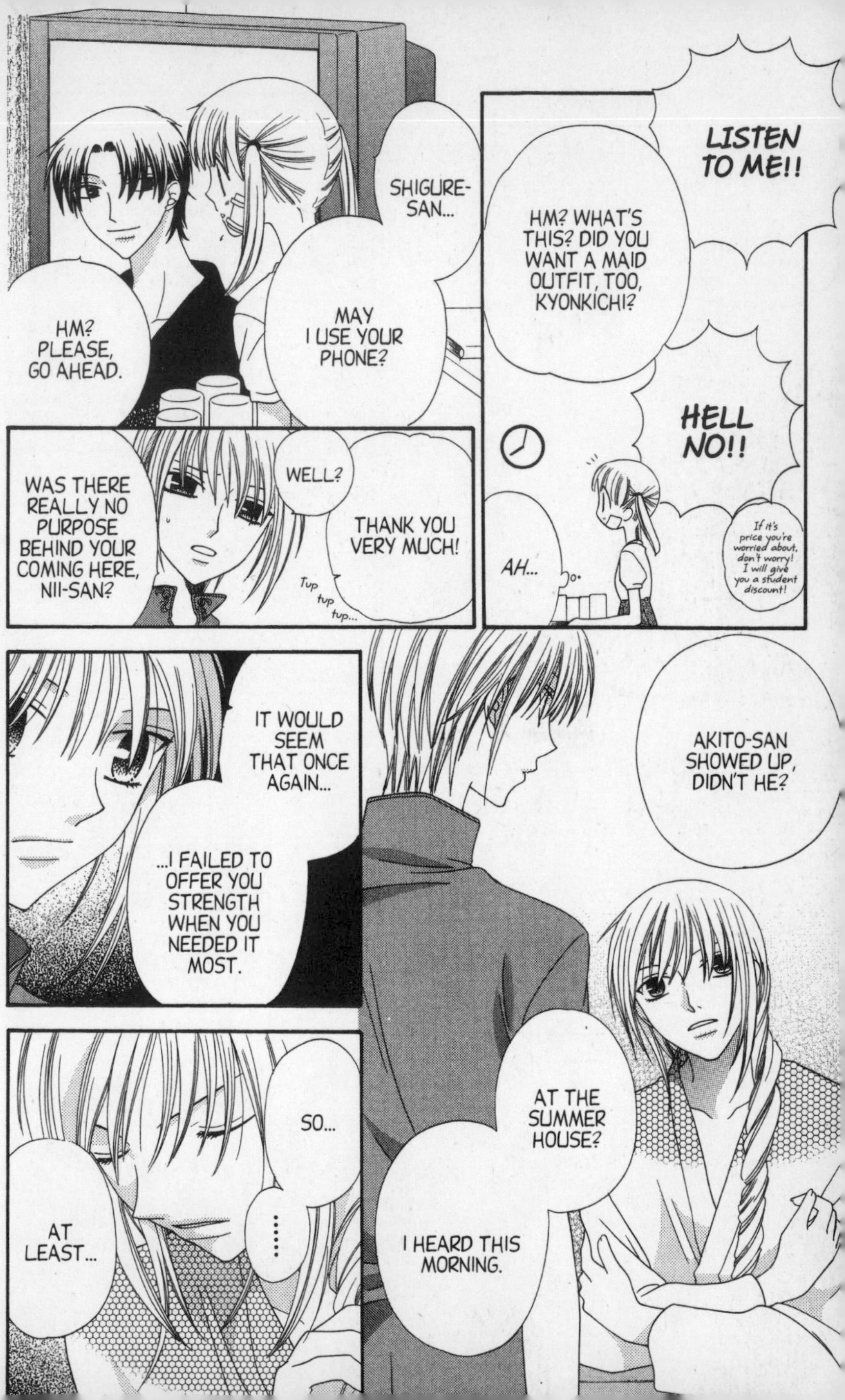
LISTEN TO ME!!
HM? WHAT'S THIS? DID YOU WANT A MAID OUTFIT, TOO, KYONKICHI?
HELL NO!!
If it's price you're worried about, don't worry! I will give you a student discount!
AH...
SHIGURE-SAN...
MAY I USE YOUR PHONE?
HM? PLEASE, GO AHEAD.
THANK YOU VERY MUCH!
Tup tup tup...
WELL?
WAS THERE REALLY NO PURPOSE BEHIND YOUR COMING HERE, NII-SAN?
AKITO-SAN SHOWED UP, DIDN'T HE?
AT THE SUMMER HOUSE?
I HEARD THIS MORNING.
IT WOULD SEEM THAT ONCE AGAIN...
...I FAILED TO OFFER YOU STRENGTH WHEN YOU NEEDED IT MOST.
SO...
......
AT LEAST...

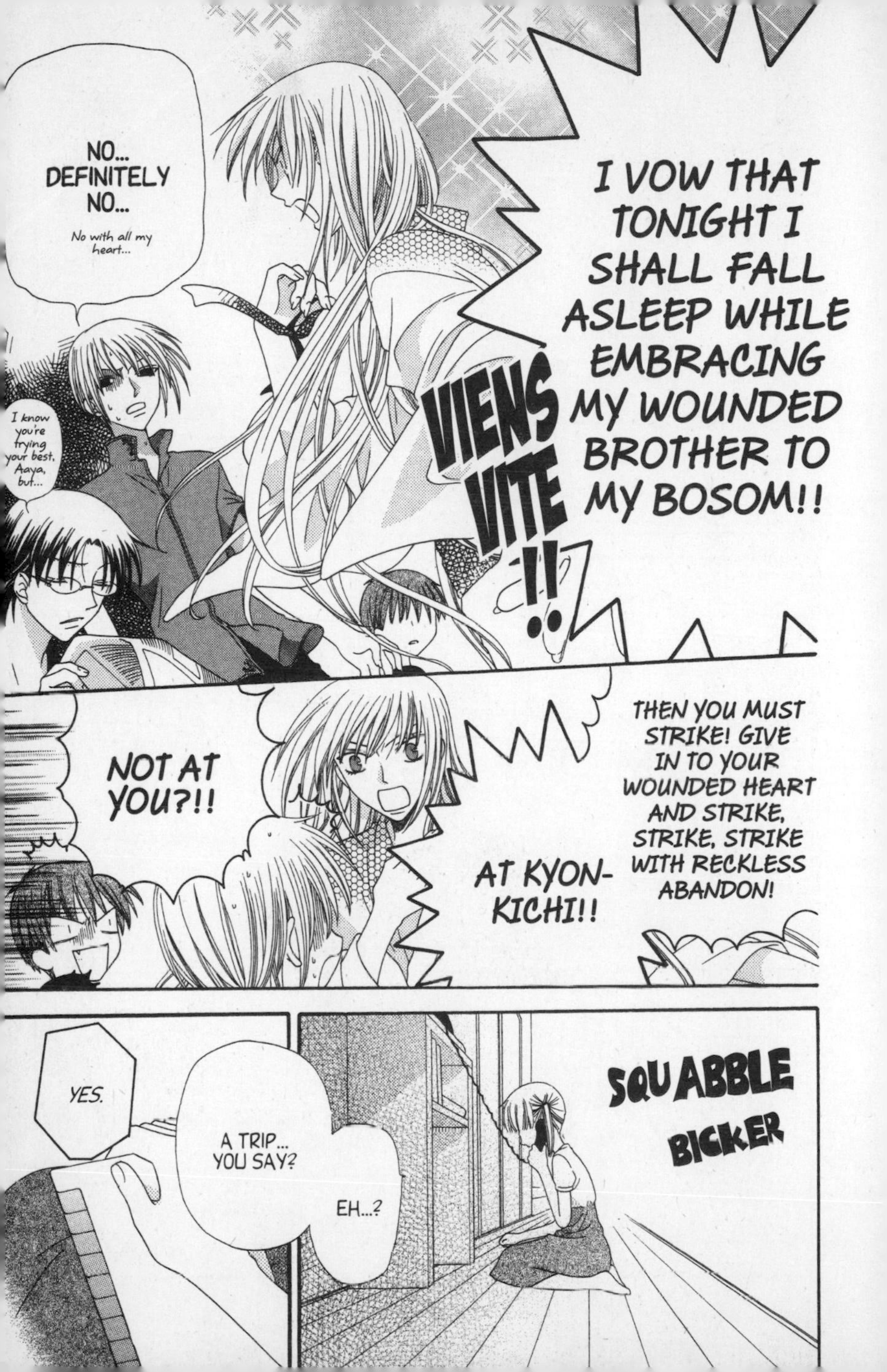
I VOW THAT TONIGHT I SHALL FALL ASLEEP WHILE EMBRACING MY WOUNDED BROTHER TO MY BOSOM!!
VIENS VITE!!
NO... DEFINITELY NO...
No with all my heart...
I know you're trying your best, Aaya, but...
THEN YOU MUST STRIKE! GIVE IN TO YOUR WOUNDED HEART AND STRIKE, STRIKE, STRIKE WITH RECKLESS ABANDON!
AT KYON-KICHI!!
NOT AT YOU?!!
SQUABBLE
BICKER
EH...?
A TRIP... YOU SAY?
YES.

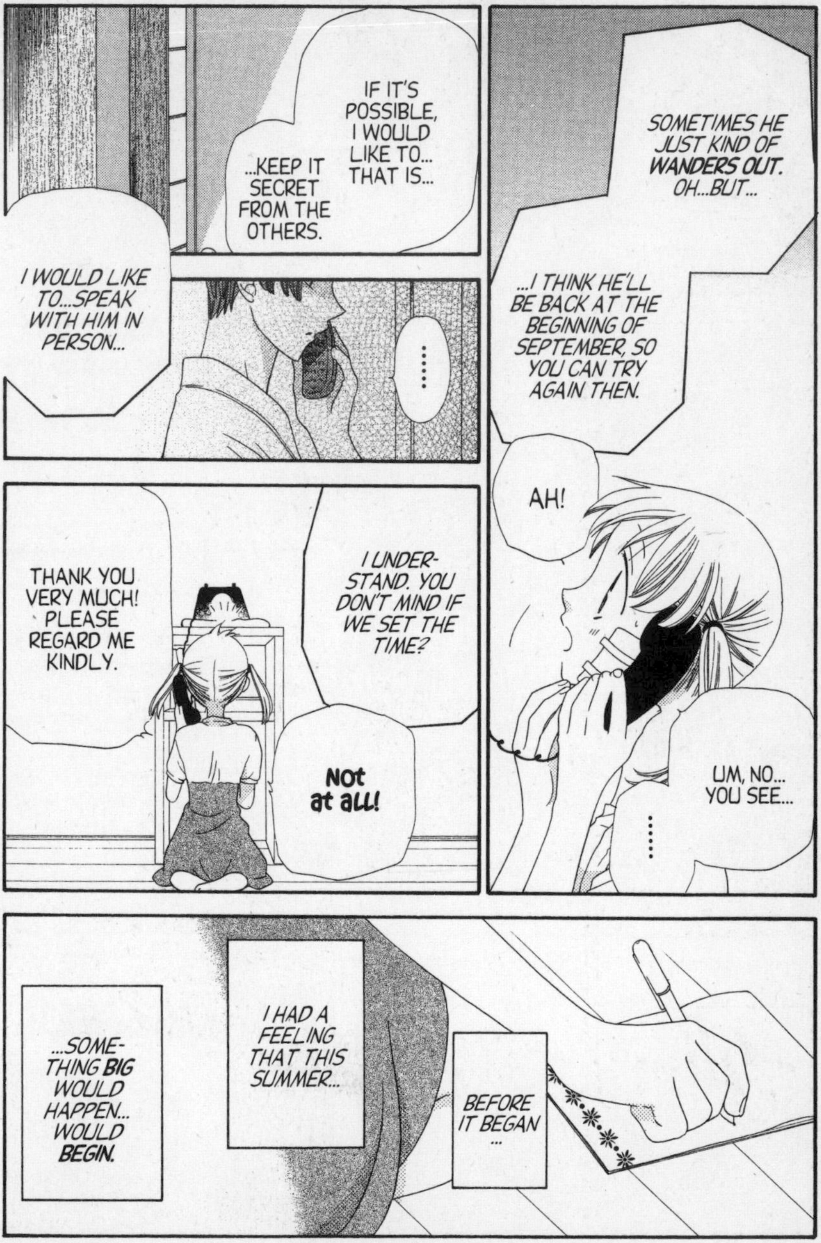
SOMETIMES HE JUST KIND OF **WANDERS OUT.** OH...BUT...
...I THINK HE'LL BE BACK AT THE BEGINNING OF SEPTEMBER, SO YOU CAN TRY AGAIN THEN.
AH!
UM, NO... YOU SEE...
......
IF IT'S POSSIBLE, I WOULD LIKE TO... THAT IS...
...KEEP IT SECRET FROM THE OTHERS.
I WOULD LIKE TO...SPEAK WITH HIM IN PERSON...
......
I UNDER-STAND. YOU DON'T MIND IF WE SET THE TIME?
Not at all!
THANK YOU VERY MUCH! PLEASE REGARD ME KINDLY.
BEFORE IT BEGAN...
I HAD A FEELING THAT THIS SUMMER...
...SOME-THING **BIG** WOULD HAPPEN... WOULD **BEGIN.**

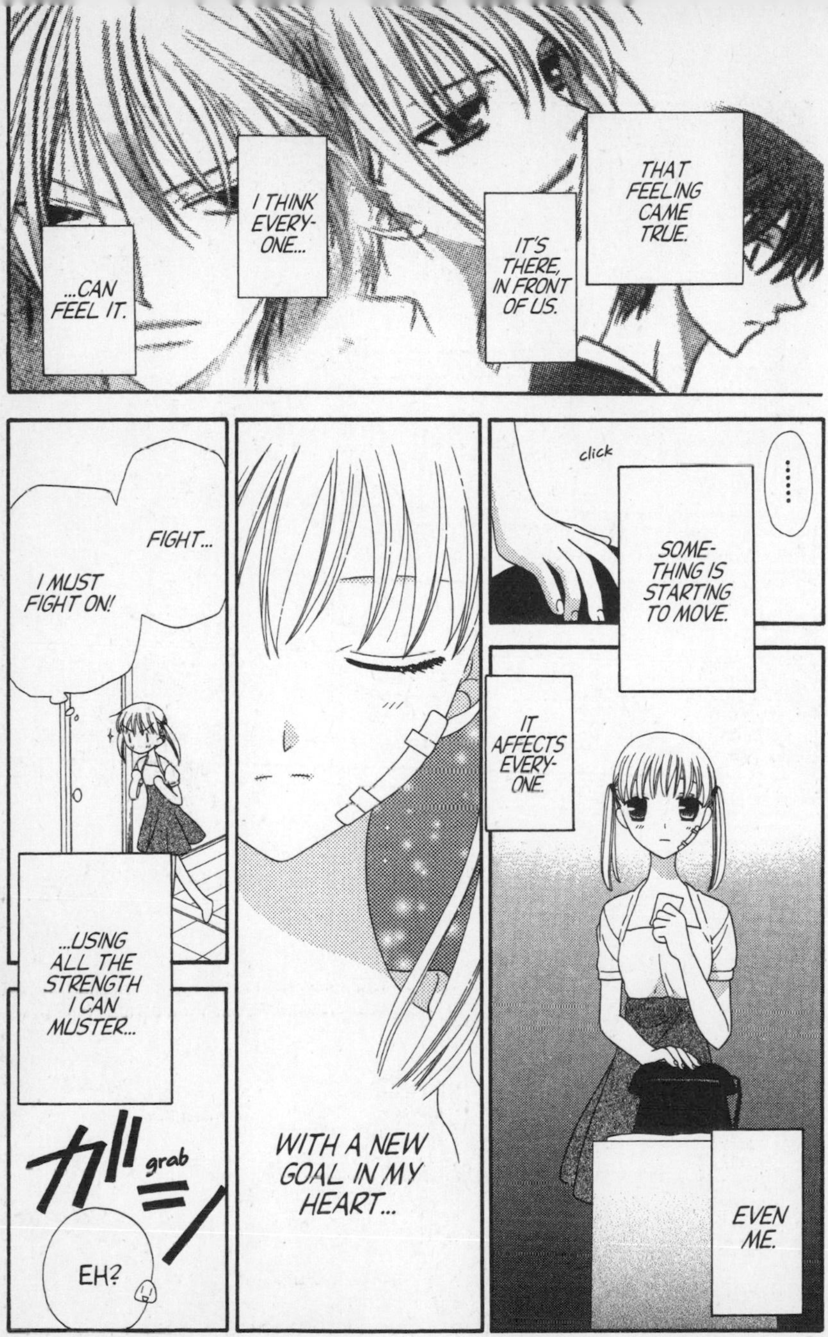
THAT FEELING CAME TRUE.
IT'S THERE, IN FRONT OF US.
I THINK EVERY-ONE...
...CAN FEEL IT.
......
click
SOME-THING IS STARTING TO MOVE.
IT AFFECTS EVERY-ONE.
EVEN ME.
WITH A NEW GOAL IN MY HEART...
FIGHT...
I MUST FIGHT ON!
...USING ALL THE STRENGTH I CAN MUSTER...
grab
EH?

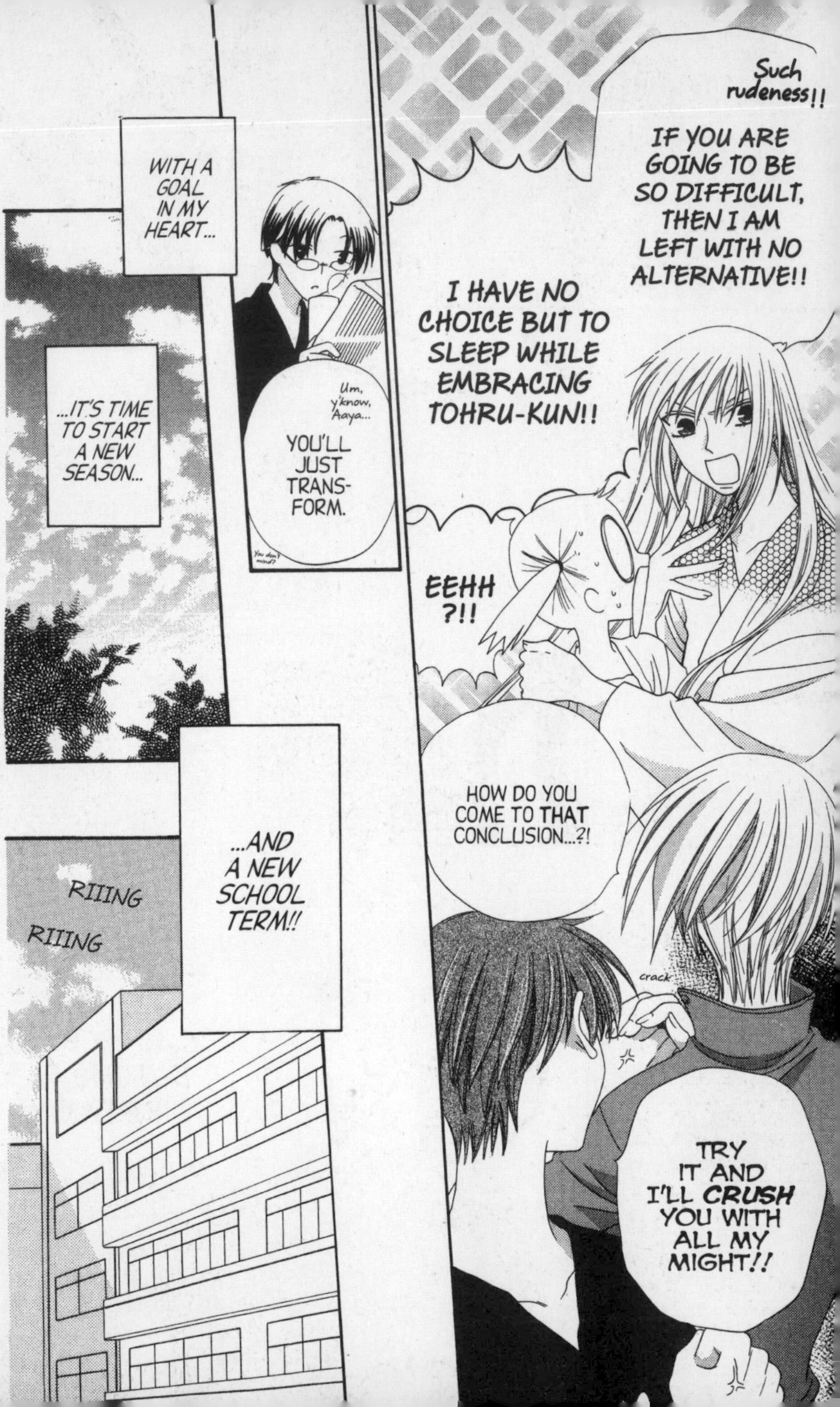
Such rudeness!!
IF YOU ARE GOING TO BE SO DIFFICULT, THEN I AM LEFT WITH NO ALTERNATIVE!!
I HAVE NO CHOICE BUT TO SLEEP WHILE EMBRACING TOHRU-KUN!!
EEHH ?!!
HOW DO YOU COME TO THAT CONCLUSION...?!
crack
TRY IT AND I'LL CRUSH YOU WITH ALL MY MIGHT!!
Um, y'know, Aaya...
YOU'LL JUST TRANS- FORM.
You don't mind?
WITH A GOAL IN MY HEART...
...IT'S TIME TO START A NEW SEASON...
...AND A NEW SCHOOL TERM!!
RIIING
RIIING

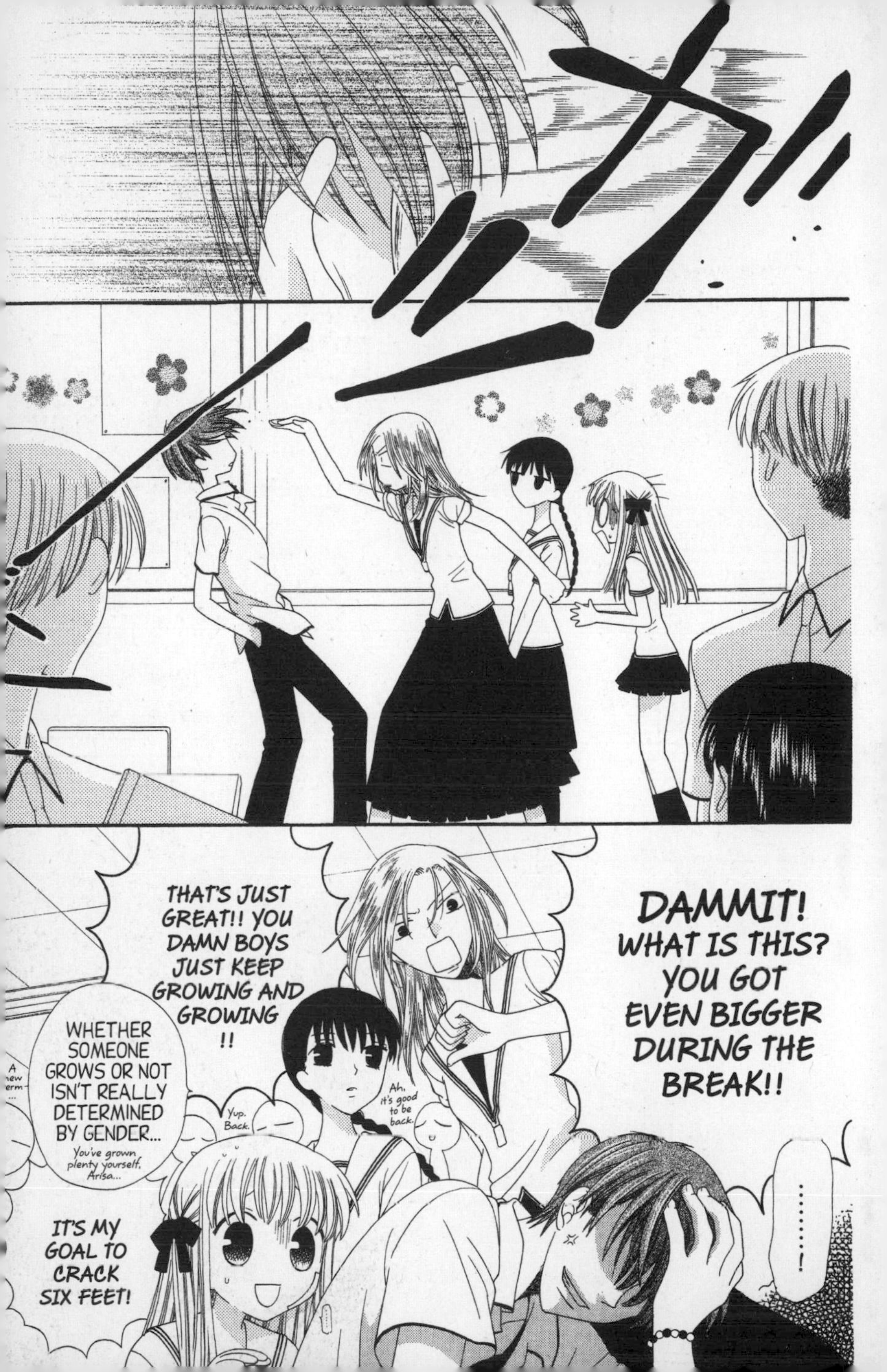
DAMMIT! WHAT IS THIS? YOU GOT EVEN BIGGER DURING THE BREAK!!
......!
THAT'S JUST GREAT!! YOU DAMN BOYS JUST KEEP GROWING AND GROWING !!
Ah, it's good to be back.
Yup. Back.
WHETHER SOMEONE GROWS OR NOT ISN'T REALLY DETERMINED BY GENDER...
You've grown plenty yourself, Arisa...
IT'S MY GOAL TO CRACK SIX FEET!

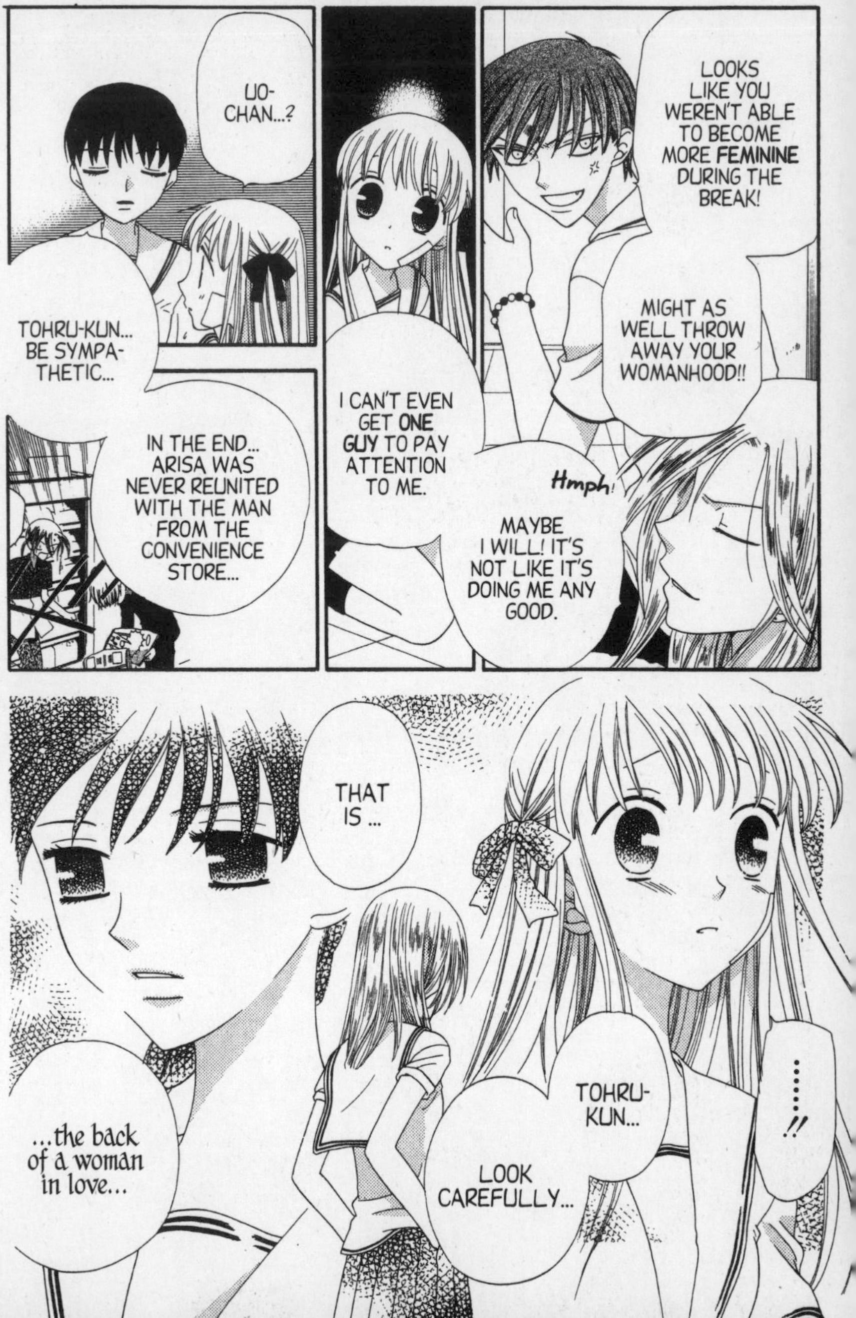
LOOKS LIKE YOU WEREN'T ABLE TO BECOME MORE FEMININE DURING THE BREAK!
MIGHT AS WELL THROW AWAY YOUR WOMANHOOD!!
Hmph!
MAYBE I WILL! IT'S NOT LIKE IT'S DOING ME ANY GOOD.
I CAN'T EVEN GET ONE GUY TO PAY ATTENTION TO ME.
UO-CHAN...?
TOHRU-KUN... BE SYMPATHETIC...
IN THE END... ARISA WAS NEVER REUNITED WITH THE MAN FROM THE CONVENIENCE STORE...
......!!
TOHRU-KUN...
LOOK CAREFULLY...
THAT IS ...
...the back of a woman in love...

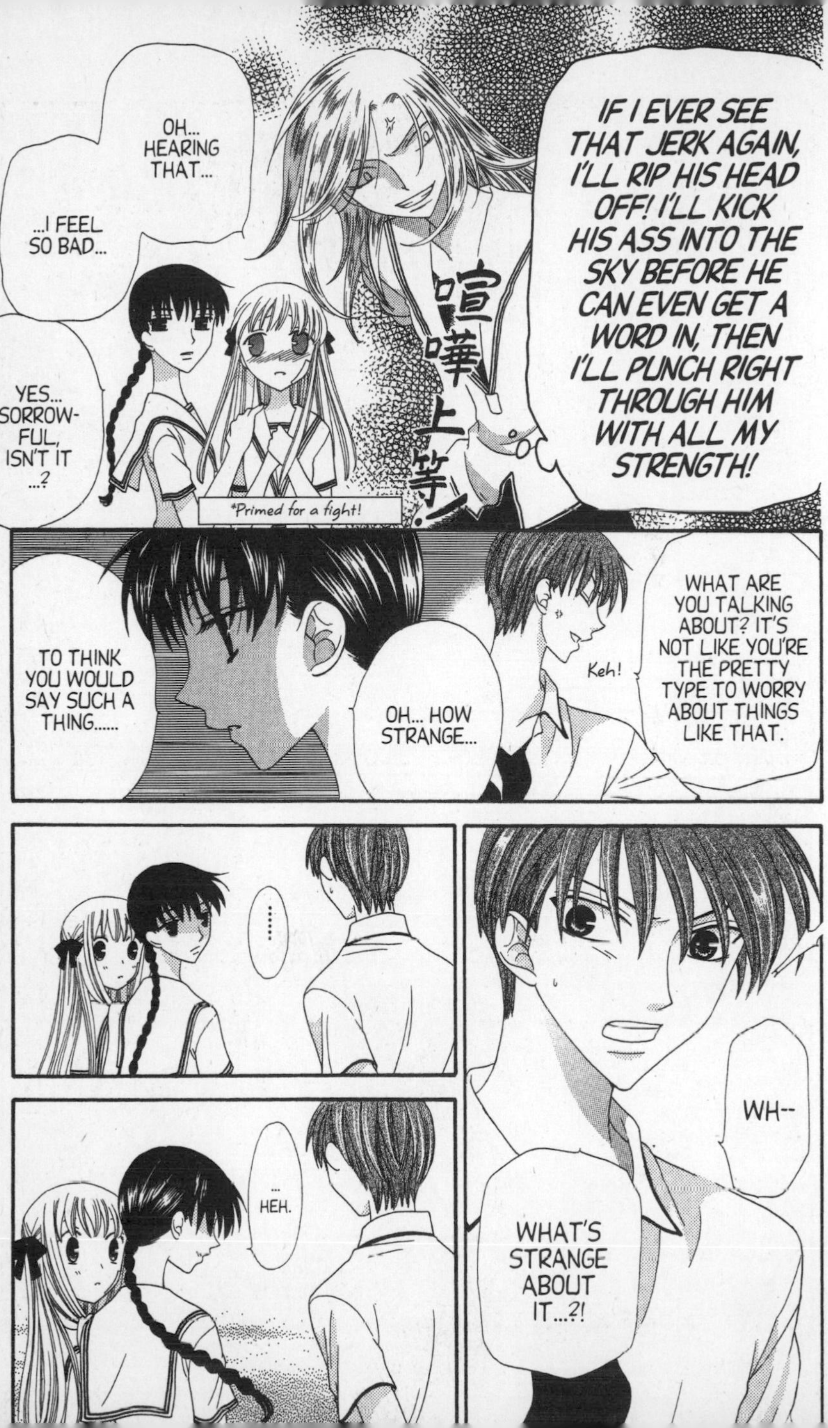
IF I EVER SEE THAT JERK AGAIN, I'LL RIP HIS HEAD OFF! I'LL KICK HIS ASS INTO THE SKY BEFORE HE CAN EVEN GET A WORD IN, THEN I'LL PUNCH RIGHT THROUGH HIM WITH ALL MY STRENGTH!
喧嘩上等!
*Primed for a fight!
OH... HEARING THAT...
...I FEEL SO BAD...
YES... SORROWFUL, ISN'T IT ...?
WHAT ARE YOU TALKING ABOUT? IT'S NOT LIKE YOU'RE THE PRETTY TYPE TO WORRY ABOUT THINGS LIKE THAT.
Keh!
OH... HOW STRANGE...
TO THINK YOU WOULD SAY SUCH A THING......
WH--
WHAT'S STRANGE ABOUT IT...?!
......
...HEH.

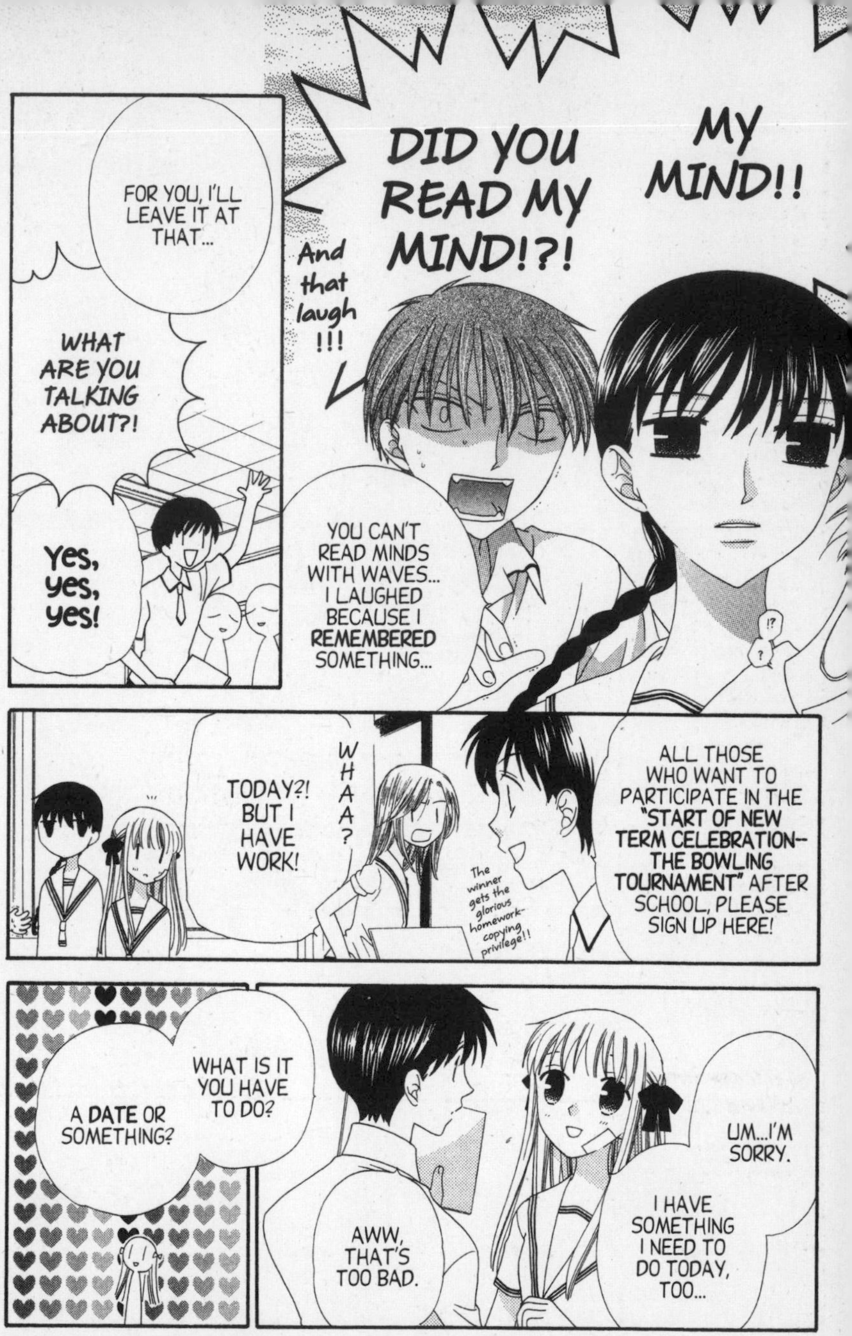
MY MIND!!
DID YOU READ MY MIND!?!
And that laugh!!!
!?
?
YOU CAN'T READ MINDS WITH WAVES... I LAUGHED BECAUSE I **REMEMBERED** SOMETHING...
FOR YOU, I'LL LEAVE IT AT THAT...
WHAT ARE YOU TALKING ABOUT?!
Yes, yes, yes!
ALL THOSE WHO WANT TO PARTICIPATE IN THE **"START OF NEW TERM CELEBRATION-- THE BOWLING TOURNAMENT"** AFTER SCHOOL, PLEASE SIGN UP HERE!
The winner gets the glorious homework-copying privilege!!
WHAAA?
TODAY?! BUT I HAVE WORK!
UM...I'M SORRY.
I HAVE SOMETHING I NEED TO DO TODAY, TOO...
AWW, THAT'S TOO BAD.
WHAT IS IT YOU HAVE TO DO?
A **DATE** OR SOMETHING?

Fruits Basket 12
Part 1:

Hajimemashite and konnichiwa! I'm Takaya. Are you doing well? I have a cold with a slight fever, so I have even less time than usual. Grroooan...
If you please. This is Furuba volume 12. 12... That's amazing! Ah, for those of you who are reading for the first time starting with 12, I wonder if you thought that Ritsu, who's on the cover, was a woman?
I understand that there were some people who thought Aaya on volume 9 was a woman, so I think it's quite likely. Somehow, I didn't hesitate to let him wear a furisode*. So, without further ado...

Let's continue volume 12!

* formal long-sleeved kimono worn by unmarried women

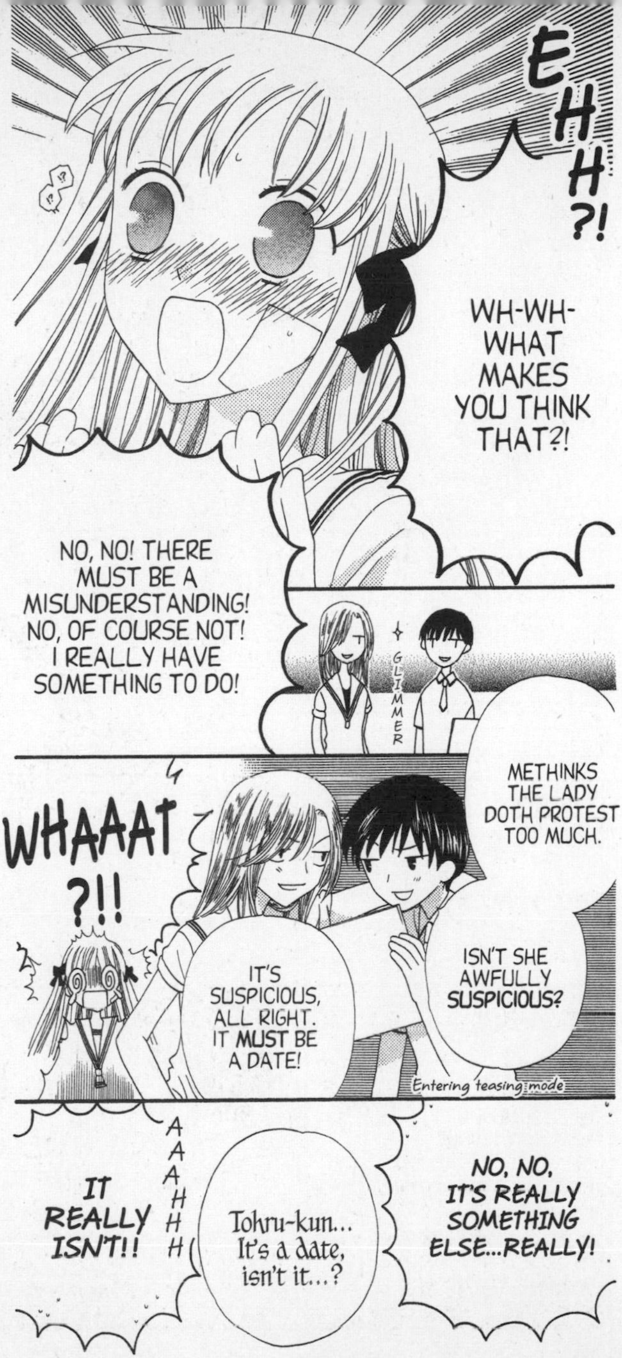
EHH?!
!? !?
WH-WH-WHAT MAKES YOU THINK THAT?!
NO, NO! THERE MUST BE A MISUNDERSTANDING! NO, OF COURSE NOT! I REALLY HAVE SOMETHING TO DO!
GLIMMER
METHINKS THE LADY DOTH PROTEST TOO MUCH.
ISN'T SHE AWFULLY SUSPICIOUS?
IT'S SUSPICIOUS, ALL RIGHT. IT MUST BE A DATE!
WHAAAT ?!!
Entering teasing mode
NO, NO, IT'S REALLY SOMETHING ELSE...REALLY!
Tohru-kun... It's a date, isn't it...?
AAAHHH
IT REALLY ISN'T!!

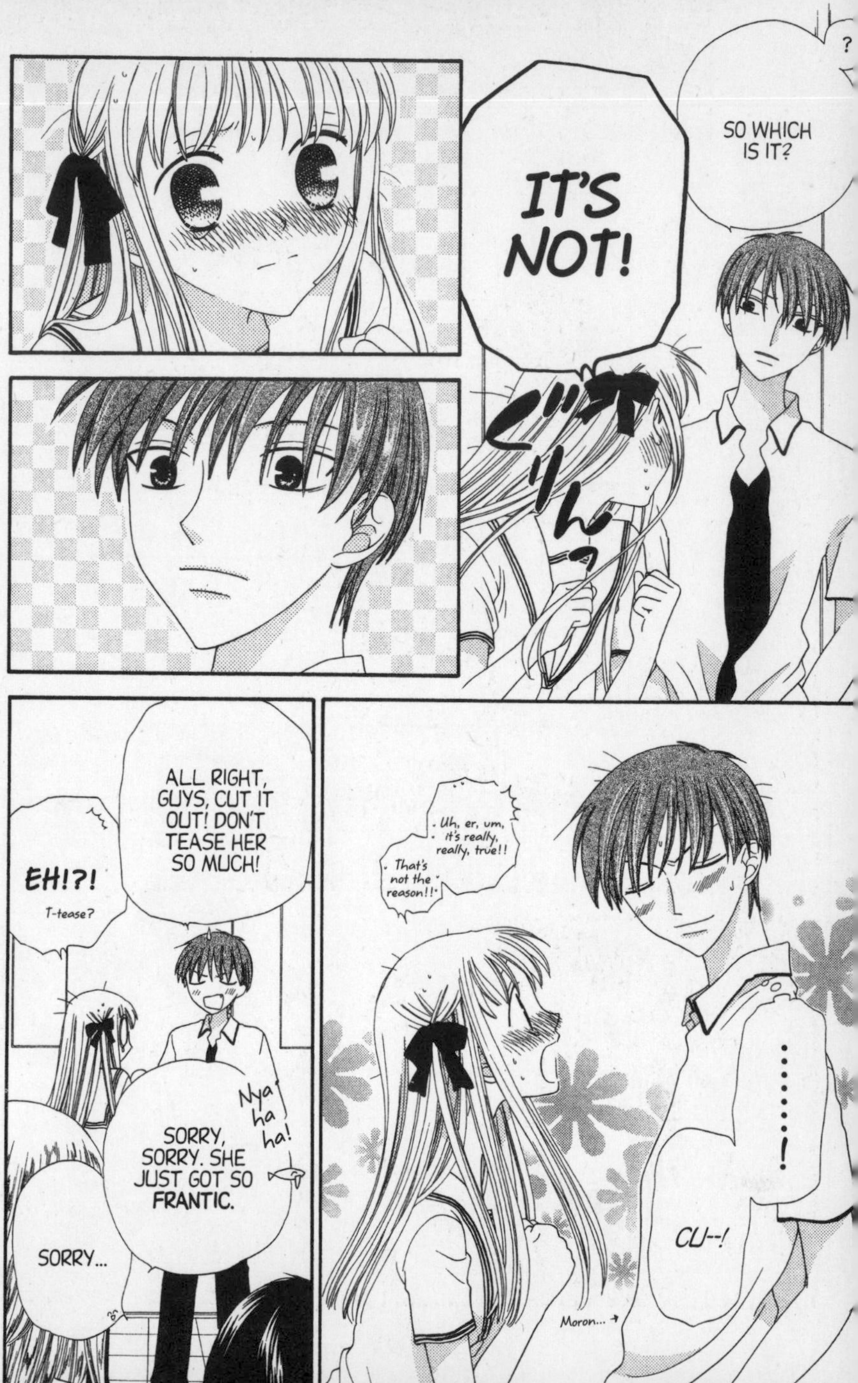
?
SO WHICH IS IT?
IT'S NOT!
ぐりんっ
Uh, er, um, it's really, really, true!!
That's not the reason!!
......!
CU--!
Moron...
ALL RIGHT, GUYS, CUT IT OUT! DON'T TEASE HER SO MUCH!
EH!?!
T-tease?
Nya ha ha!
SORRY, SORRY. SHE JUST GOT SO FRANTIC.
SORRY...

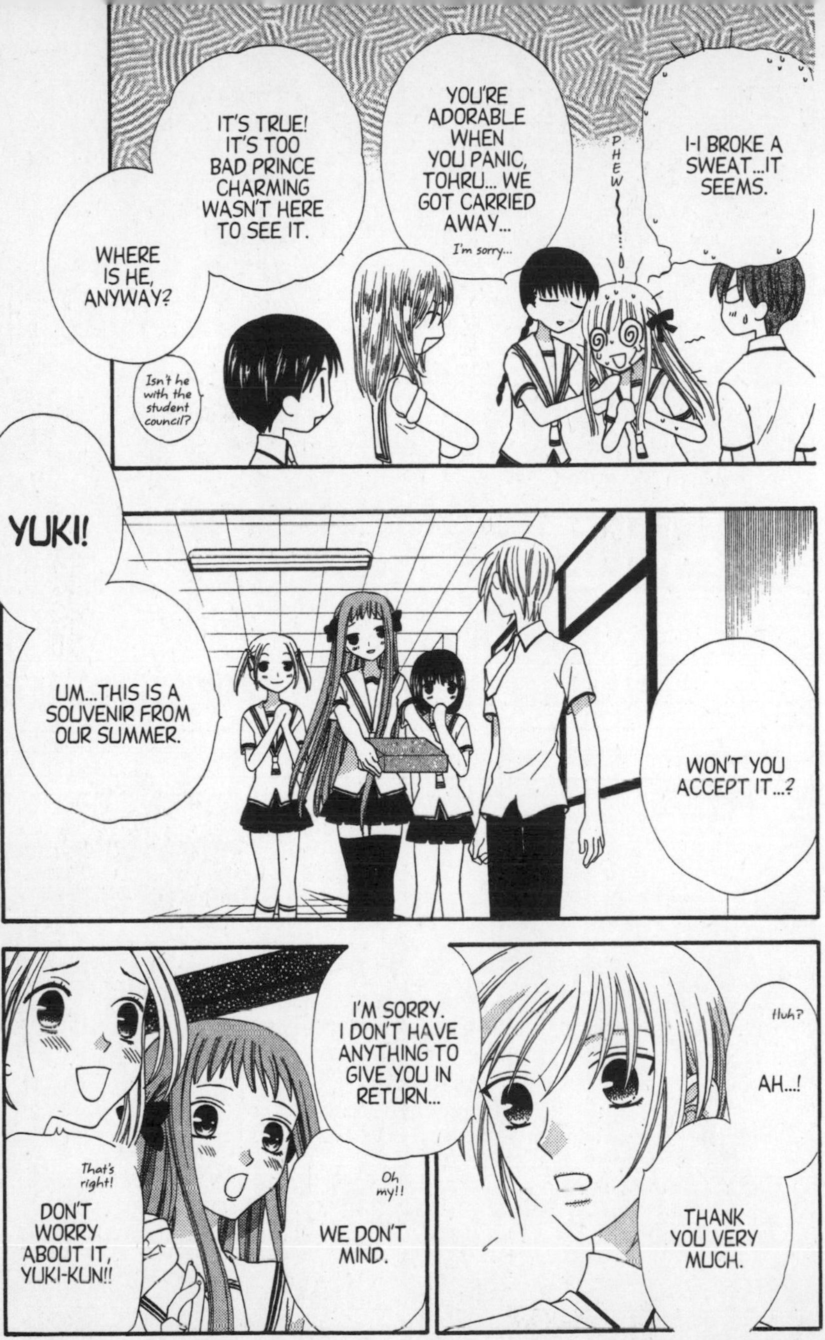
I-I BROKE A SWEAT...IT SEEMS.
PHEW~~...
YOU'RE ADORABLE WHEN YOU PANIC, TOHRU... WE GOT CARRIED AWAY...
I'm sorry...
IT'S TRUE! IT'S TOO BAD PRINCE CHARMING WASN'T HERE TO SEE IT.
WHERE IS HE, ANYWAY?
Isn't he with the student council?
YUKI!
UM...THIS IS A SOUVENIR FROM OUR SUMMER.
WON'T YOU ACCEPT IT...?
Huh?
AH...!
THANK YOU VERY MUCH.
I'M SORRY. I DON'T HAVE ANYTHING TO GIVE YOU IN RETURN...
Oh my!!
WE DON'T MIND.
That's right!
DON'T WORRY ABOUT IT, YUKI-KUN!!

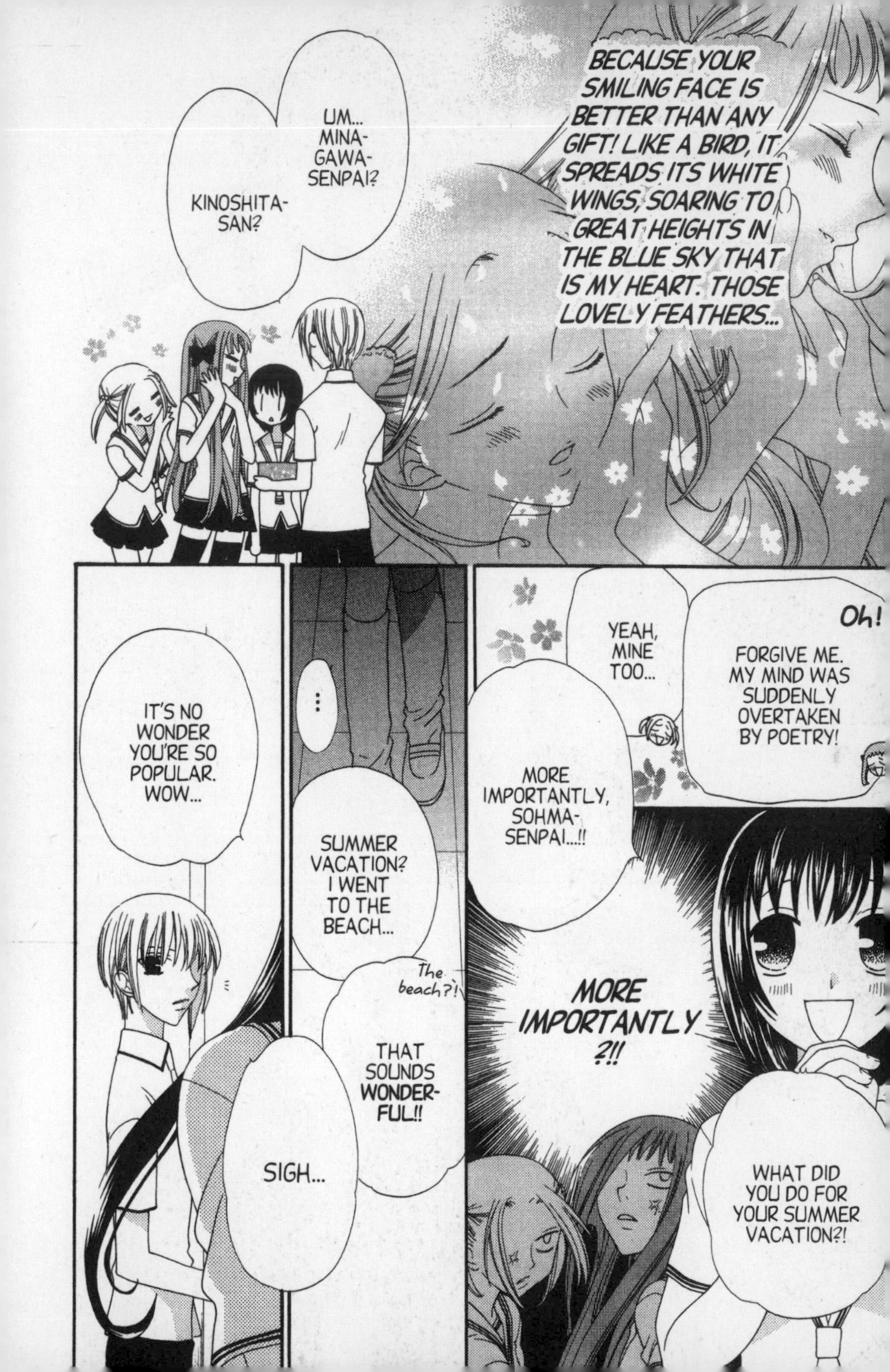
BECAUSE YOUR SMILING FACE IS BETTER THAN ANY GIFT! LIKE A BIRD, IT SPREADS ITS WHITE WINGS, SOARING TO GREAT HEIGHTS IN THE BLUE SKY THAT IS MY HEART. THOSE LOVELY FEATHERS...
UM... MINA-GAWA-SENPAI?
KINOSHITA-SAN?
Oh!
FORGIVE ME. MY MIND WAS SUDDENLY OVERTAKEN BY POETRY!
YEAH, MINE TOO...
MORE IMPORTANTLY, SOHMA-SENPAI...!!
WHAT DID YOU DO FOR YOUR SUMMER VACATION?!
MORE IMPORTANTLY?!!
...
SUMMER VACATION? I WENT TO THE BEACH...
The beach?!
THAT SOUNDS WONDERFUL!!
IT'S NO WONDER YOU'RE SO POPULAR. WOW...
SIGH...

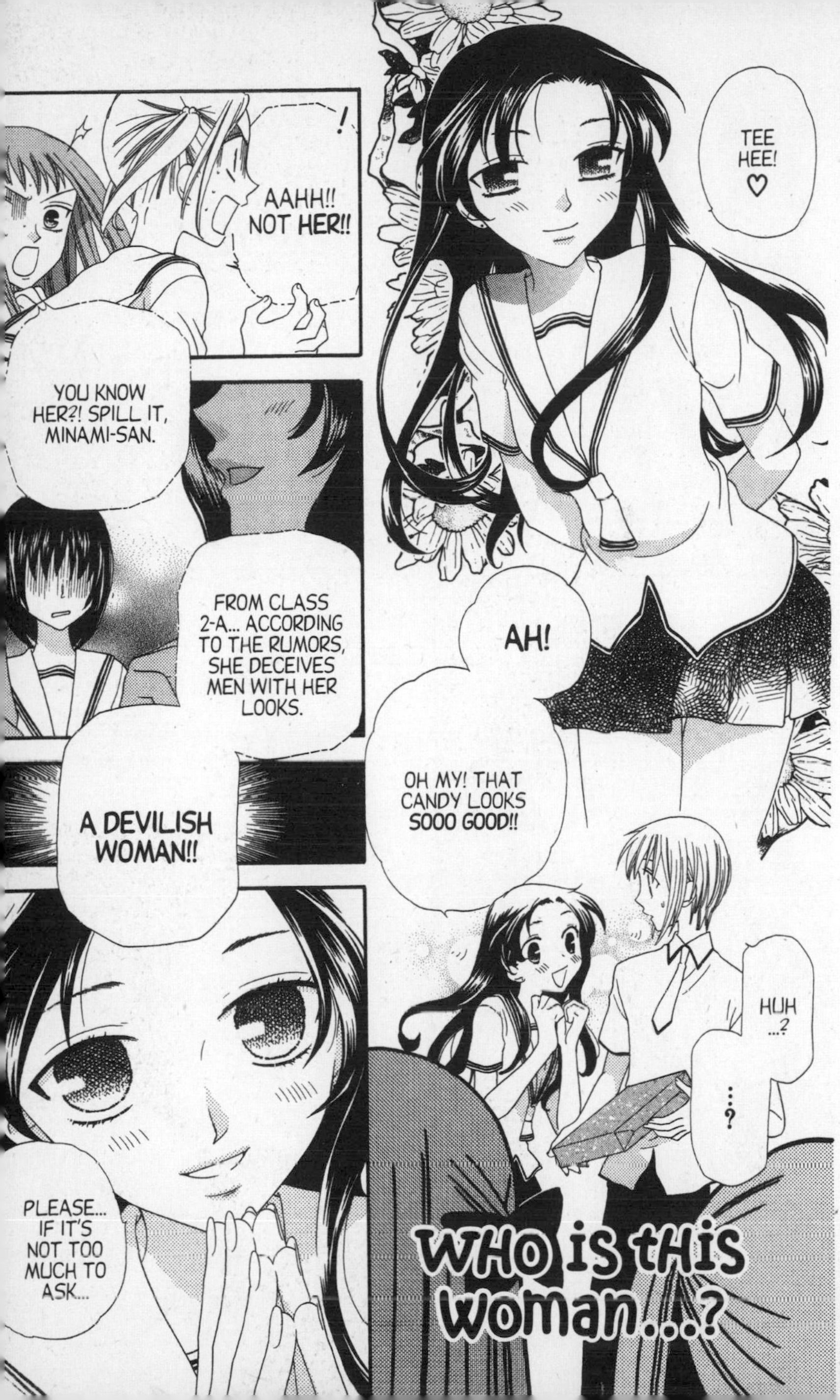
TEE HEE! ♡
AH!
OH MY! THAT CANDY LOOKS SOOO GOOD!!
HUH ...?
...?
WHO IS THIS WOMAN...?
!
AAHH!! NOT HER!!
YOU KNOW HER?! SPILL IT, MINAMI-SAN.
FROM CLASS 2-A... ACCORDING TO THE RUMORS, SHE DECEIVES MEN WITH HER LOOKS.
A DEVILISH WOMAN!!
PLEASE... IF IT'S NOT TOO MUCH TO ASK...

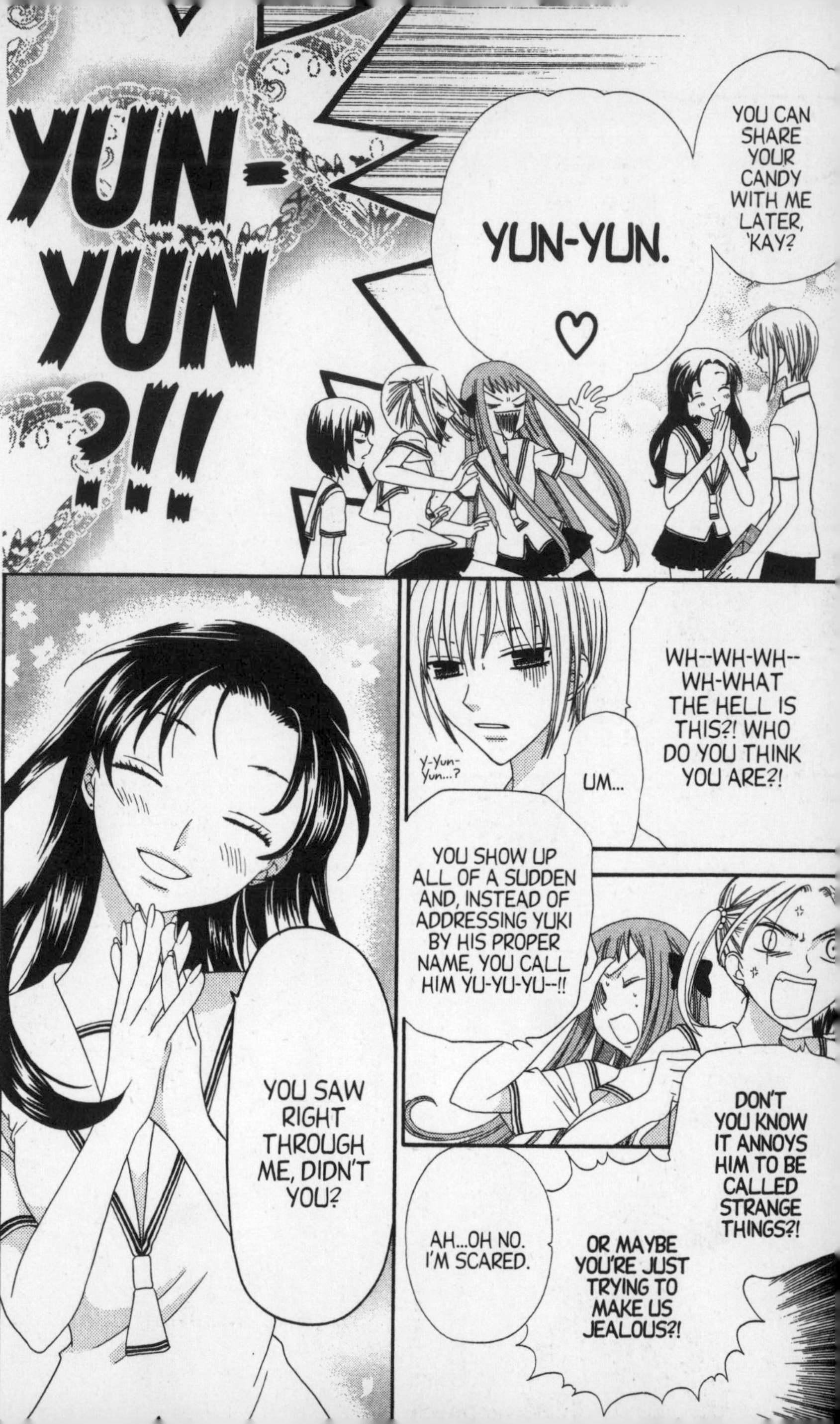
YOU CAN SHARE YOUR CANDY WITH ME LATER, 'KAY?
YUN-YUN. ♡
YUN-YUN?!!
WH--WH-WH-- WH-WHAT THE HELL IS THIS?! WHO DO YOU THINK YOU ARE?!
UM...
Y-Yun-Yun...?
YOU SHOW UP ALL OF A SUDDEN AND, INSTEAD OF ADDRESSING YUKI BY HIS PROPER NAME, YOU CALL HIM YU-YU-YU--!!
DON'T YOU KNOW IT ANNOYS HIM TO BE CALLED STRANGE THINGS?!
OR MAYBE YOU'RE JUST TRYING TO MAKE US JEALOUS?!
AH...OH NO. I'M SCARED.
YOU SAW RIGHT THROUGH ME, DIDN'T YOU?

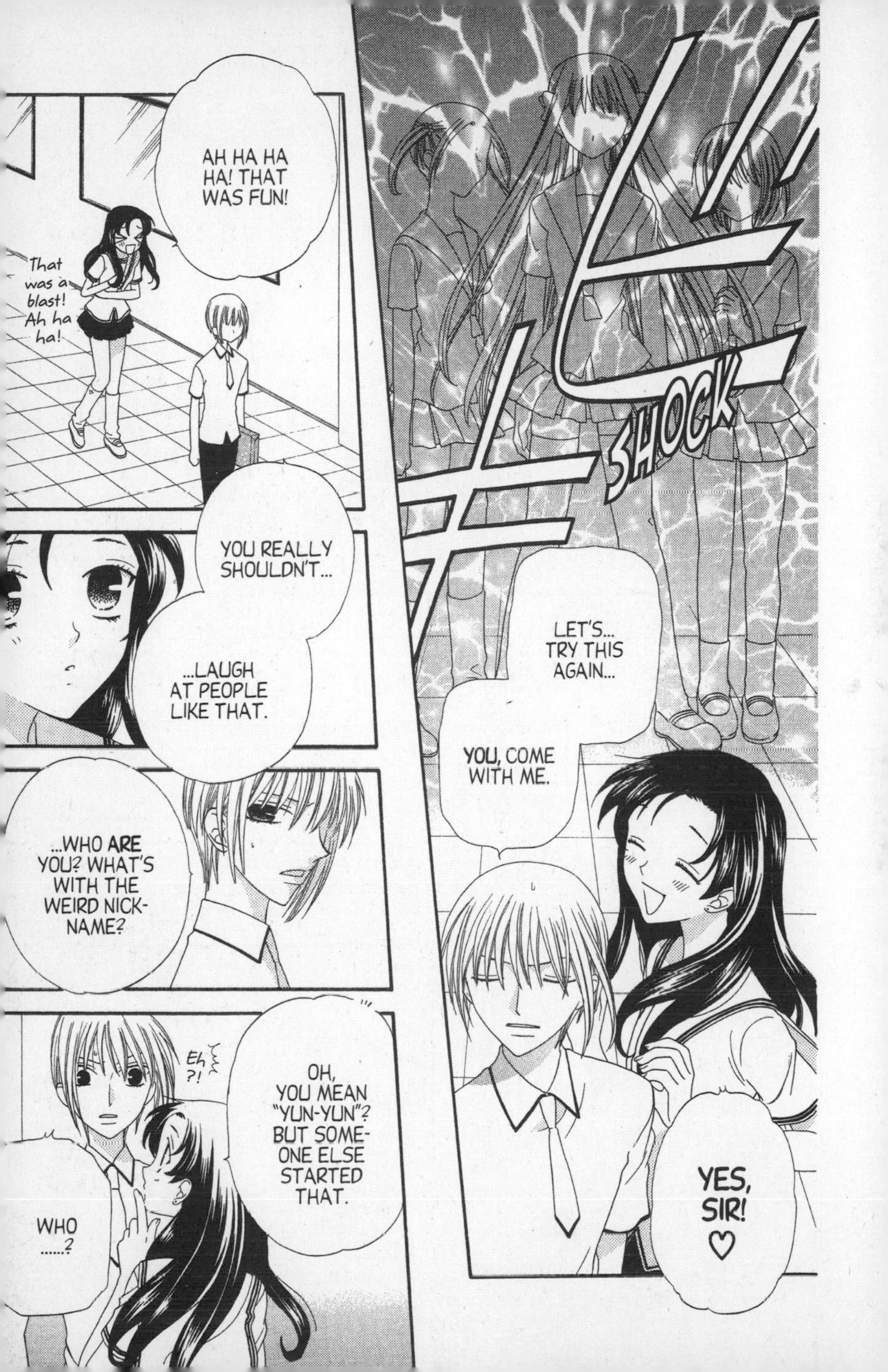
SHOCK
LET'S... TRY THIS AGAIN...
YOU, COME WITH ME.
YES, SIR! ♡
AH HA HA HA! THAT WAS FUN!
That was a blast! Ah ha ha!
YOU REALLY SHOULDN'T...
...LAUGH AT PEOPLE LIKE THAT.
...WHO ARE YOU? WHAT'S WITH THE WEIRD NICK-NAME?
OH, YOU MEAN "YUN-YUN"? BUT SOME-ONE ELSE STARTED THAT.
Eh?!
WHO ......?

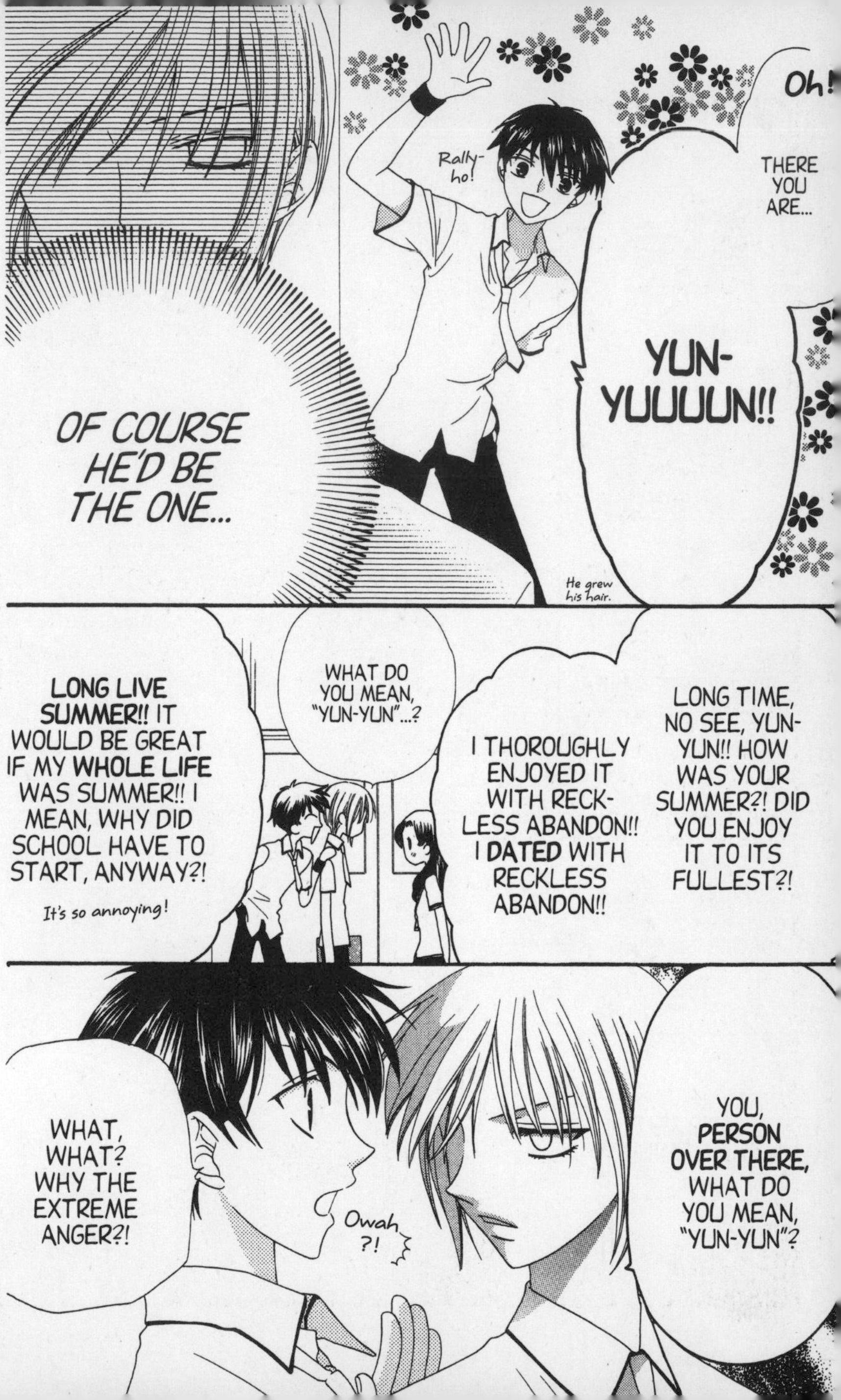
Oh!
THERE YOU ARE...
YUN-YUUUUN!!
Rally-ho!
He grew his hair.
OF COURSE HE'D BE THE ONE...
LONG TIME, NO SEE, YUN-YUN!! HOW WAS YOUR SUMMER?! DID YOU ENJOY IT TO ITS FULLEST?!
I THOROUGHLY ENJOYED IT WITH RECK-LESS ABANDON!! I DATED WITH RECKLESS ABANDON!!
WHAT DO YOU MEAN, "YUN-YUN"...?
LONG LIVE SUMMER!! IT WOULD BE GREAT IF MY WHOLE LIFE WAS SUMMER!! I MEAN, WHY DID SCHOOL HAVE TO START, ANYWAY?!
It's so annoying!
YOU, PERSON OVER THERE, WHAT DO YOU MEAN, "YUN-YUN"?
Owah?!
WHAT, WHAT? WHY THE EXTREME ANGER?!

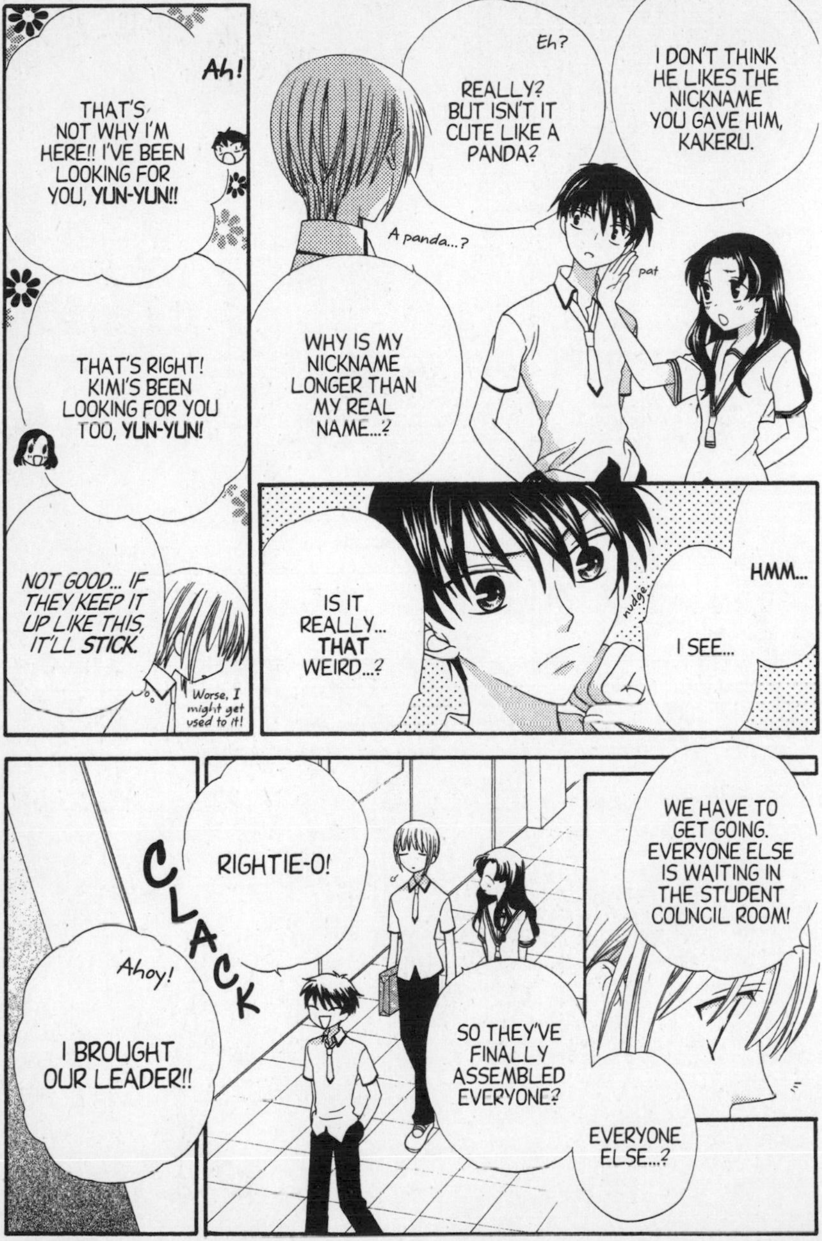
I DON'T THINK HE LIKES THE NICKNAME YOU GAVE HIM, KAKERU.
Eh?
REALLY? BUT ISN'T IT CUTE LIKE A PANDA?
pat
A panda...?
WHY IS MY NICKNAME LONGER THAN MY REAL NAME...?
HMM...
I SEE...
nudge
IS IT REALLY... THAT WEIRD...?
Ah!
THAT'S NOT WHY I'M HERE!! I'VE BEEN LOOKING FOR YOU, YUN-YUN!!
THAT'S RIGHT! KIMI'S BEEN LOOKING FOR YOU TOO, YUN-YUN!
NOT GOOD... IF THEY KEEP IT UP LIKE THIS, IT'LL STICK.
Worse, I might get used to it!
WE HAVE TO GET GOING. EVERYONE ELSE IS WAITING IN THE STUDENT COUNCIL ROOM!
SO THEY'VE FINALLY ASSEMBLED EVERYONE?
EVERYONE ELSE...?
RIGHTIE-O!
CLACK
Ahoy!
I BROUGHT OUR LEADER!!

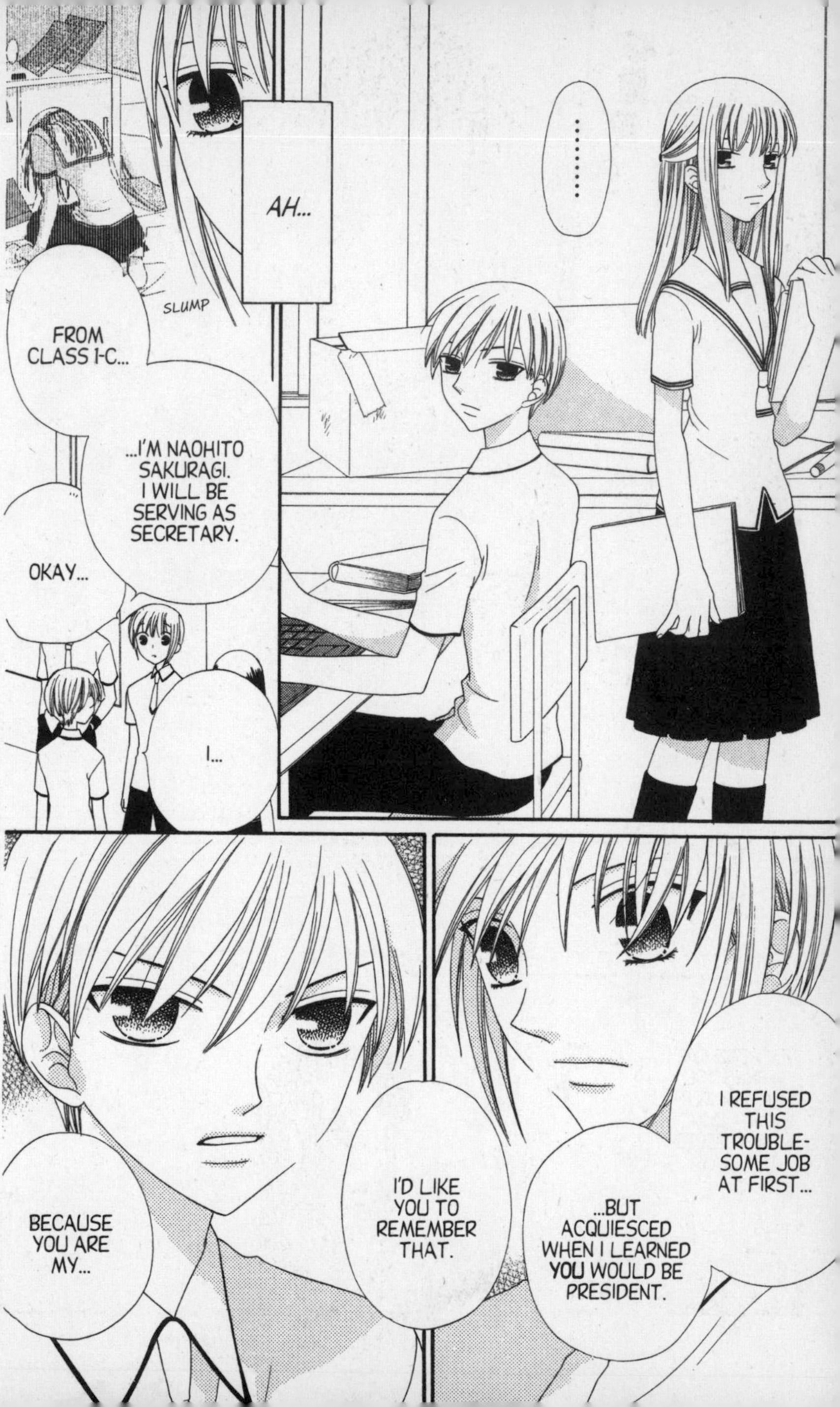
......
AH...
SLUMP
FROM CLASS 1-C...
...I'M NAOHITO SAKURAGI. I WILL BE SERVING AS SECRETARY.
OKAY...
I...
I REFUSED THIS TROUBLE-SOME JOB AT FIRST...
...BUT ACQUIESCED WHEN I LEARNED **YOU** WOULD BE PRESIDENT.
I'D LIKE YOU TO REMEMBER THAT.
BECAUSE YOU ARE MY...

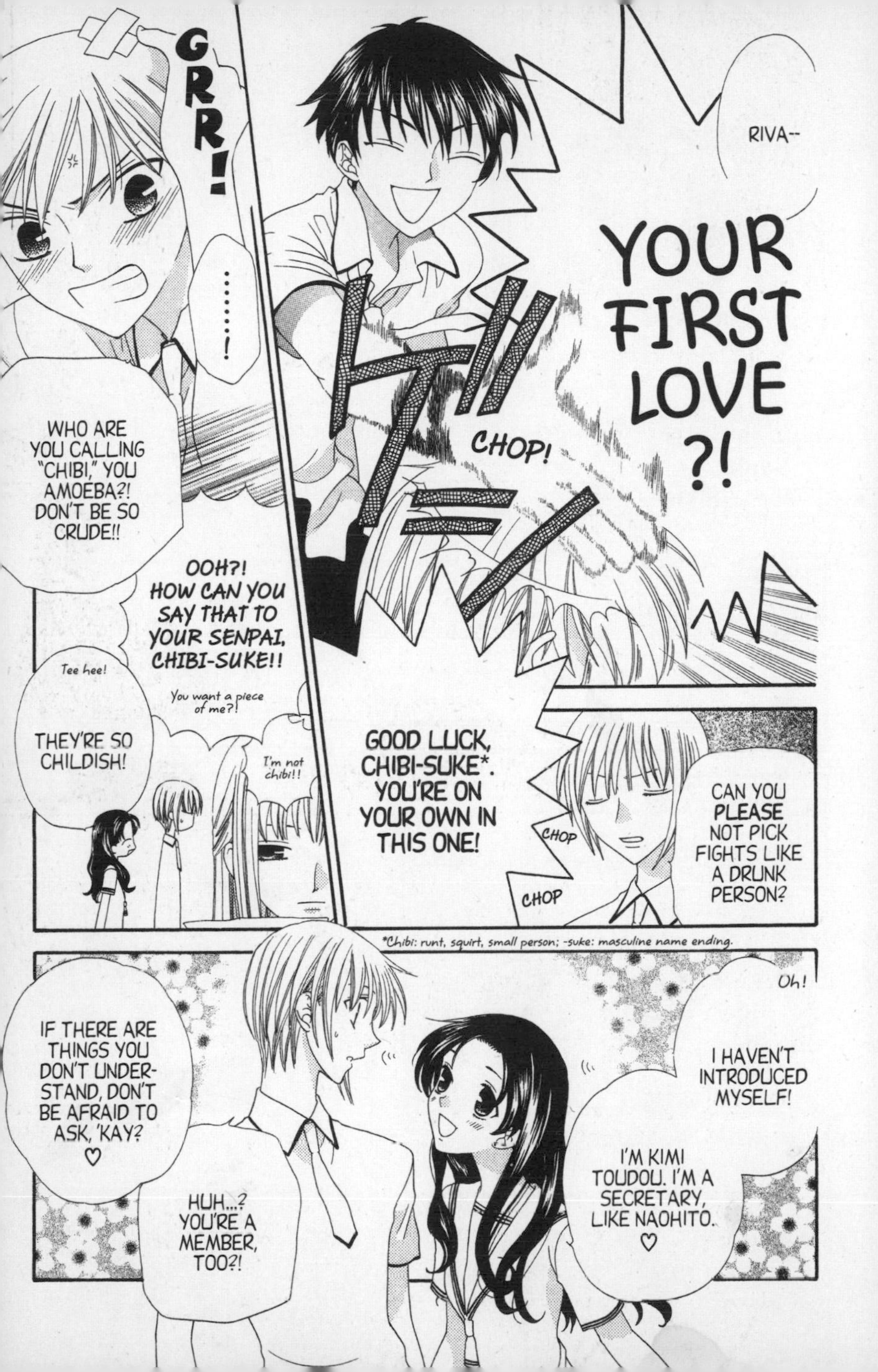
RIVA--
YOUR FIRST LOVE ?!
CHOP!
CAN YOU PLEASE NOT PICK FIGHTS LIKE A DRUNK PERSON?
CHOP
CHOP
GOOD LUCK, CHIBI-SUKE*. YOU'RE ON YOUR OWN IN THIS ONE!
GRR!
......!
WHO ARE YOU CALLING "CHIBI," YOU AMOEBA?! DON'T BE SO CRUDE!!
OOH?! HOW CAN YOU SAY THAT TO YOUR SENPAI, CHIBI-SUKE!!
You want a piece of me?!
I'm not chibi!!
Tee hee!
THEY'RE SO CHILDISH!
Oh!
I HAVEN'T INTRODUCED MYSELF!
I'M KIMI TOUDOU. I'M A SECRETARY, LIKE NAOHITO. ♡
IF THERE ARE THINGS YOU DON'T UNDER-STAND, DON'T BE AFRAID TO ASK, 'KAY? ♡
HUH...? YOU'RE A MEMBER, TOO?!
*Chibi: runt, squirt, small person; -suke: masculine name ending.

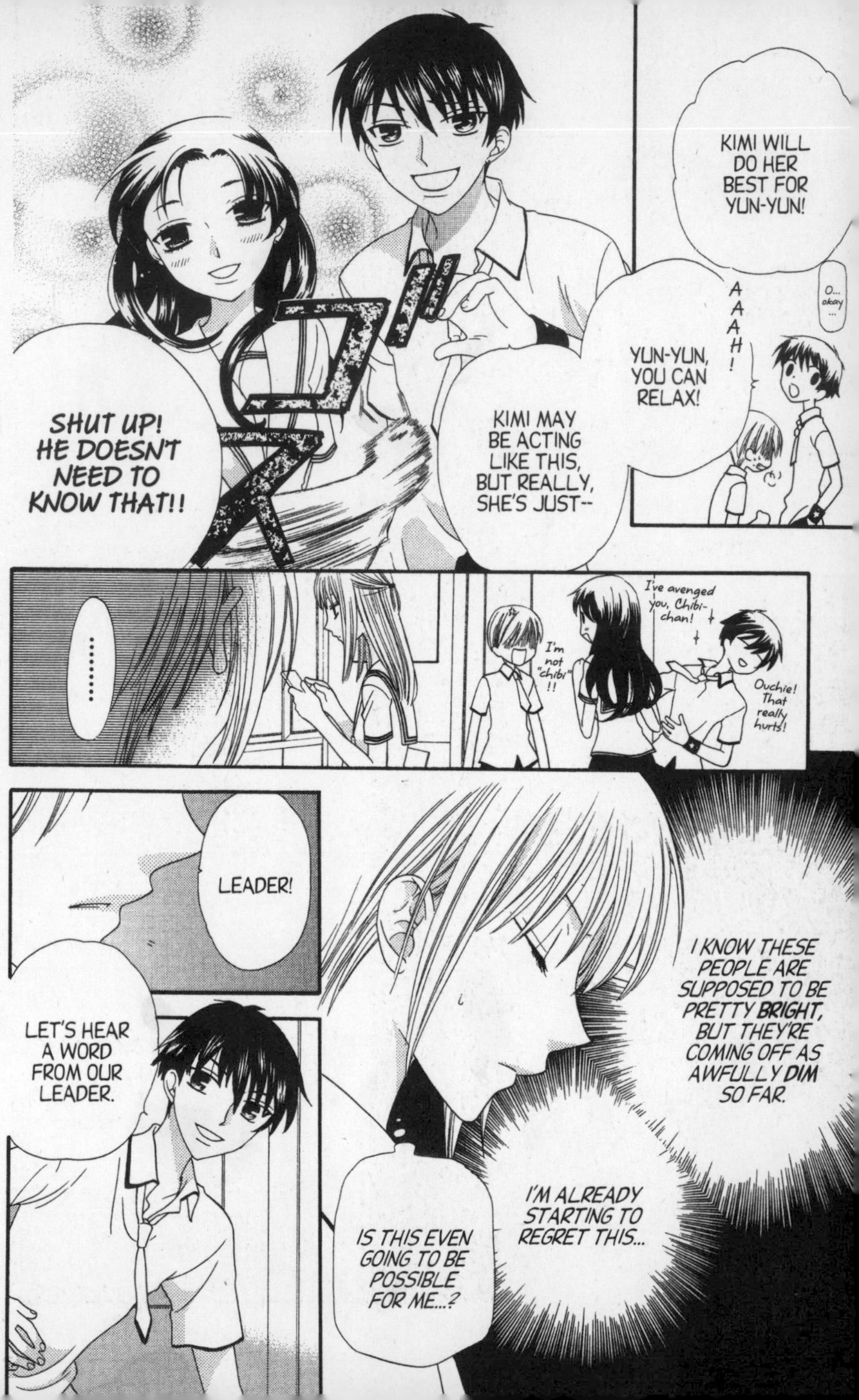

KIMI WILL DO HER BEST FOR YUN-YUN!
O... okay ...
YUN-YUN, YOU CAN RELAX!
KIMI MAY BE ACTING LIKE THIS, BUT REALLY, SHE'S JUST--
AAAH!
SHUT UP! HE DOESN'T NEED TO KNOW THAT!!
I've avenged you, Chibi-chan!
Ouchie! That really hurts!
I'm not "chibi"!!
......
I KNOW THESE PEOPLE ARE SUPPOSED TO BE PRETTY BRIGHT, BUT THEY'RE COMING OFF AS AWFULLY DIM SO FAR.
I'M ALREADY STARTING TO REGRET THIS...
IS THIS EVEN GOING TO BE POSSIBLE FOR ME...?
LEADER!
LET'S HEAR A WORD FROM OUR LEADER.

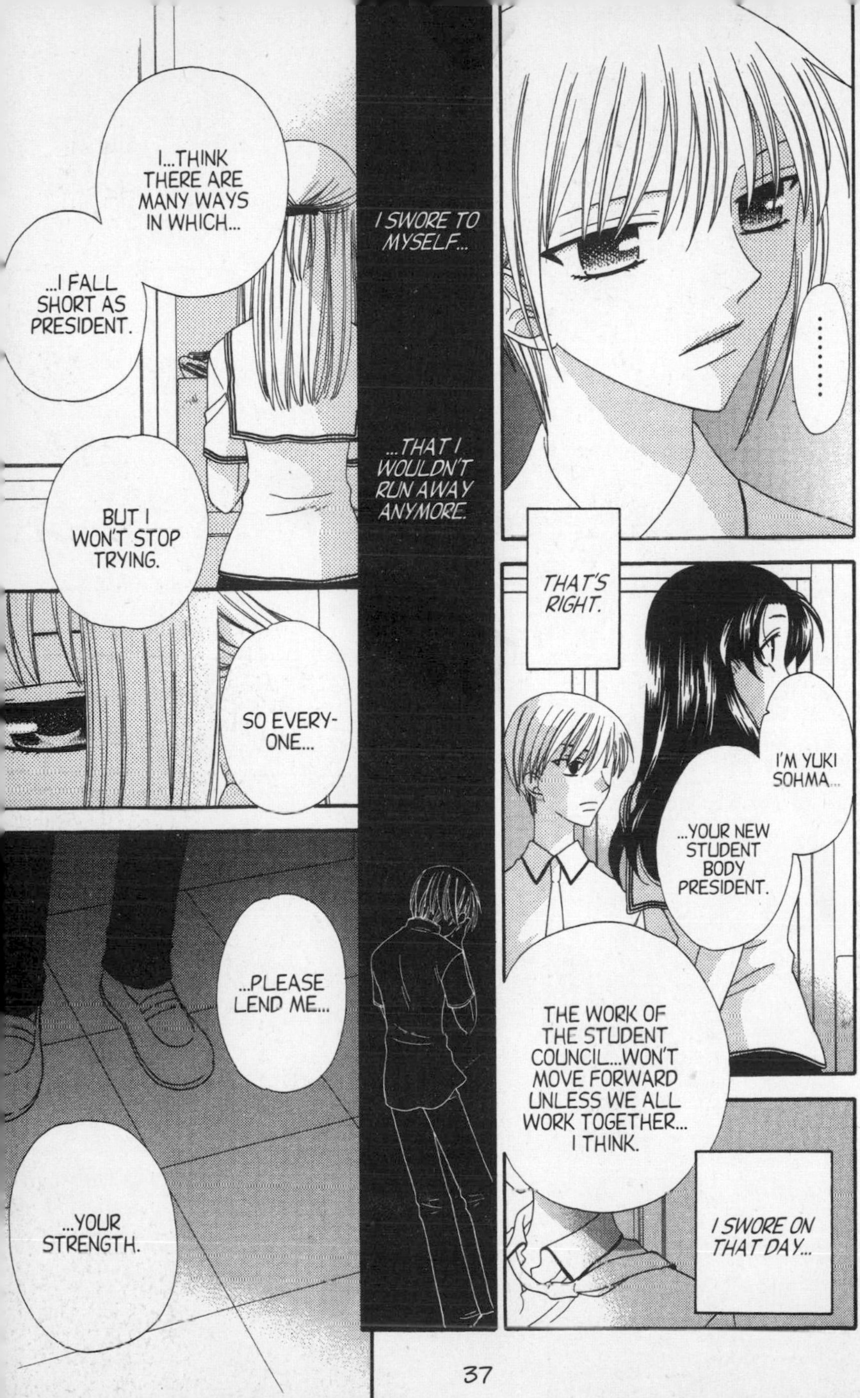
......
THAT'S RIGHT.
I'M YUKI SOHMA...
...YOUR NEW STUDENT BODY PRESIDENT.
THE WORK OF THE STUDENT COUNCIL...WON'T MOVE FORWARD UNLESS WE ALL WORK TOGETHER... I THINK.
I SWORE ON THAT DAY...
I SWORE TO MYSELF...
...THAT I WOULDN'T RUN AWAY ANYMORE.
I...THINK THERE ARE MANY WAYS IN WHICH...
...I FALL SHORT AS PRESIDENT.
BUT I WON'T STOP TRYING.
SO EVERY-ONE...
...PLEASE LEND ME...
...YOUR STRENGTH.

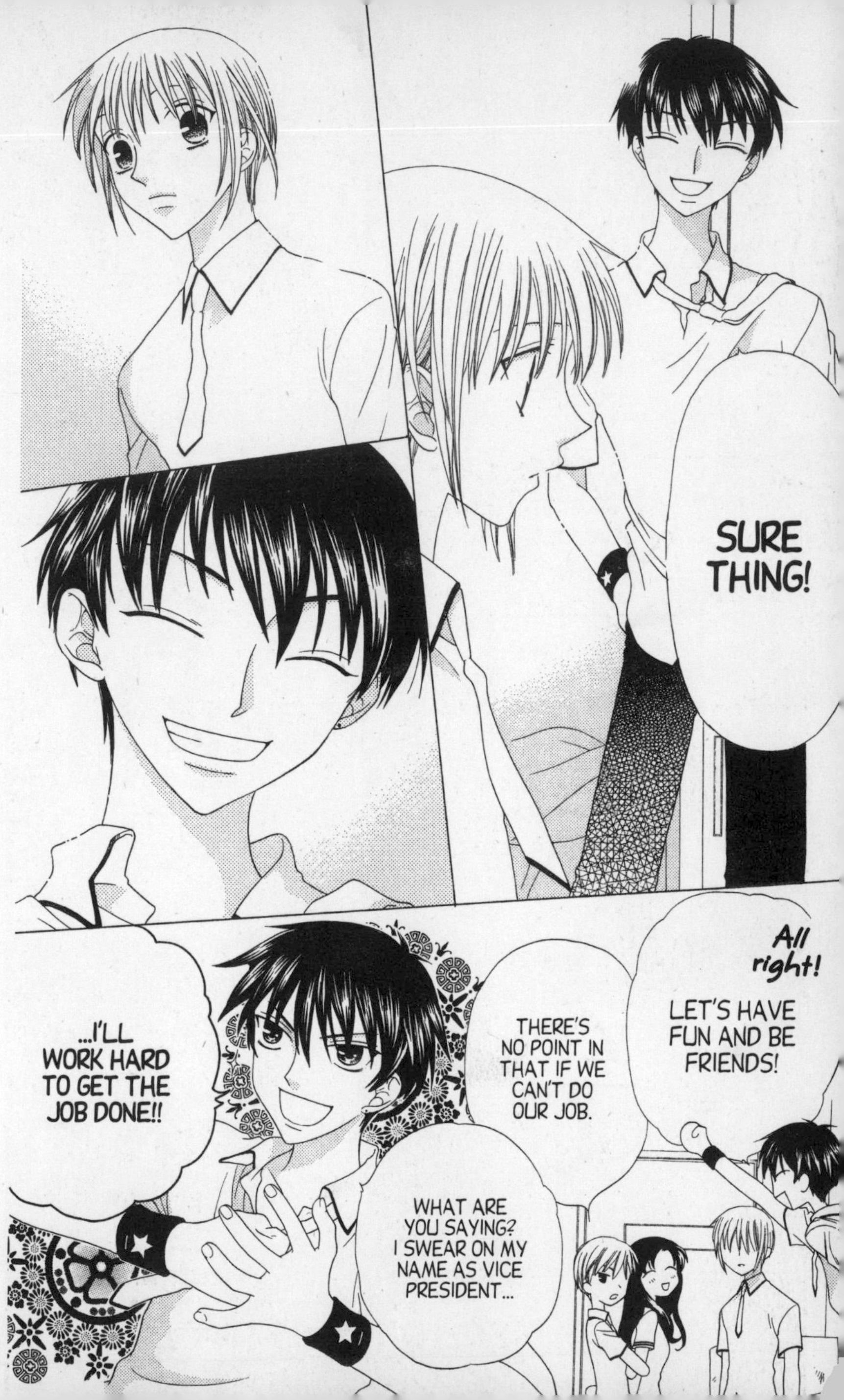
SURE THING!
All right!
LET'S HAVE FUN AND BE FRIENDS!
THERE'S NO POINT IN THAT IF WE CAN'T DO OUR JOB.
WHAT ARE YOU SAYING? I SWEAR ON MY NAME AS VICE PRESIDENT...
...I'LL WORK HARD TO GET THE JOB DONE!!

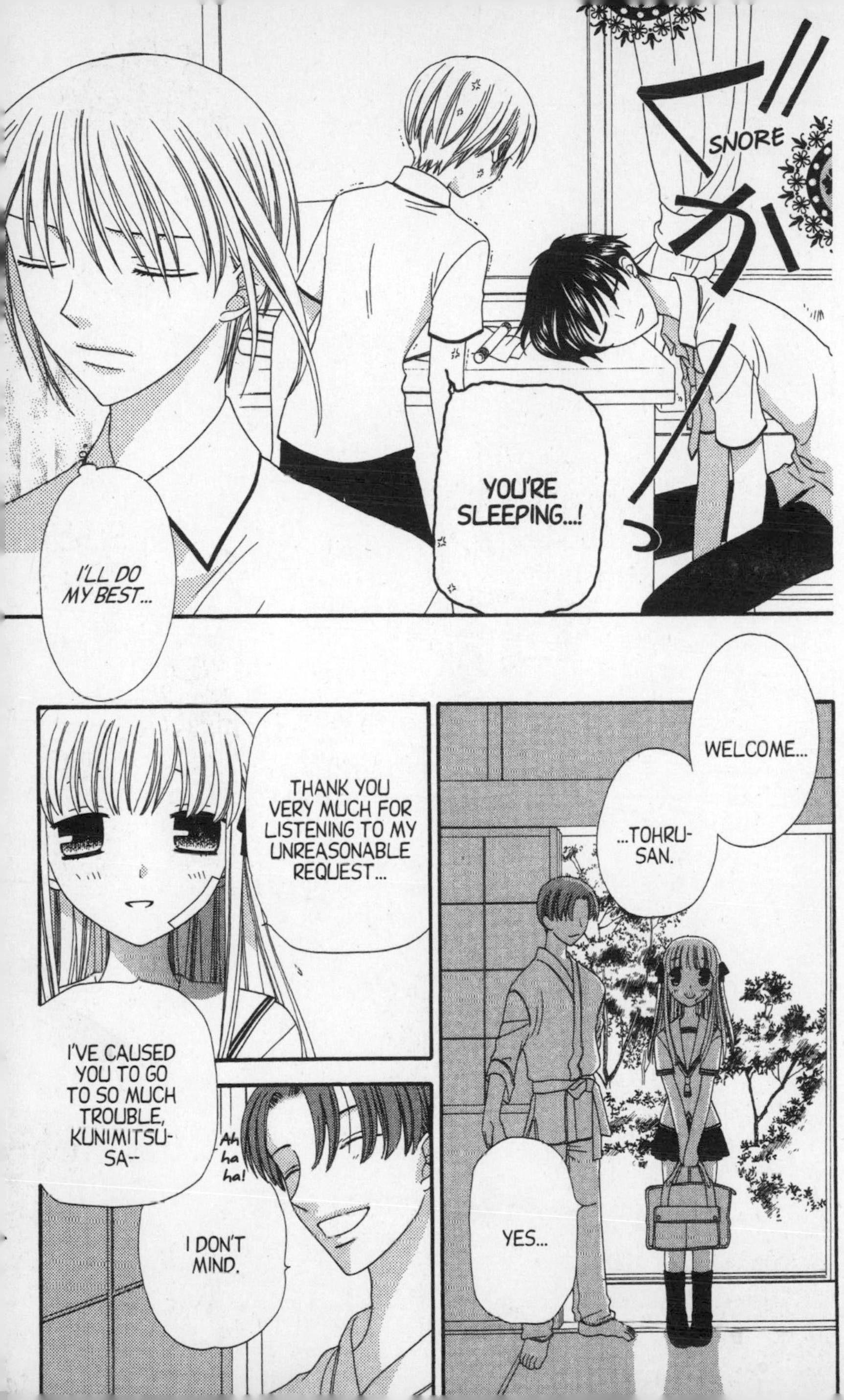
SNORE
YOU'RE SLEEPING...!
I'LL DO MY BEST...
WELCOME...
...TOHRU-SAN.
YES...
THANK YOU VERY MUCH FOR LISTENING TO MY UNREASONABLE REQUEST...
I'VE CAUSED YOU TO GO TO SO MUCH TROUBLE, KUNIMITSU-SA--
Ah ha ha!
I DON'T MIND.

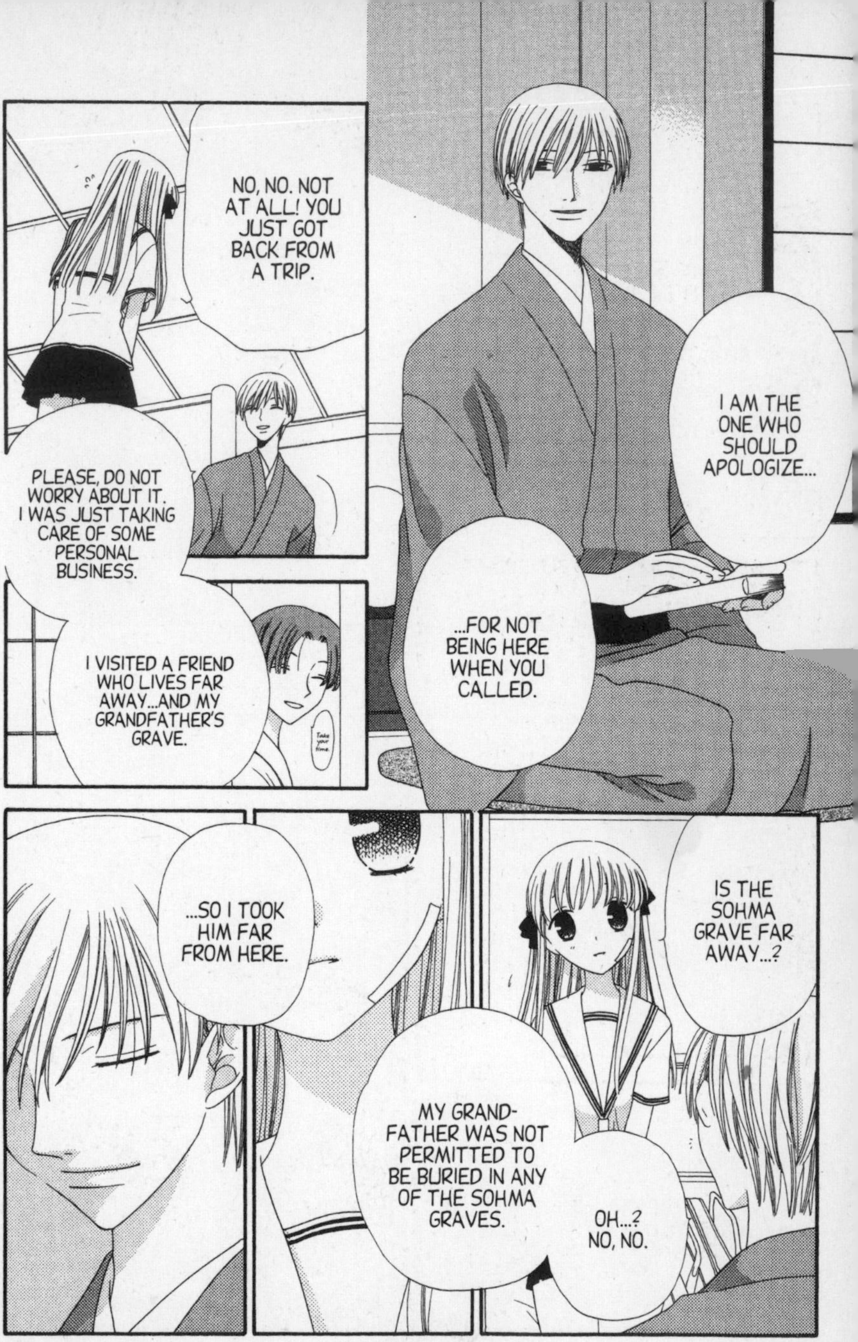
I AM THE ONE WHO SHOULD APOLOGIZE...
...FOR NOT BEING HERE WHEN YOU CALLED.
NO, NO. NOT AT ALL! YOU JUST GOT BACK FROM A TRIP.
PLEASE, DO NOT WORRY ABOUT IT. I WAS JUST TAKING CARE OF SOME PERSONAL BUSINESS.
I VISITED A FRIEND WHO LIVES FAR AWAY...AND MY GRANDFATHER'S GRAVE.
Take your time.
IS THE SOHMA GRAVE FAR AWAY...?
OH...? NO, NO.
MY GRANDFATHER WAS NOT PERMITTED TO BE BURIED IN ANY OF THE SOHMA GRAVES.
...SO I TOOK HIM FAR FROM HERE.

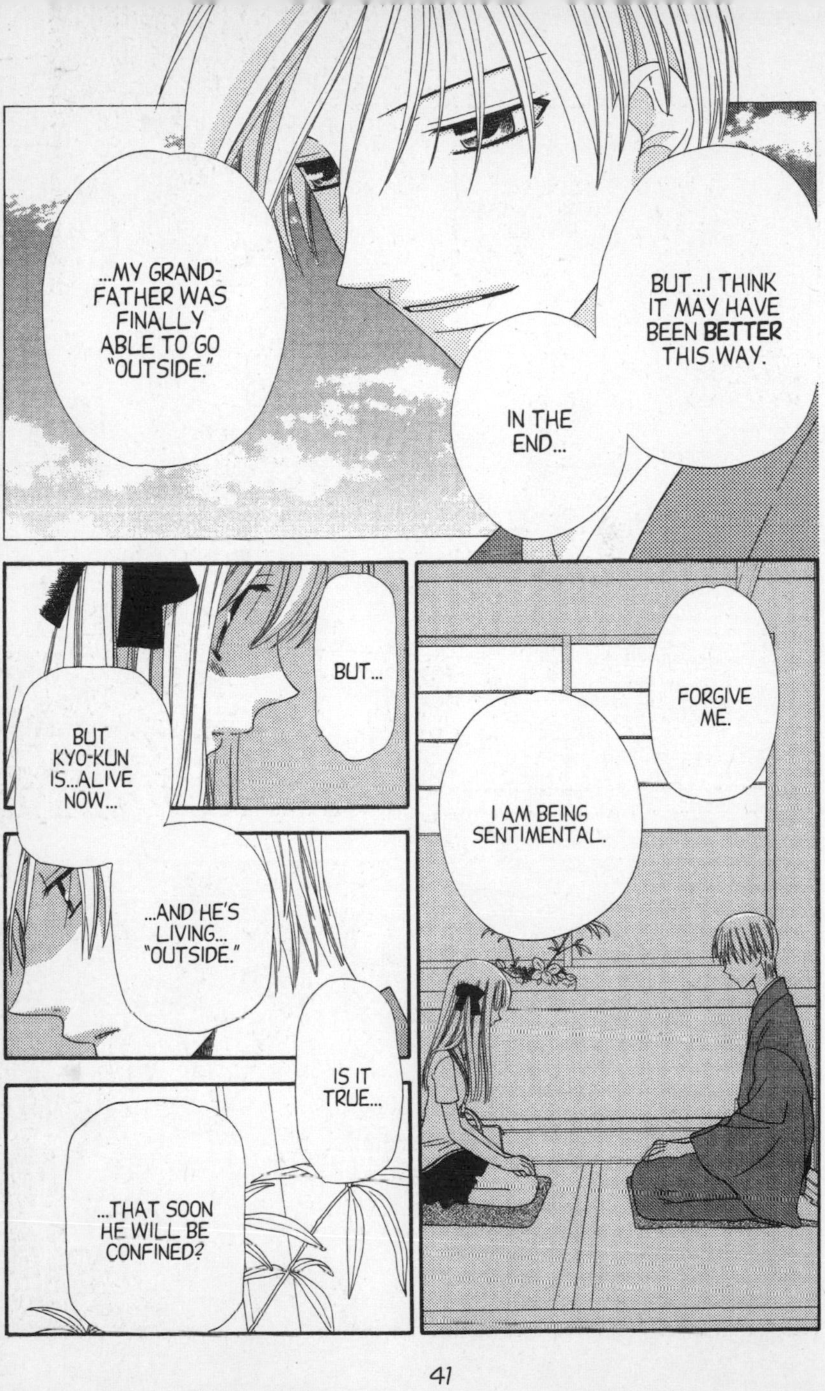
BUT...I THINK IT MAY HAVE BEEN **BETTER** THIS WAY.
IN THE END...
...MY GRAND-FATHER WAS FINALLY ABLE TO GO "OUTSIDE."
FORGIVE ME.
I AM BEING SENTIMENTAL.
BUT...
BUT KYO-KUN IS...ALIVE NOW...
...AND HE'S LIVING... "OUTSIDE."
IS IT TRUE...
...THAT SOON HE WILL BE CONFINED?

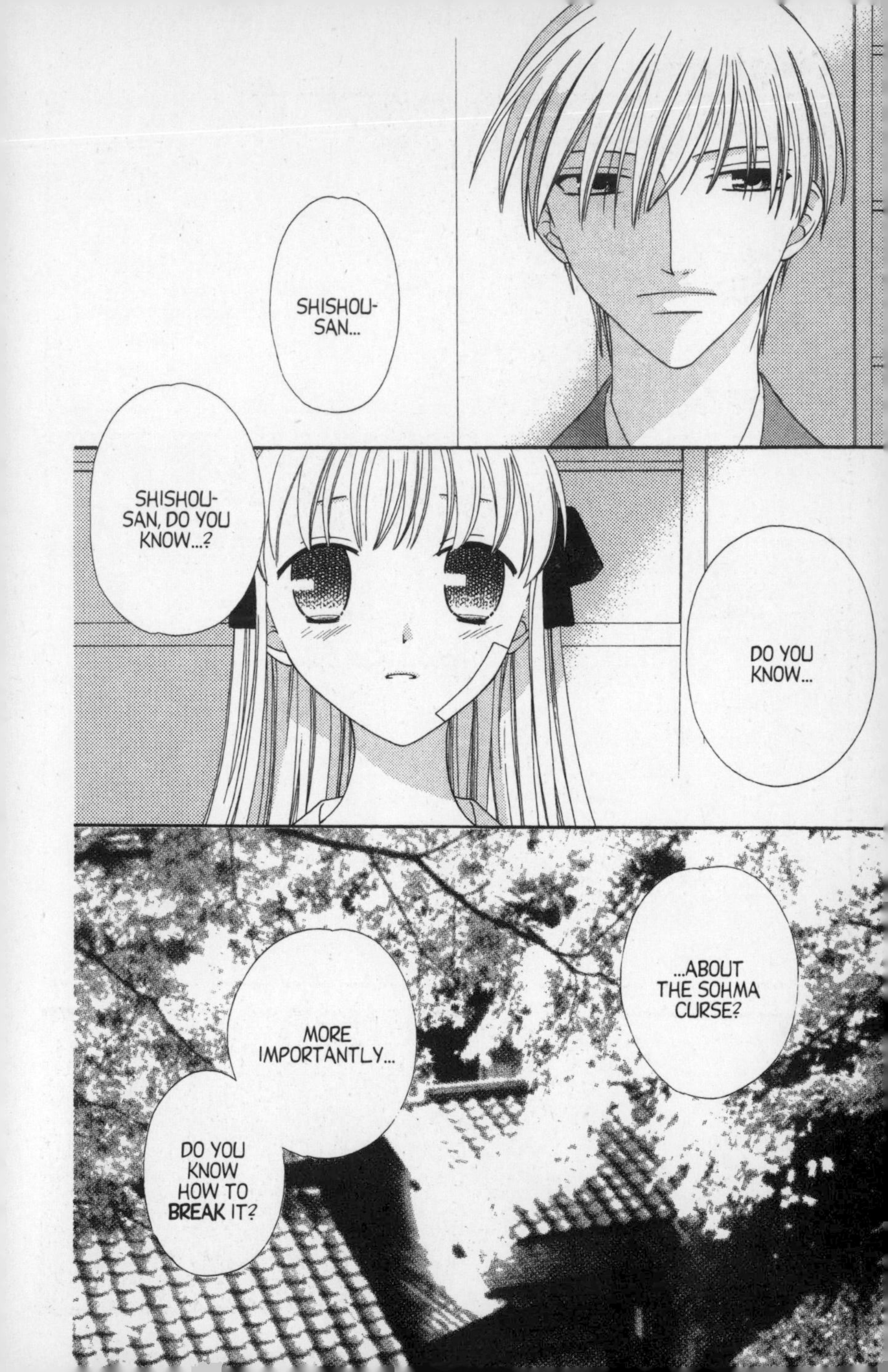
SHISHOU-SAN...
SHISHOU-SAN, DO YOU KNOW...?
DO YOU KNOW...
...ABOUT THE SOHMA CURSE?
MORE IMPORTANTLY...
DO YOU KNOW HOW TO **BREAK** IT?

Chapter 67

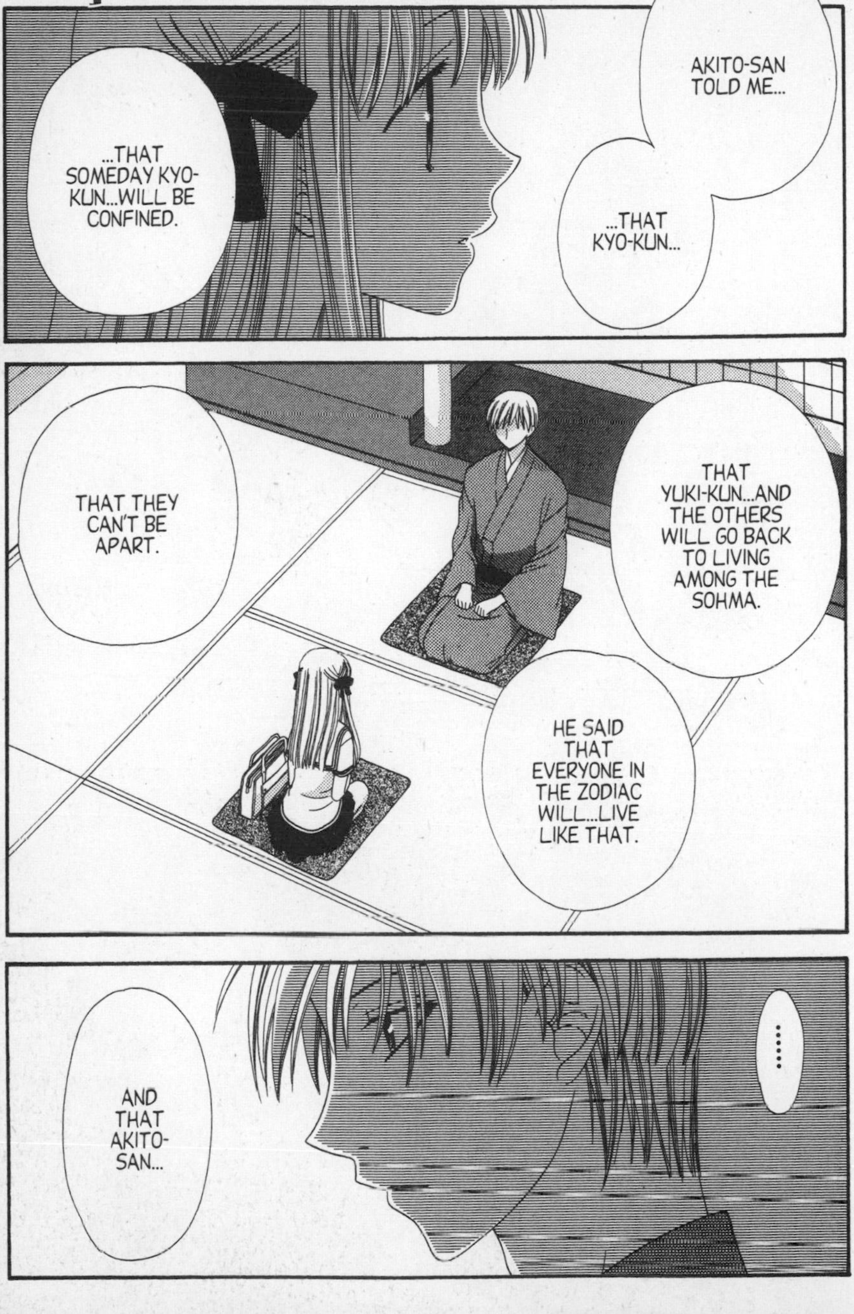
AKITO-SAN TOLD ME...
...THAT KYO-KUN...
...THAT SOMEDAY KYO-KUN...WILL BE CONFINED.
THAT YUKI-KUN...AND THE OTHERS WILL GO BACK TO LIVING AMONG THE SOHMA.
HE SAID THAT EVERYONE IN THE ZODIAC WILL...LIVE LIKE THAT.
THAT THEY CAN'T BE APART.
......
AND THAT AKITO-SAN...

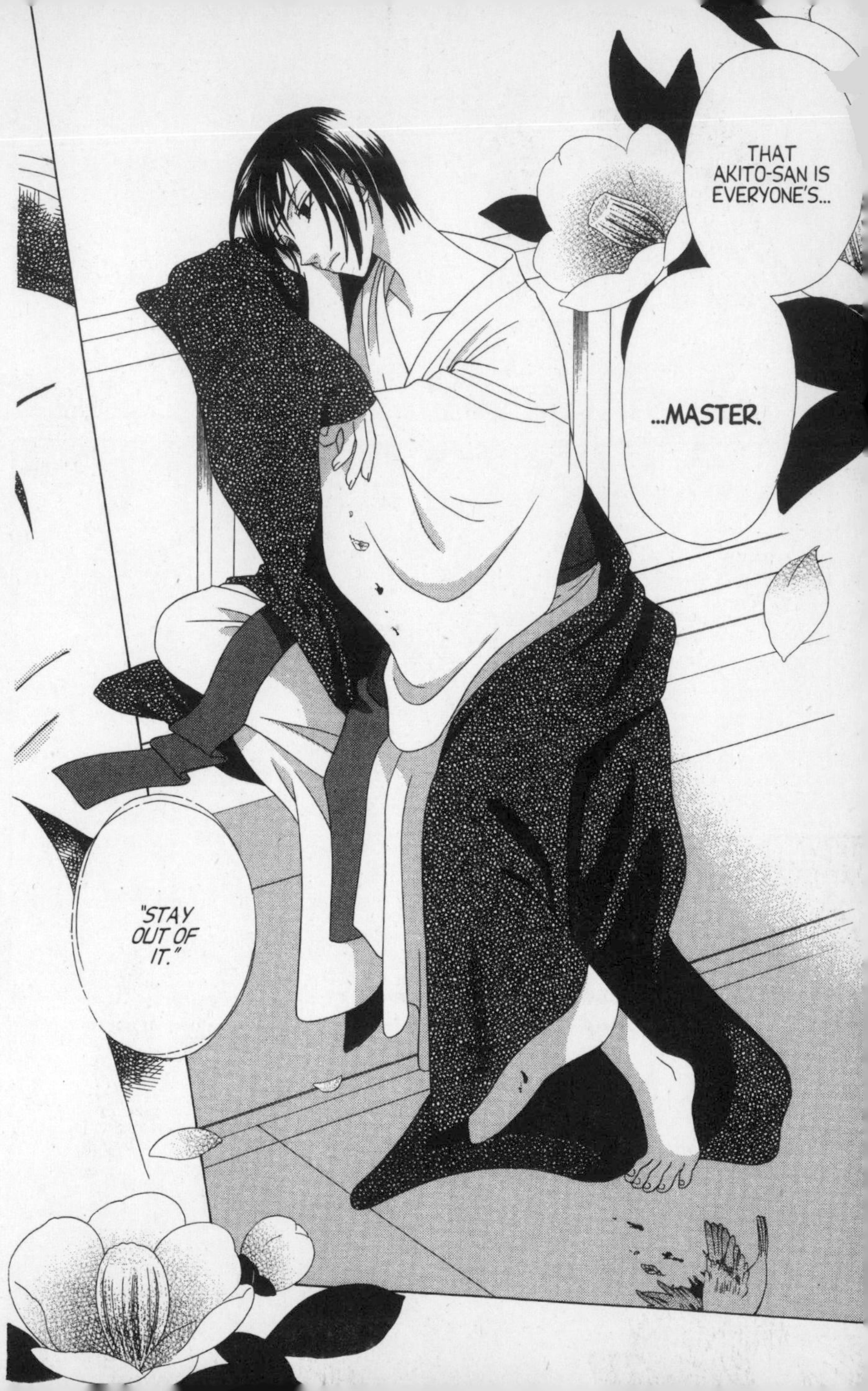
THAT AKITO-SAN IS EVERYONE'S...
...MASTER.
"STAY OUT OF IT."

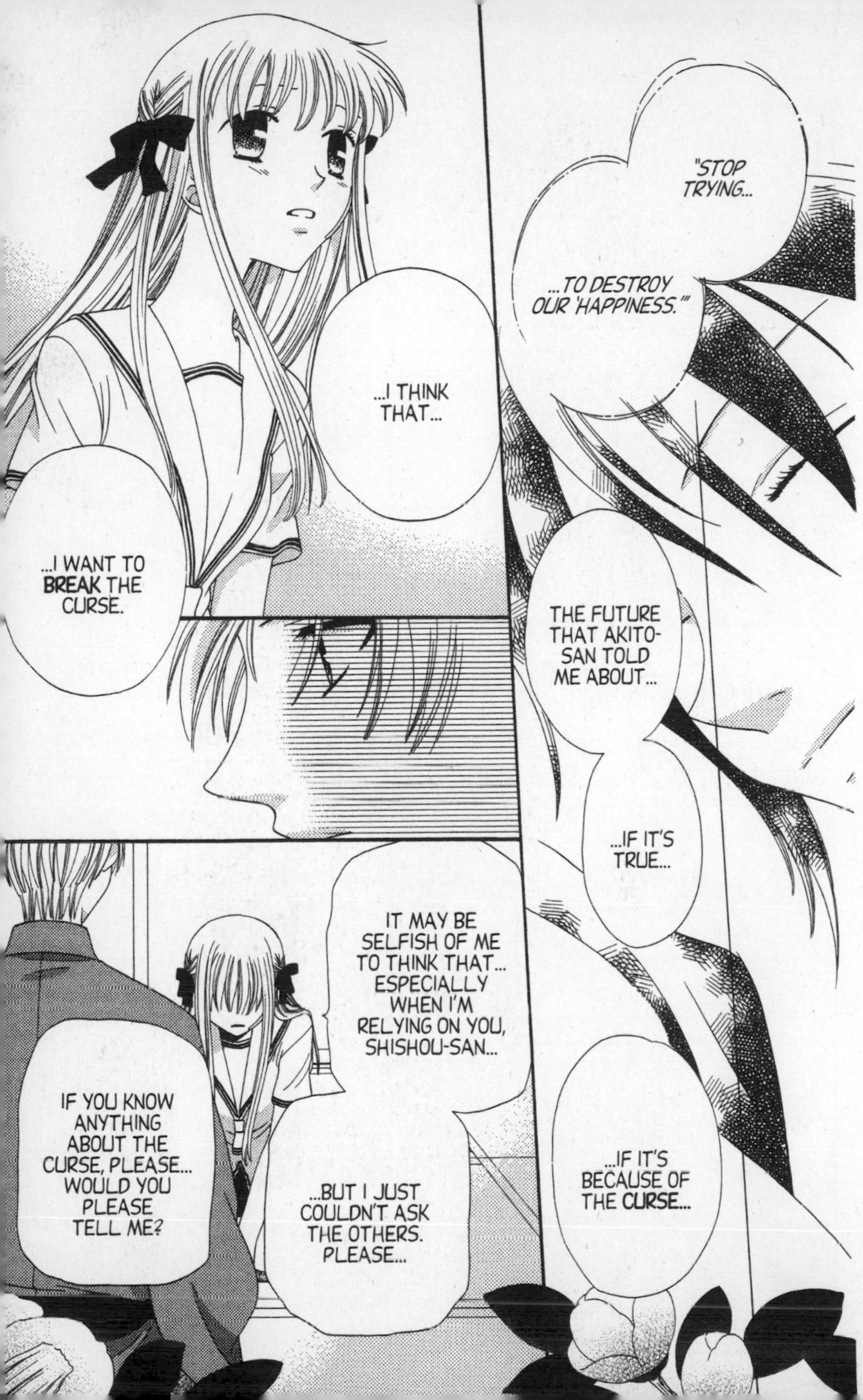
"STOP TRYING...
...TO DESTROY OUR 'HAPPINESS.'"
THE FUTURE THAT AKITO-SAN TOLD ME ABOUT...
...IF IT'S TRUE...
...IF IT'S BECAUSE OF THE CURSE...
...I THINK THAT...
...I WANT TO BREAK THE CURSE.
IT MAY BE SELFISH OF ME TO THINK THAT... ESPECIALLY WHEN I'M RELYING ON YOU, SHISHOU-SAN...
...BUT I JUST COULDN'T ASK THE OTHERS. PLEASE...
IF YOU KNOW ANYTHING ABOUT THE CURSE, PLEASE... WOULD YOU PLEASE TELL ME?

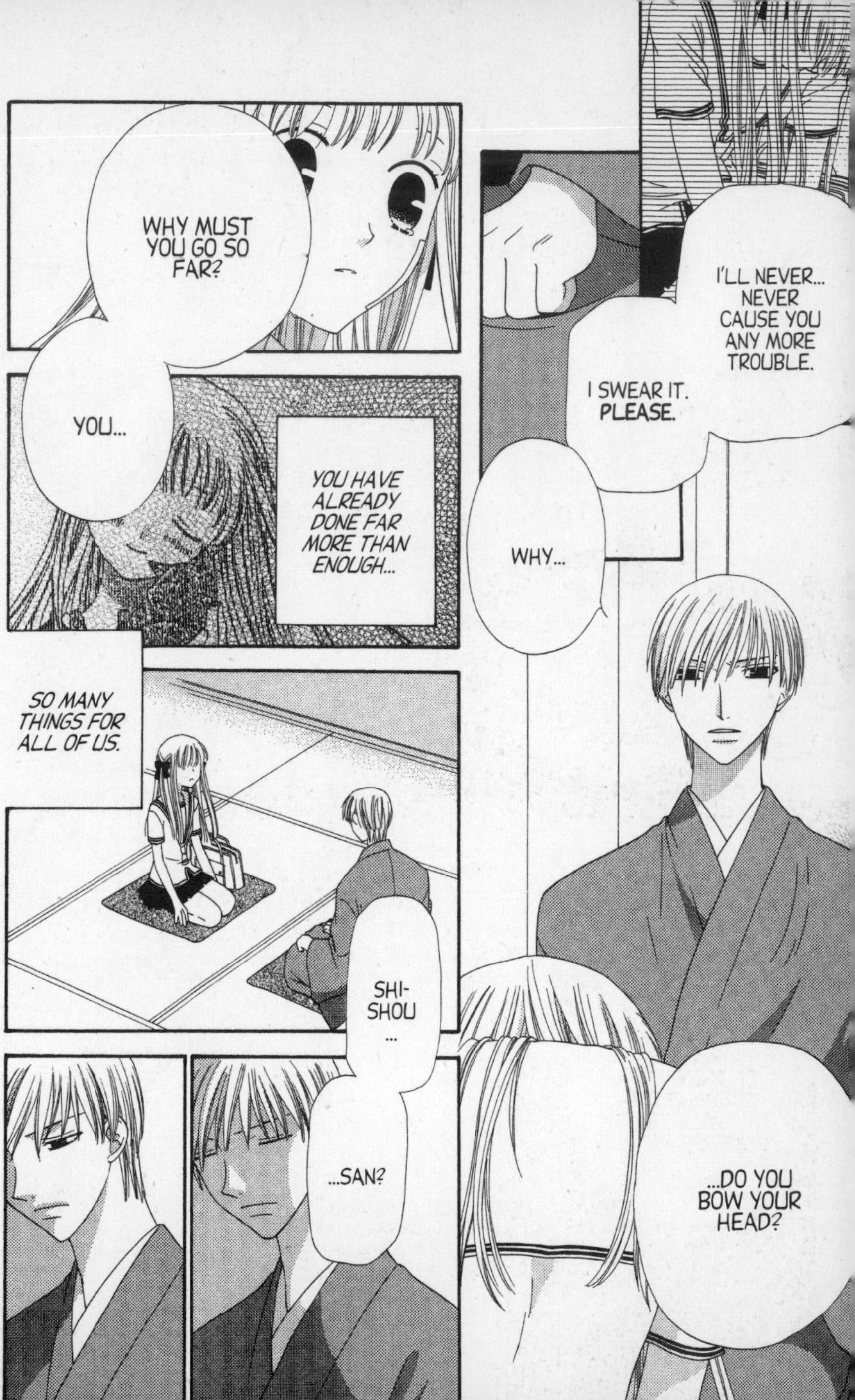
I'LL NEVER... NEVER CAUSE YOU ANY MORE TROUBLE.
I SWEAR IT. PLEASE.
WHY...
...DO YOU BOW YOUR HEAD?
WHY MUST YOU GO SO FAR?
YOU...
YOU HAVE ALREADY DONE FAR MORE THAN ENOUGH...
SO MANY THINGS FOR ALL OF US.
SHI-SHOU...
...SAN?

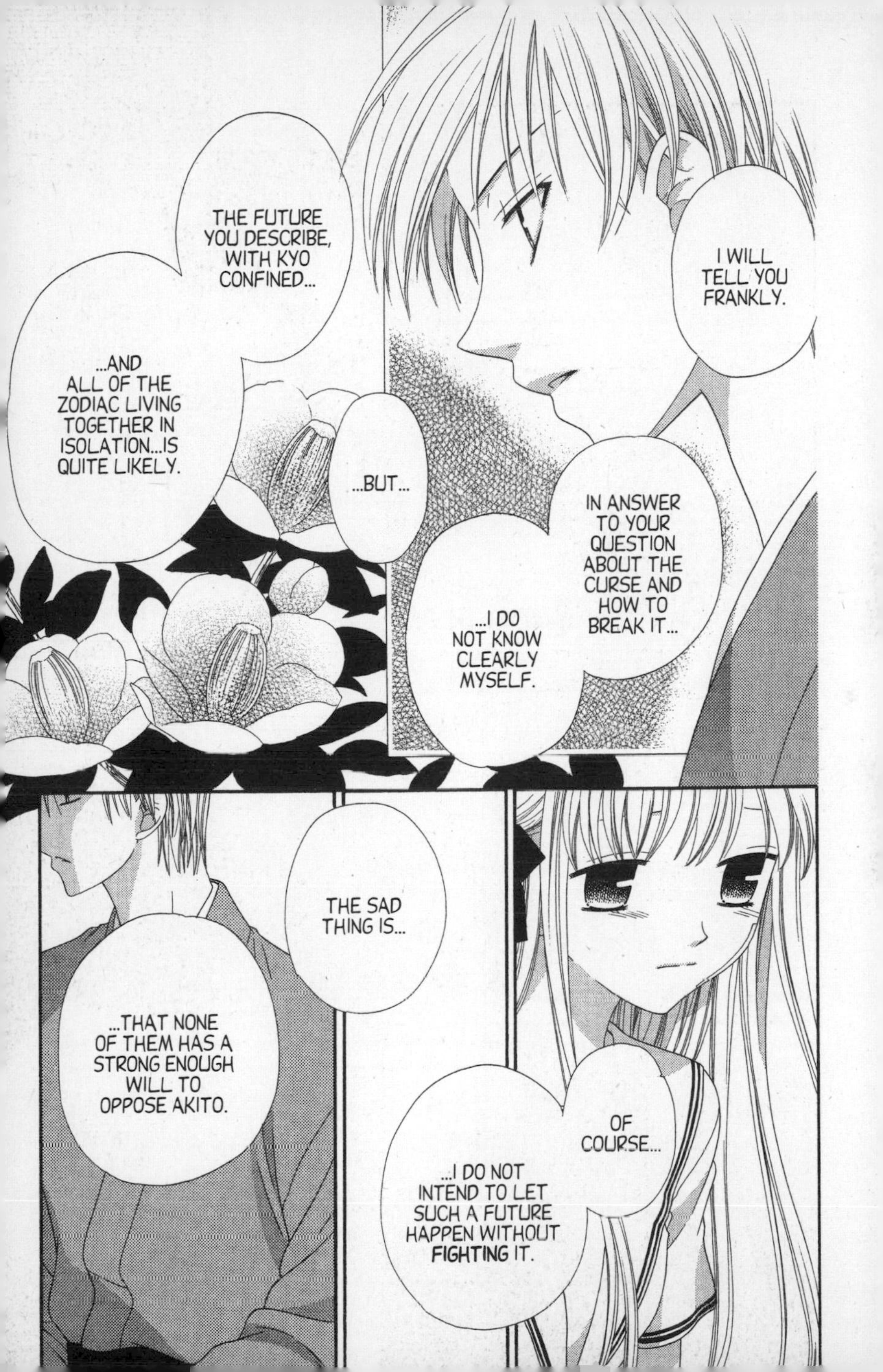
I WILL TELL YOU FRANKLY.
IN ANSWER TO YOUR QUESTION ABOUT THE CURSE AND HOW TO BREAK IT...
...I DO NOT KNOW CLEARLY MYSELF.
...BUT...
THE FUTURE YOU DESCRIBE, WITH KYO CONFINED...
...AND ALL OF THE ZODIAC LIVING TOGETHER IN ISOLATION...IS QUITE LIKELY.
OF COURSE...
...I DO NOT INTEND TO LET SUCH A FUTURE HAPPEN WITHOUT **FIGHTING** IT.
THE SAD THING IS...
...THAT NONE OF THEM HAS A STRONG ENOUGH WILL TO OPPOSE AKITO.

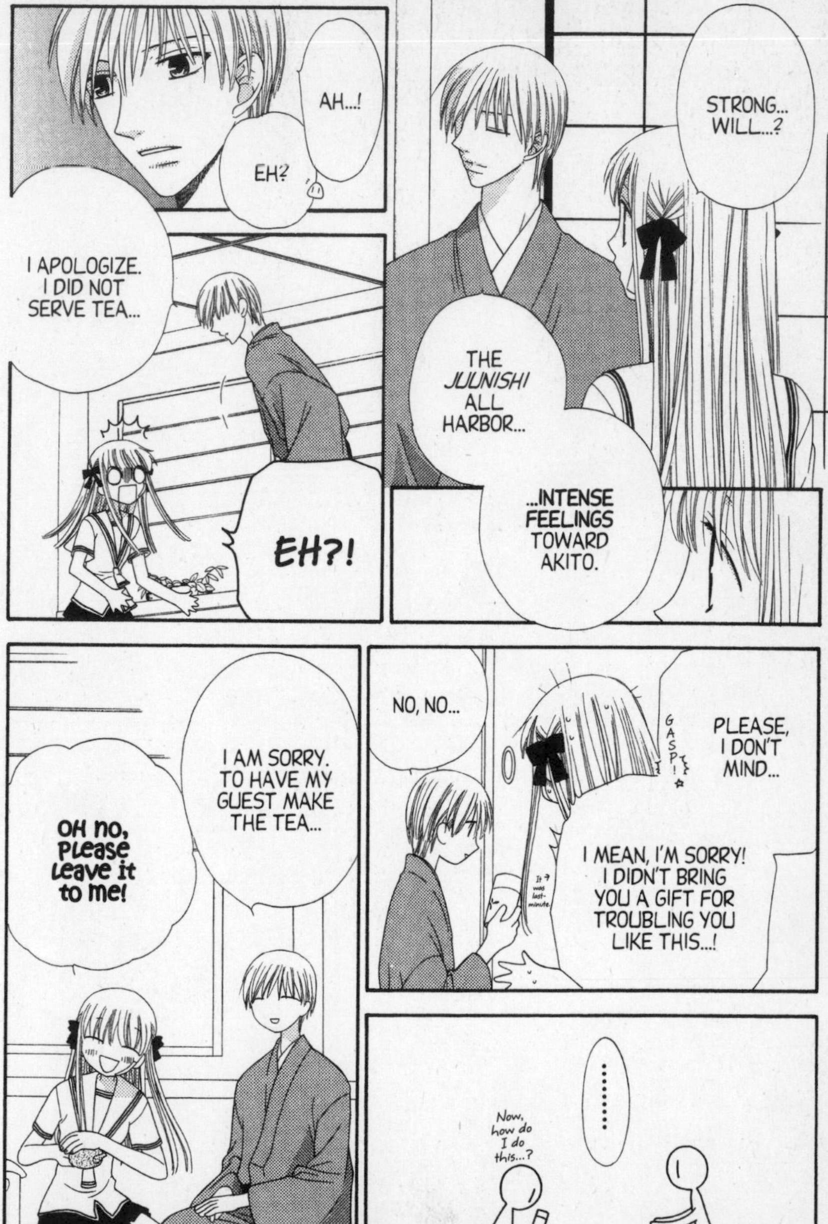
STRONG... WILL...?
THE JUUNISHI ALL HARBOR...
...INTENSE FEELINGS TOWARD AKITO.
AH...!
EH?
I APOLOGIZE. I DID NOT SERVE TEA...
EH?!
PLEASE, I DON'T MIND...
GASP!
NO, NO...
It was last-minute.
I MEAN, I'M SORRY! I DIDN'T BRING YOU A GIFT FOR TROUBLING YOU LIKE THIS...!
....
Now, how do I do this...?
I AM SORRY. TO HAVE MY GUEST MAKE THE TEA...
OH no, PLease Leave it to me!

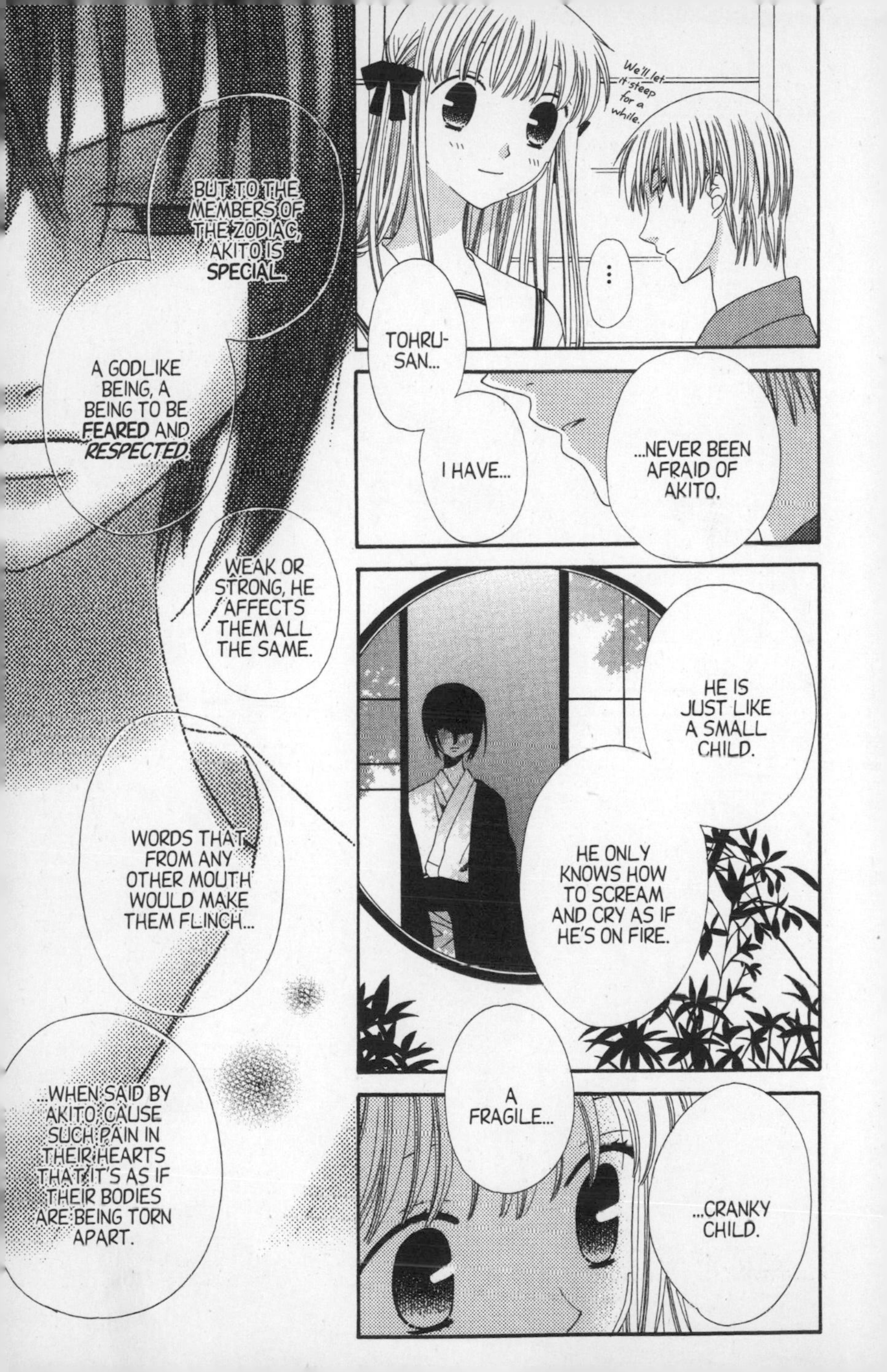
We'll let it steep for a while.
...
TOHRU-SAN...
I HAVE...
...NEVER BEEN AFRAID OF AKITO.
HE IS JUST LIKE A SMALL CHILD.
HE ONLY KNOWS HOW TO SCREAM AND CRY AS IF HE'S ON FIRE.
A FRAGILE...
...CRANKY CHILD.
BUT TO THE MEMBERS OF THE ZODIAC, AKITO IS **SPECIAL**.
A GODLIKE BEING, A BEING TO BE **FEARED** AND ***RESPECTED***.
WEAK OR STRONG, HE AFFECTS THEM ALL THE SAME.
WORDS THAT FROM ANY OTHER MOUTH WOULD MAKE THEM FLINCH...
...WHEN SAID BY AKITO CAUSE SUCH PAIN IN THEIR HEARTS THAT IT'S AS IF THEIR BODIES ARE BEING TORN APART.

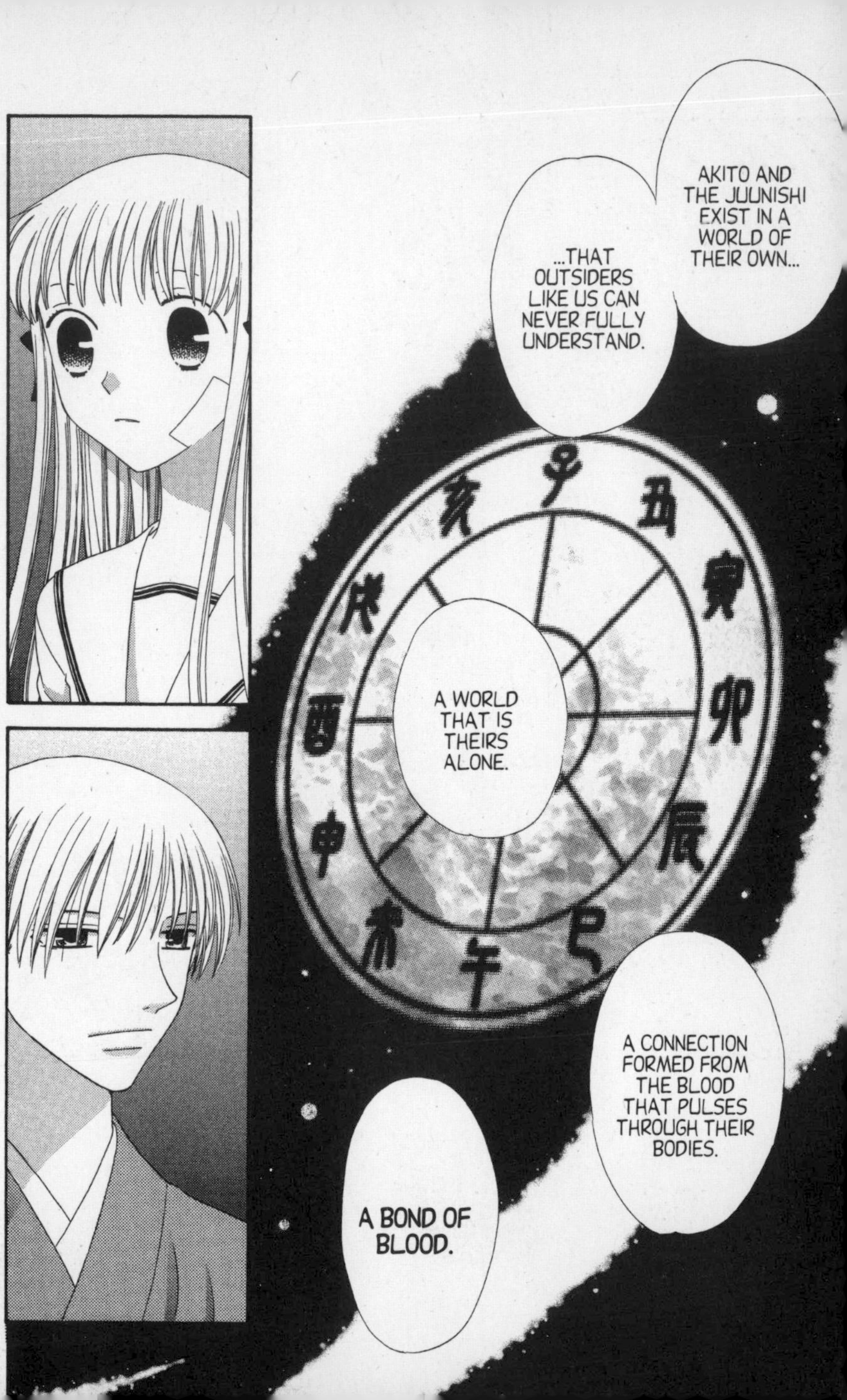
AKITO AND THE JUUNISHI EXIST IN A WORLD OF THEIR OWN...
...THAT OUTSIDERS LIKE US CAN NEVER FULLY UNDERSTAND.
子 丑 寅 卯 辰 巳 午 未 申 酉 戌 亥
A WORLD THAT IS THEIRS ALONE.
A CONNECTION FORMED FROM THE BLOOD THAT PULSES THROUGH THEIR BODIES.
A BOND OF BLOOD.

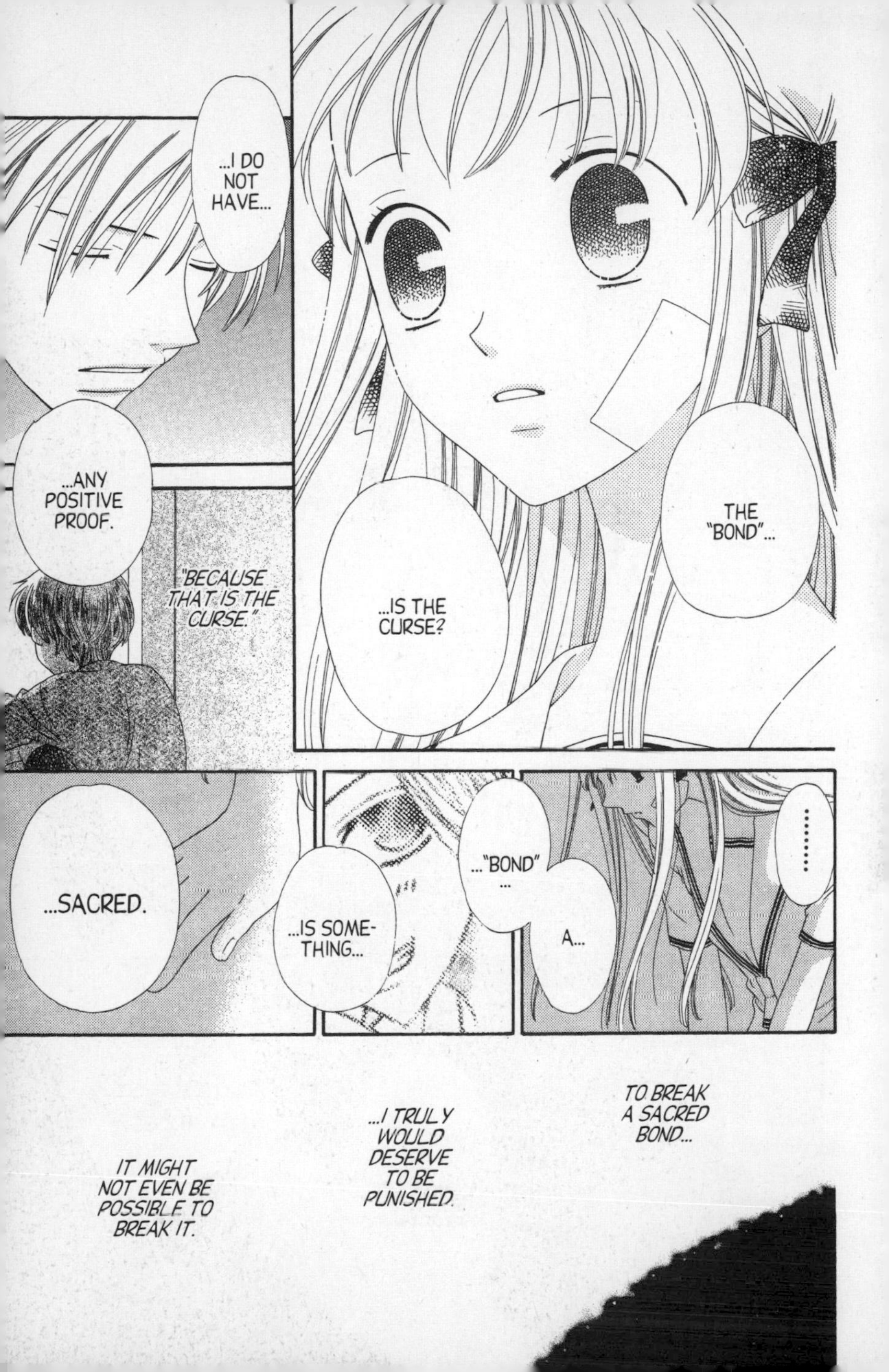
THE "BOND"...
...IS THE CURSE?
...I DO NOT HAVE...
...ANY POSITIVE PROOF.
"BECAUSE THAT IS THE CURSE."
......
..."BOND" ...
A...
...IS SOME-THING...
...SACRED.
TO BREAK A SACRED BOND...
...I TRULY WOULD DESERVE TO BE PUNISHED.
IT MIGHT NOT EVEN BE POSSIBLE TO BREAK IT.

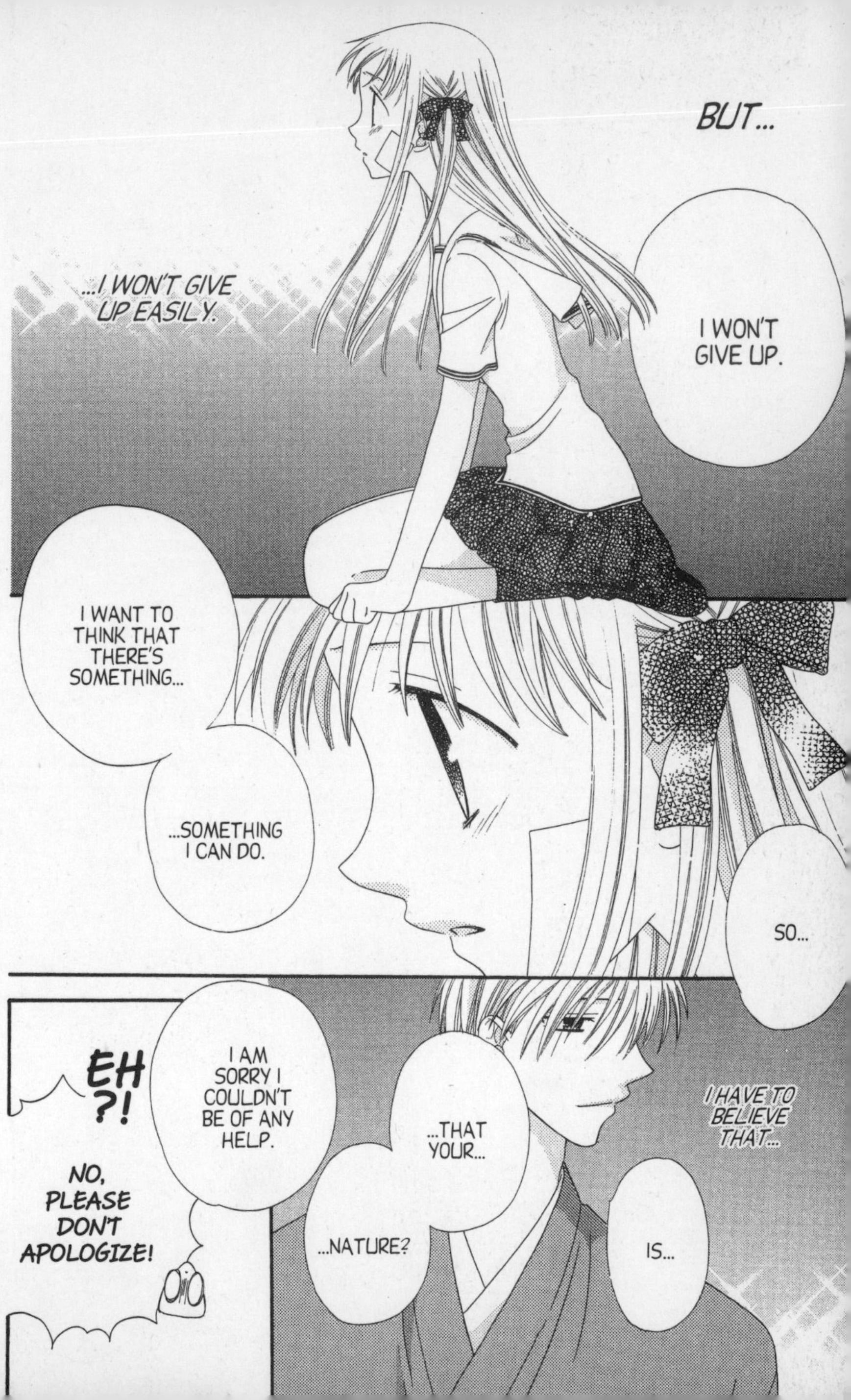
BUT...
I WON'T GIVE UP.
...I WON'T GIVE UP EASILY.
I WANT TO THINK THAT THERE'S SOMETHING...
...SOMETHING I CAN DO.
SO...
I HAVE TO BELIEVE THAT...
IS...
...THAT YOUR...
...NATURE?
I AM SORRY I COULDN'T BE OF ANY HELP.
EH?!
NO, PLEASE DON'T APOLOGIZE!

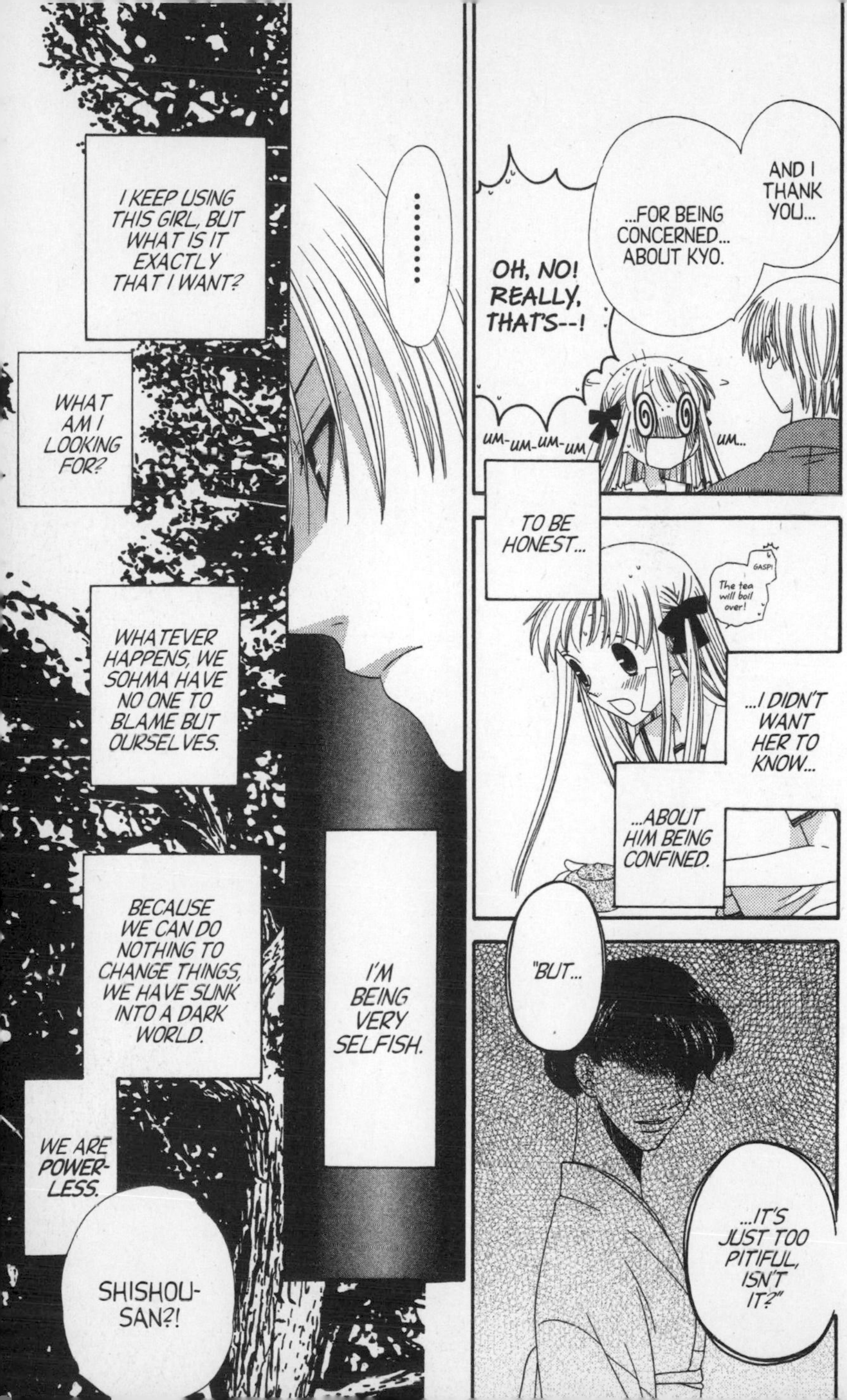
AND I THANK YOU...
...FOR BEING CONCERNED... ABOUT KYO.
OH, NO! REALLY, THAT'S--!
UM...
UM-UM-UM-UM
TO BE HONEST...
GASP! The tea will boil over!
...I DIDN'T WANT HER TO KNOW...
...ABOUT HIM BEING CONFINED.
"BUT...
...IT'S JUST TOO PITIFUL, ISN'T IT?"
....
I KEEP USING THIS GIRL, BUT WHAT IS IT EXACTLY THAT I WANT?
WHAT AM I LOOKING FOR?
WHATEVER HAPPENS, WE SOHMA HAVE NO ONE TO BLAME BUT OURSELVES.
I'M BEING VERY SELFISH.
BECAUSE WE CAN DO NOTHING TO CHANGE THINGS, WE HAVE SUNK INTO A DARK WORLD.
WE ARE POWER-LESS.
SHISHOU-SAN?!

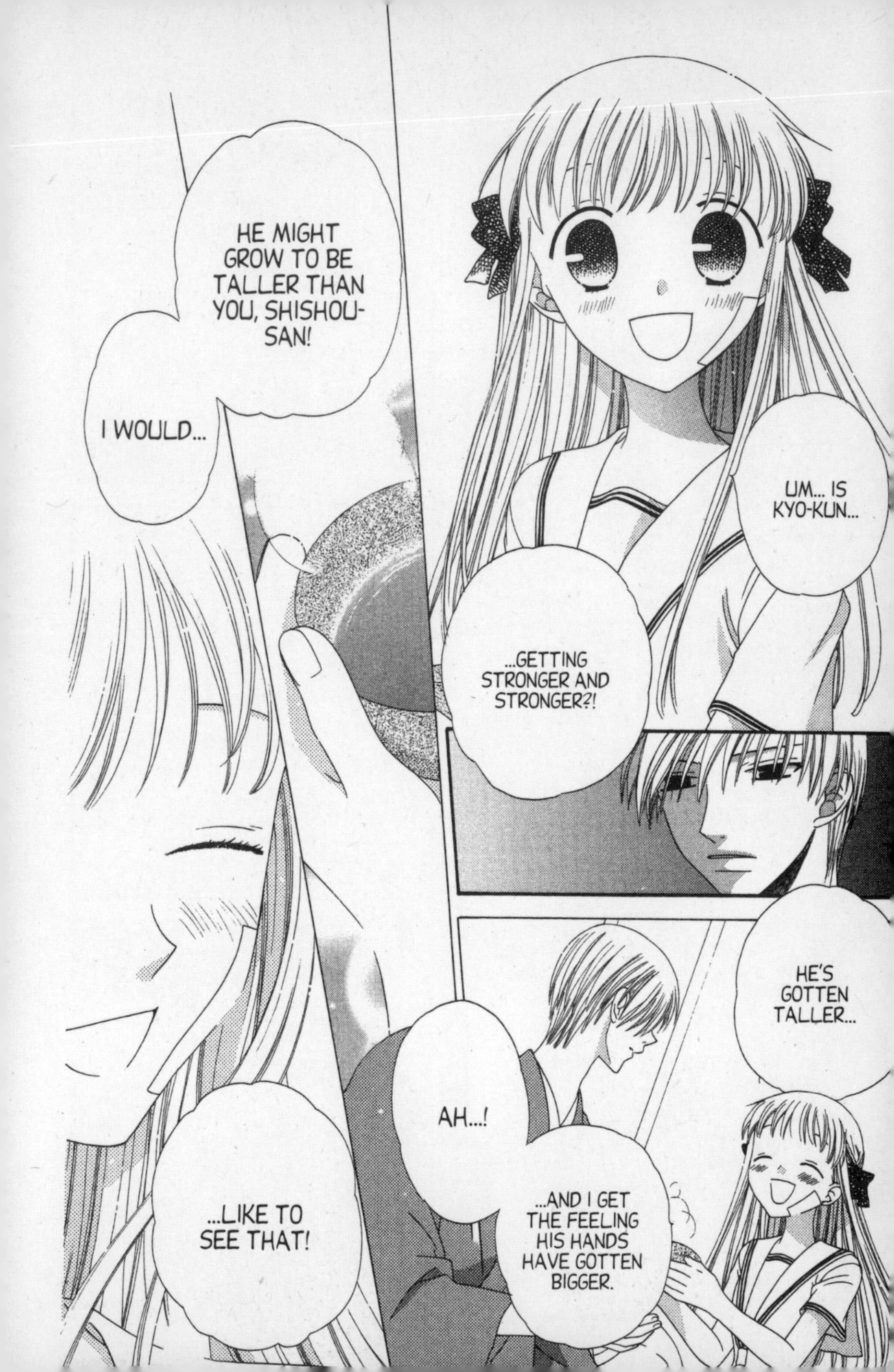
UM... IS KYO-KUN...
...GETTING STRONGER AND STRONGER?!
HE'S GOTTEN TALLER...
...AND I GET THE FEELING HIS HANDS HAVE GOTTEN BIGGER.
AH...!
HE MIGHT GROW TO BE TALLER THAN YOU, SHISHOU-SAN!
I WOULD...
...LIKE TO SEE THAT!

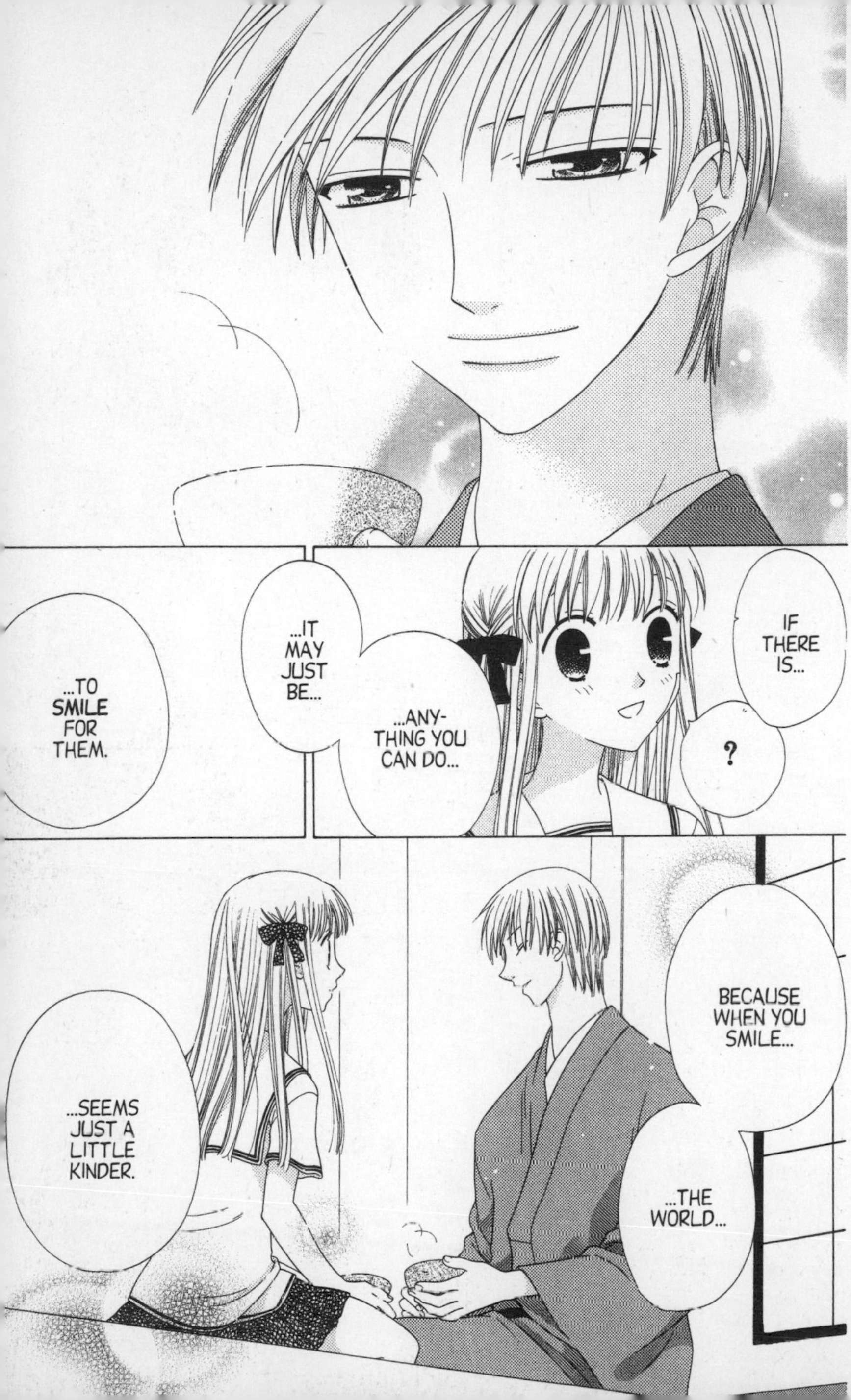
IF THERE IS...
?
...ANY-THING YOU CAN DO...
...IT MAY JUST BE...
...TO SMILE FOR THEM.
BECAUSE WHEN YOU SMILE...
...THE WORLD...
...SEEMS JUST A LITTLE KINDER.

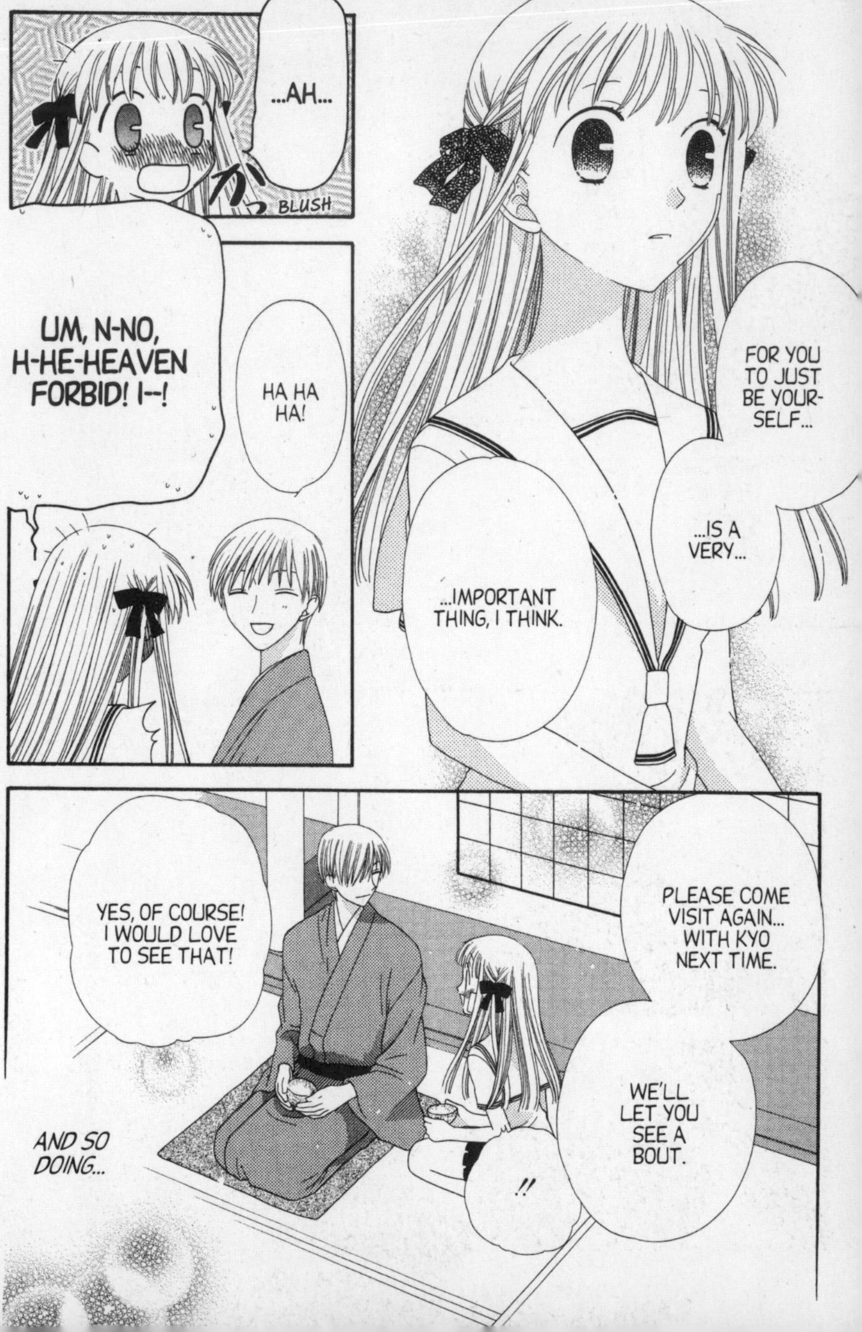
FOR YOU TO JUST BE YOUR-SELF...
...IS A VERY...
...IMPORTANT THING, I THINK.
...AH...
かっ
BLUSH
HA HA HA!
UM, N-NO, H-HE-HEAVEN FORBID! I--!
PLEASE COME VISIT AGAIN... WITH KYO NEXT TIME.
WE'LL LET YOU SEE A BOUT.
!!
YES, OF COURSE! I WOULD LOVE TO SEE THAT!
AND SO DOING...

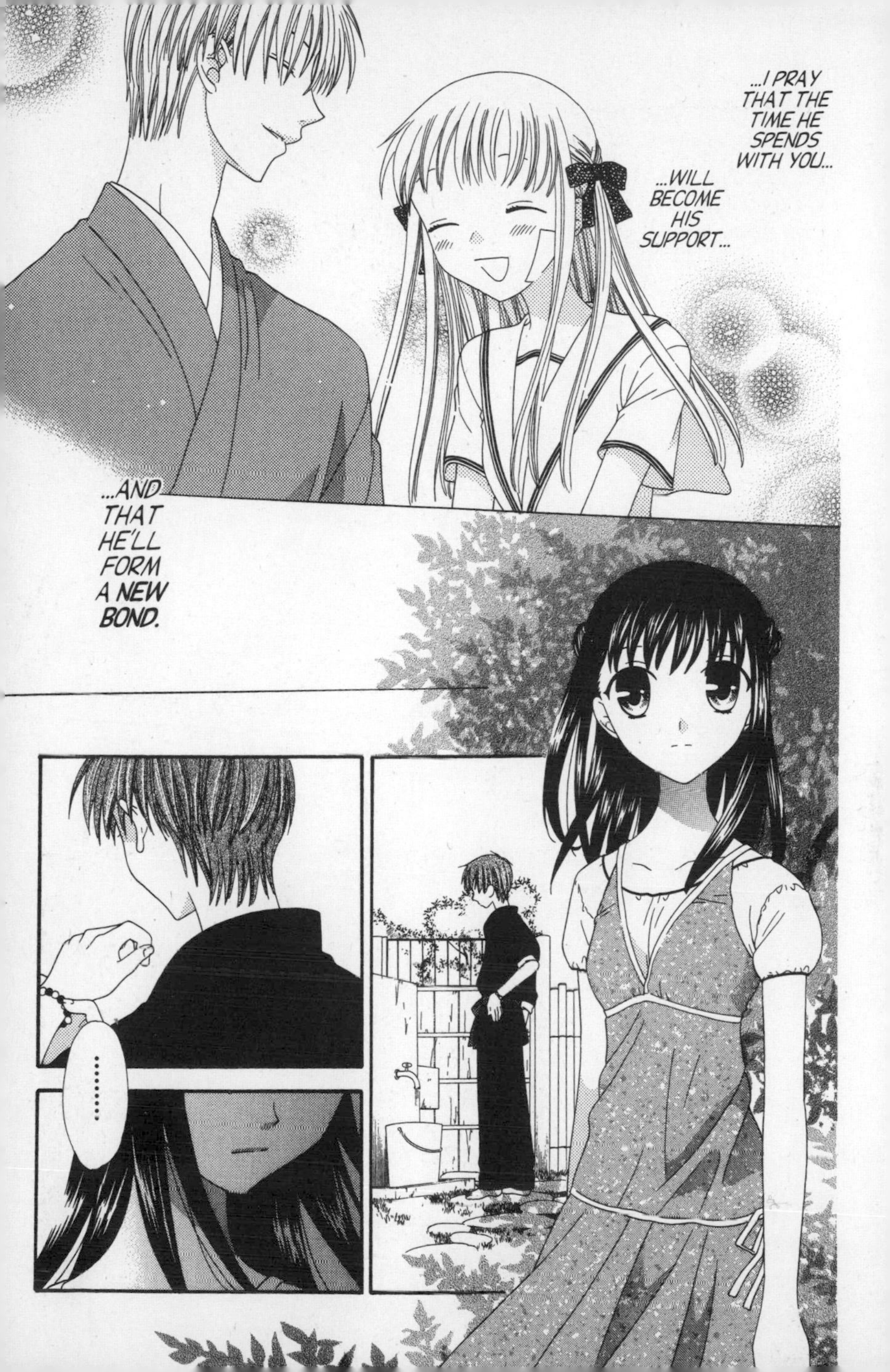
...I PRAY THAT THE TIME HE SPENDS WITH YOU...
...WILL BECOME HIS SUPPORT...
...AND THAT HE'LL FORM A NEW BOND.
....

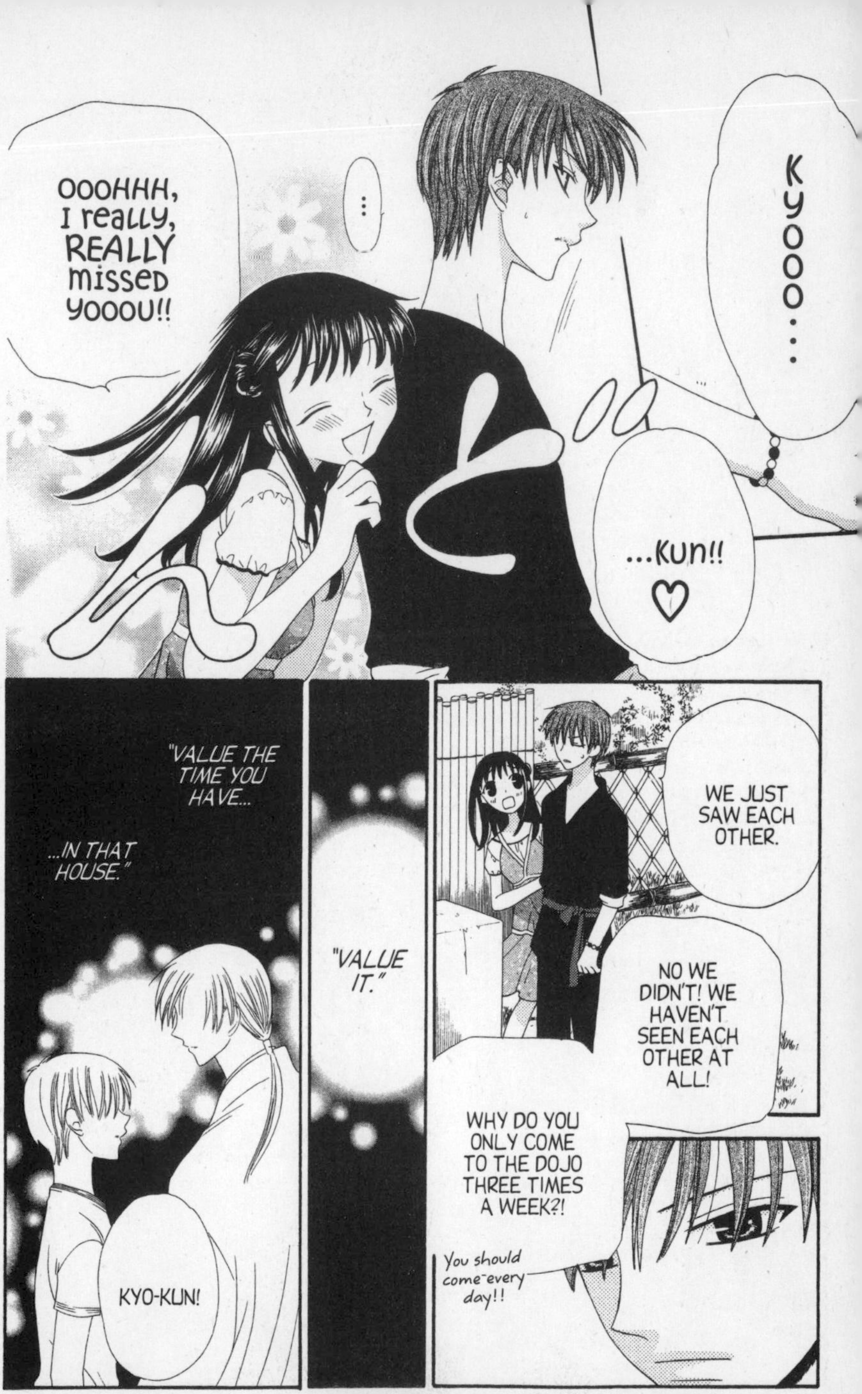
KYOOO...
...KUN!! ♡
...
OOOHHH, I really, REALLY missed yooou!!
WE JUST SAW EACH OTHER.
NO WE DIDN'T! WE HAVEN'T SEEN EACH OTHER AT ALL!
WHY DO YOU ONLY COME TO THE DOJO THREE TIMES A WEEK?!
You should come every day!!
"VALUE IT."
"VALUE THE TIME YOU HAVE...
...IN THAT HOUSE."
KYO-KUN!

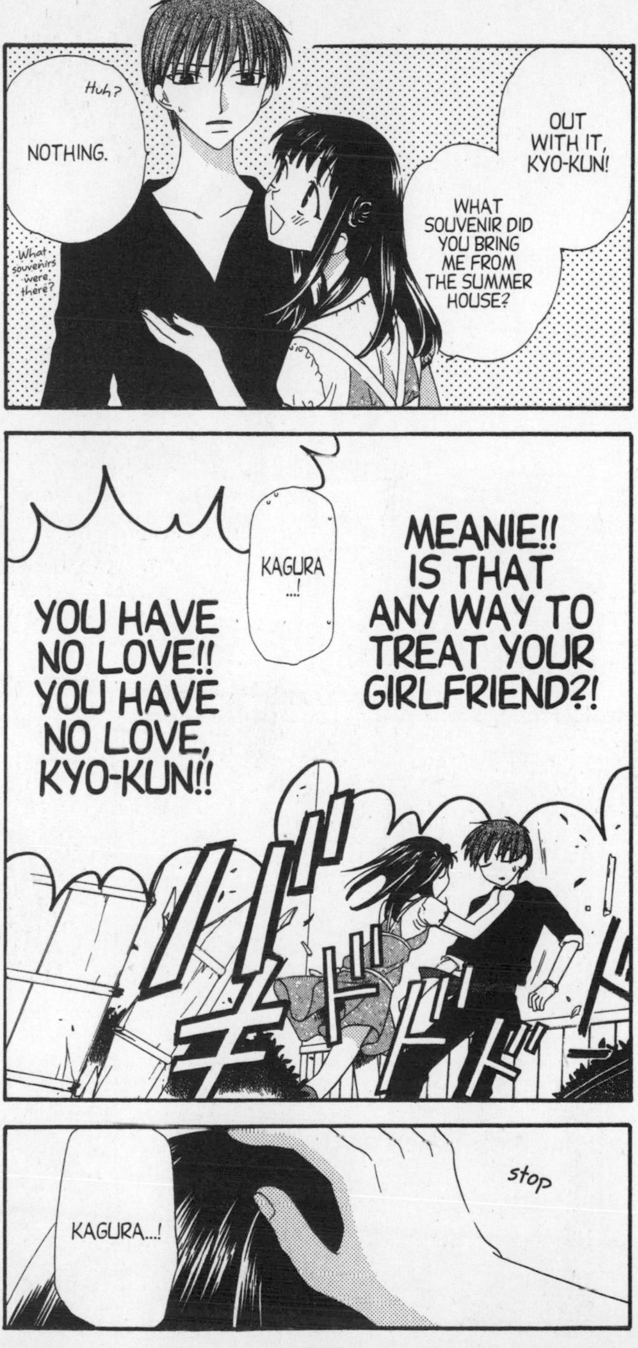
OUT WITH IT, KYO-KUN!
WHAT SOUVENIR DID YOU BRING ME FROM THE SUMMER HOUSE?
Huh?
NOTHING.
What souvenirs were there?
MEANIE!! IS THAT ANY WAY TO TREAT YOUR GIRLFRIEND?!
KAGURA ...!
YOU HAVE NO LOVE!! YOU HAVE NO LOVE, KYO-KUN!!
stop
KAGURA...!

Mitchan

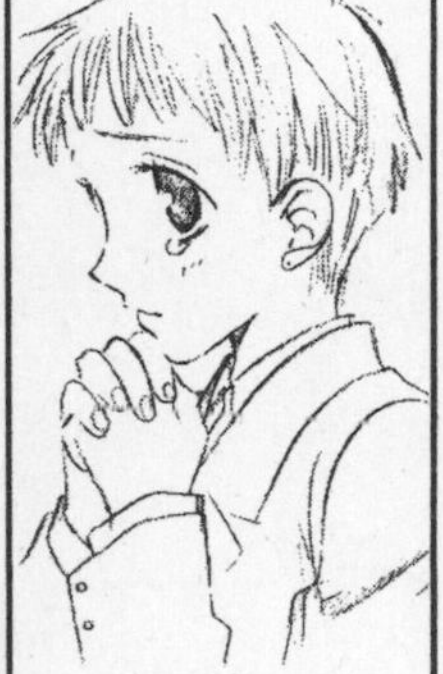

Just because the cover is Ritchan (laugh). His honey. Her name is Mitsuru, but I haven't decided on a surname. When she first saw him, she was slightly attracted to Shigure, but now she strongly, deeply regrets that. Now she thinks he's **evil**...

Shigure makes her go to all that trouble to come get his manuscripts just to kill time. He really is evil!

There are some heartwarming(?) episodes left between her and Ritchan, but now that the main story has progressed so far, there might not be time to draw them...

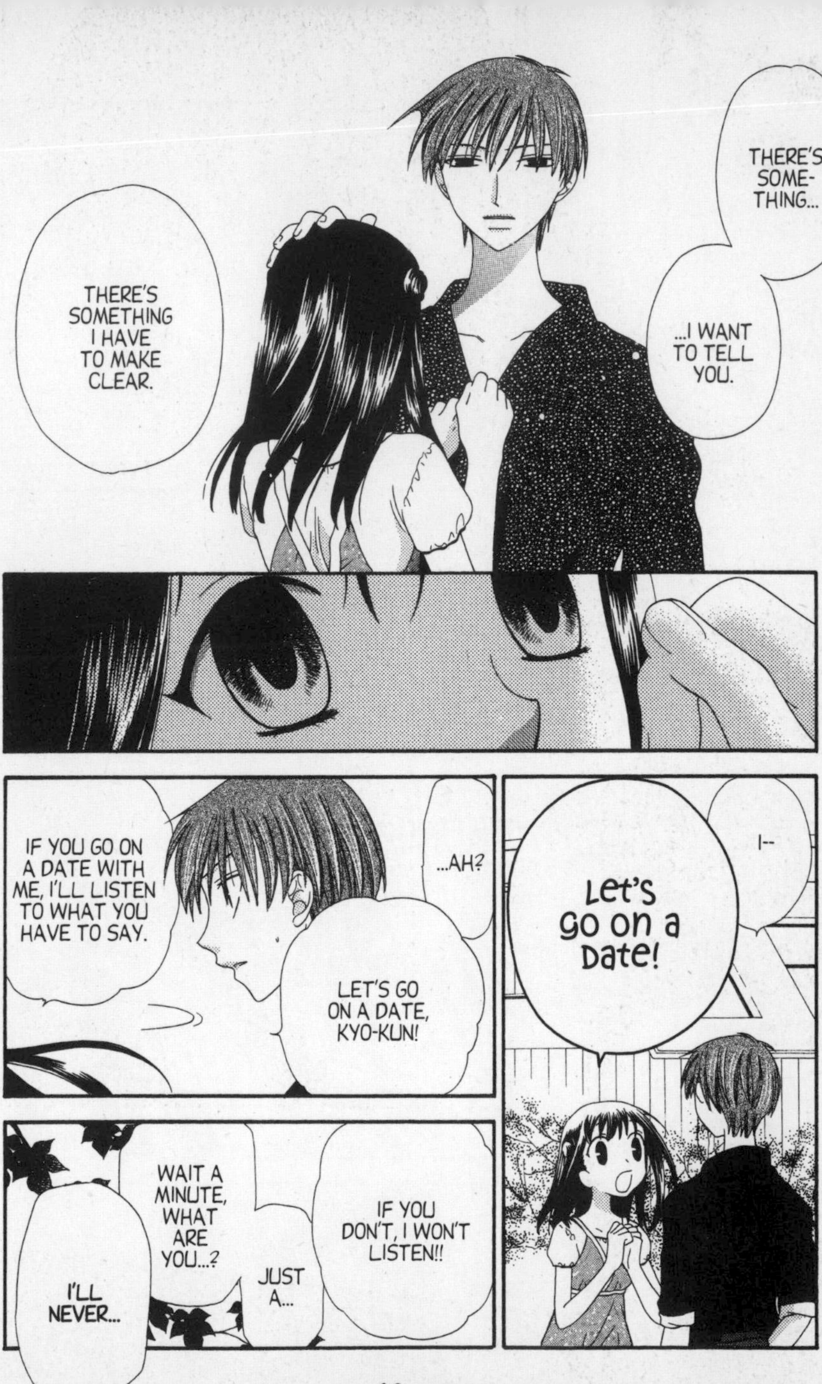
THERE'S SOME-THING...
...I WANT TO TELL YOU.
THERE'S SOMETHING I HAVE TO MAKE CLEAR.
I--
Let's go on a Date!
...AH?
LET'S GO ON A DATE, KYO-KUN!
IF YOU GO ON A DATE WITH ME, I'LL LISTEN TO WHAT YOU HAVE TO SAY.
IF YOU DON'T, I WON'T LISTEN!!
WAIT A MINUTE, WHAT ARE YOU...?
JUST A...
I'LL NEVER...

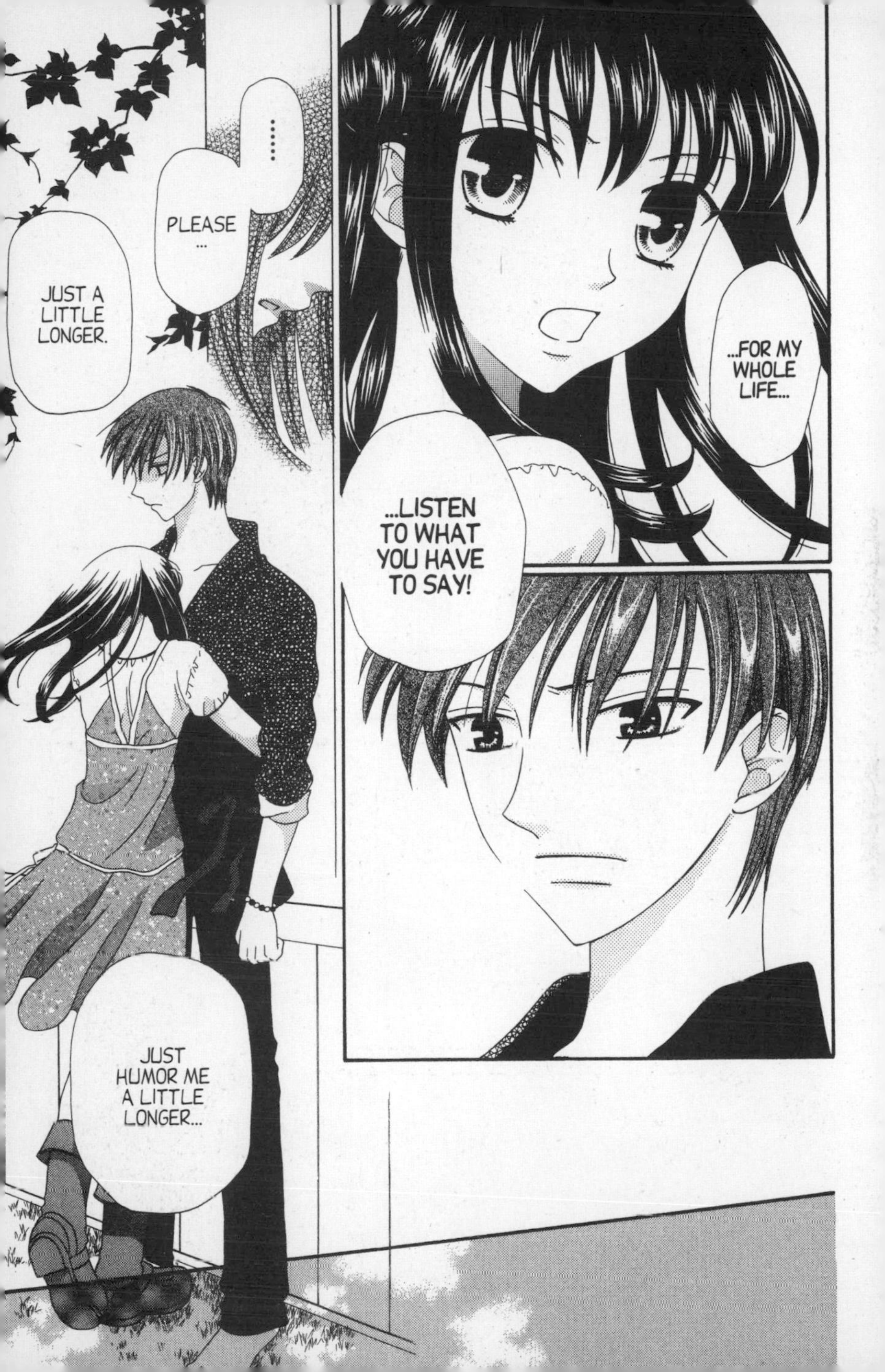
...FOR MY WHOLE LIFE...
...LISTEN TO WHAT YOU HAVE TO SAY!
......
PLEASE ...
JUST A LITTLE LONGER.
JUST HUMOR ME A LITTLE LONGER...

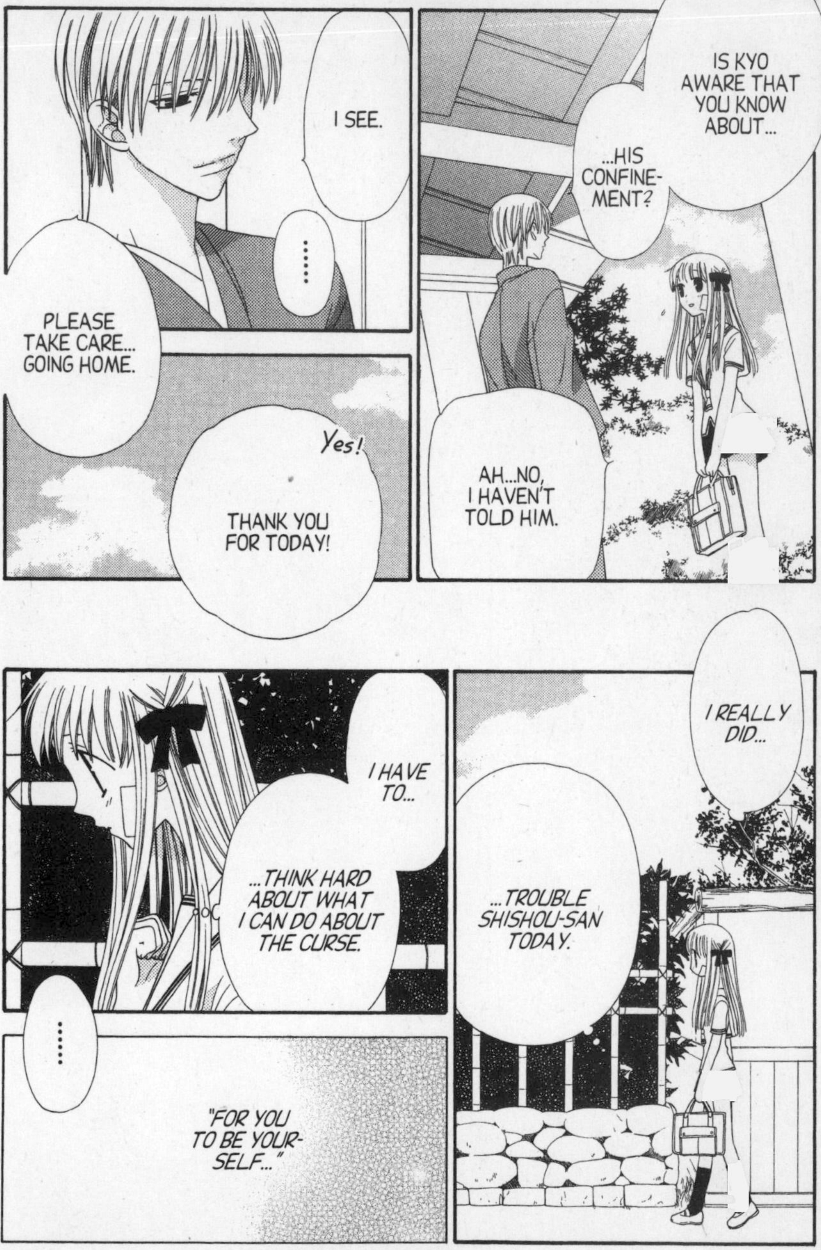
IS KYO AWARE THAT YOU KNOW ABOUT...
...HIS CONFINE-MENT?
AH...NO, I HAVEN'T TOLD HIM.
I SEE.
......
PLEASE TAKE CARE... GOING HOME.
Yes!
THANK YOU FOR TODAY!
I REALLY DID...
...TROUBLE SHISHOU-SAN TODAY.
I HAVE TO...
...THINK HARD ABOUT WHAT I CAN DO ABOUT THE CURSE.
......
"FOR YOU TO BE YOUR-SELF..."

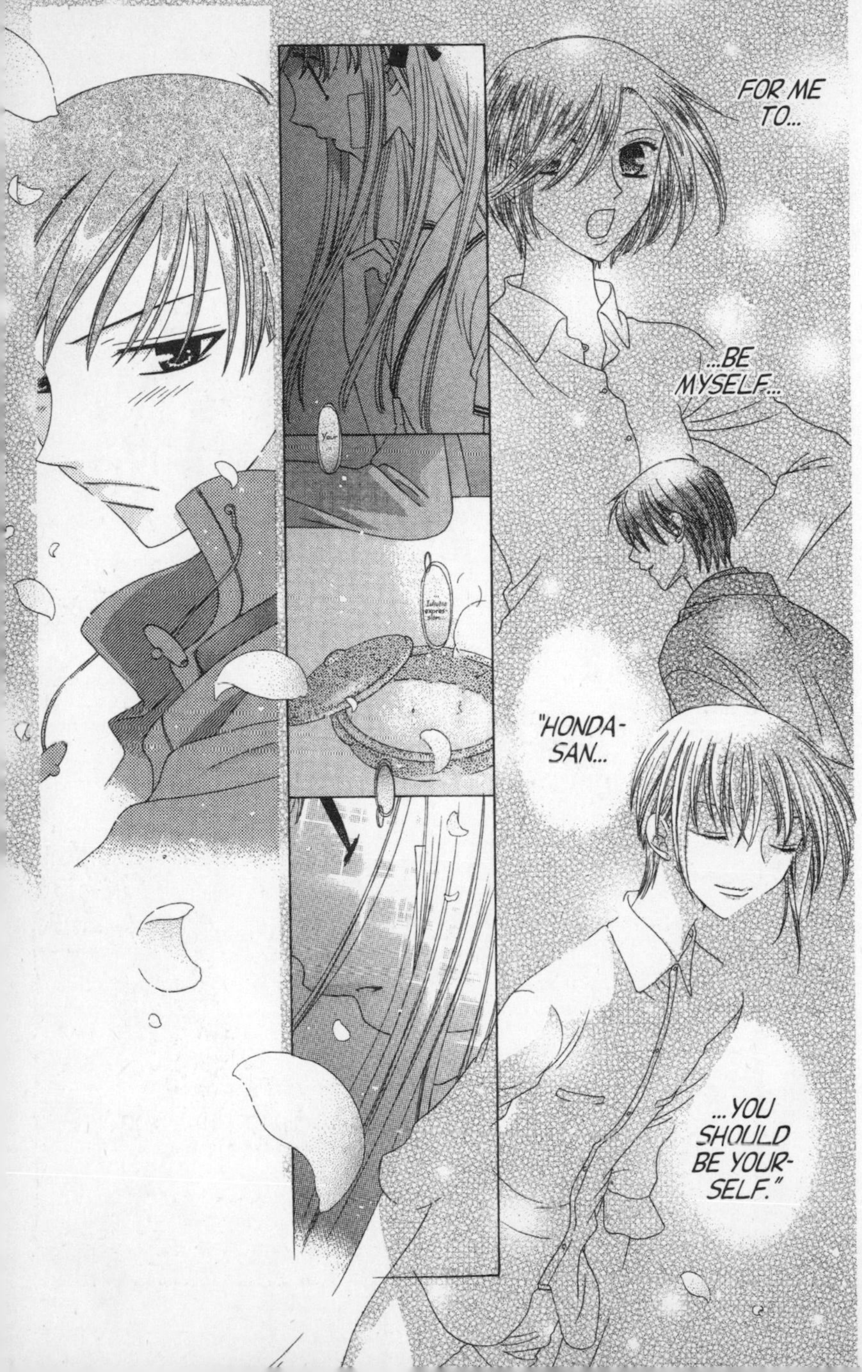
FOR ME TO...
...BE MYSELF...
"HONDA-SAN...
...YOU SHOULD BE YOURSELF."
Your

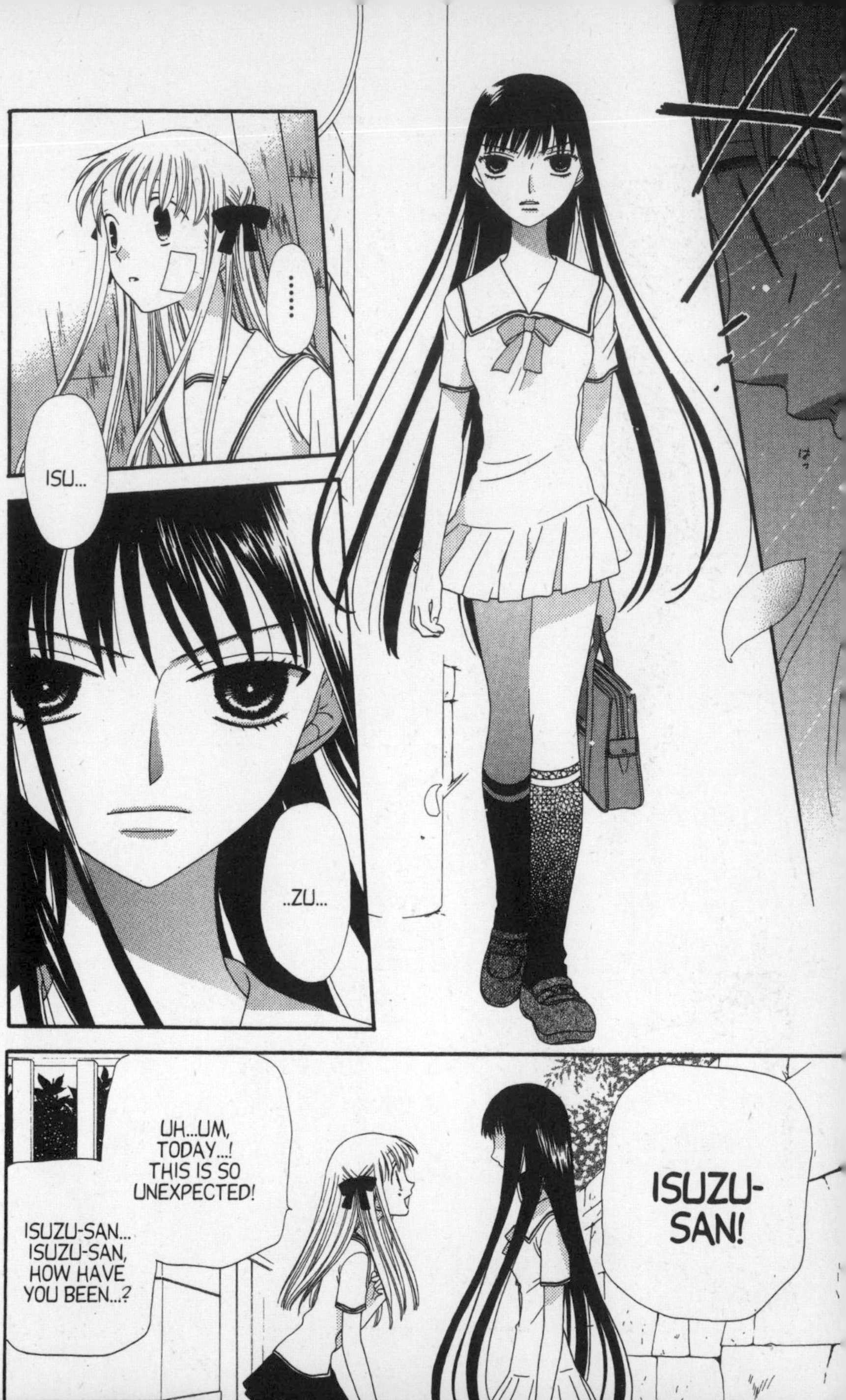
......
ISU...
..ZU...
ISUZU-SAN!
UH...UM, TODAY...! THIS IS SO UNEXPECTED!
ISUZU-SAN... ISUZU-SAN, HOW HAVE YOU BEEN...?

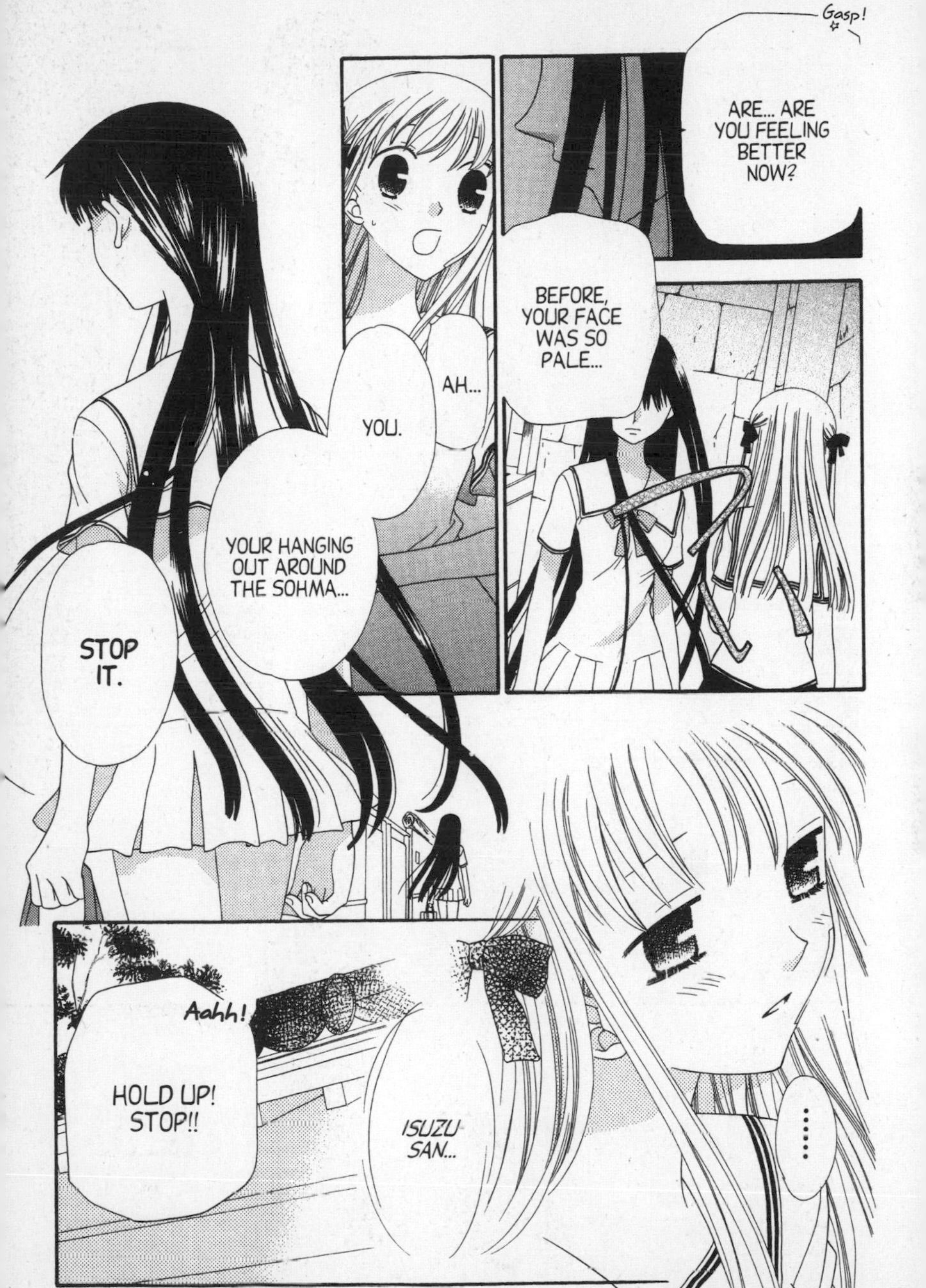
Gasp!
ARE... ARE YOU FEELING BETTER NOW?
BEFORE, YOUR FACE WAS SO PALE...
AH...
YOU.
YOUR HANGING OUT AROUND THE SOHMA...
STOP IT.
......
ISUZU SAN...
Aahh!
HOLD UP! STOP!!

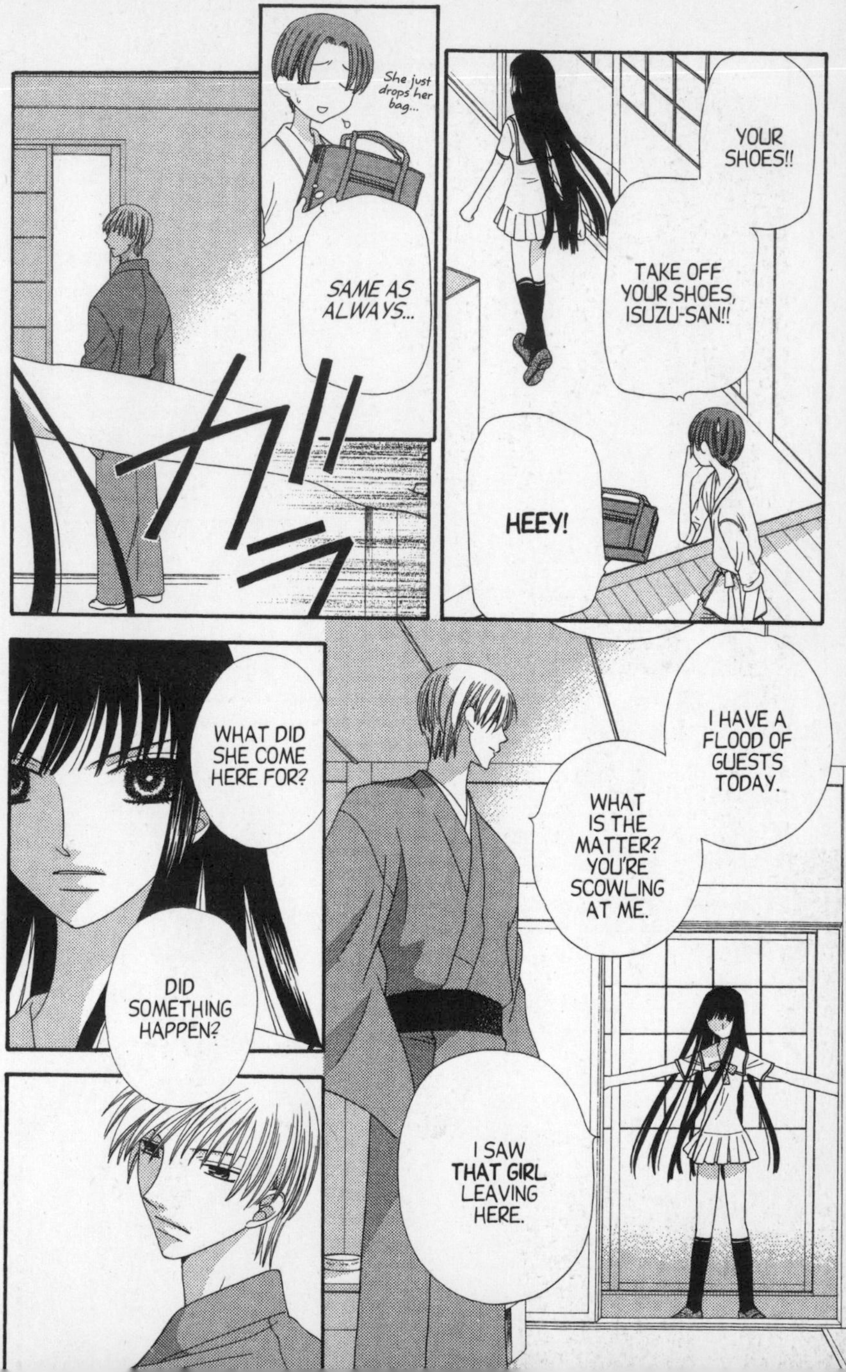
YOUR SHOES!!
TAKE OFF YOUR SHOES, ISUZU-SAN!!
HEEY!
She just drops her bag...
SAME AS ALWAYS...
I HAVE A FLOOD OF GUESTS TODAY.
WHAT IS THE MATTER? YOU'RE SCOWLING AT ME.
I SAW THAT GIRL LEAVING HERE.
WHAT DID SHE COME HERE FOR?
DID SOMETHING HAPPEN?

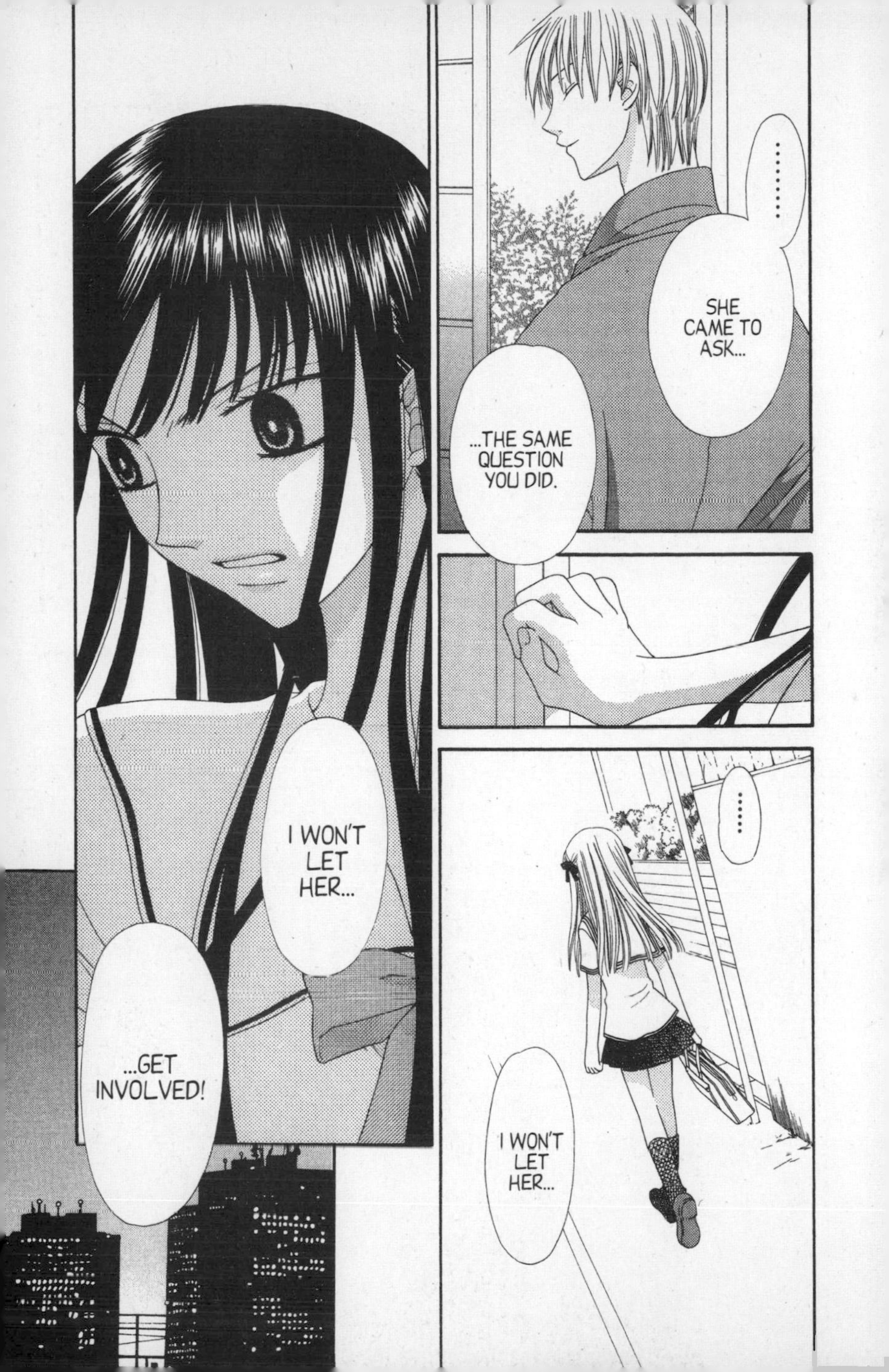
......
SHE CAME TO ASK...
...THE SAME QUESTION YOU DID.
......
I WON'T LET HER...
I WON'T LET HER...
...GET INVOLVED!

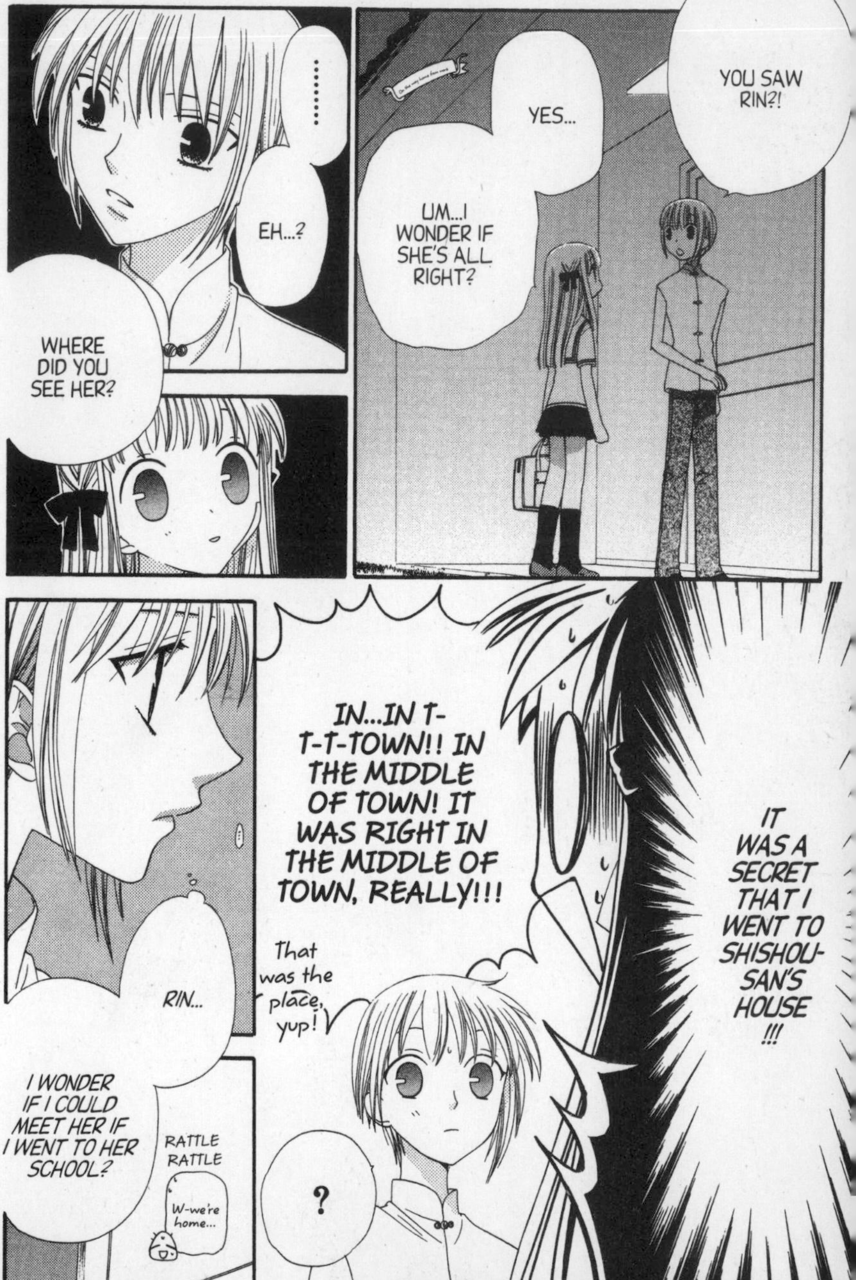
YOU SAW RIN?!
YES...
UM...I WONDER IF SHE'S ALL RIGHT?
......
EH...?
WHERE DID YOU SEE HER?
IT WAS A SECRET THAT I WENT TO SHISHOU-SAN'S HOUSE!!!
IN...IN T-T-T-TOWN!! IN THE MIDDLE OF TOWN! IT WAS RIGHT IN THE MIDDLE OF TOWN, REALLY!!!
That was the place, yup!
?
...
RIN...
I WONDER IF I COULD MEET HER IF I WENT TO HER SCHOOL?
RATTLE RATTLE
W-we're home...

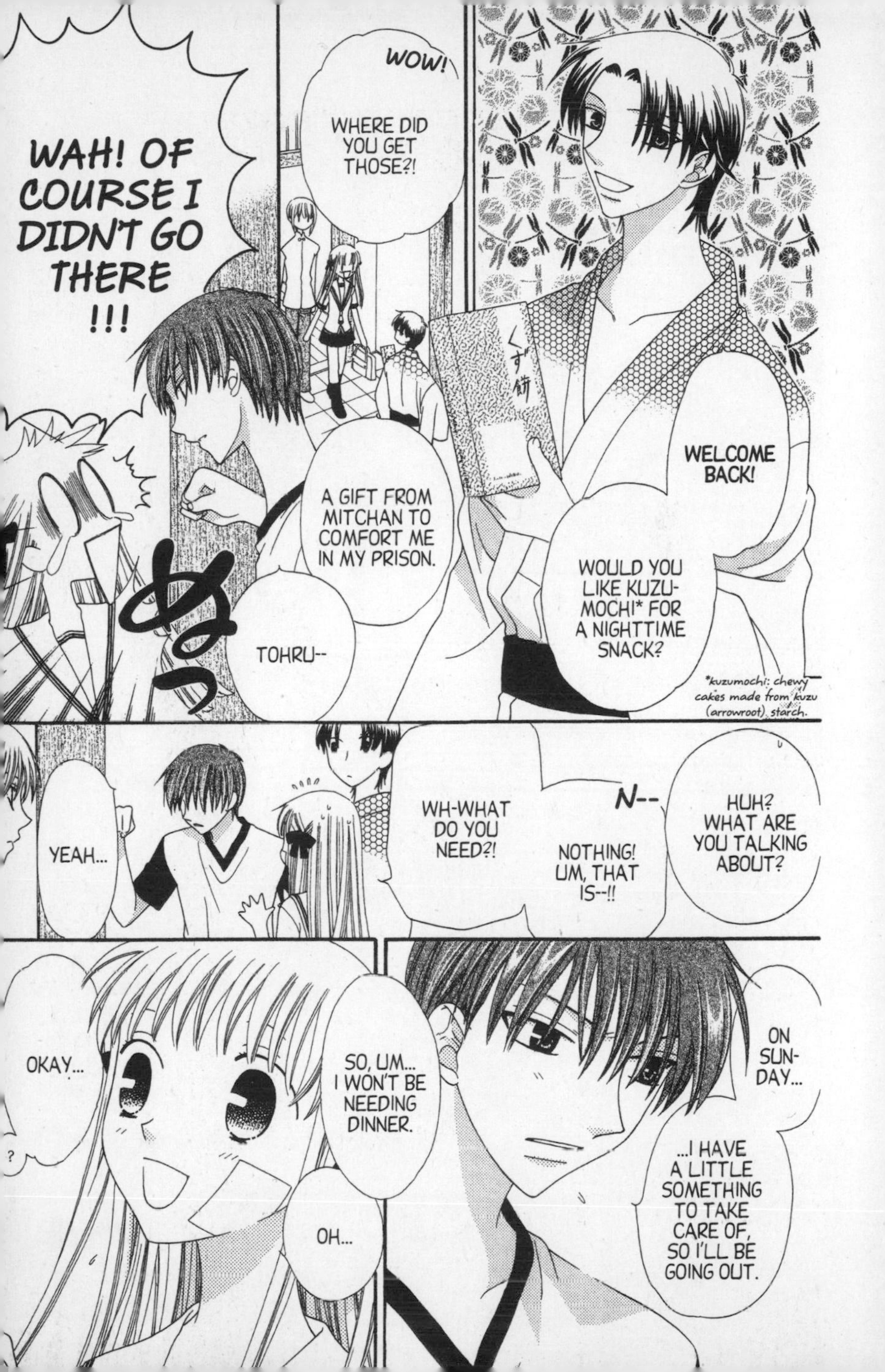

WELCOME BACK!
WOULD YOU LIKE KUZU-MOCHI* FOR A NIGHTTIME SNACK?
くず餅
*kuzumochi: chewy cakes made from kuzu (arrowroot) starch.
WOW!
WHERE DID YOU GET THOSE?!
A GIFT FROM MITCHAN TO COMFORT ME IN MY PRISON.
WAH! OF COURSE I DIDN'T GO THERE !!!
TOHRU--
めっ
HUH? WHAT ARE YOU TALKING ABOUT?
N--
NOTHING! UM, THAT IS--!!
WH-WHAT DO YOU NEED?!
YEAH...
ON SUNDAY...
...I HAVE A LITTLE SOMETHING TO TAKE CARE OF, SO I'LL BE GOING OUT.
SO, UM... I WON'T BE NEEDING DINNER.
OH...
OKAY...
?

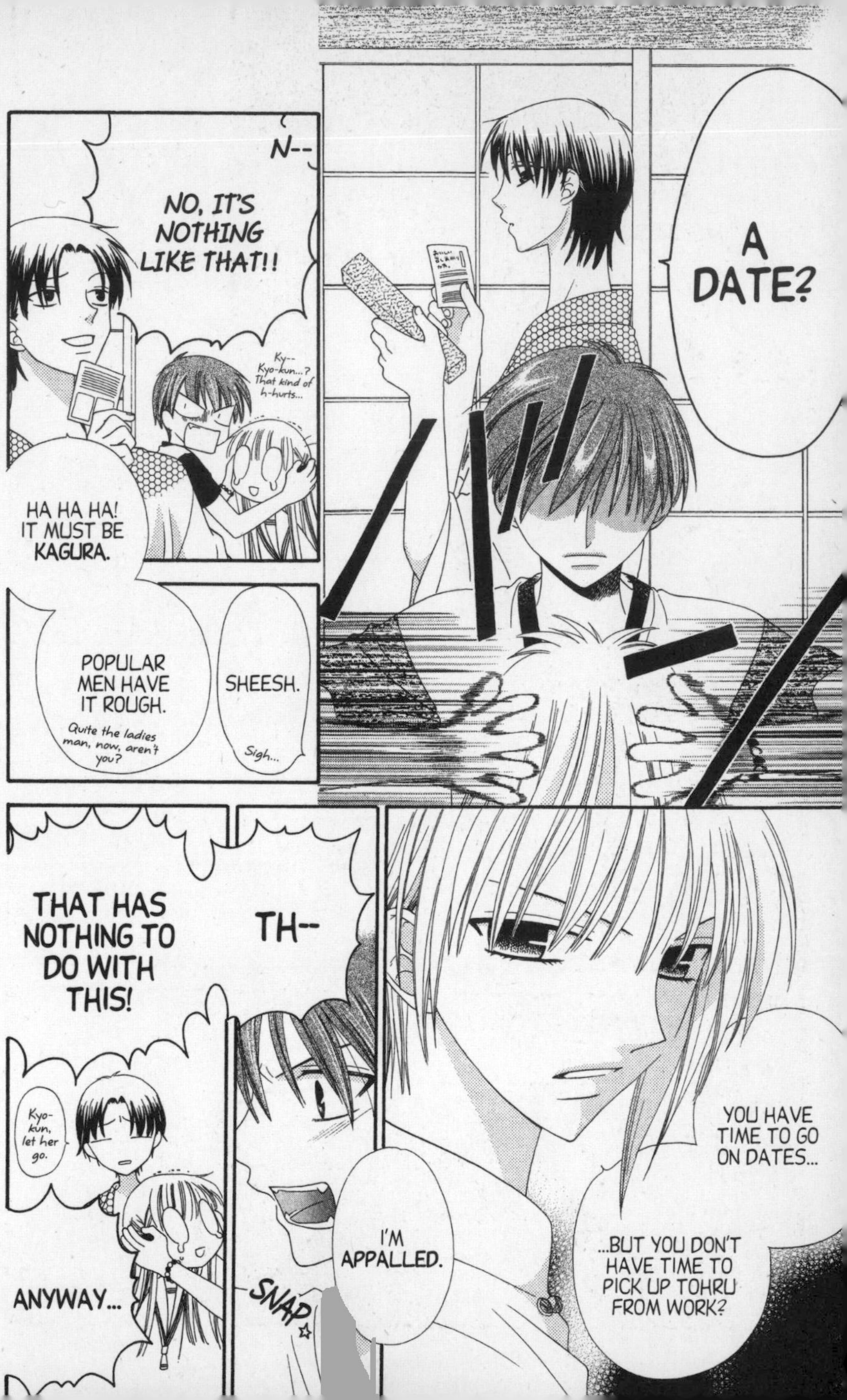
A DATE?
N--
NO, IT'S NOTHING LIKE THAT!!
Ky-- Kyo-kun...? That kind of h-hurts...
HA HA HA! IT MUST BE KAGURA.
SHEESH.
Sigh...
POPULAR MEN HAVE IT ROUGH.
Quite the ladies man, now, aren't you?
YOU HAVE TIME TO GO ON DATES...
...BUT YOU DON'T HAVE TIME TO PICK UP TOHRU FROM WORK?
I'M APPALLED.
SNAP
TH--
THAT HAS NOTHING TO DO WITH THIS!
Kyo-kun, let her go.
ANYWAY...

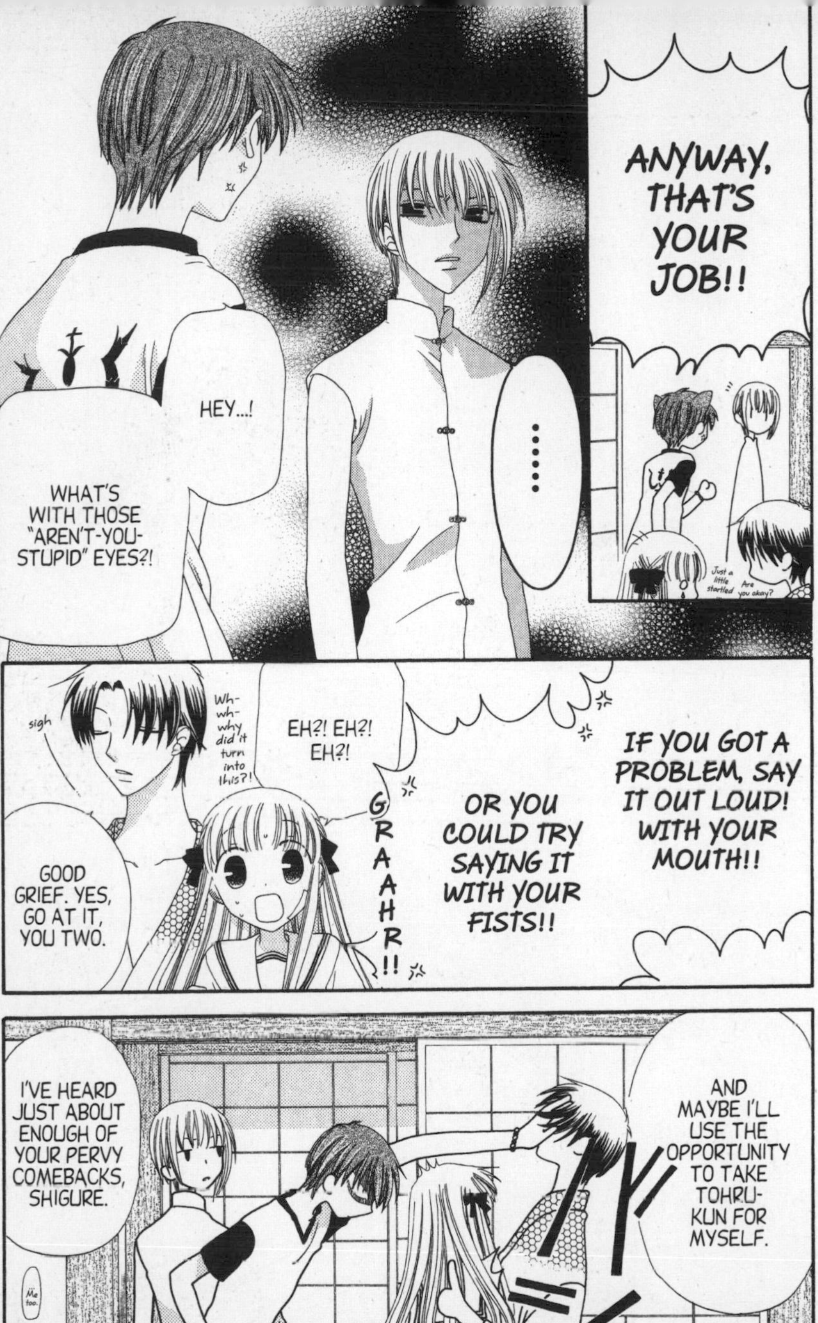
ANYWAY, THAT'S YOUR JOB!!
Are you okay?
Just a little startled
......
HEY...!
WHAT'S WITH THOSE "AREN'T-YOU-STUPID" EYES?!
IF YOU GOT A PROBLEM, SAY IT OUT LOUD! WITH YOUR MOUTH!!
OR YOU COULD TRY SAYING IT WITH YOUR FISTS!!
GRAAHR!!
EH?! EH?! EH?!
Wh-wh-why did it turn into this?!
sigh
GOOD GRIEF. YES, GO AT IT, YOU TWO.
AND MAYBE I'LL USE THE OPPORTUNITY TO TAKE TOHRU-KUN FOR MYSELF.
I'VE HEARD JUST ABOUT ENOUGH OF YOUR PERVY COMEBACKS, SHIGURE.
Me too.

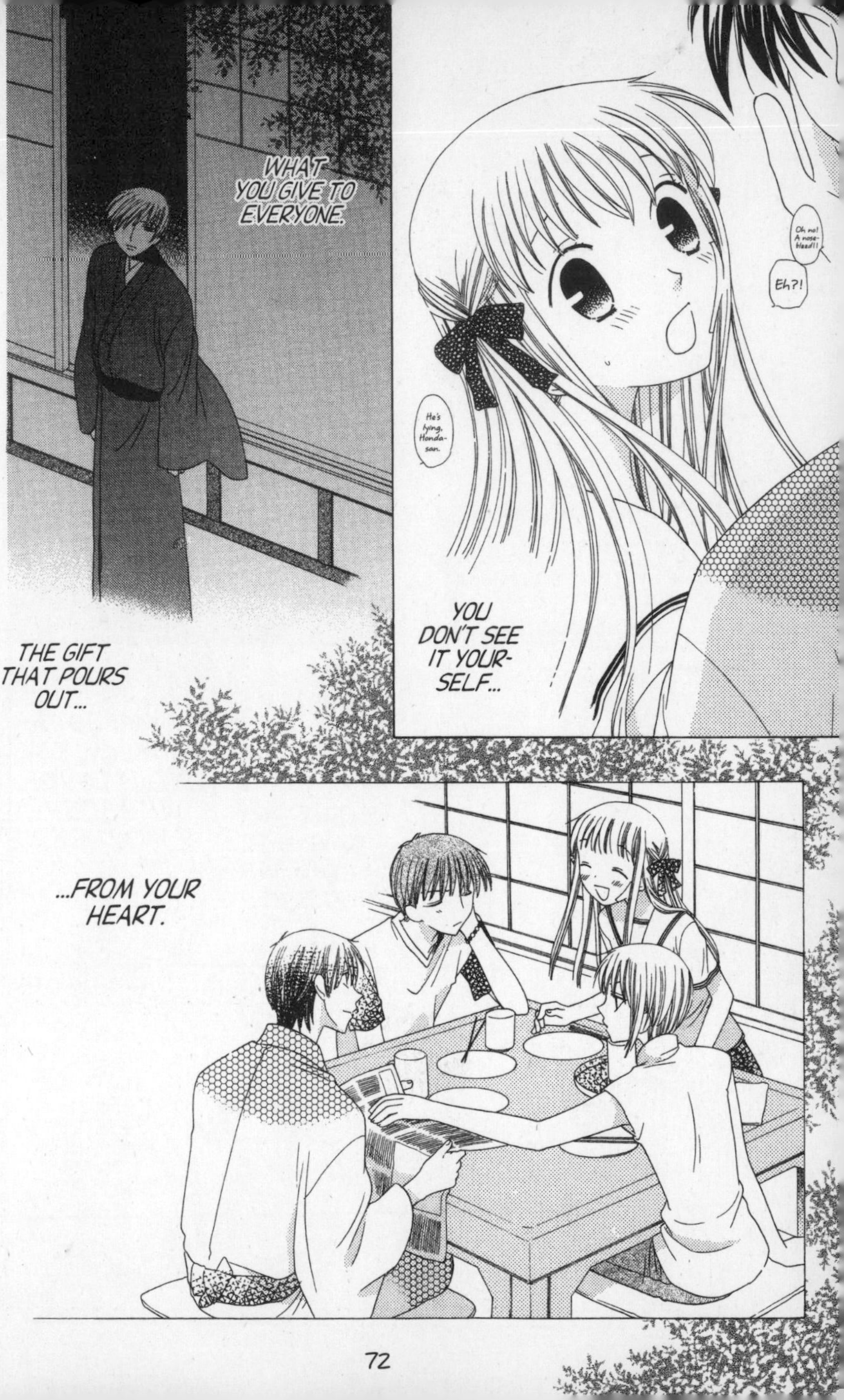
Oh no! A nose-bleed!!
Eh?!
He's lying, Honda-san.
YOU DON'T SEE IT YOUR-SELF...
WHAT YOU GIVE TO EVERYONE.
THE GIFT THAT POURS OUT...
...FROM YOUR HEART.

Chapter 68

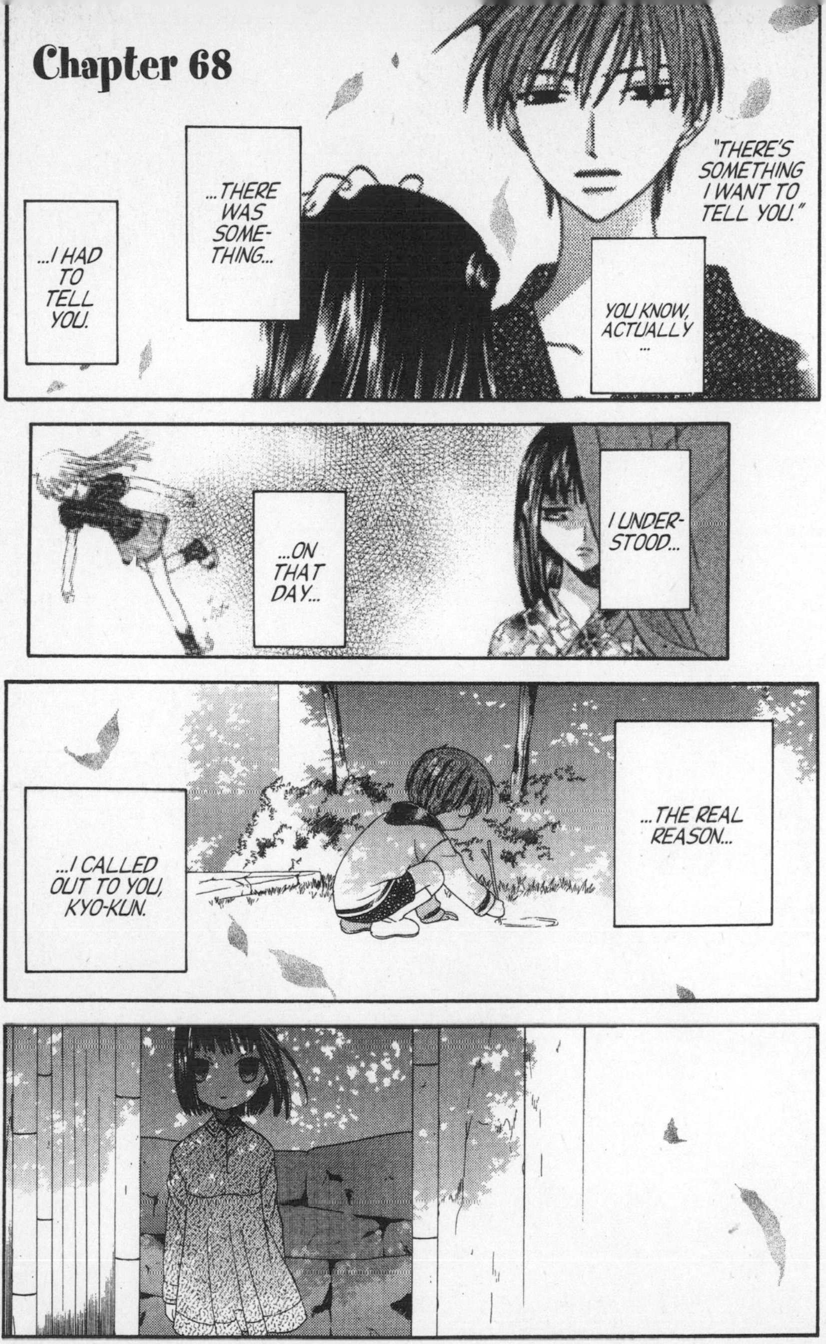
"THERE'S SOMETHING I WANT TO TELL YOU."
YOU KNOW, ACTUALLY ...
...THERE WAS SOME-THING...
...I HAD TO TELL YOU.
I UNDER-STOOD...
...ON THAT DAY...
...THE REAL REASON...
...I CALLED OUT TO YOU, KYO-KUN.

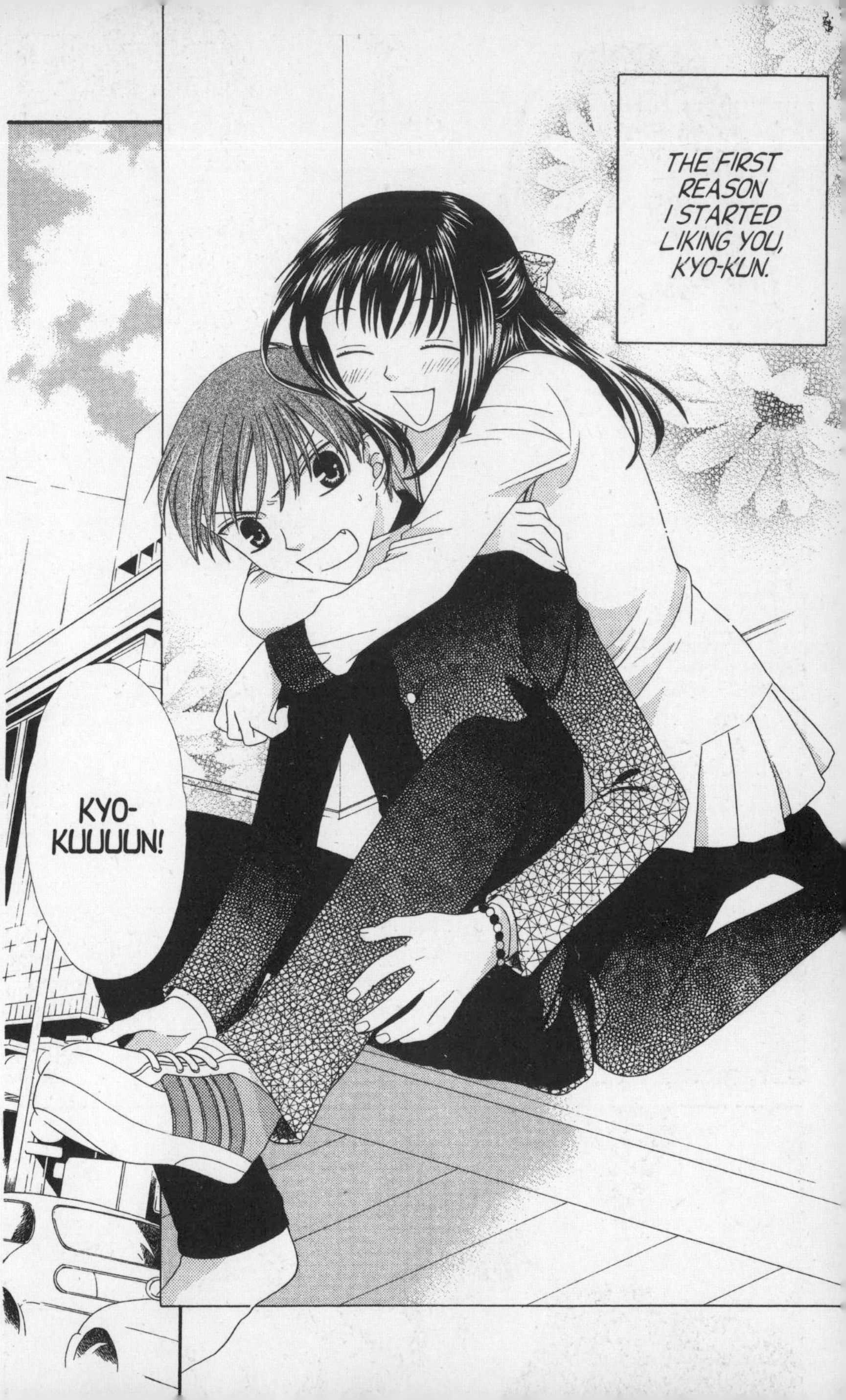
THE FIRST REASON I STARTED LIKING YOU, KYO-KUN.
KYO-KUUUUN!

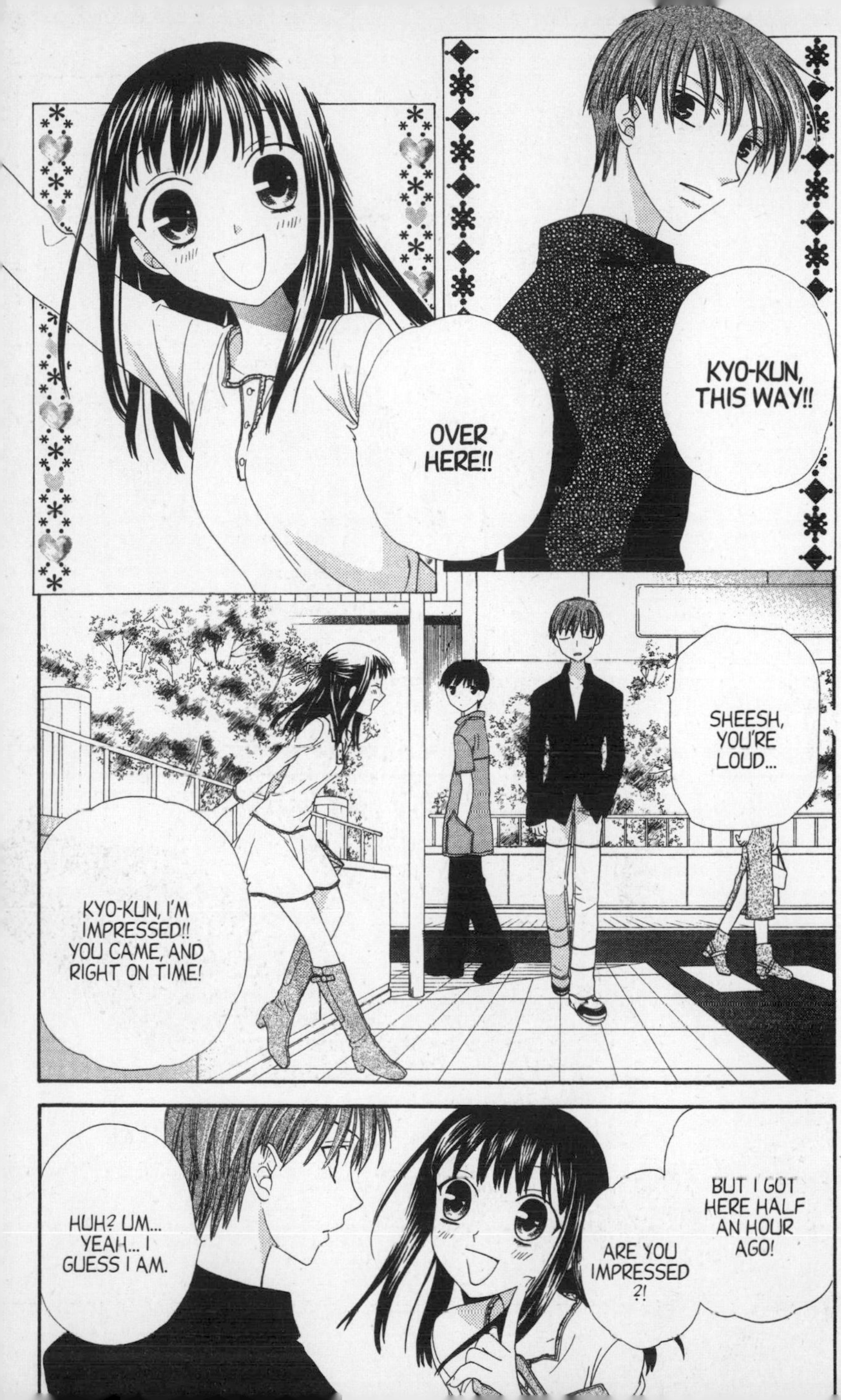
KYO-KUN, THIS WAY!!
OVER HERE!!
SHEESH, YOU'RE LOUD...
KYO-KUN, I'M IMPRESSED!! YOU CAME, AND RIGHT ON TIME!
BUT I GOT HERE HALF AN HOUR AGO!
ARE YOU IMPRESSED?!
HUH? UM... YEAH... I GUESS I AM.

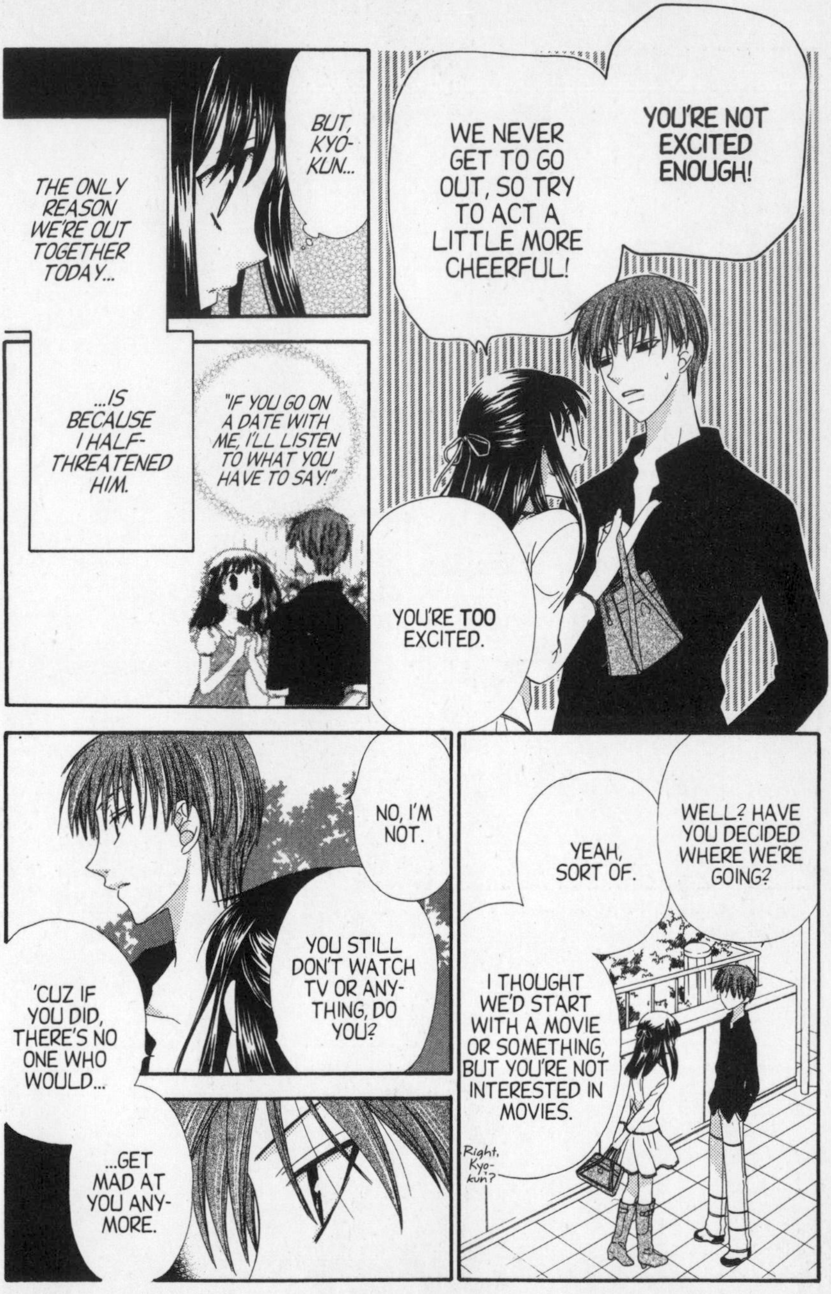
YOU'RE NOT EXCITED ENOUGH!
WE NEVER GET TO GO OUT, SO TRY TO ACT A LITTLE MORE CHEERFUL!
YOU'RE TOO EXCITED.
BUT, KYO-KUN...
THE ONLY REASON WE'RE OUT TOGETHER TODAY...
...IS BECAUSE I HALF-THREATENED HIM.
"IF YOU GO ON A DATE WITH ME, I'LL LISTEN TO WHAT YOU HAVE TO SAY!"
WELL? HAVE YOU DECIDED WHERE WE'RE GOING?
YEAH, SORT OF.
I THOUGHT WE'D START WITH A MOVIE OR SOMETHING, BUT YOU'RE NOT INTERESTED IN MOVIES.
Right, Kyo-kun?
NO, I'M NOT.
YOU STILL DON'T WATCH TV OR ANY-THING, DO YOU?
'CUZ IF YOU DID, THERE'S NO ONE WHO WOULD...
...GET MAD AT YOU ANY-MORE.

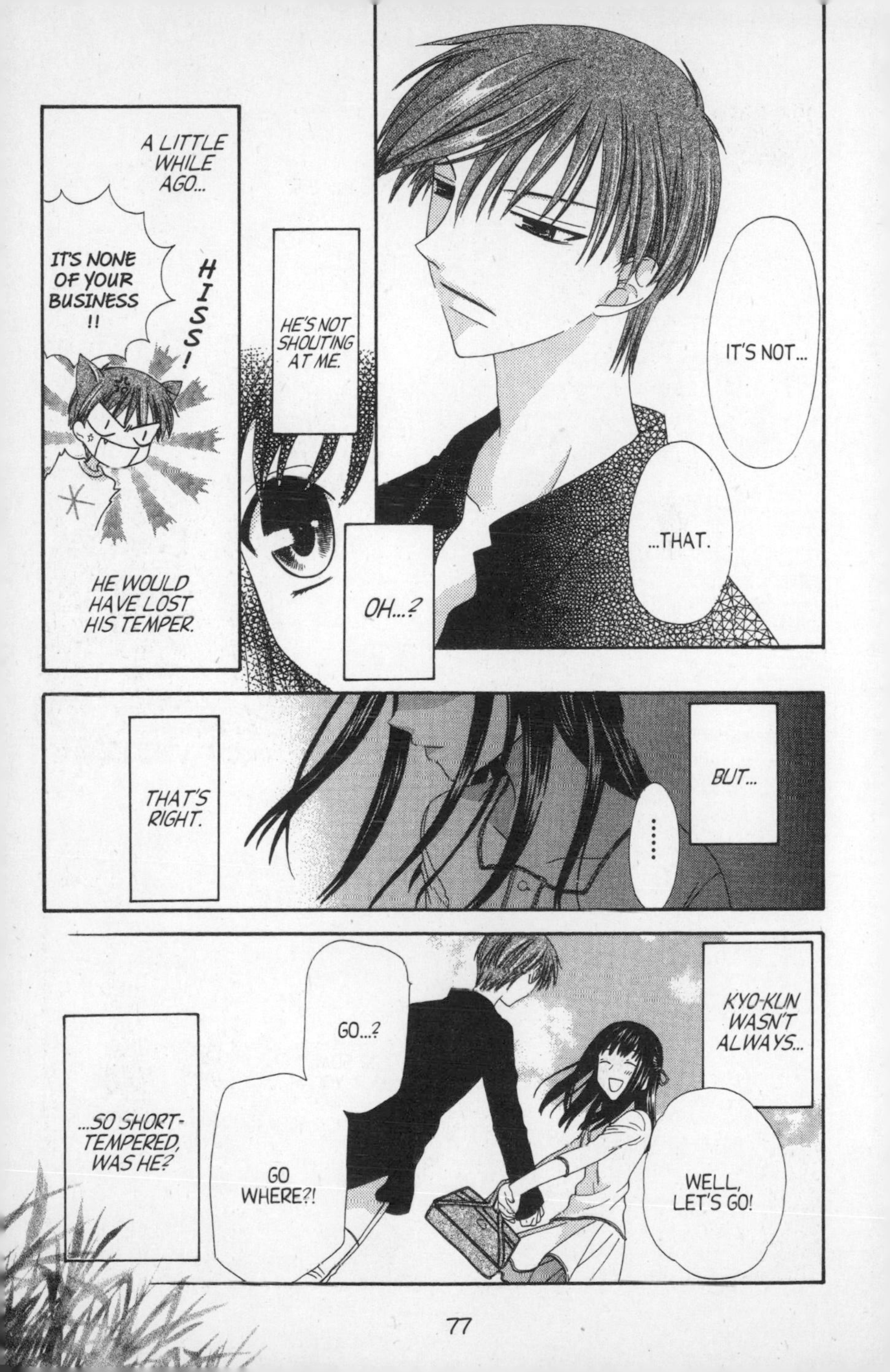
IT'S NOT...
...THAT.
HE'S NOT SHOUTING AT ME.
OH...?
A LITTLE WHILE AGO...
IT'S NONE OF YOUR BUSINESS !!
HISS!
HE WOULD HAVE LOST HIS TEMPER.
BUT...
......
THAT'S RIGHT.
KYO-KUN WASN'T ALWAYS...
WELL, LET'S GO!
GO...?
GO WHERE?!
...SO SHORT-TEMPERED, WAS HE?

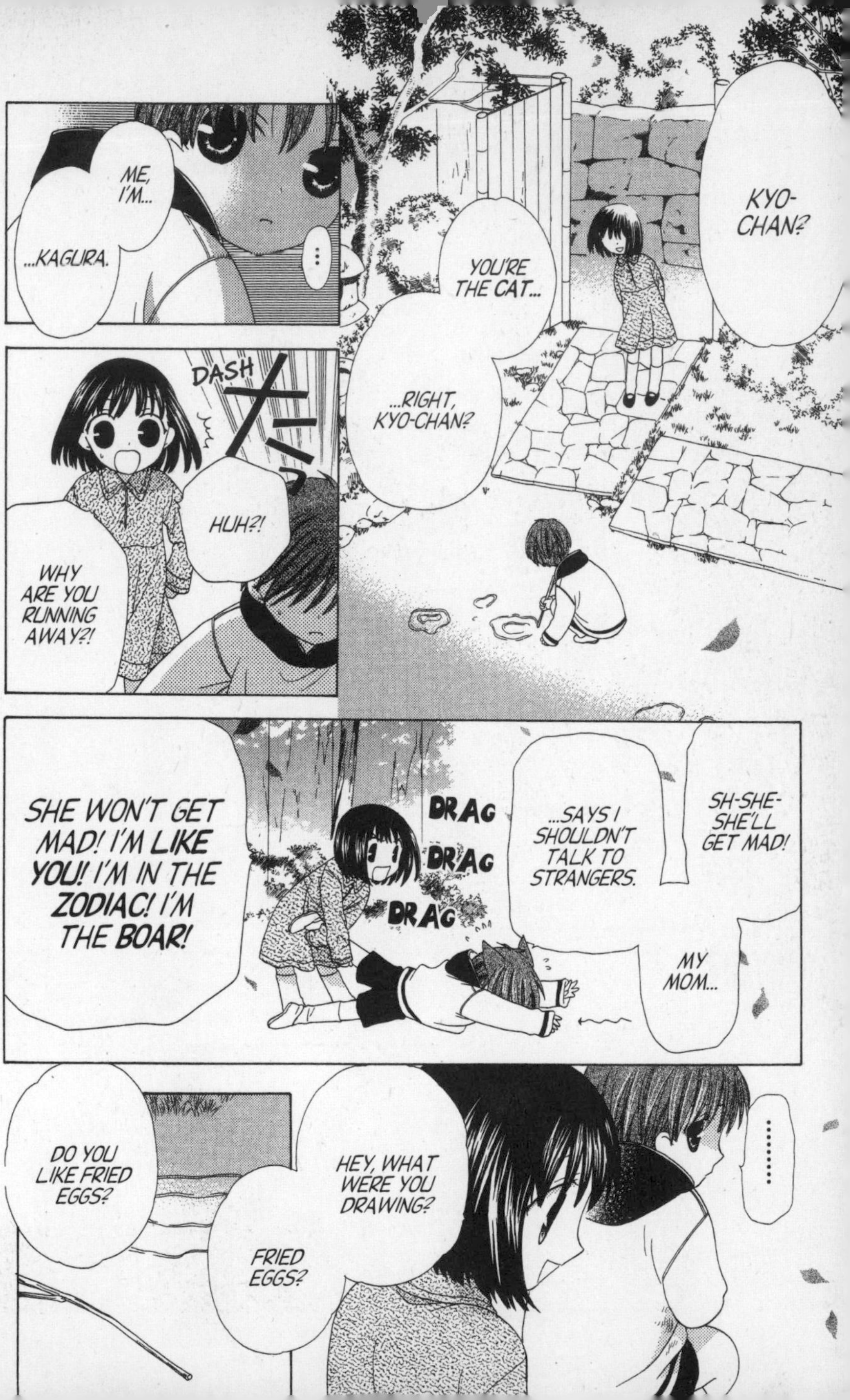
KYO-CHAN?
YOU'RE THE CAT...
...RIGHT, KYO-CHAN?
ME, I'M...
...KAGURA.
…
DASH
HUH?!
WHY ARE YOU RUNNING AWAY?!
SH-SHE-SHE'LL GET MAD!
MY MOM...
...SAYS I SHOULDN'T TALK TO STRANGERS.
DRAG
DRAG
DRAG
SHE WON'T GET MAD! I'M LIKE YOU! I'M IN THE ZODIAC! I'M THE BOAR!
……
HEY, WHAT WERE YOU DRAWING?
FRIED EGGS?
DO YOU LIKE FRIED EGGS?

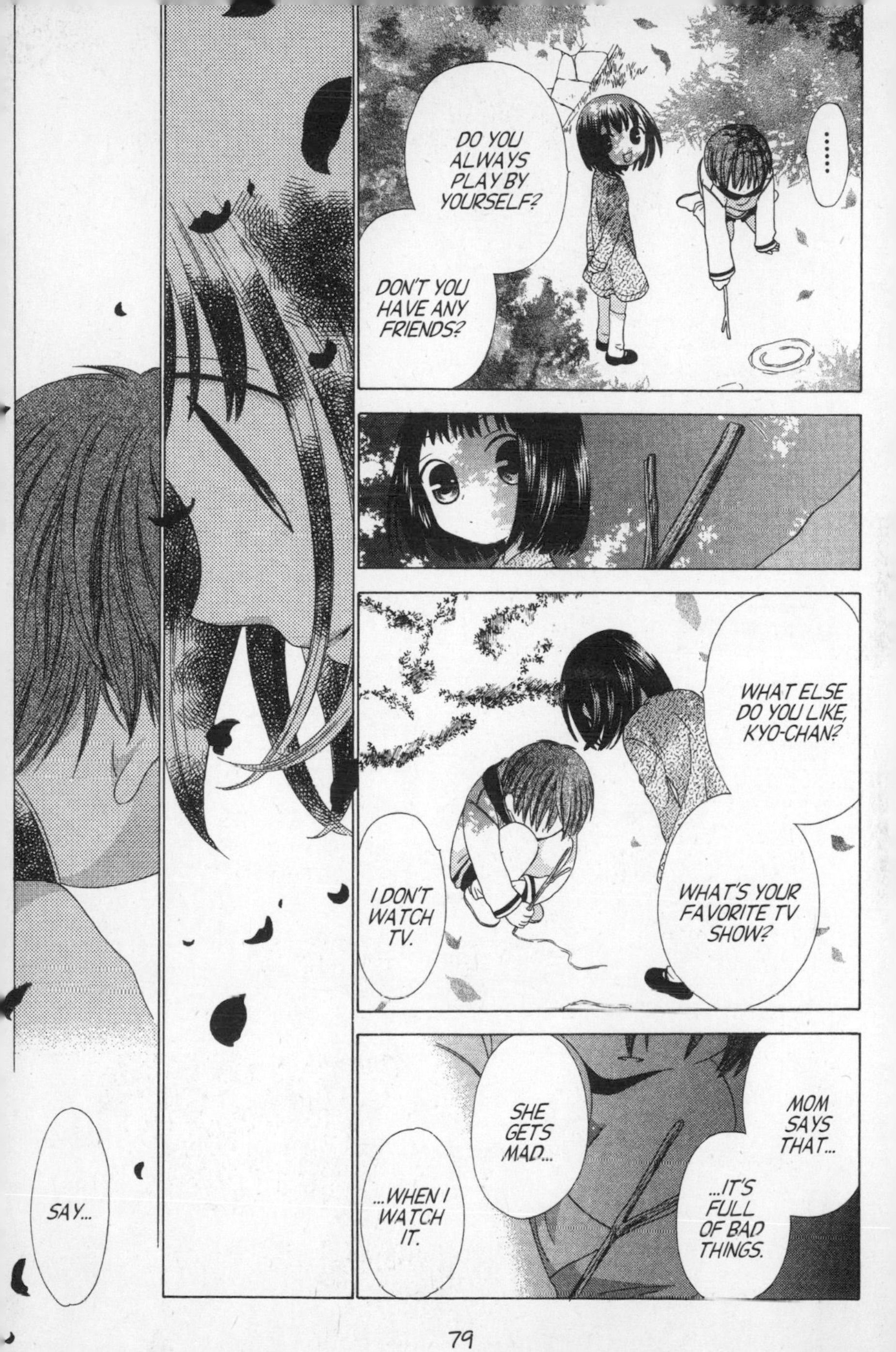
......
DO YOU ALWAYS PLAY BY YOURSELF?
DON'T YOU HAVE ANY FRIENDS?
WHAT ELSE DO YOU LIKE, KYO-CHAN?
WHAT'S YOUR FAVORITE TV SHOW?
I DON'T WATCH TV.
MOM SAYS THAT...
...IT'S FULL OF BAD THINGS.
SHE GETS MAD...
...WHEN I WATCH IT.
SAY...

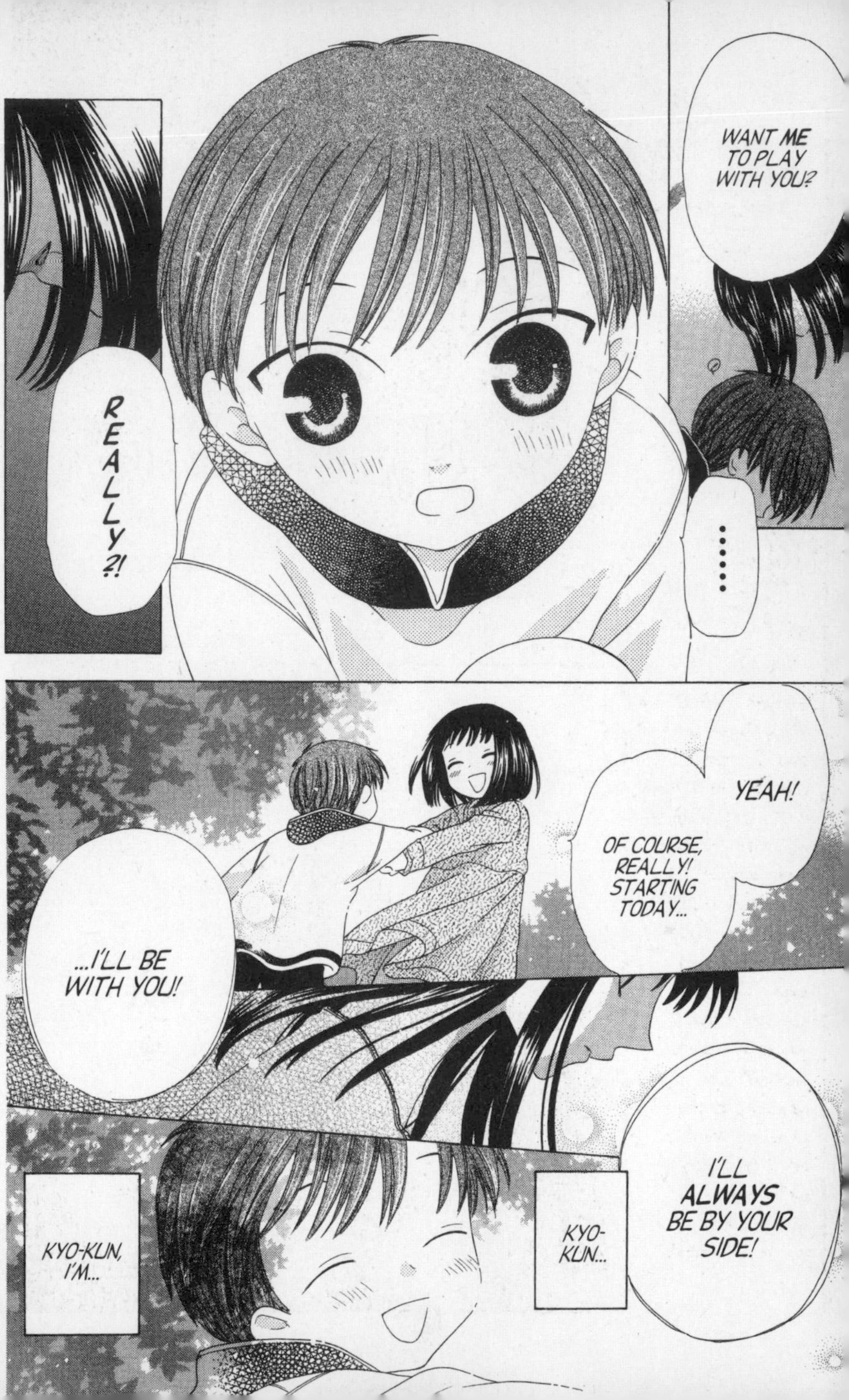
WANT ME TO PLAY WITH YOU?
......
REALLY?!
YEAH!
OF COURSE, REALLY! STARTING TODAY...
...I'LL BE WITH YOU!
I'LL ALWAYS BE BY YOUR SIDE!
KYO-KUN...
KYO-KUN, I'M...

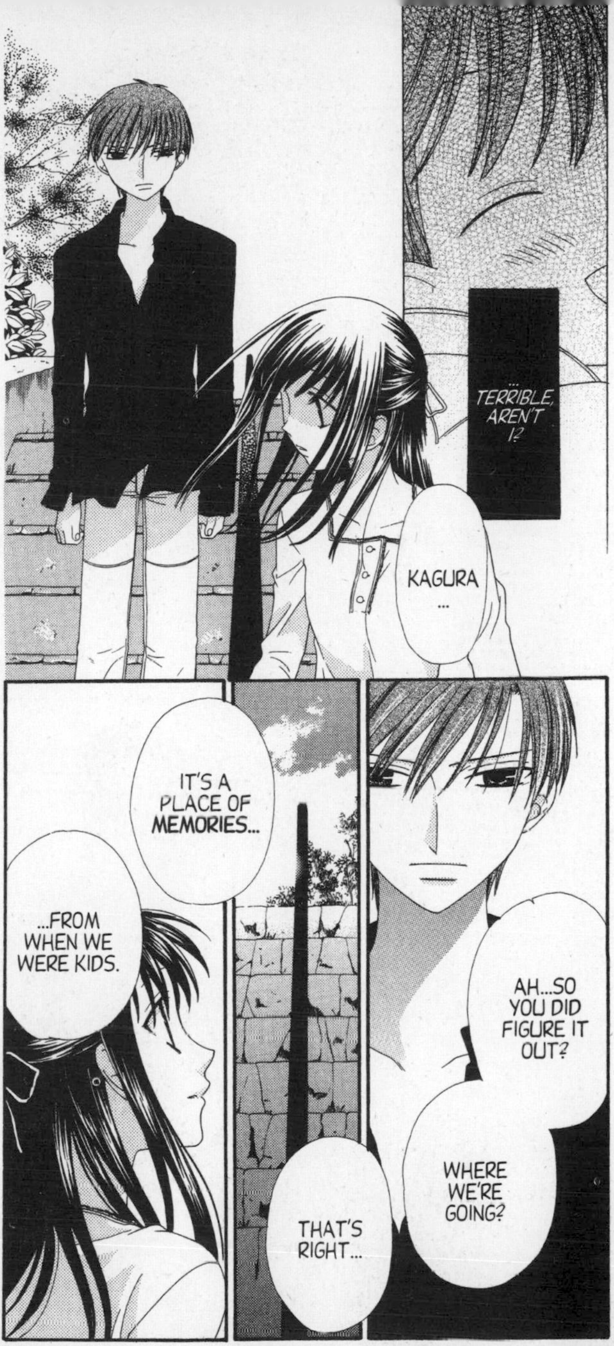
...TERRIBLE, AREN'T I?
KAGURA...
AH...SO YOU DID FIGURE IT OUT?
WHERE WE'RE GOING?
THAT'S RIGHT...
IT'S A PLACE OF MEMORIES...
...FROM WHEN WE WERE KIDS.

Motoko Minagawa

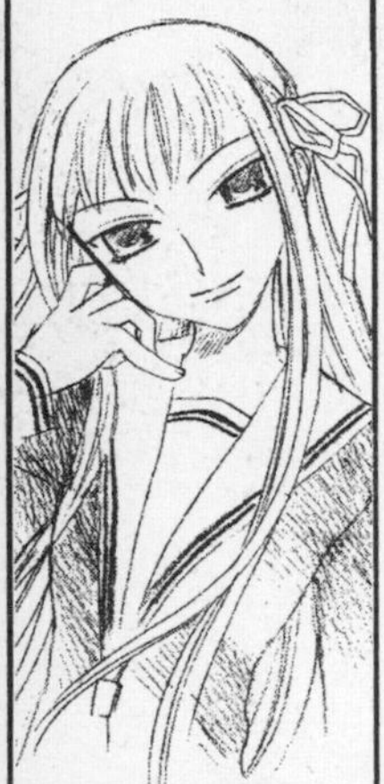

Motoko "Yuki is my life!" Minagawa-san. I predicted this, but when she first showed up, I got a lot of letters from people saying they hated her. One of my favorite letters said, "She's the rival, so why do you draw her so pretty?" Of course, I enjoy drawing Motoko. Well, basically, I enjoy drawing girls (laugh). So, you go, Motoko!

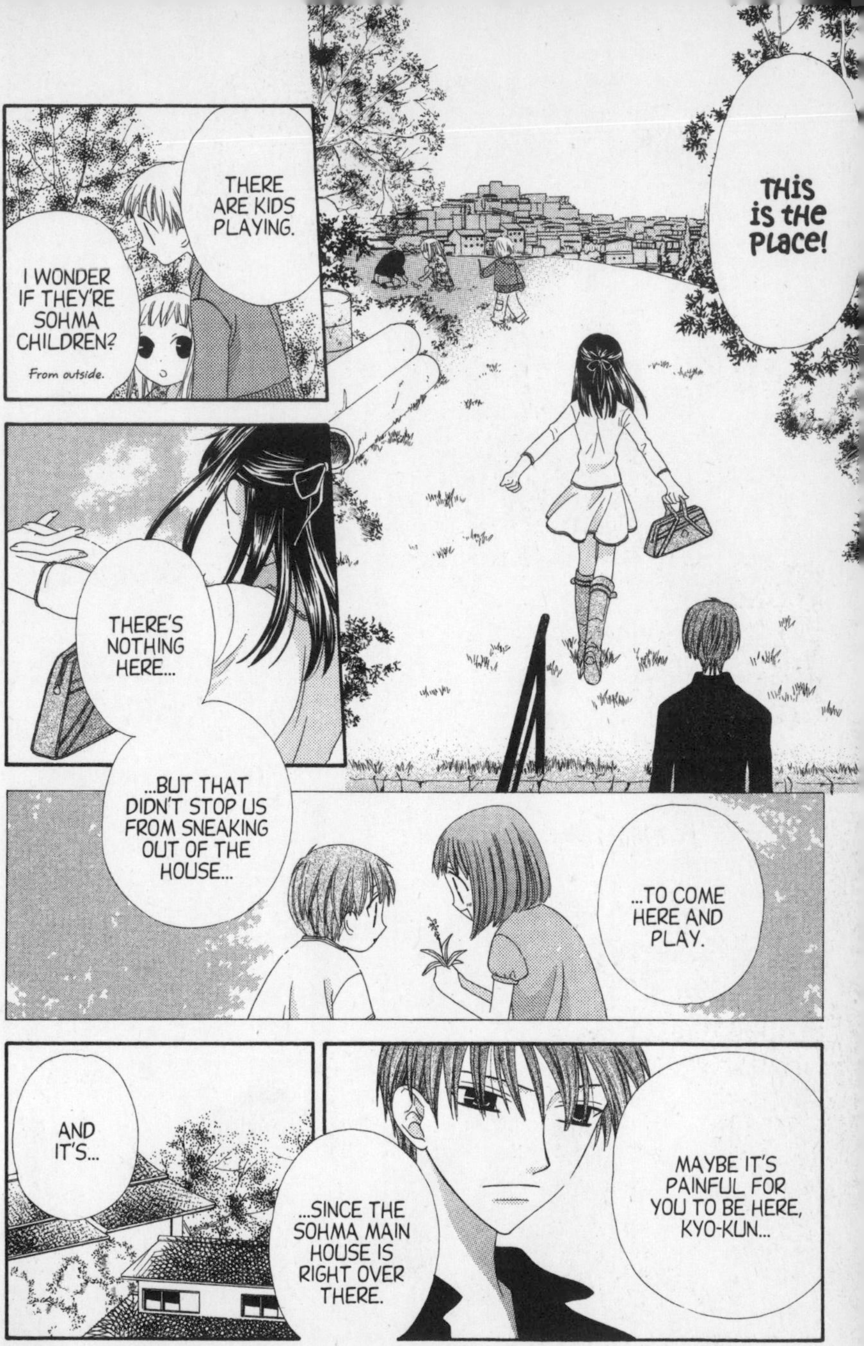
THIS IS THE PLACE!
THERE ARE KIDS PLAYING.
I WONDER IF THEY'RE SOHMA CHILDREN?
From outside.
THERE'S NOTHING HERE...
...BUT THAT DIDN'T STOP US FROM SNEAKING OUT OF THE HOUSE...
...TO COME HERE AND PLAY.
MAYBE IT'S PAINFUL FOR YOU TO BE HERE, KYO-KUN...
...SINCE THE SOHMA MAIN HOUSE IS RIGHT OVER THERE.
AND IT'S...

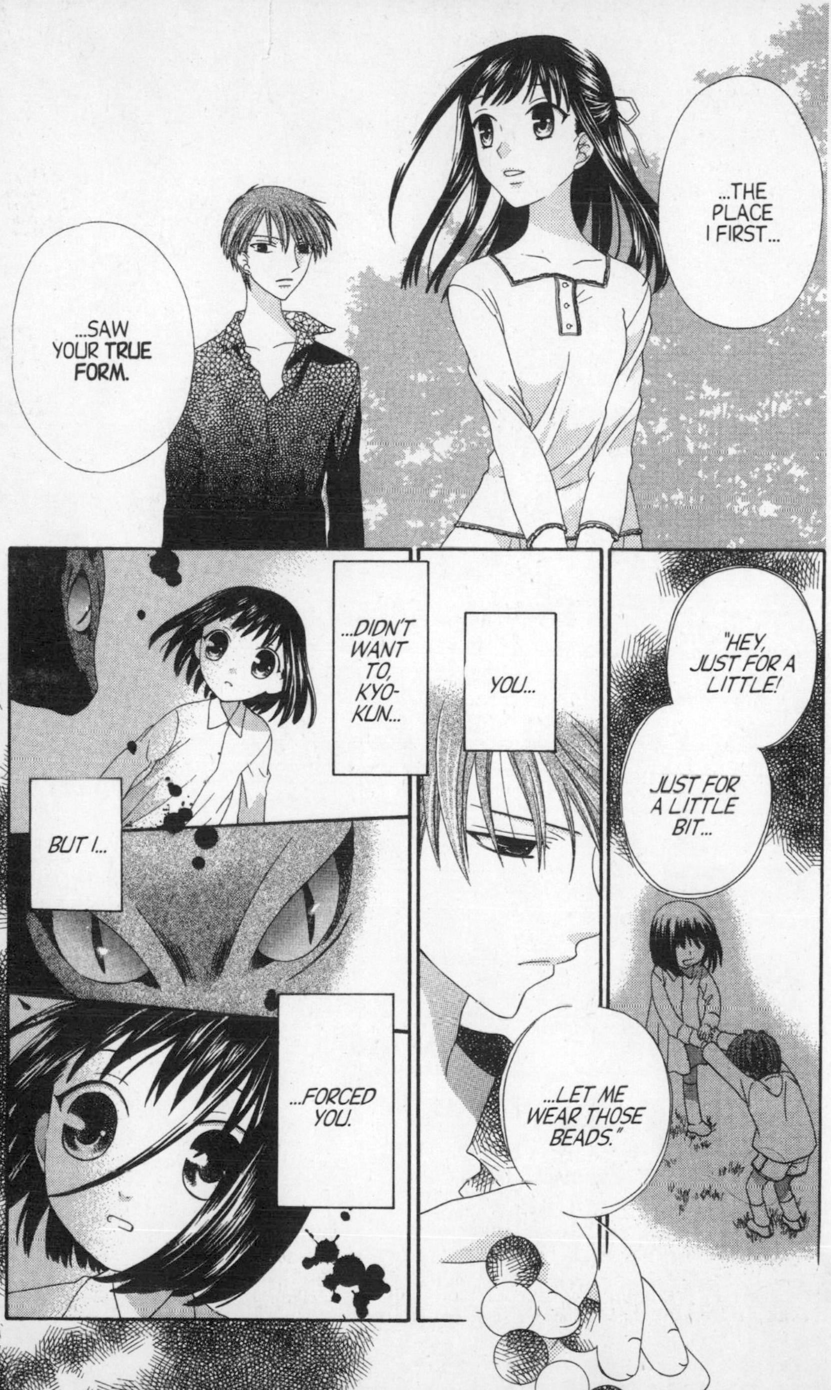
...THE PLACE I FIRST...
...SAW YOUR TRUE FORM.
"HEY, JUST FOR A LITTLE!
JUST FOR A LITTLE BIT...
...LET ME WEAR THOSE BEADS."
YOU...
...DIDN'T WANT TO, KYO-KUN...
BUT I...
...FORCED YOU.

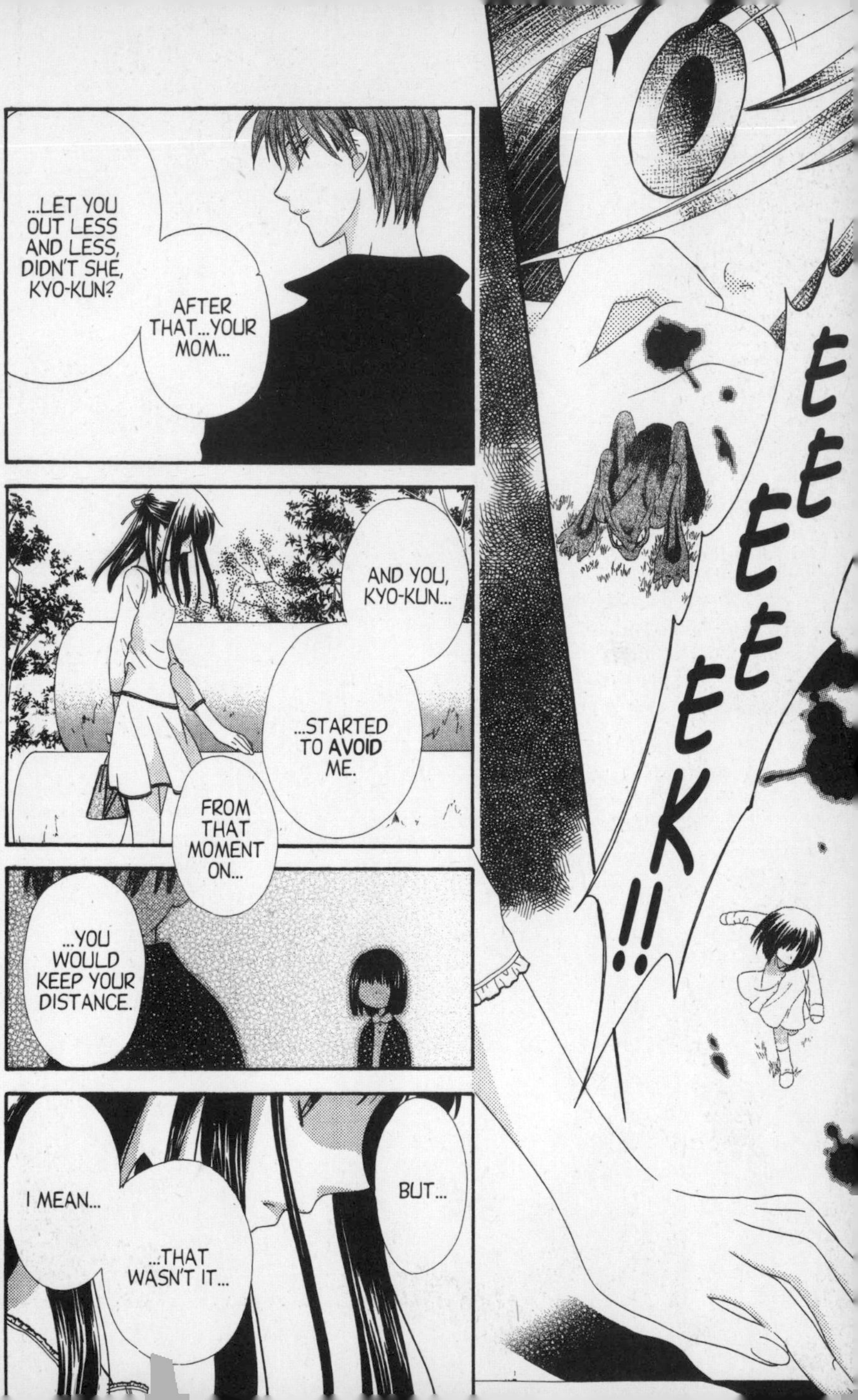
EEEEEEK!!
AFTER THAT...YOUR MOM...
...LET YOU OUT LESS AND LESS, DIDN'T SHE, KYO-KUN?
AND YOU, KYO-KUN...
...STARTED TO AVOID ME.
FROM THAT MOMENT ON...
...YOU WOULD KEEP YOUR DISTANCE.
BUT...
I MEAN...
...THAT WASN'T IT...

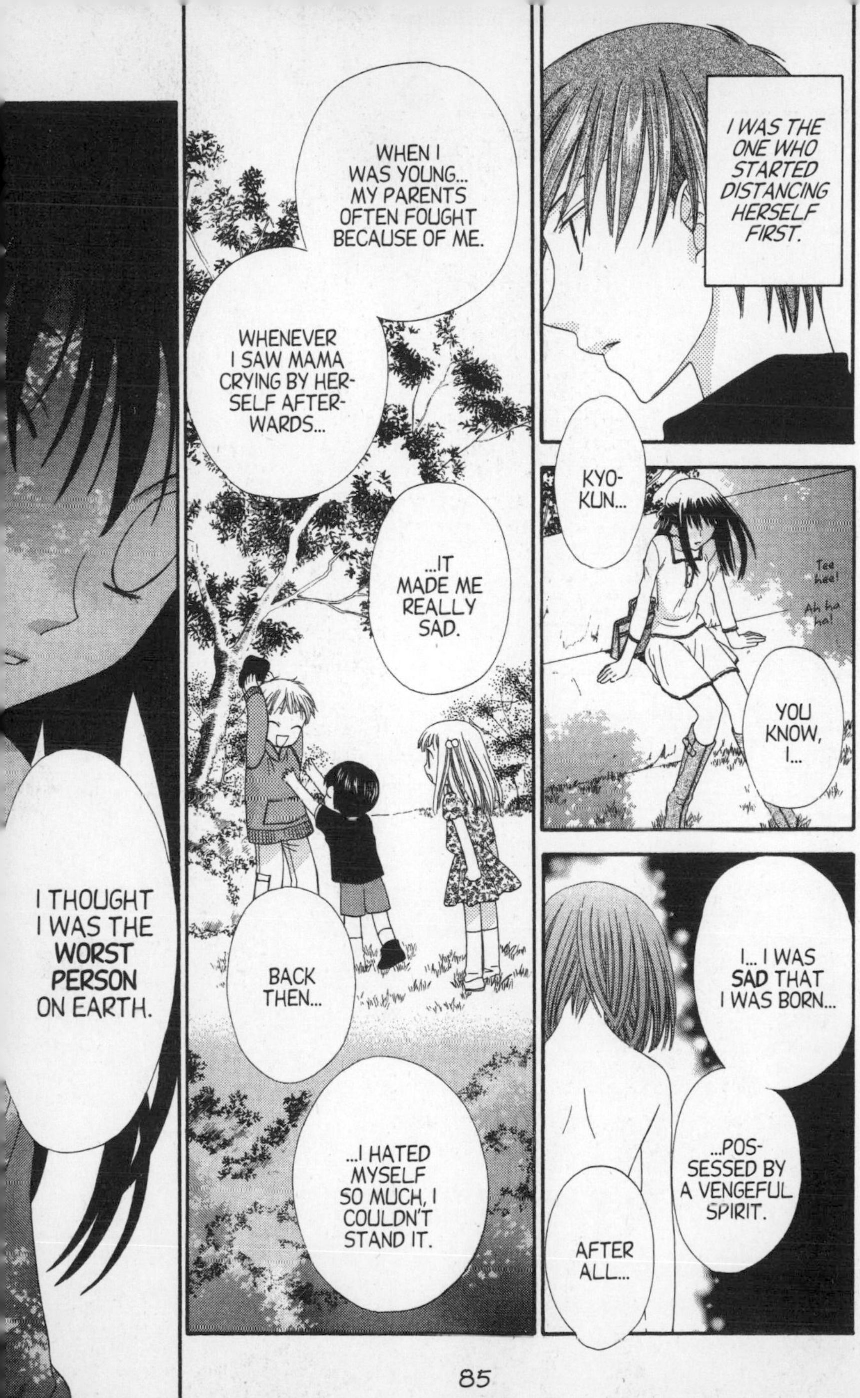
I WAS THE ONE WHO STARTED DISTANCING HERSELF FIRST.
KYO-KUN...
Tee hee!
Ah ha ha!
YOU KNOW, I...
I... I WAS **SAD** THAT I WAS BORN...
...POSSESSED BY A VENGEFUL SPIRIT.
AFTER ALL...
WHEN I WAS YOUNG... MY PARENTS OFTEN FOUGHT BECAUSE OF ME.
WHENEVER I SAW MAMA CRYING BY HERSELF AFTERWARDS...
...IT MADE ME REALLY SAD.
BACK THEN...
...I HATED MYSELF SO MUCH, I COULDN'T STAND IT.
I THOUGHT I WAS THE **WORST PERSON** ON EARTH.

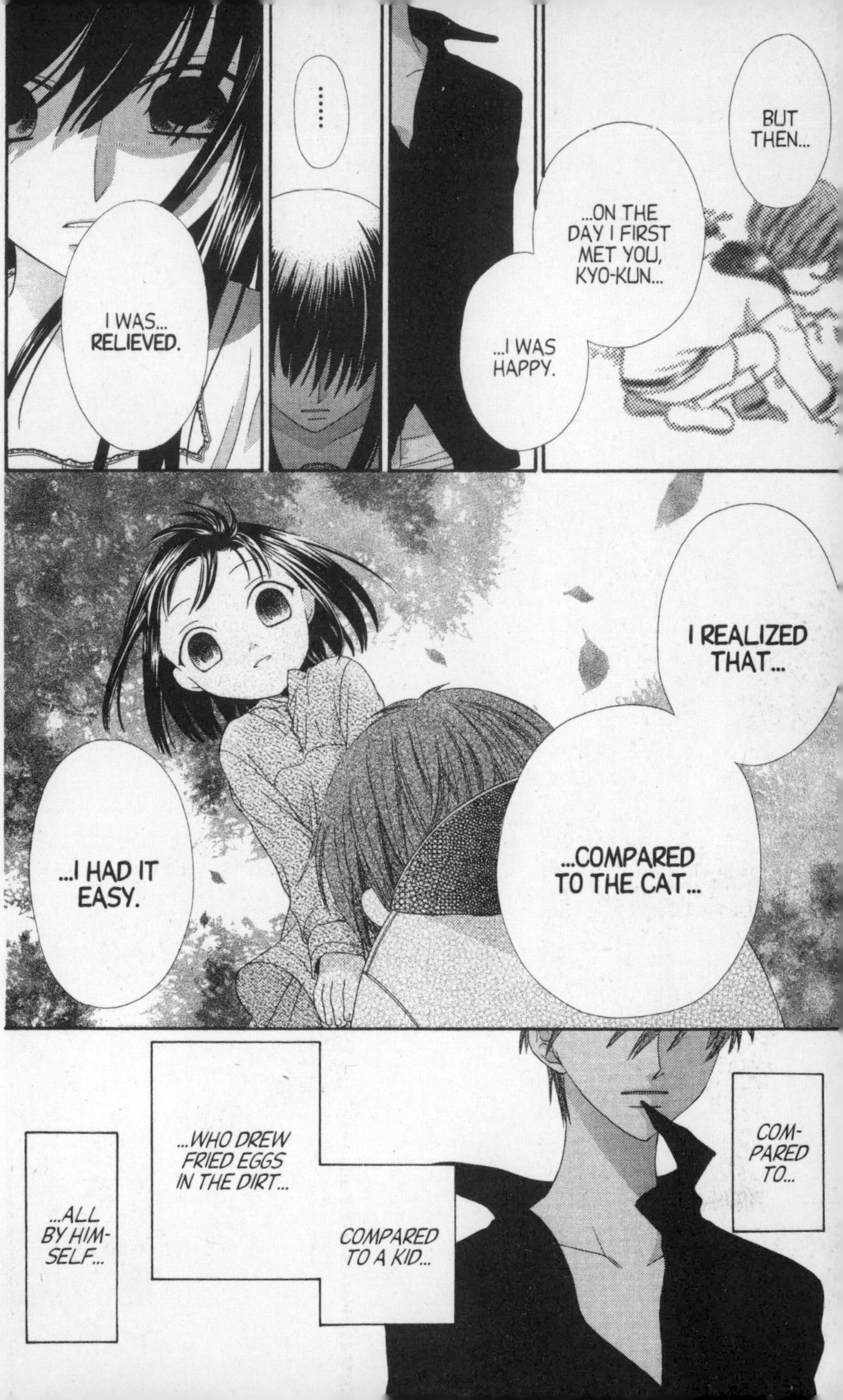

BUT THEN...
...ON THE DAY I FIRST MET YOU, KYO-KUN...
...I WAS HAPPY.
......
I WAS... RELIEVED.
I REALIZED THAT...
...COMPARED TO THE CAT...
...I HAD IT EASY.
COM-PARED TO...
COMPARED TO A KID...
...WHO DREW FRIED EGGS IN THE DIRT...
...ALL BY HIM-SELF...

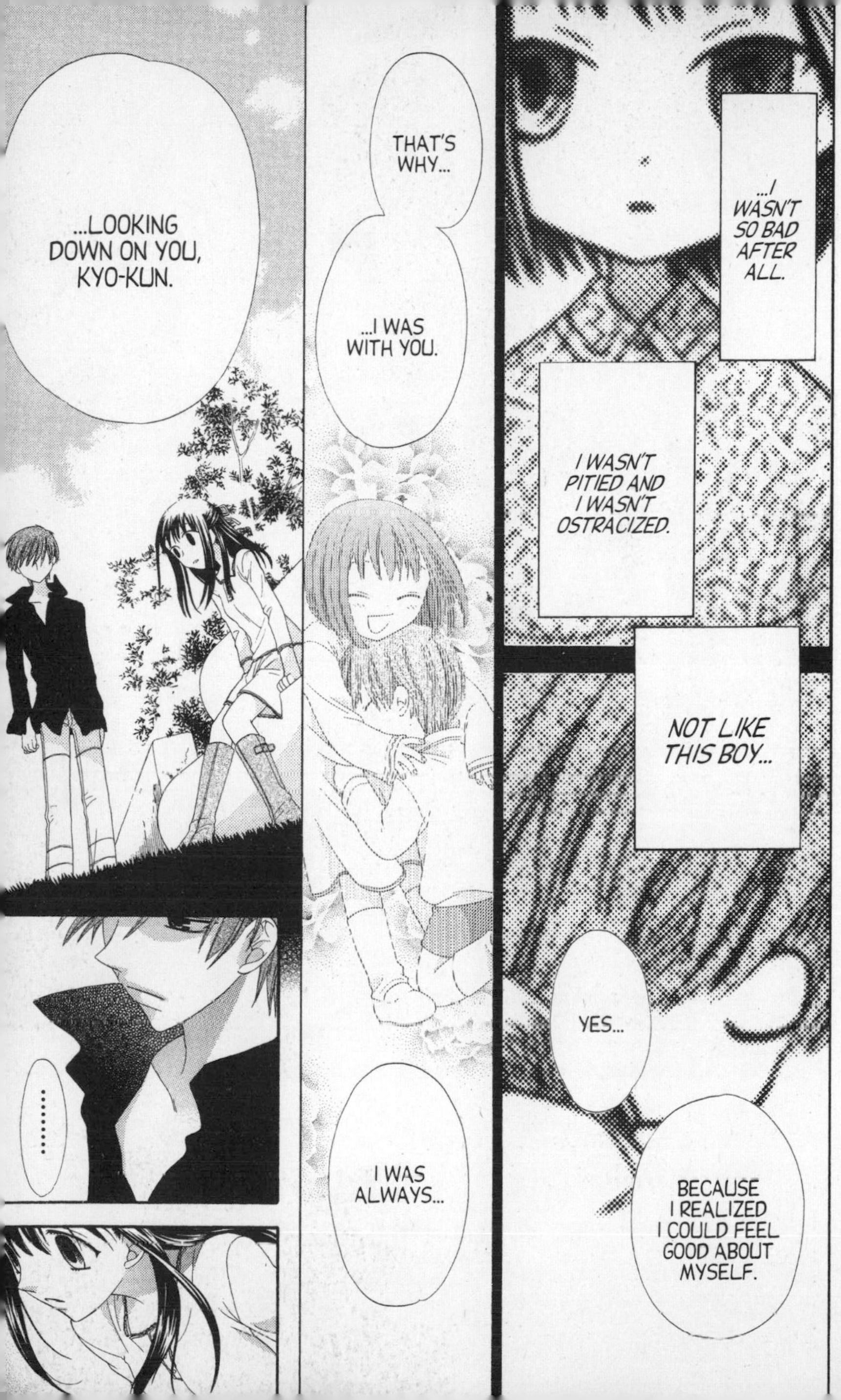
...I WASN'T SO BAD AFTER ALL.
I WASN'T PITIED AND I WASN'T OSTRACIZED.
NOT LIKE THIS BOY...
YES...
BECAUSE I REALIZED I COULD FEEL GOOD ABOUT MYSELF.
THAT'S WHY...
...I WAS WITH YOU.
I WAS ALWAYS...
...LOOKING DOWN ON YOU, KYO-KUN.
....

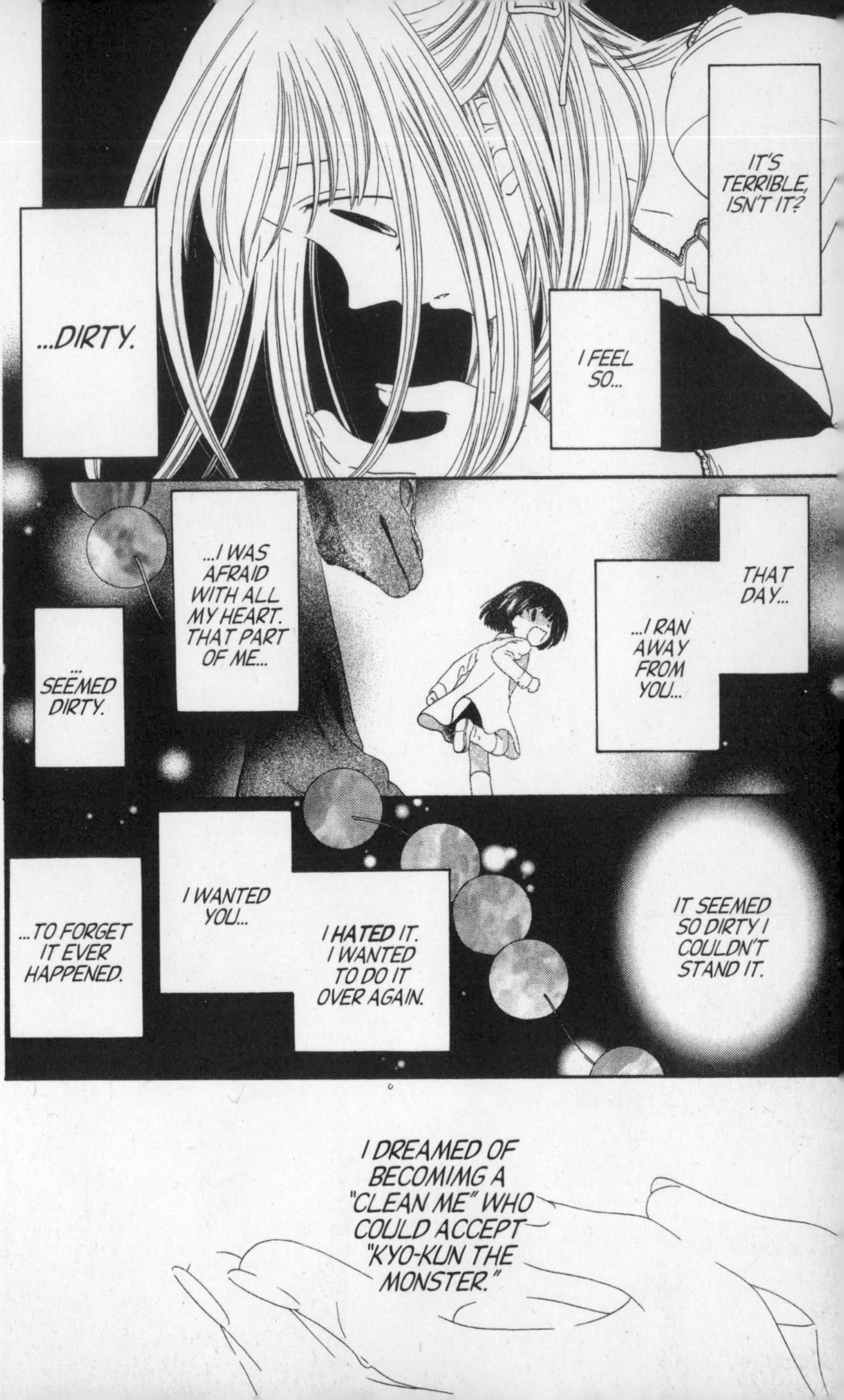
IT'S TERRIBLE, ISN'T IT?
I FEEL SO...
...DIRTY.
THAT DAY...
...I RAN AWAY FROM YOU...
...I WAS AFRAID WITH ALL MY HEART. THAT PART OF ME...
...SEEMED DIRTY.
IT SEEMED SO DIRTY I COULDN'T STAND IT.
I HATED IT. I WANTED TO DO IT OVER AGAIN.
I WANTED YOU...
...TO FORGET IT EVER HAPPENED.
I DREAMED OF BECOMIMG A "CLEAN ME" WHO COULD ACCEPT "KYO-KUN THE MONSTER."

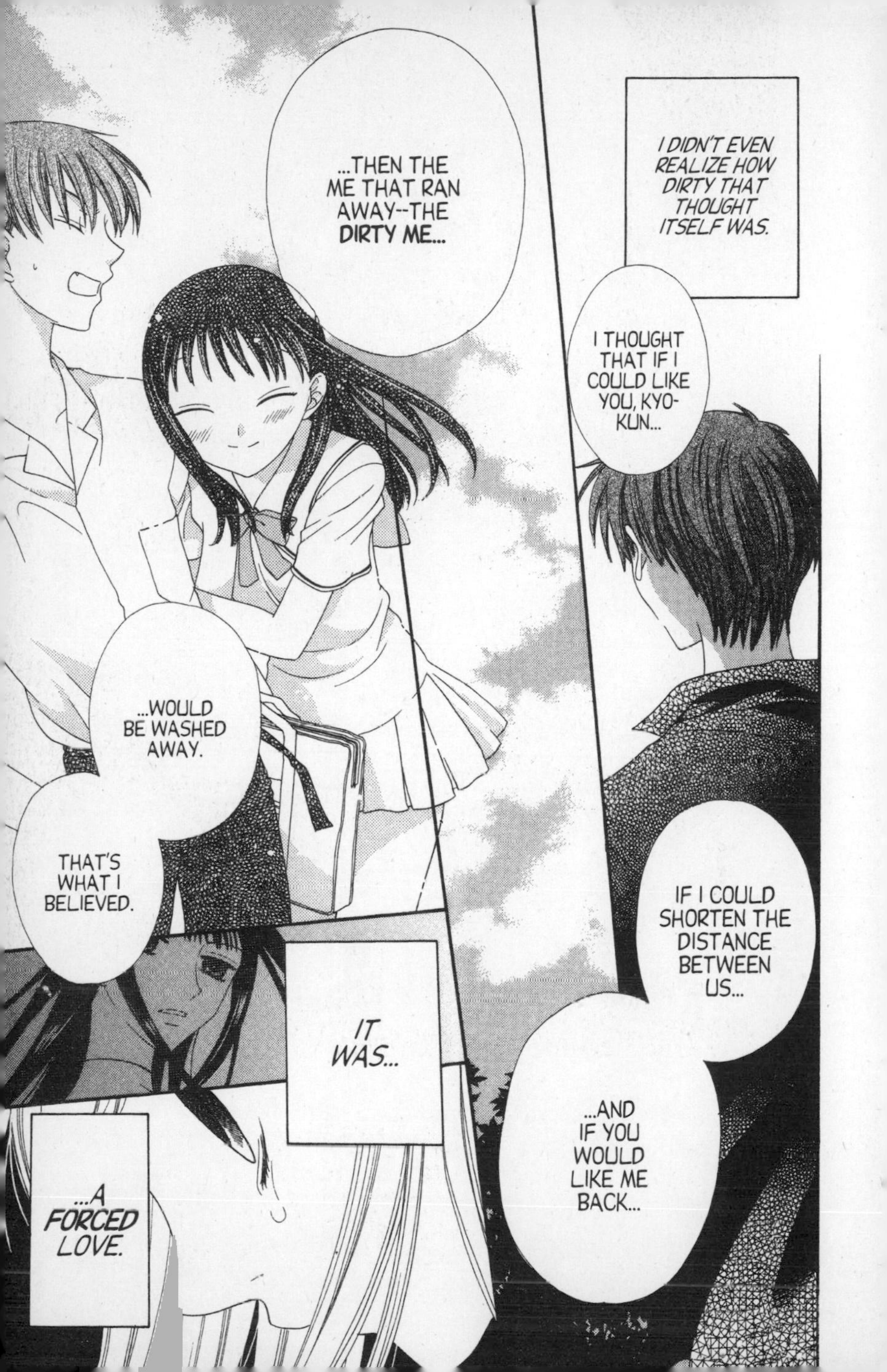

I DIDN'T EVEN REALIZE HOW DIRTY THAT THOUGHT ITSELF WAS.
I THOUGHT THAT IF I COULD LIKE YOU, KYO-KUN...
IF I COULD SHORTEN THE DISTANCE BETWEEN US...
...AND IF YOU WOULD LIKE ME BACK...
...THEN THE ME THAT RAN AWAY--THE DIRTY ME...
...WOULD BE WASHED AWAY.
THAT'S WHAT I BELIEVED.
IT WAS...
...A FORCED LOVE.

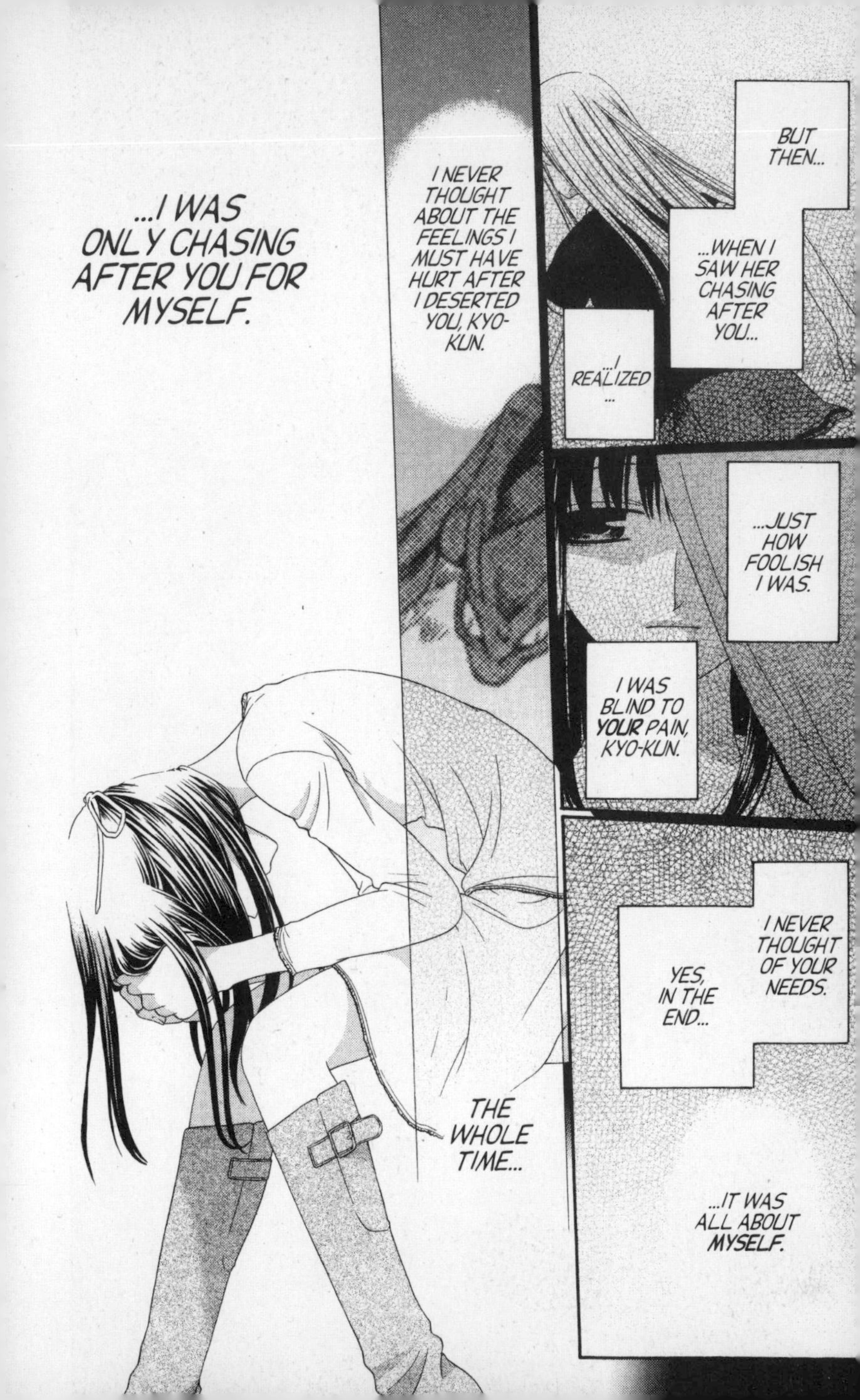
BUT THEN...
...WHEN I SAW HER CHASING AFTER YOU...
...I REALIZED...
...JUST HOW FOOLISH I WAS.
I WAS BLIND TO **YOUR** PAIN, KYO-KUN.
I NEVER THOUGHT OF YOUR NEEDS.
YES, IN THE END...
...IT WAS ALL ABOUT MYSELF.
I NEVER THOUGHT ABOUT THE FEELINGS I MUST HAVE HURT AFTER I DESERTED YOU, KYO-KUN.
...I WAS ONLY CHASING AFTER YOU FOR MYSELF.
THE WHOLE TIME...

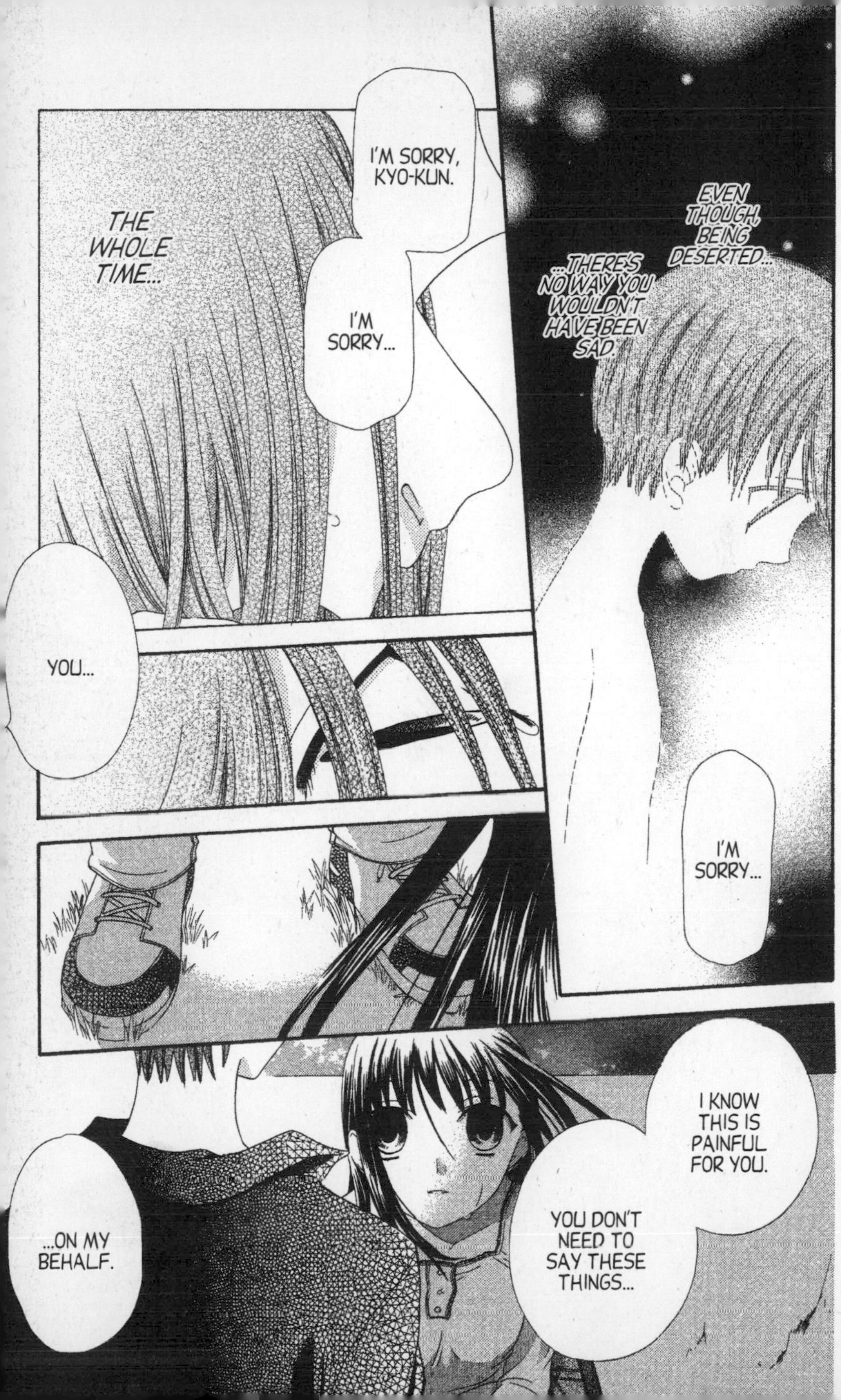
EVEN THOUGH, BEING DESERTED...
...THERE'S NO WAY YOU WOULDN'T HAVE BEEN SAD.
I'M SORRY...
I'M SORRY, KYO-KUN.
I'M SORRY...
THE WHOLE TIME...
YOU...
I KNOW THIS IS PAINFUL FOR YOU.
YOU DON'T NEED TO SAY THESE THINGS...
...ON MY BEHALF.

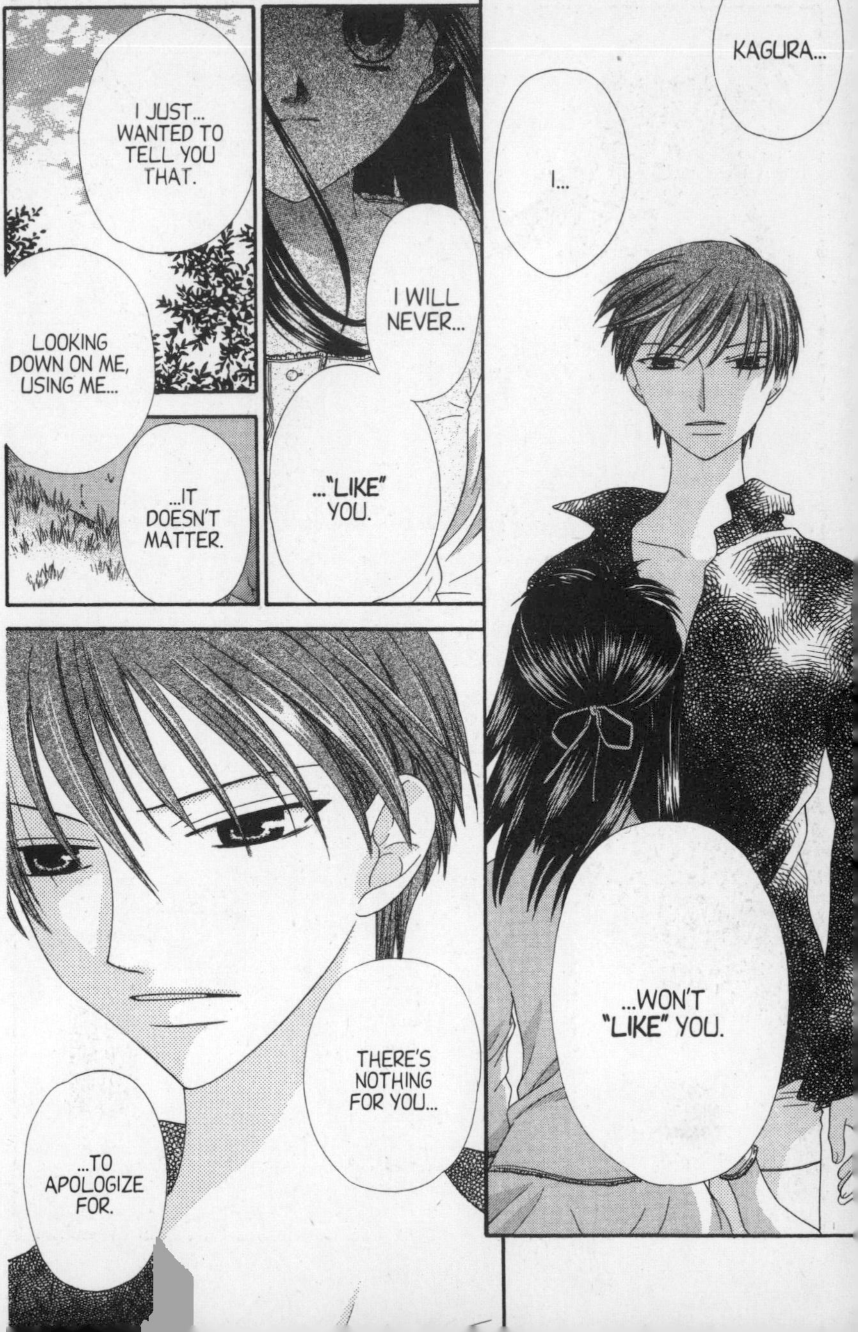
KAGURA...
I...
...WON'T "LIKE" YOU.
I WILL NEVER...
..."LIKE" YOU.
I JUST... WANTED TO TELL YOU THAT.
LOOKING DOWN ON ME, USING ME...
...IT DOESN'T MATTER.
THERE'S NOTHING FOR YOU...
...TO APOLOGIZE FOR.

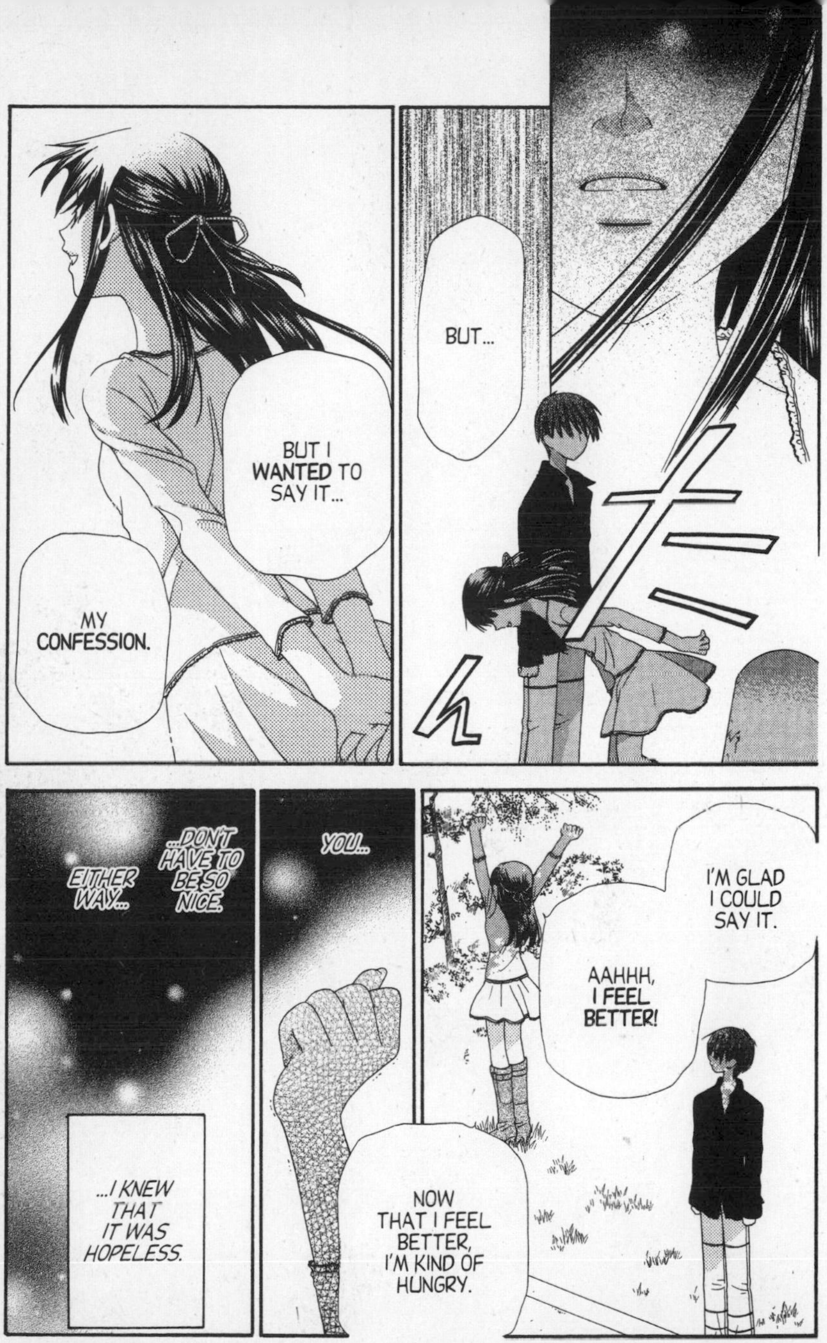
BUT...
BUT I WANTED TO SAY IT...
MY CONFESSION.
I'M GLAD I COULD SAY IT.
AAHHH, I FEEL BETTER!
NOW THAT I FEEL BETTER, I'M KIND OF HUNGRY.
YOU...
...DON'T HAVE TO BE SO NICE.
EITHER WAY...
...I KNEW THAT IT WAS HOPELESS.

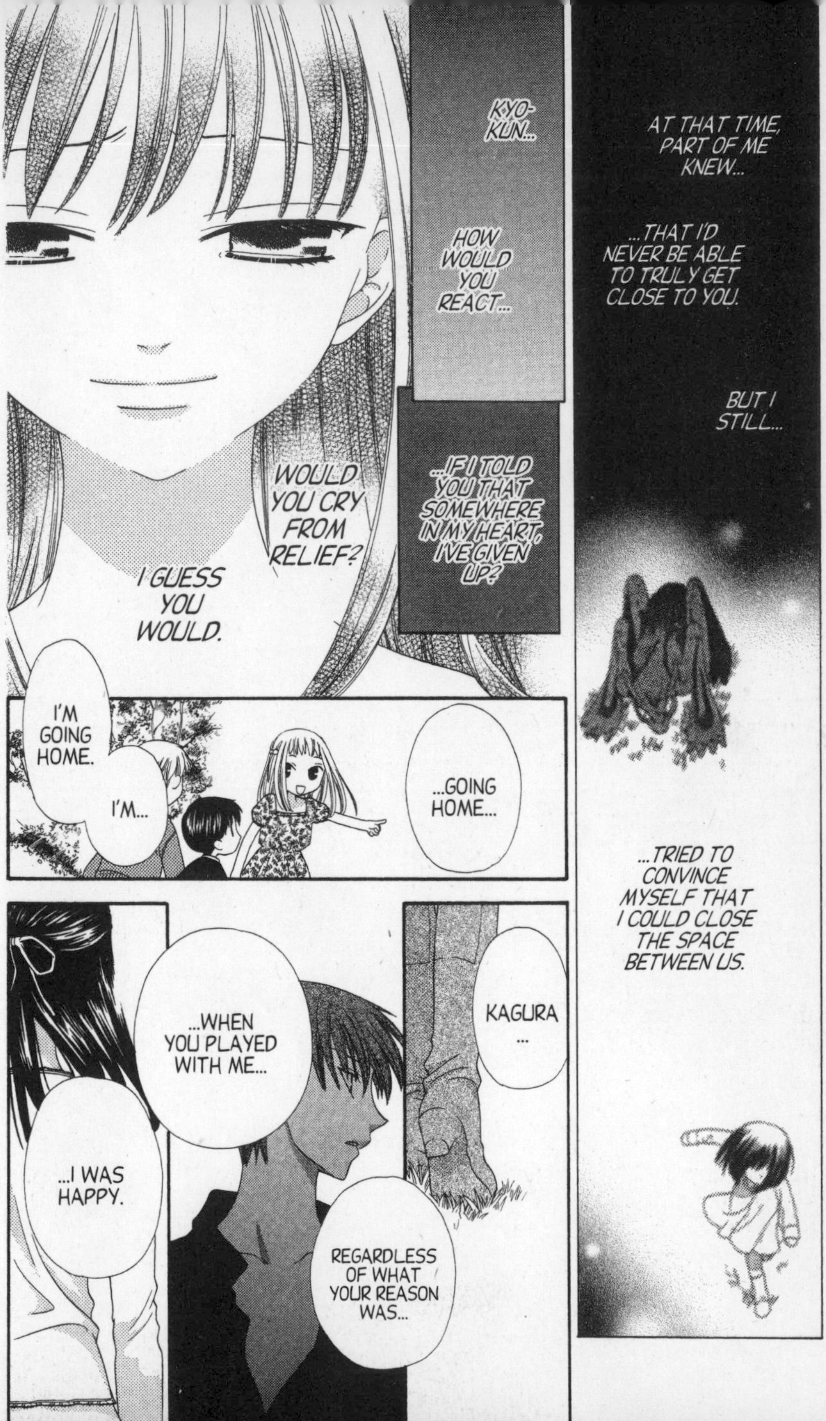
AT THAT TIME, PART OF ME KNEW...
...THAT I'D NEVER BE ABLE TO TRULY GET CLOSE TO YOU.
BUT I STILL...
...TRIED TO CONVINCE MYSELF THAT I COULD CLOSE THE SPACE BETWEEN US.
KYO-KUN...
HOW WOULD YOU REACT...
...IF I TOLD YOU THAT SOMEWHERE IN MY HEART, I'VE GIVEN UP?
WOULD YOU CRY FROM RELIEF?
I GUESS YOU WOULD.
...GOING HOME...
I'M...
I'M GOING HOME.
KAGURA ...
...WHEN YOU PLAYED WITH ME...
...I WAS HAPPY.
REGARDLESS OF WHAT YOUR REASON WAS...

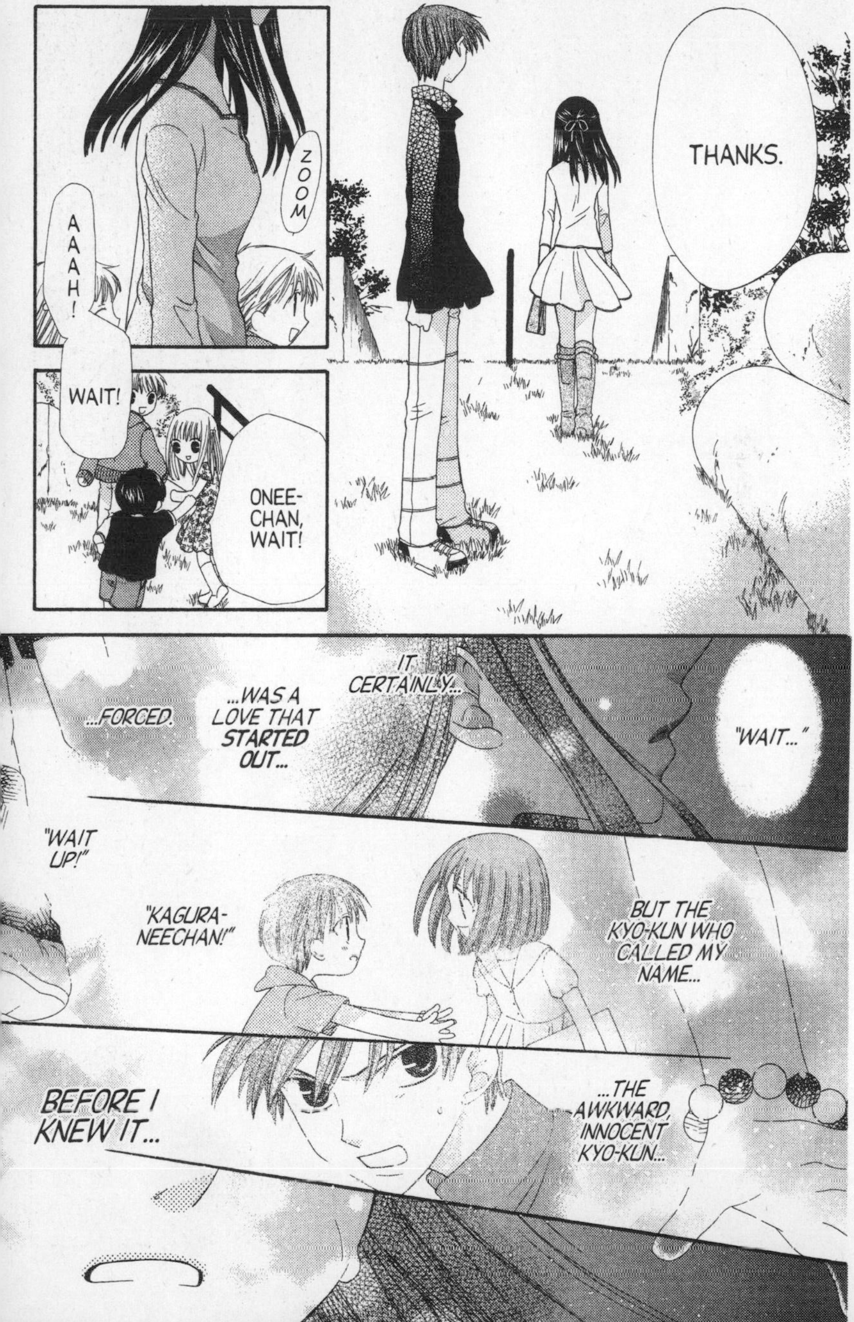
THANKS.
ZOOM
AAAH!
WAIT!
ONEE-CHAN, WAIT!
"WAIT..."
IT CERTAINLY...
...WAS A LOVE THAT STARTED OUT...
...FORCED.
BUT THE KYO-KUN WHO CALLED MY NAME...
"KAGURA-NEECHAN!"
"WAIT UP!"
...THE AWKWARD, INNOCENT KYO-KUN...
BEFORE I KNEW IT...

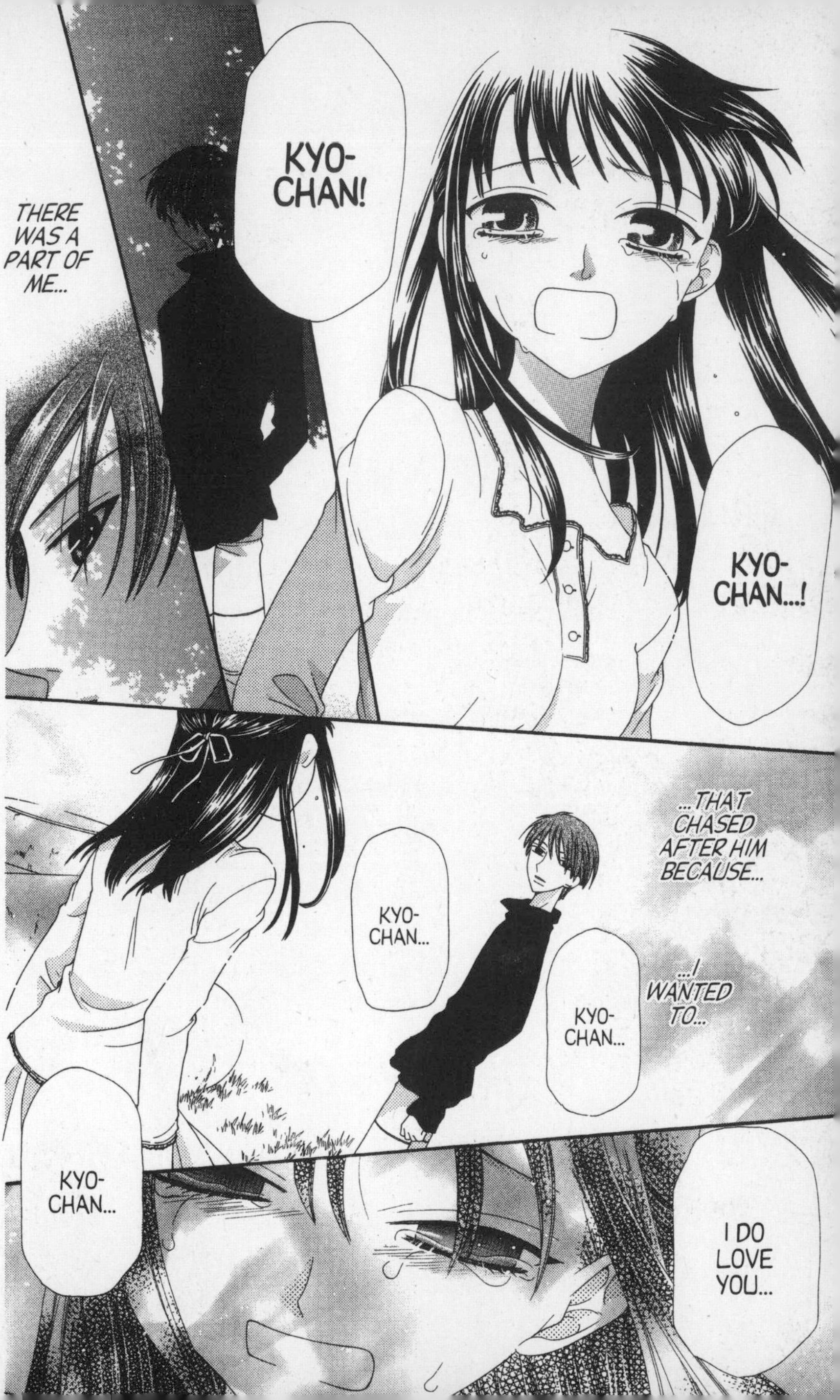
KYO-CHAN!
KYO-CHAN...!
THERE WAS A PART OF ME...
...THAT CHASED AFTER HIM BECAUSE...
...I WANTED TO...
KYO-CHAN...
KYO-CHAN...
KYO-CHAN...
I DO LOVE YOU...

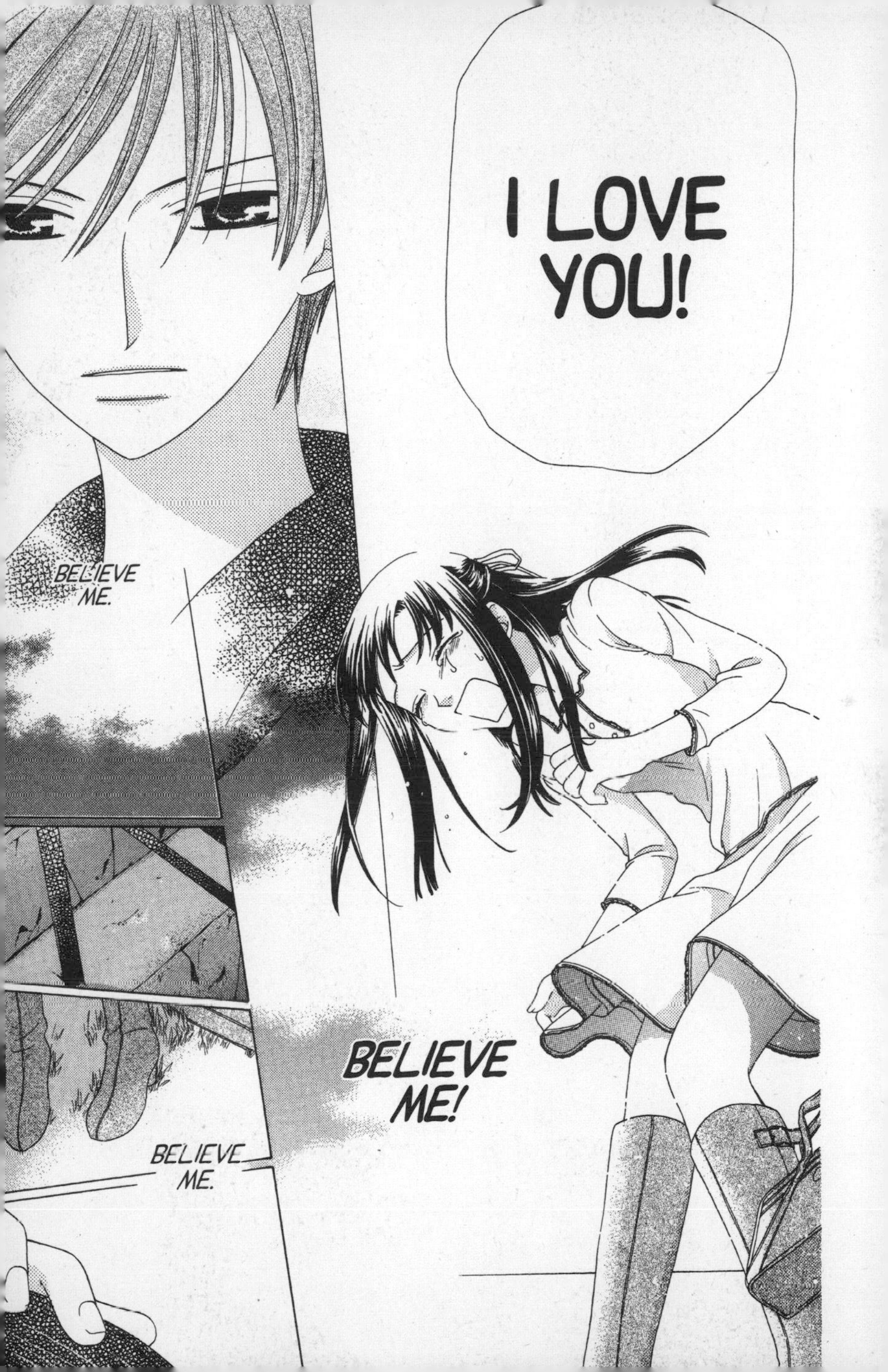
I LOVE YOU!
BELIEVE ME!
BELIEVE ME.
BELIEVE ME.

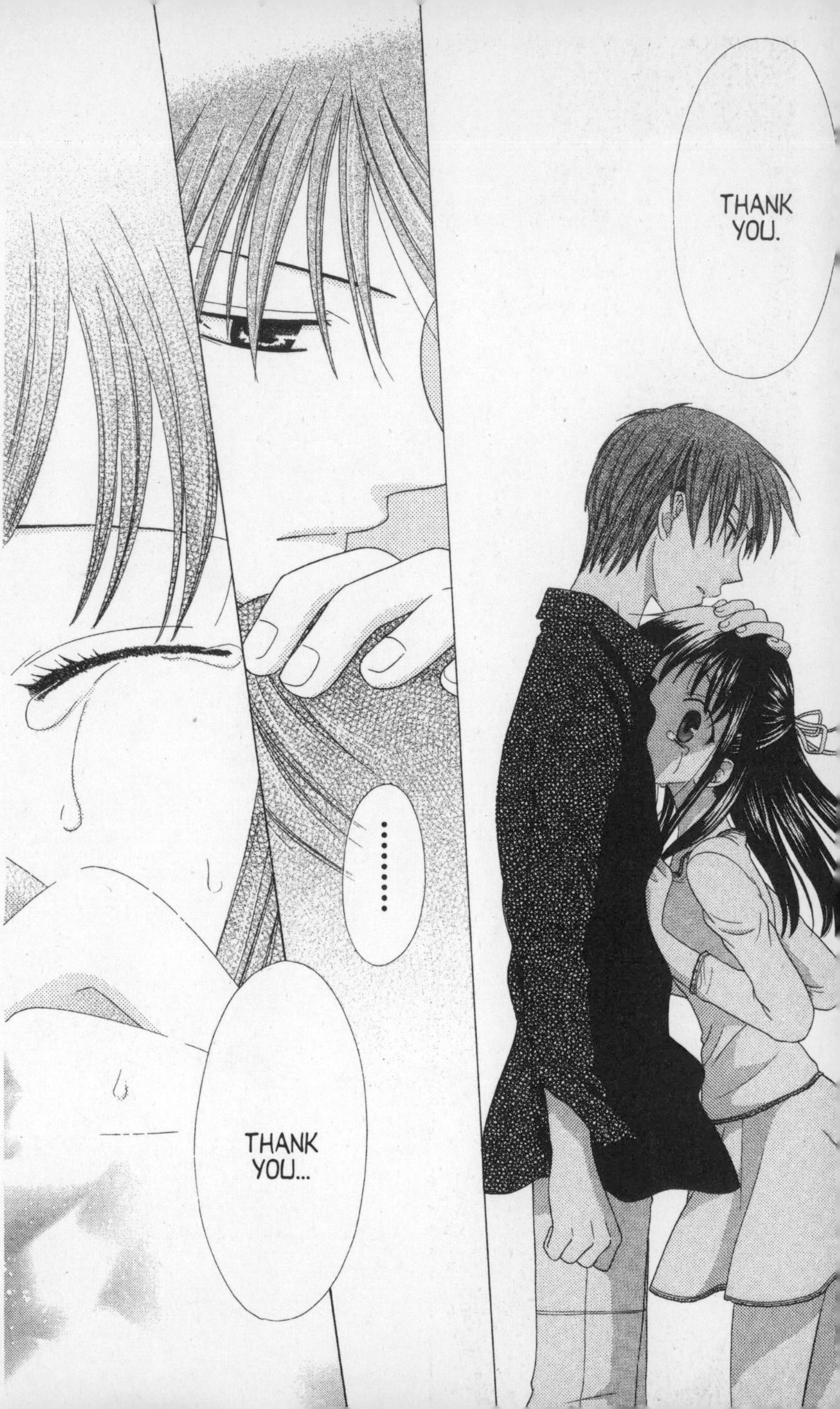
THANK YOU.
......
THANK YOU...

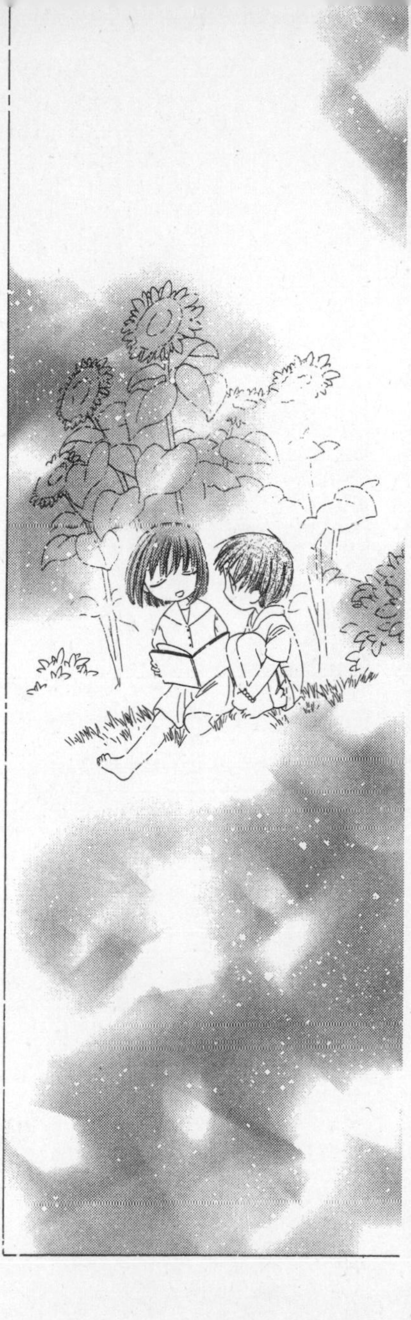

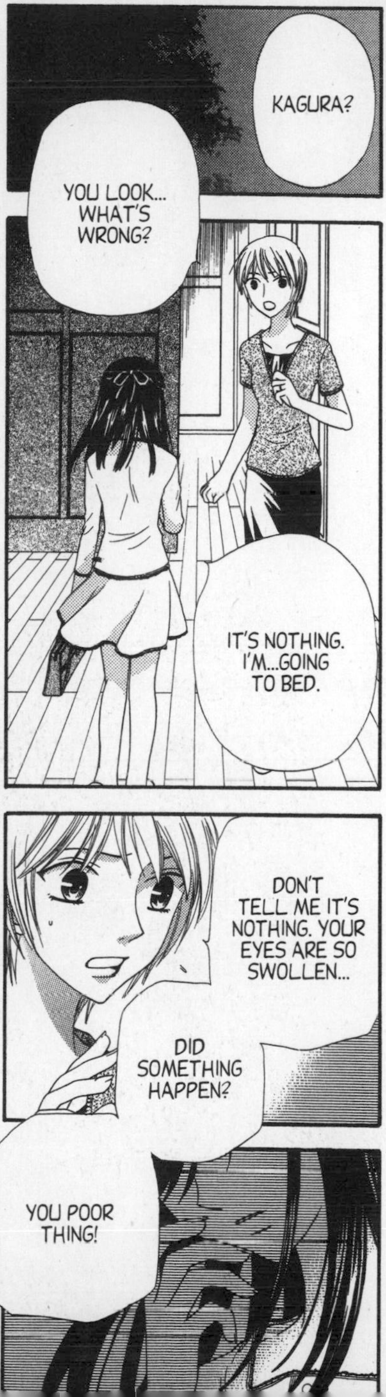
KAGURA?
YOU LOOK... WHAT'S WRONG?
IT'S NOTHING. I'M...GOING TO BED.
DON'T TELL ME IT'S NOTHING. YOUR EYES ARE SO SWOLLEN...
DID SOMETHING HAPPEN?
YOU POOR THING!

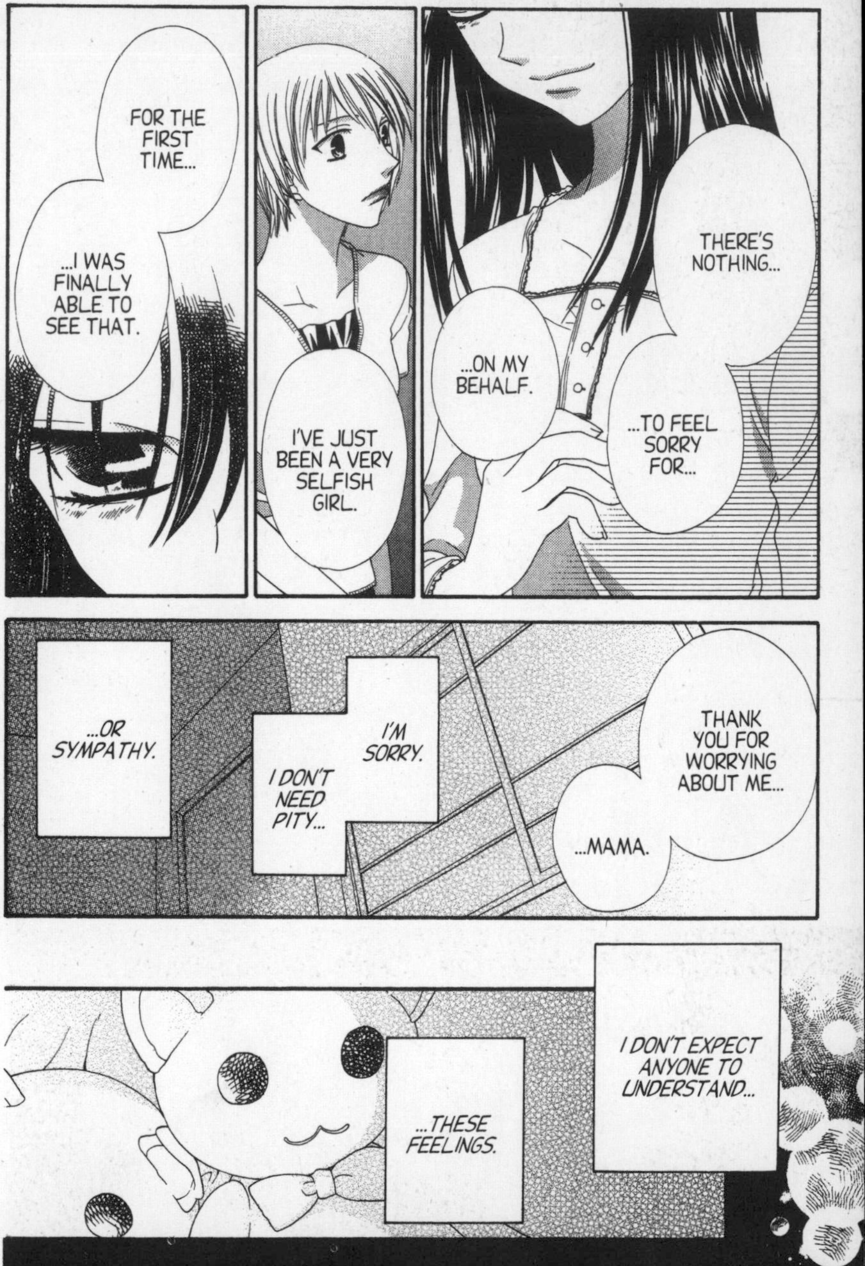
THERE'S NOTHING...
...TO FEEL SORRY FOR...
...ON MY BEHALF.
I'VE JUST BEEN A VERY SELFISH GIRL.
FOR THE FIRST TIME...
...I WAS FINALLY ABLE TO SEE THAT.
THANK YOU FOR WORRYING ABOUT ME...
...MAMA.
I'M SORRY.
I DON'T NEED PITY...
...OR SYMPATHY.
I DON'T EXPECT ANYONE TO UNDERSTAND...
...THESE FEELINGS.

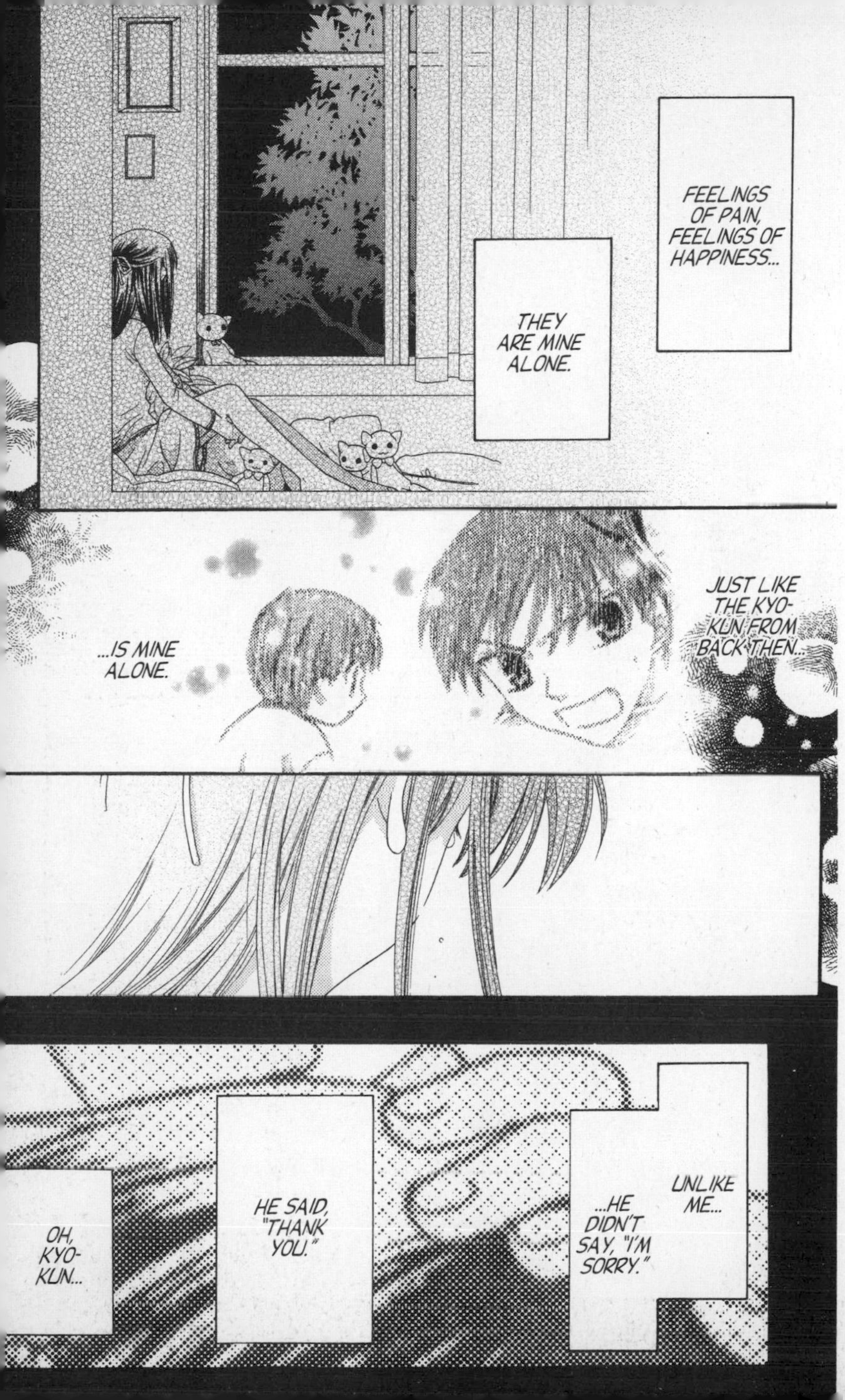
FEELINGS OF PAIN, FEELINGS OF HAPPINESS...
THEY ARE MINE ALONE.
JUST LIKE THE KYO-KUN FROM BACK THEN...
...IS MINE ALONE.
UNLIKE ME...
...HE DIDN'T SAY, "I'M SORRY."
HE SAID, "THANK YOU."
OH, KYO-KUN...

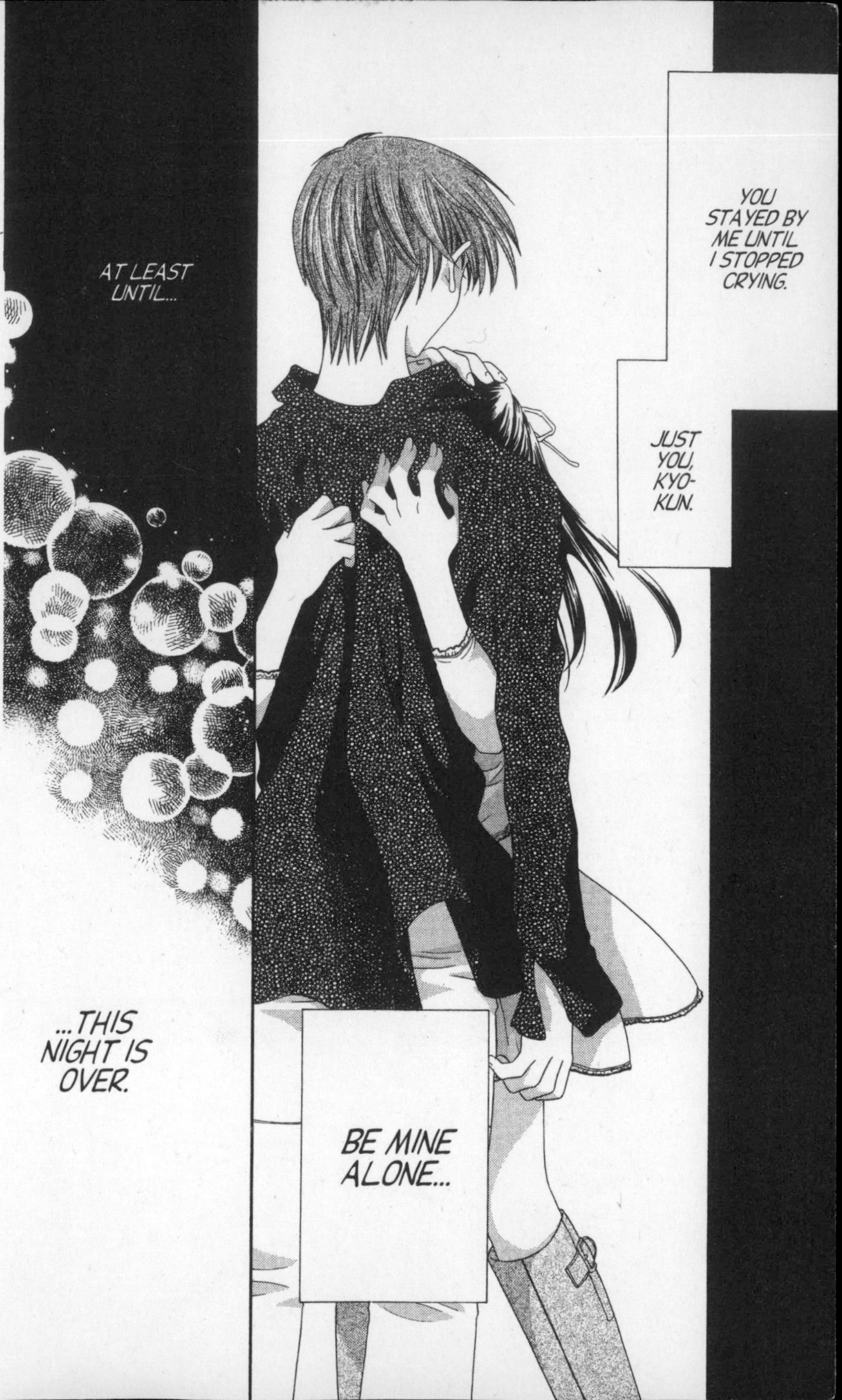
YOU STAYED BY ME UNTIL I STOPPED CRYING.
JUST YOU, KYO-KUN.
BE MINE ALONE...
AT LEAST UNTIL...
...THIS NIGHT IS OVER.

Filler Sketch

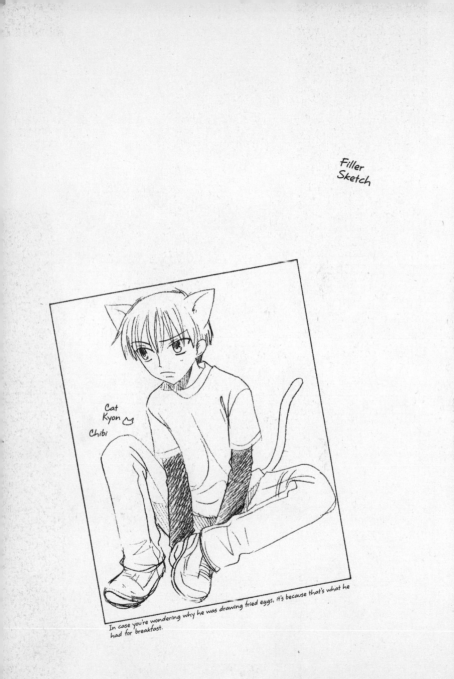

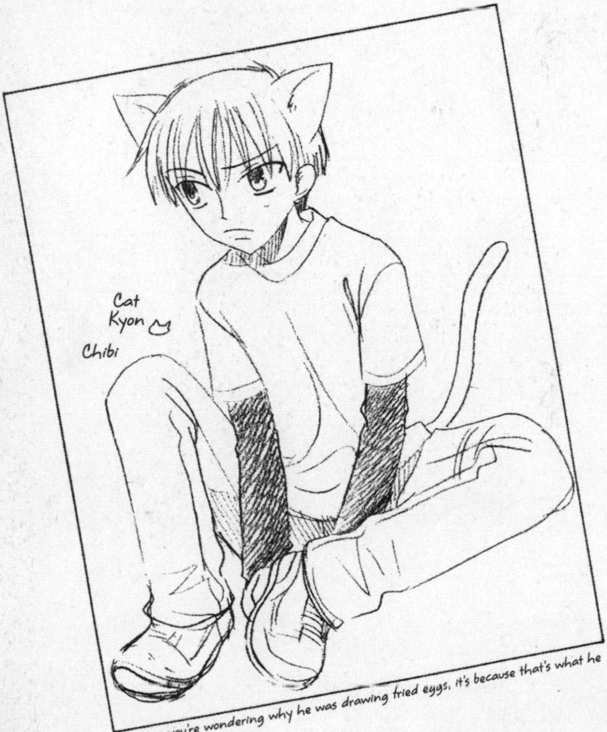
Cat Kyon
Chibi

In case you're wondering why he was drawing fried eggs, it's because that's what he had for breakfast.

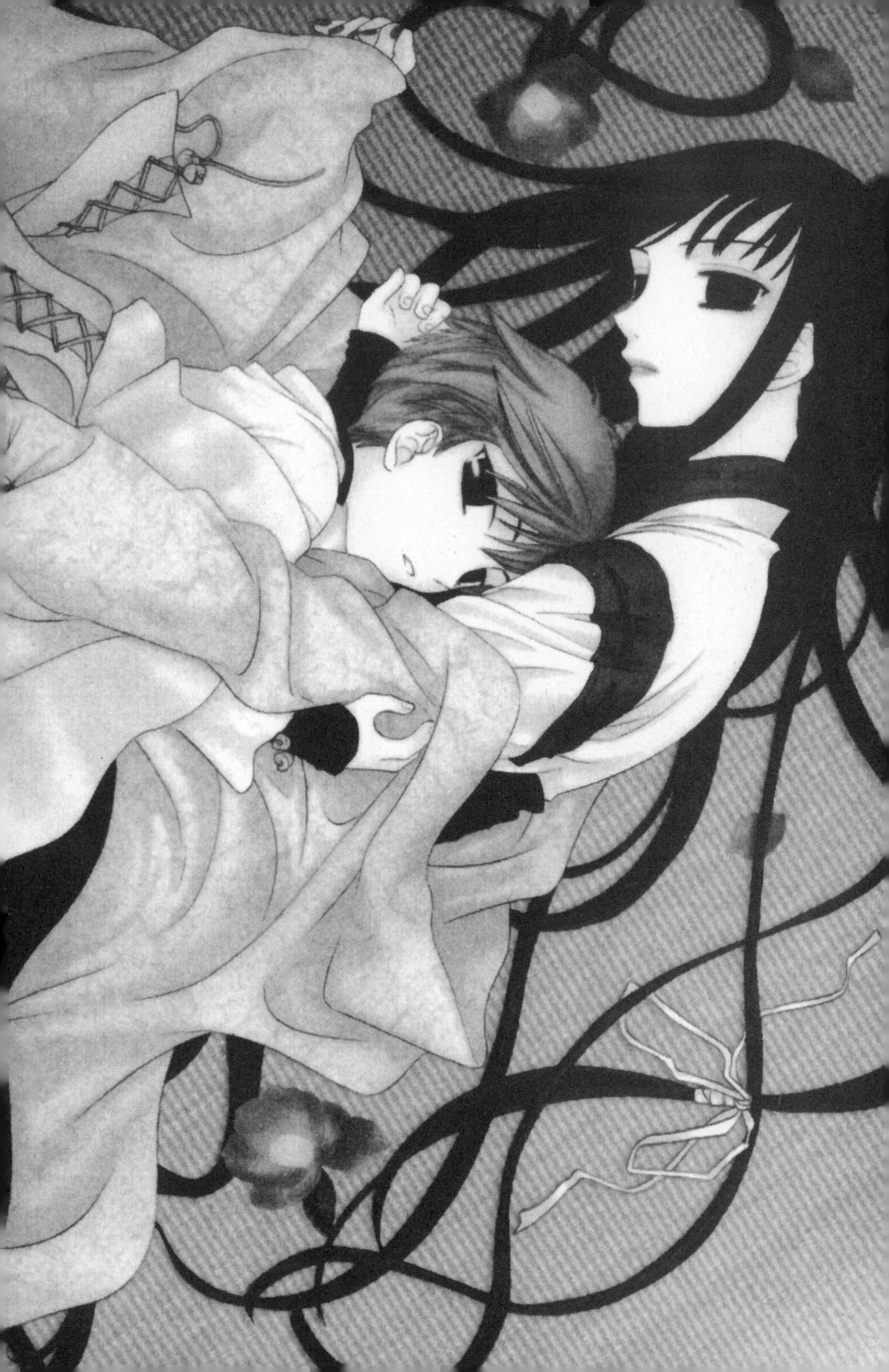

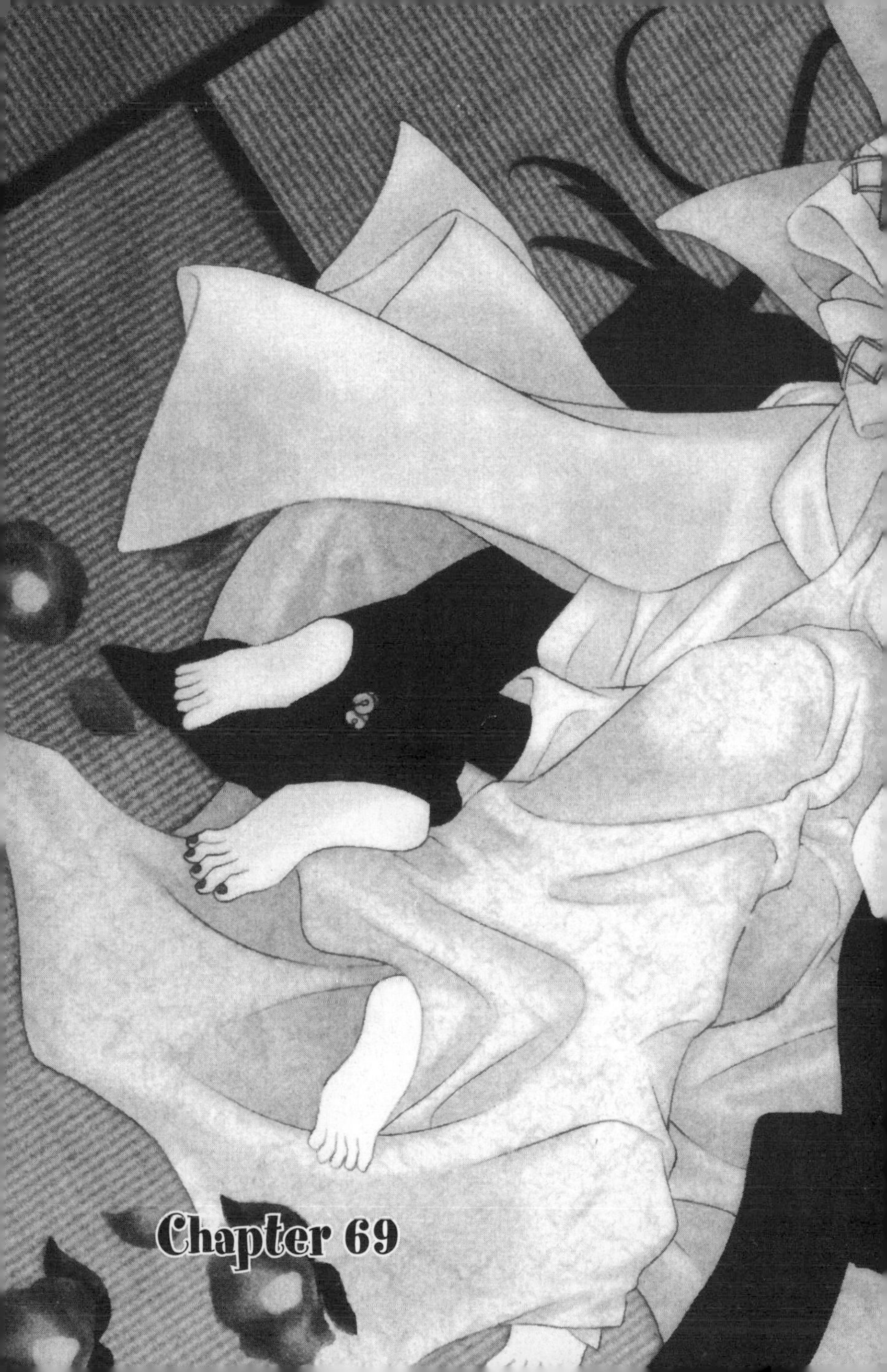
Chapter 69

Filler
Sketch

It's Rin. Drawing her is fun, but inking her in is too hard!

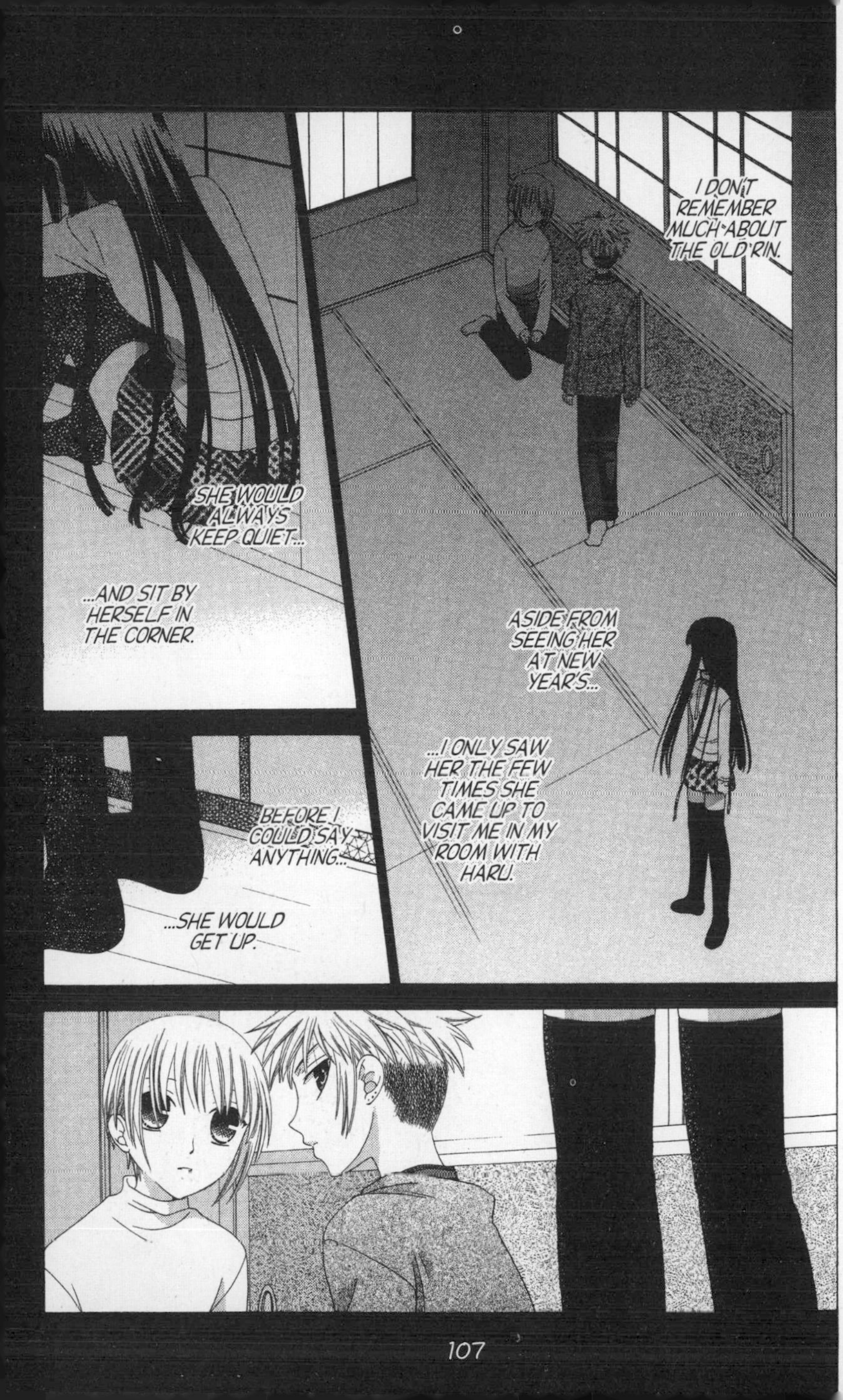
I DON'T REMEMBER MUCH ABOUT THE OLD RIN.
ASIDE FROM SEEING HER AT NEW YEAR'S...
...I ONLY SAW HER THE FEW TIMES SHE CAME UP TO VISIT ME IN MY ROOM WITH HARU.
SHE WOULD ALWAYS KEEP QUIET...
...AND SIT BY HERSELF IN THE CORNER.
BEFORE I COULD SAY ANYTHING...
...SHE WOULD GET UP.

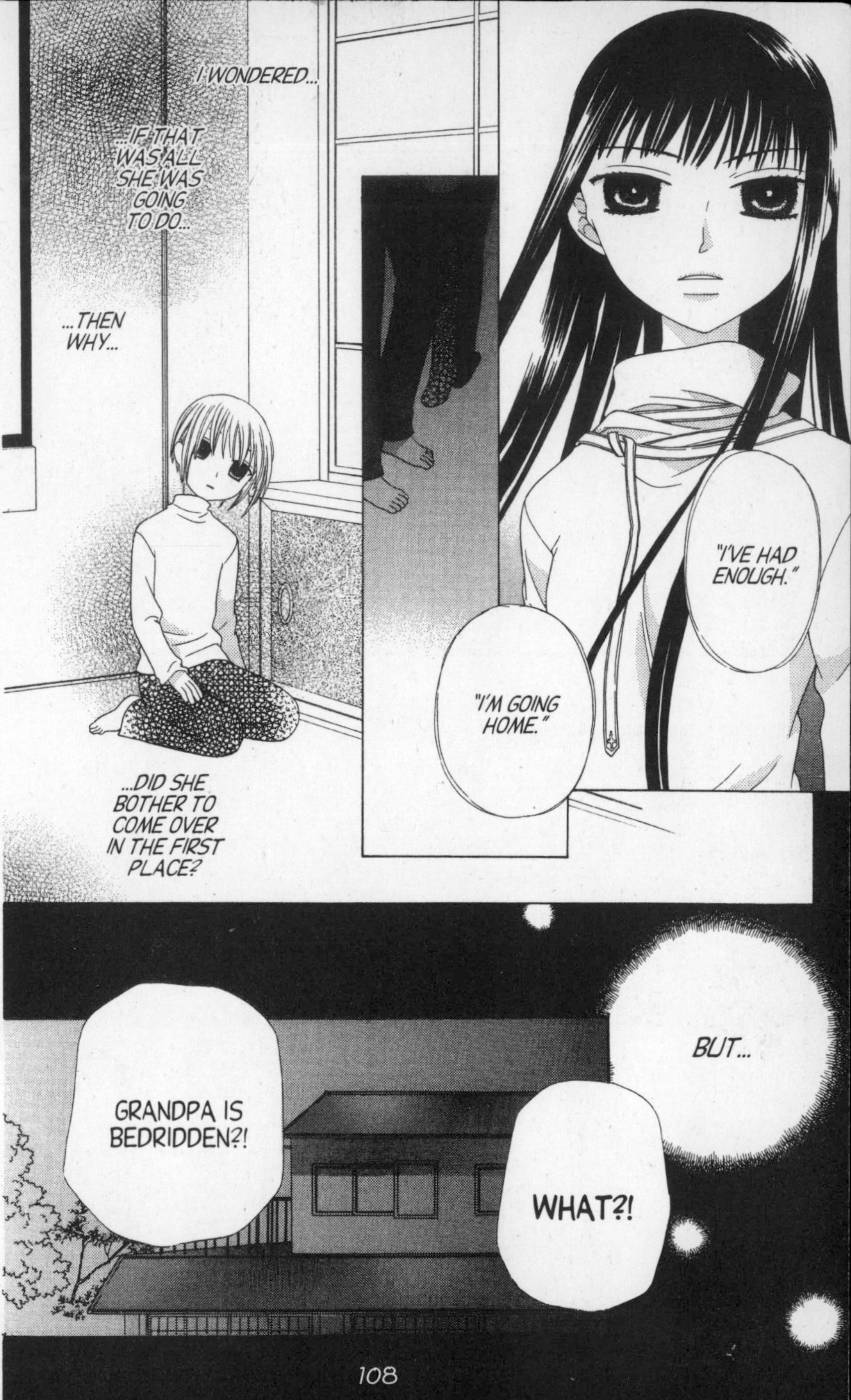
"I'VE HAD ENOUGH."
"I'M GOING HOME."
I WONDERED...
...IF THAT WAS ALL SHE WAS GOING TO DO...
...THEN WHY...
...DID SHE BOTHER TO COME OVER IN THE FIRST PLACE?
BUT...
WHAT?!
GRANDPA IS BEDRIDDEN?!

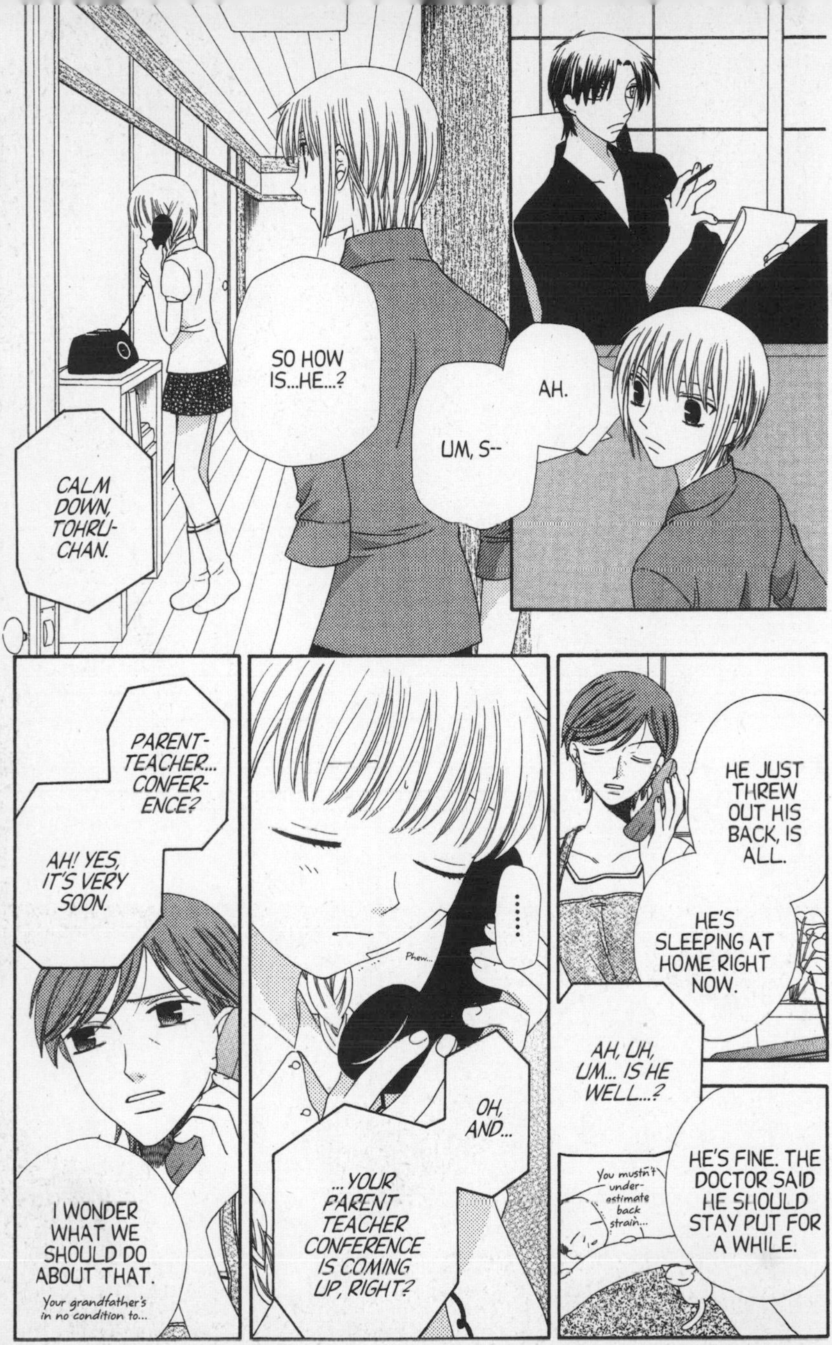
AH.
UM, S--
SO HOW IS...HE...?
CALM DOWN, TOHRU-CHAN.
HE JUST THREW OUT HIS BACK, IS ALL.
HE'S SLEEPING AT HOME RIGHT NOW.
AH, UH, UM... IS HE WELL...?
HE'S FINE. THE DOCTOR SAID HE SHOULD STAY PUT FOR A WHILE.
You mustn't under-estimate back strain...
......
Phew...
OH, AND...
...YOUR PARENT TEACHER CONFERENCE IS COMING UP, RIGHT?
PARENT-TEACHER... CONFERENCE?
AH! YES, IT'S VERY SOON.
I WONDER WHAT WE SHOULD DO ABOUT THAT.
Your grandfather's in no condition to...

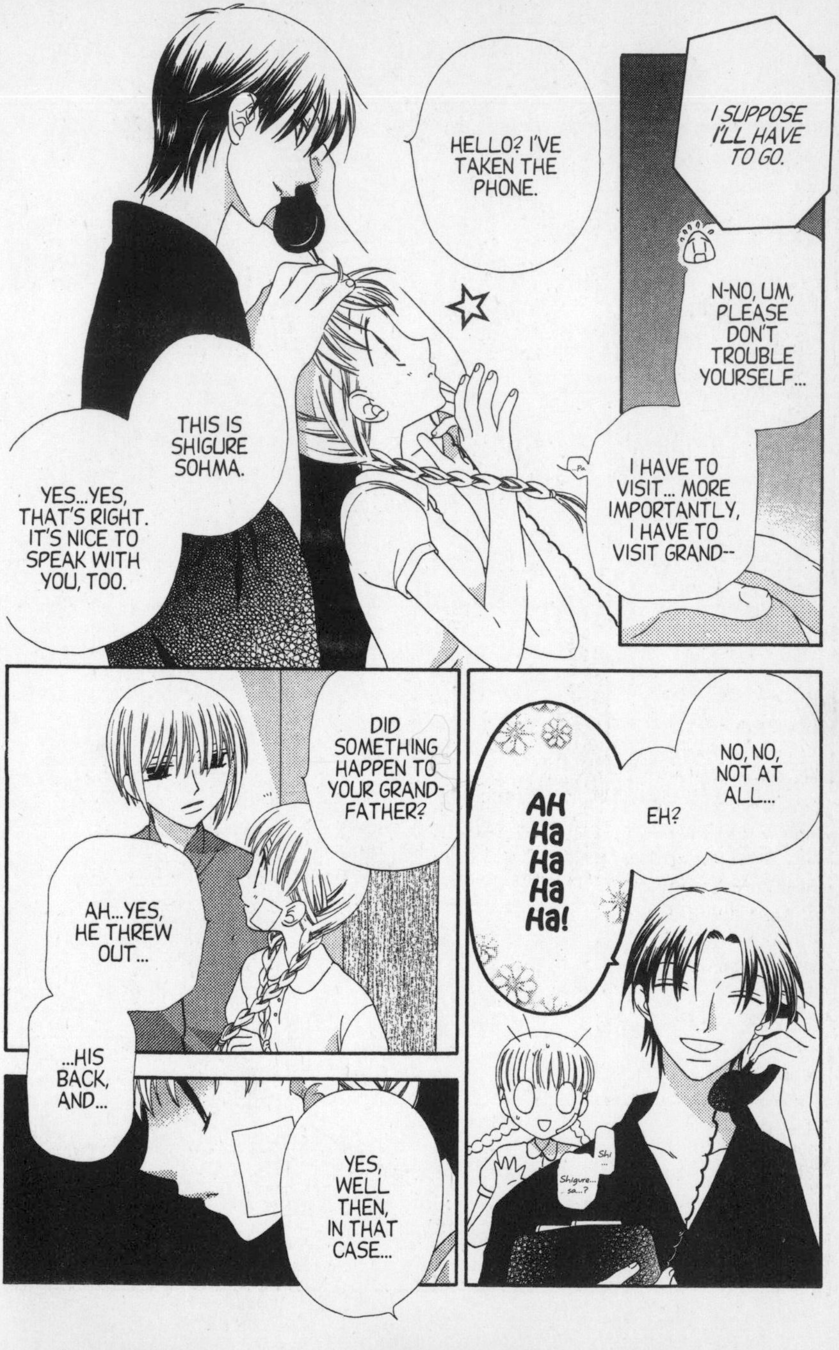
I SUPPOSE I'LL HAVE TO GO.
N-NO, UM, PLEASE DON'T TROUBLE YOURSELF...
I HAVE TO VISIT... MORE IMPORTANTLY, I HAVE TO VISIT GRAND--
HELLO? I'VE TAKEN THE PHONE.
THIS IS SHIGURE SOHMA.
YES...YES, THAT'S RIGHT. IT'S NICE TO SPEAK WITH YOU, TOO.
NO, NO, NOT AT ALL...
EH?
AH Ha Ha Ha Ha!
Shi...
Shigure... sa...?
DID SOMETHING HAPPEN TO YOUR GRAND-FATHER?
...
AH...YES, HE THREW OUT...
...HIS BACK, AND...
YES, WELL THEN, IN THAT CASE...

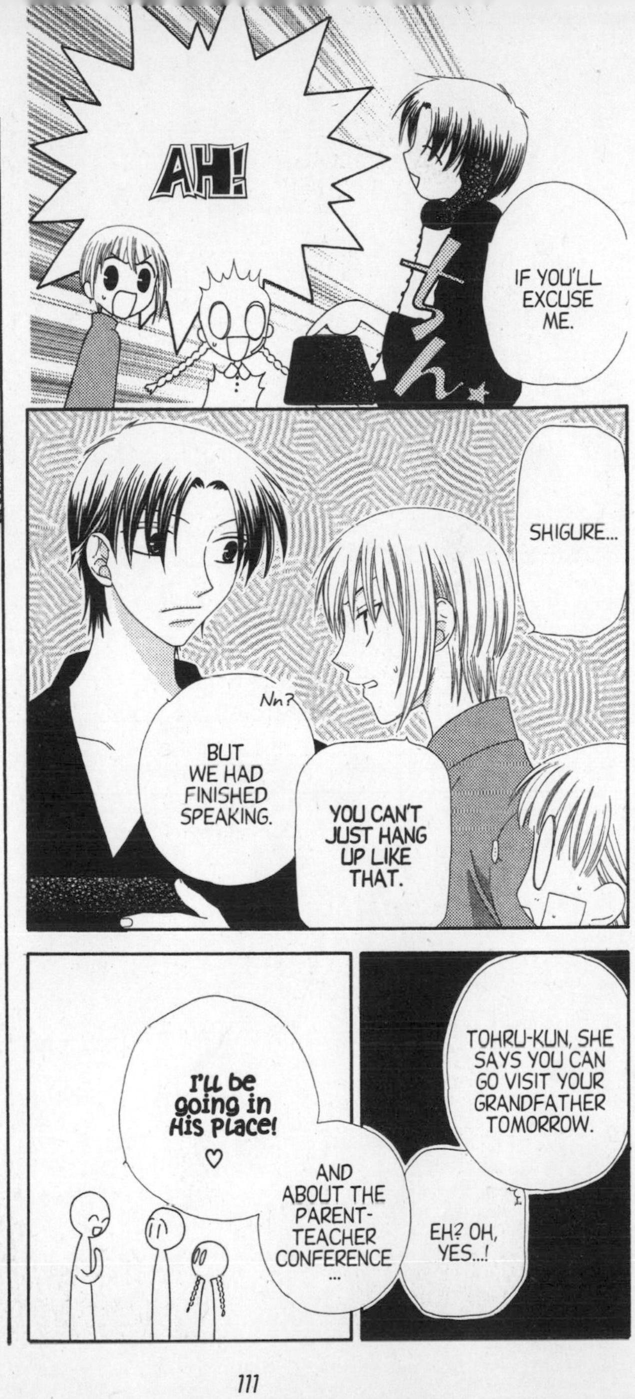
AH!
IF YOU'LL EXCUSE ME.
SHIGURE...
YOU CAN'T JUST HANG UP LIKE THAT.
Nn?
BUT WE HAD FINISHED SPEAKING.
TOHRU-KUN, SHE SAYS YOU CAN GO VISIT YOUR GRANDFATHER TOMORROW.
EH? OH, YES...!
AND ABOUT THE PARENT-TEACHER CONFERENCE ...
I'll be going in His place! ♡

Mio Yamagishi

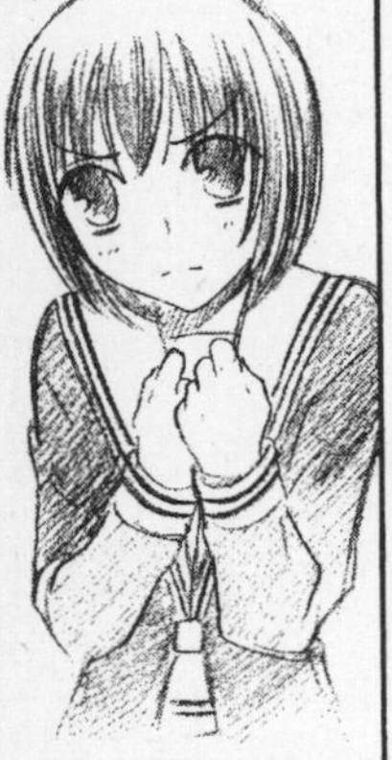

Well, I drew Motoko, so let's do Mio while I'm at it (laugh). Mio is the lowest-ranking and most docile member of the Prince Yuki Club, but I think she may also be the slyest. Kind of like, "When I'm gonna do it, I'm gonna do it, even if I have to drag others down!" (Do what?) But really...I think I wrote this before, but when Mio becomes the president of Pri-Yuki, Yuki will have already graduated! ...What will she do? (laugh)

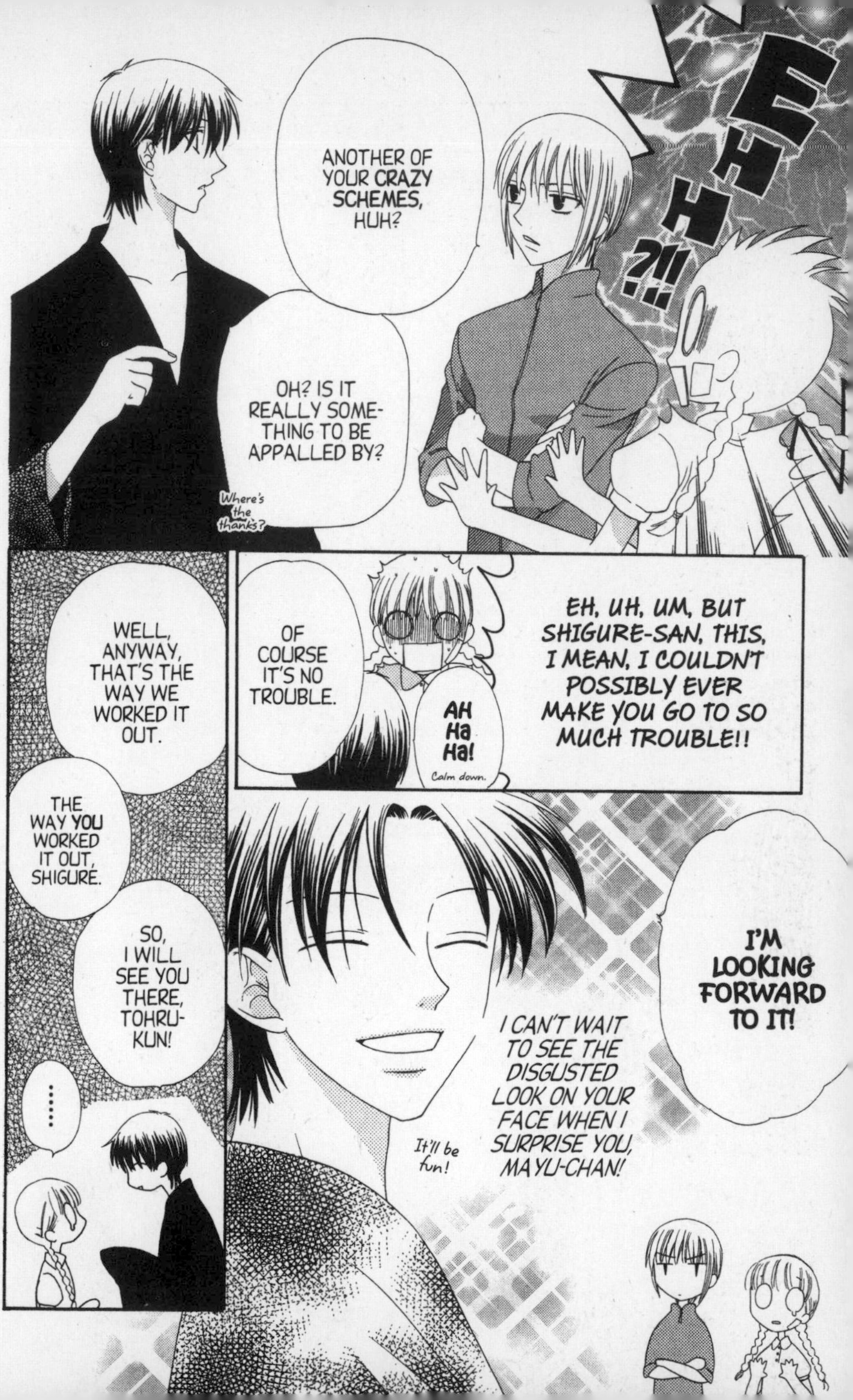
EHH?!!
ANOTHER OF YOUR CRAZY SCHEMES, HUH?
OH? IS IT REALLY SOME-THING TO BE APPALLED BY?
Where's the thanks?
EH, UH, UM, BUT SHIGURE-SAN, THIS, I MEAN, I COULDN'T POSSIBLY EVER MAKE YOU GO TO SO MUCH TROUBLE!!
OF COURSE IT'S NO TROUBLE.
AH Ha Ha!
Calm down.
I'M LOOKING FORWARD TO IT!
I CAN'T WAIT TO SEE THE DISGUSTED LOOK ON YOUR FACE WHEN I SURPRISE YOU, MAYU-CHAN!
It'll be fun!
WELL, ANYWAY, THAT'S THE WAY WE WORKED IT OUT.
THE WAY YOU WORKED IT OUT, SHIGURE.
SO, I WILL SEE YOU THERE, TOHRU-KUN!
......

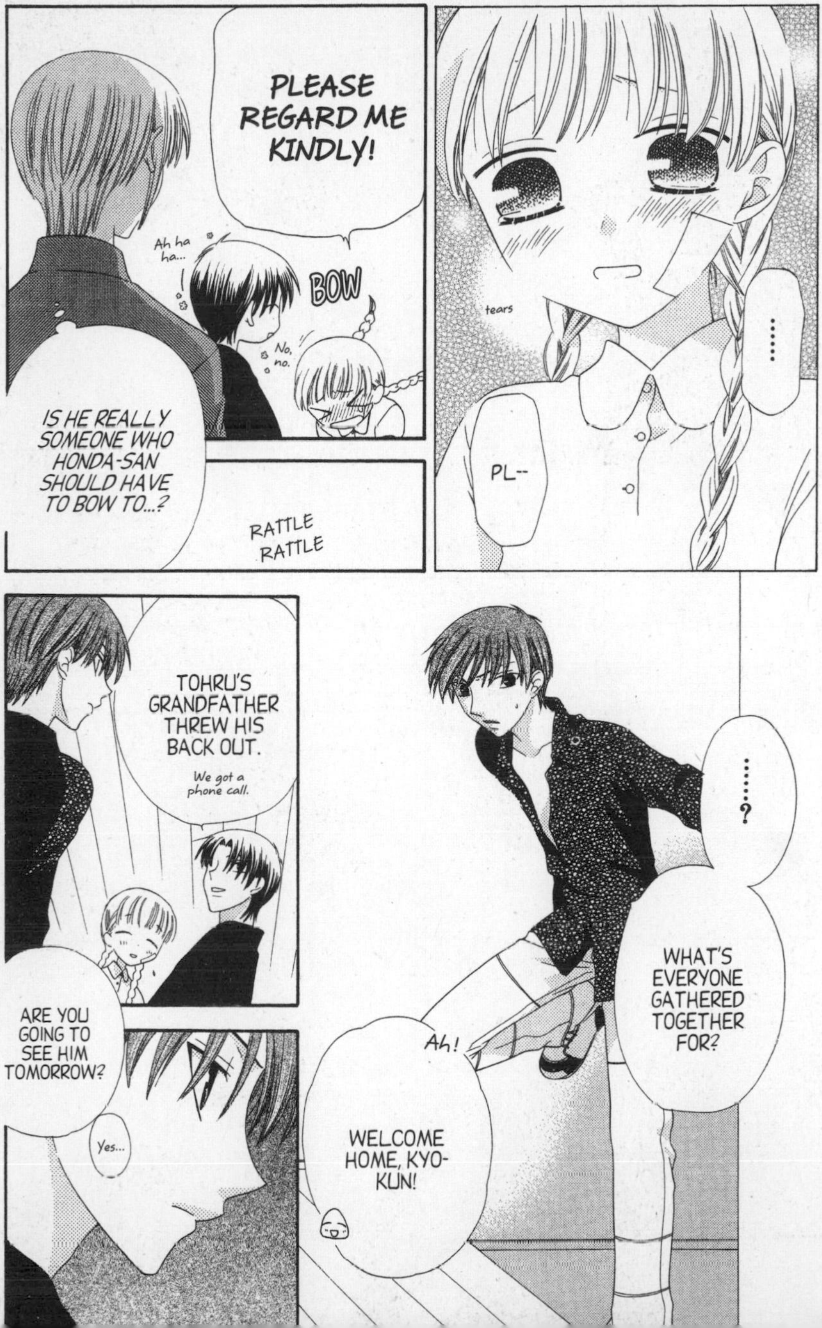
......
tears
PL--
PLEASE REGARD ME KINDLY!
BOW
Ah ha ha...
No, no.
IS HE REALLY SOMEONE WHO HONDA-SAN SHOULD HAVE TO BOW TO...?
RATTLE RATTLE
......?
WHAT'S EVERYONE GATHERED TOGETHER FOR?
Ah!
WELCOME HOME, KYO-KUN!
TOHRU'S GRANDFATHER THREW HIS BACK OUT.
We got a phone call.
ARE YOU GOING TO SEE HIM TOMORROW?
Yes...

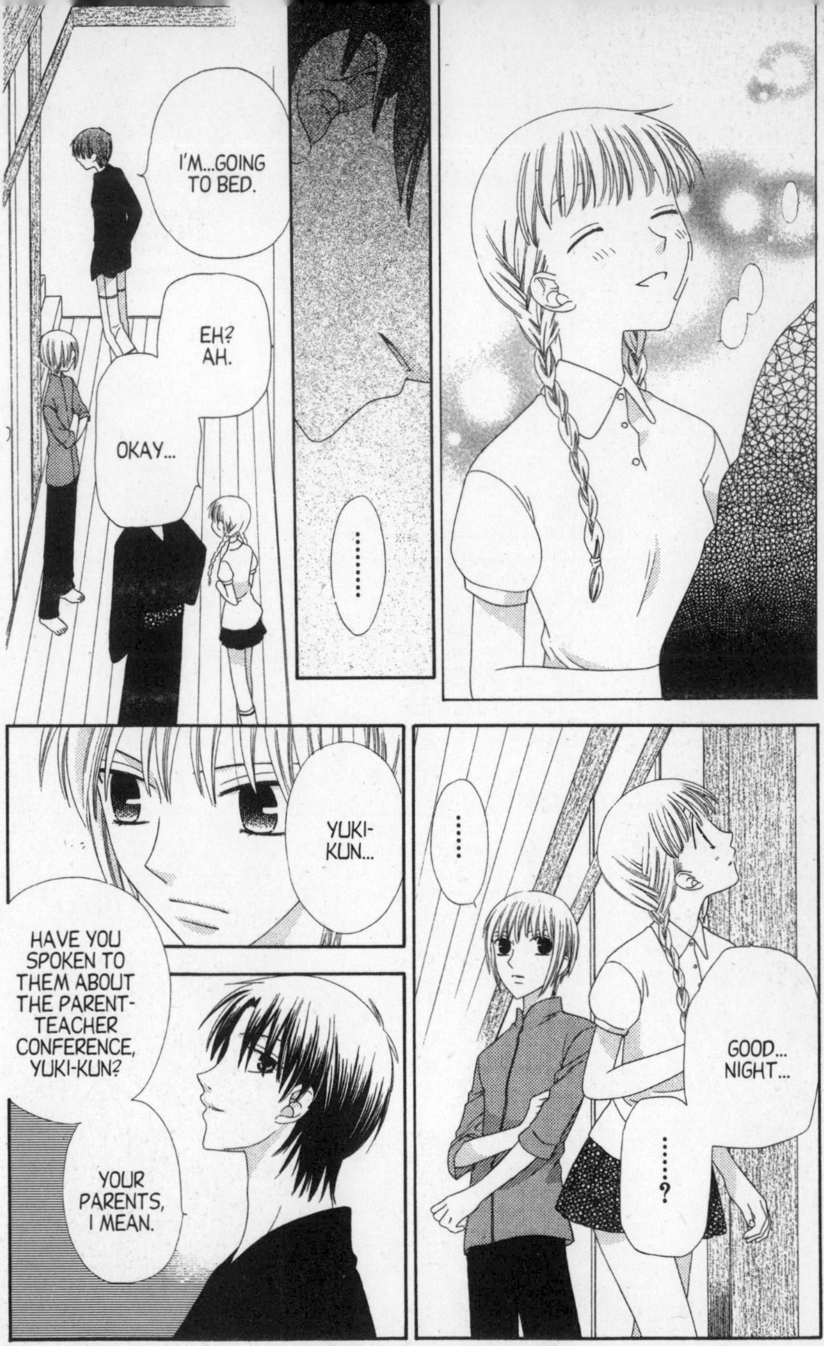
……
I'M...GOING TO BED.
EH? AH.
OKAY...
……
GOOD... NIGHT...
……?
YUKI-KUN...
HAVE YOU SPOKEN TO THEM ABOUT THE PARENT-TEACHER CONFERENCE, YUKI-KUN?
YOUR PARENTS, I MEAN.

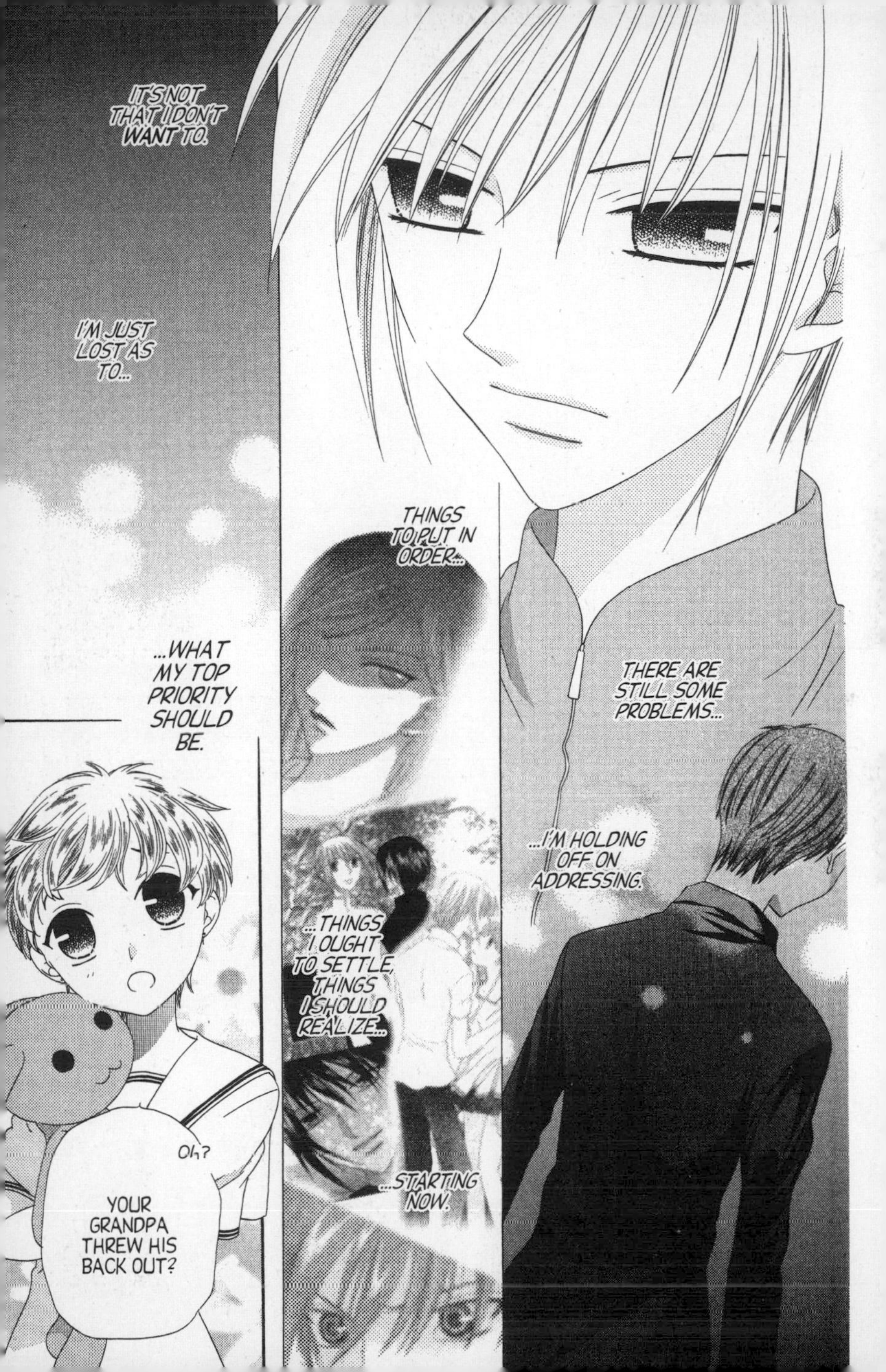
THERE ARE STILL SOME PROBLEMS...
...I'M HOLDING OFF ON ADDRESSING.
THINGS TO PUT IN ORDER...
...THINGS I OUGHT TO SETTLE, THINGS I SHOULD REALIZE...
...STARTING NOW.
IT'S NOT THAT I DON'T WANT TO.
I'M JUST LOST AS TO...
...WHAT MY TOP PRIORITY SHOULD BE.
Oh?
YOUR GRANDPA THREW HIS BACK OUT?

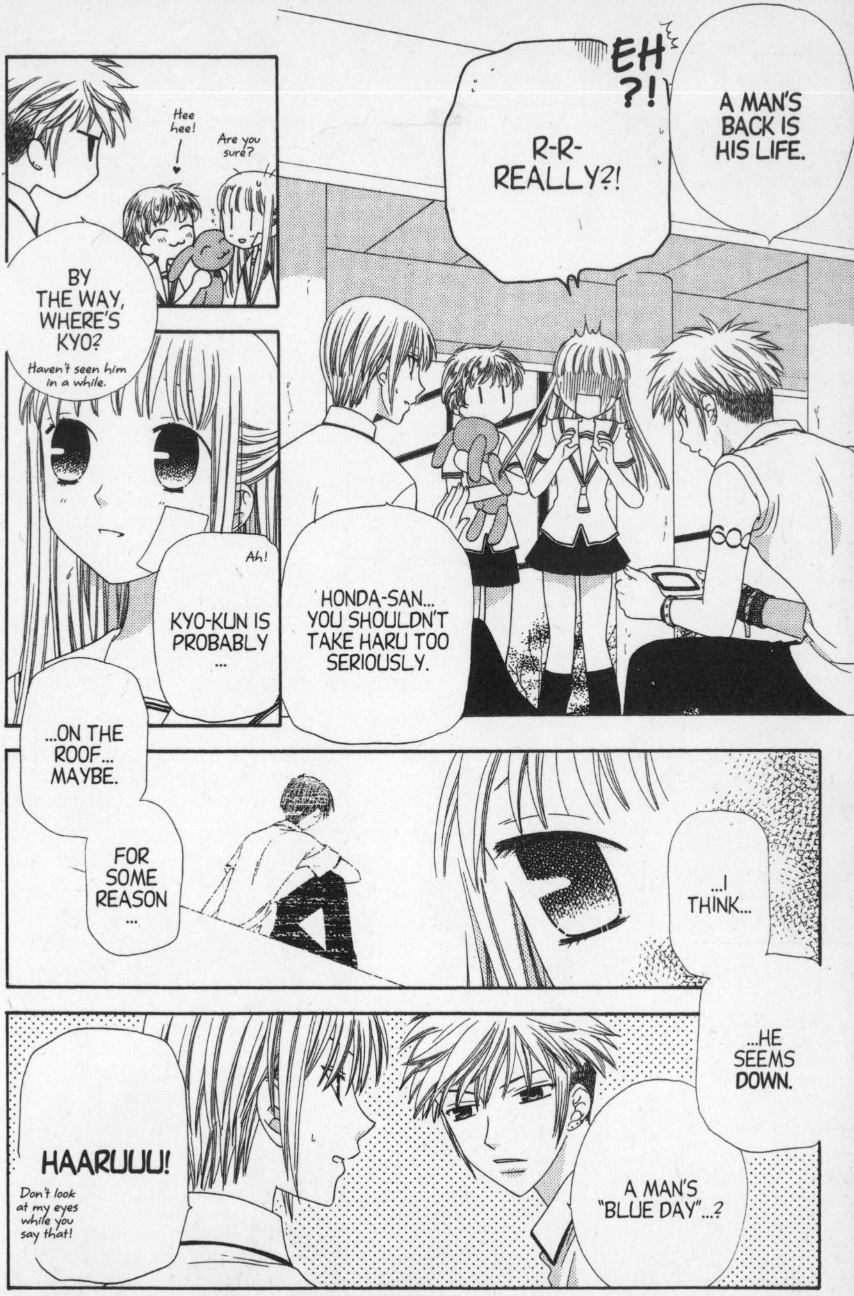
A MAN'S BACK IS HIS LIFE.
EH?!
R-R-REALLY?!
HONDA-SAN... YOU SHOULDN'T TAKE HARU TOO SERIOUSLY.
Hee hee!
Are you sure?
BY THE WAY, WHERE'S KYO?
Haven't seen him in a while.
Ah!
KYO-KUN IS PROBABLY ...
...ON THE ROOF... MAYBE.
...I THINK...
FOR SOME REASON ...
...HE SEEMS DOWN.
A MAN'S "BLUE DAY"...?
HAARUUU!
Don't look at my eyes while you say that!

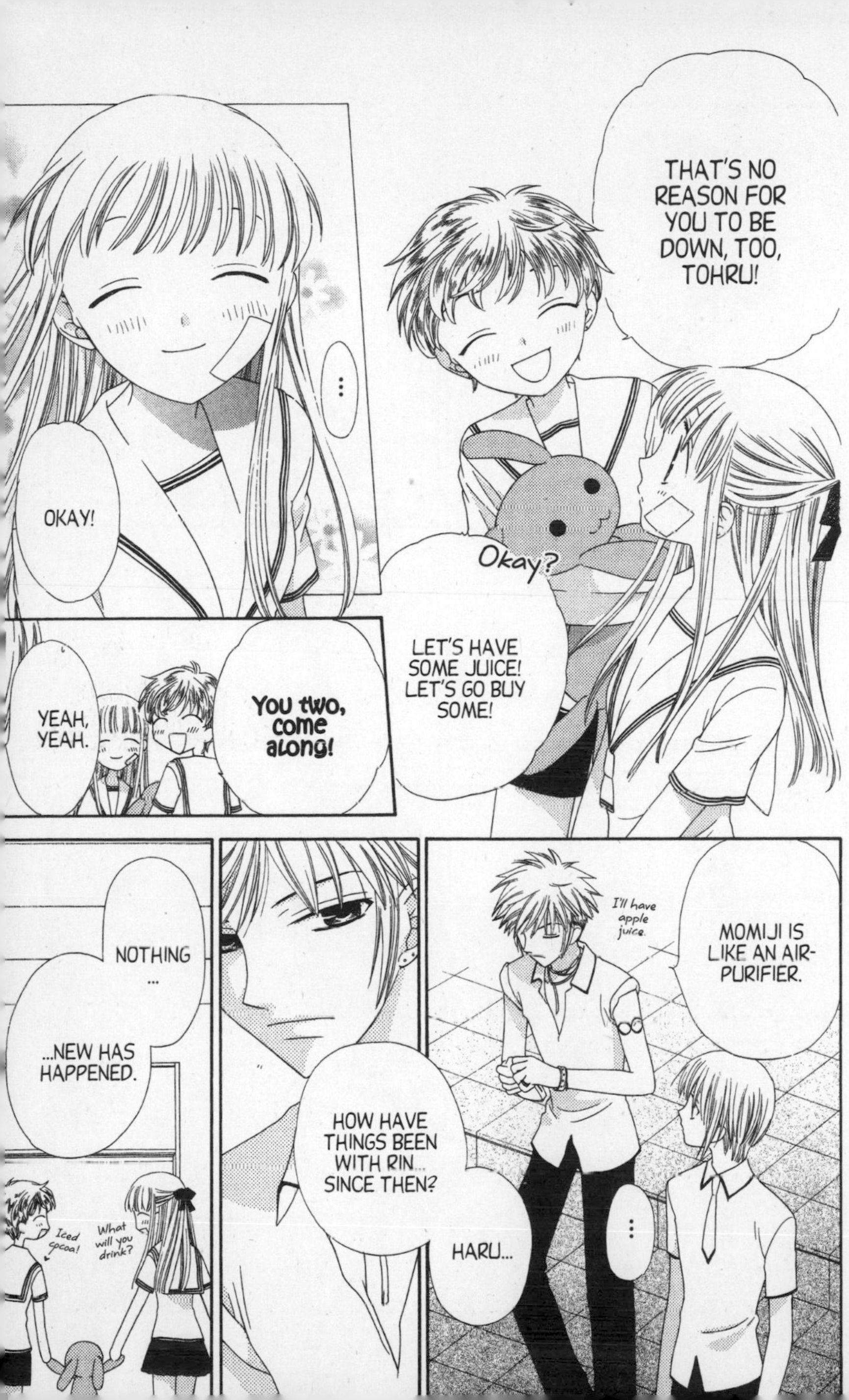
THAT'S NO REASON FOR YOU TO BE DOWN, TOO, TOHRU!
Okay?
...
OKAY!
LET'S HAVE SOME JUICE! LET'S GO BUY SOME!
You two, come along!
YEAH, YEAH.
MOMIJI IS LIKE AN AIR-PURIFIER.
I'll have apple juice.
...
HARU...
HOW HAVE THINGS BEEN WITH RIN... SINCE THEN?
NOTHING ...
...NEW HAS HAPPENED.
What will you drink?
Iced cocoa!

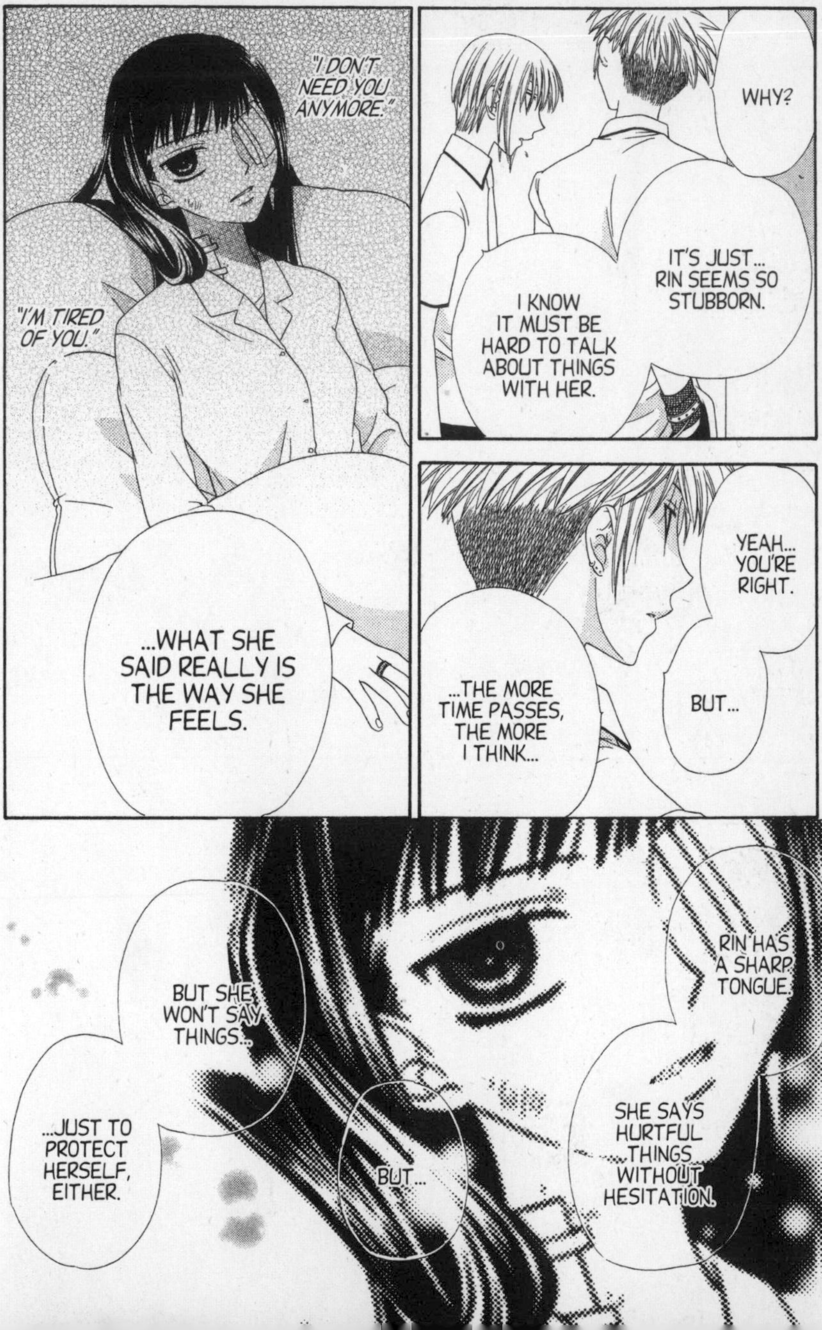
WHY?
IT'S JUST... RIN SEEMS SO STUBBORN.
I KNOW IT MUST BE HARD TO TALK ABOUT THINGS WITH HER.
YEAH... YOU'RE RIGHT.
BUT...
...THE MORE TIME PASSES, THE MORE I THINK...
"I DON'T NEED YOU ANYMORE."
"I'M TIRED OF YOU."
...WHAT SHE SAID REALLY IS THE WAY SHE FEELS.
RIN HAS A SHARP TONGUE.
SHE SAYS HURTFUL THINGS WITHOUT HESITATION.
BUT...
BUT SHE WON'T SAY THINGS...
...JUST TO PROTECT HERSELF, EITHER.

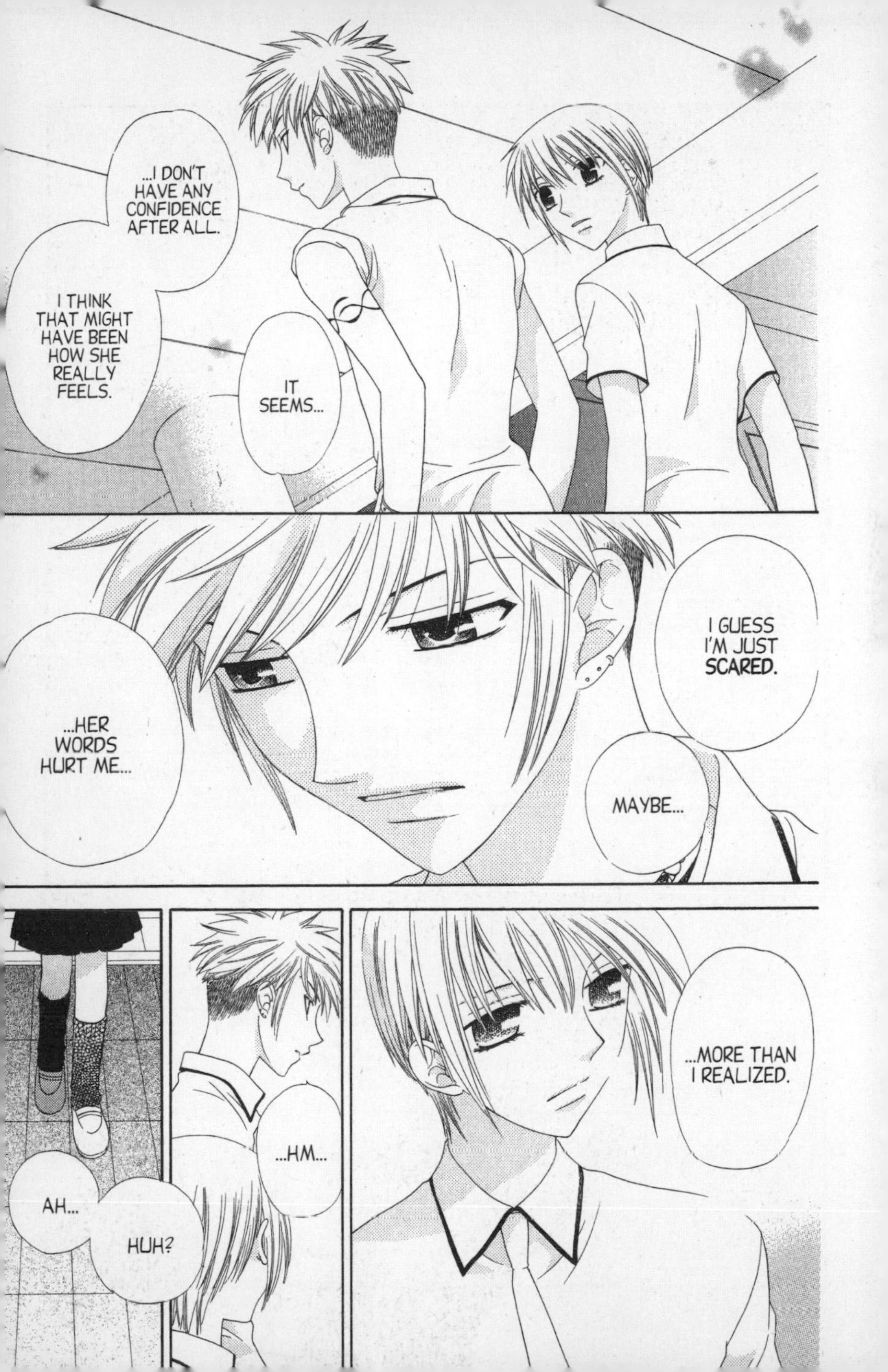
IT SEEMS...
...I DON'T HAVE ANY CONFIDENCE AFTER ALL.
I THINK THAT MIGHT HAVE BEEN HOW SHE REALLY FEELS.
I GUESS I'M JUST SCARED.
MAYBE...
...HER WORDS HURT ME...
...MORE THAN I REALIZED.
...HM...
HUH?
AH...

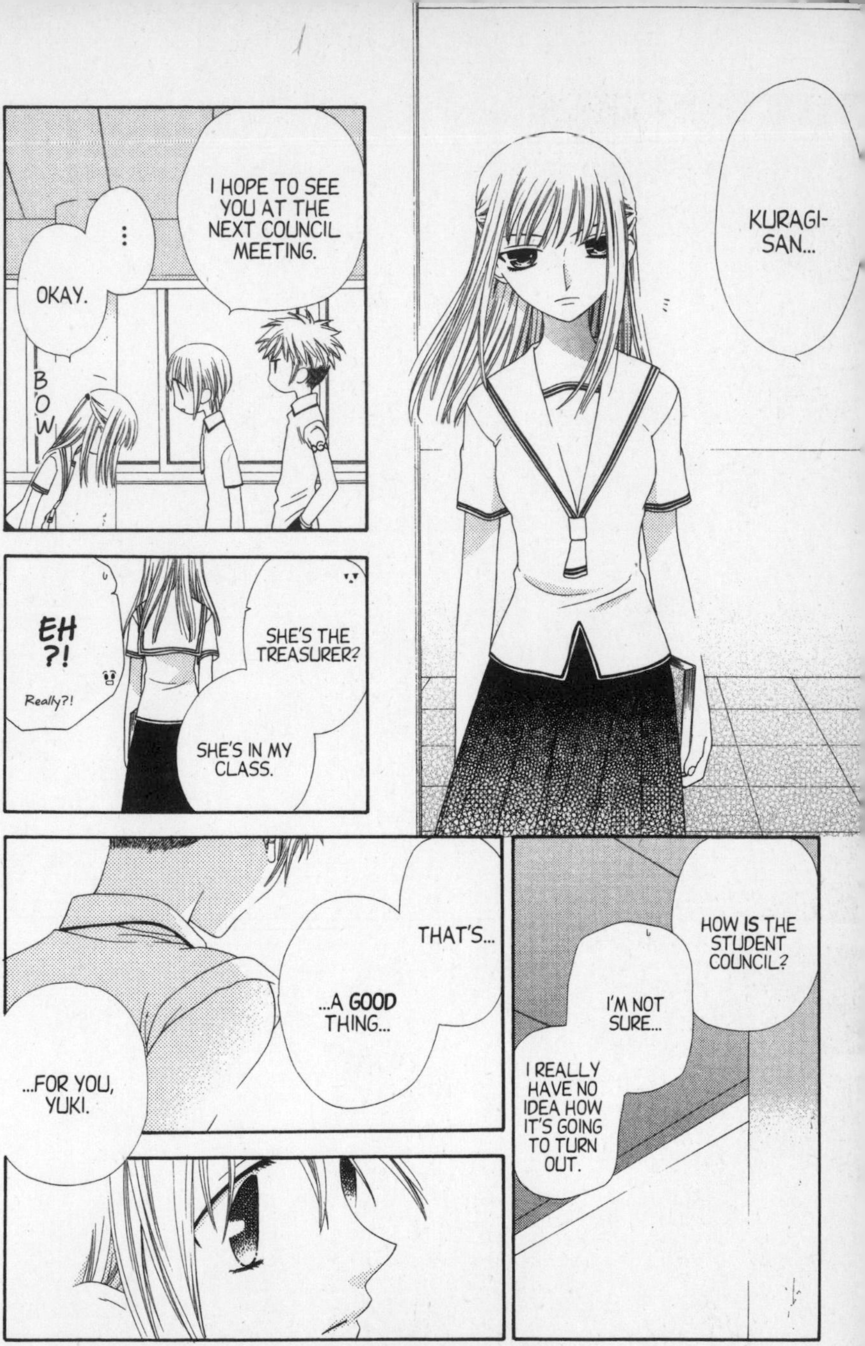
KURAGI-SAN...
I HOPE TO SEE YOU AT THE NEXT COUNCIL MEETING.
...
OKAY.
BOW
SHE'S THE TREASURER?
SHE'S IN MY CLASS.
EH ?!
Really?!
HOW IS THE STUDENT COUNCIL?
I'M NOT SURE...
I REALLY HAVE NO IDEA HOW IT'S GOING TO TURN OUT.
THAT'S...
...A GOOD THING...
...FOR YOU, YUKI.

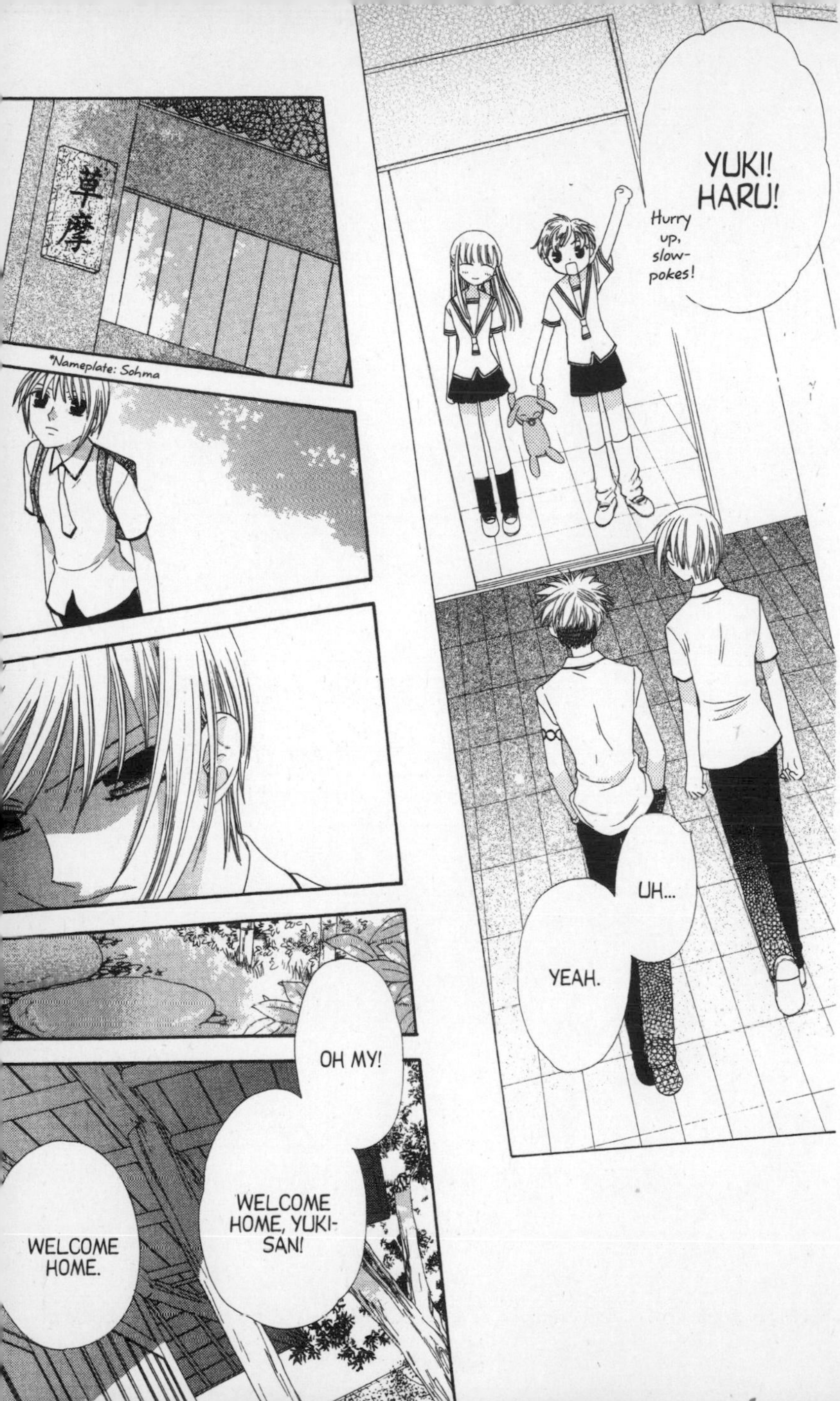
YUKI! HARU!
Hurry up, slow-pokes!
UH...
YEAH.
*Nameplate: Sohma
OH MY!
WELCOME HOME, YUKI-SAN!
WELCOME HOME.

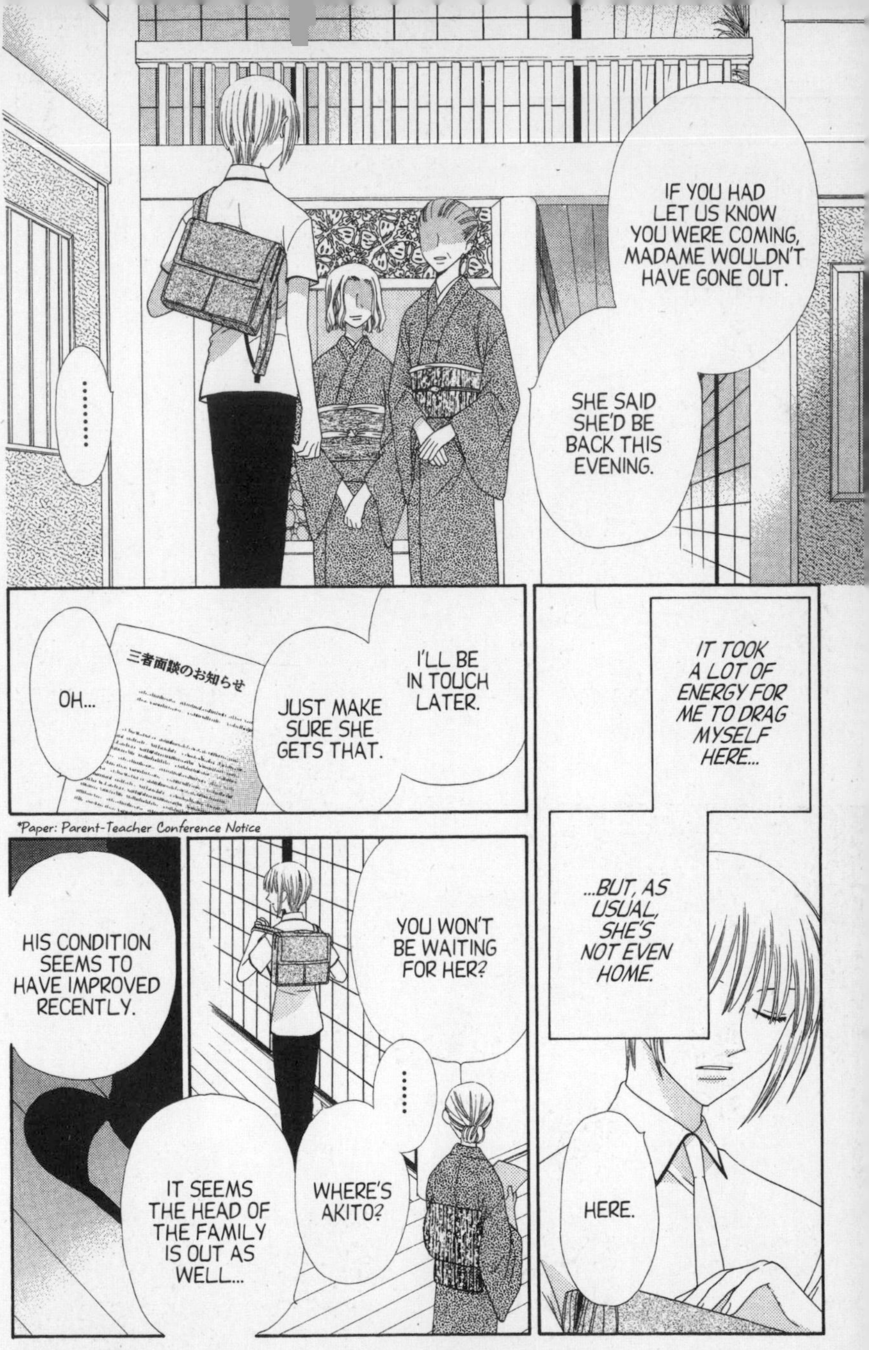
IF YOU HAD LET US KNOW YOU WERE COMING, MADAME WOULDN'T HAVE GONE OUT.
SHE SAID SHE'D BE BACK THIS EVENING.
......
IT TOOK A LOT OF ENERGY FOR ME TO DRAG MYSELF HERE...
...BUT, AS USUAL, SHE'S NOT EVEN HOME.
HERE.
I'LL BE IN TOUCH LATER.
JUST MAKE SURE SHE GETS THAT.
三者面談のお知らせ
OH...
YOU WON'T BE WAITING FOR HER?
......
WHERE'S AKITO?
IT SEEMS THE HEAD OF THE FAMILY IS OUT AS WELL...
HIS CONDITION SEEMS TO HAVE IMPROVED RECENTLY.

*Paper: Parent-Teacher Conference Notice

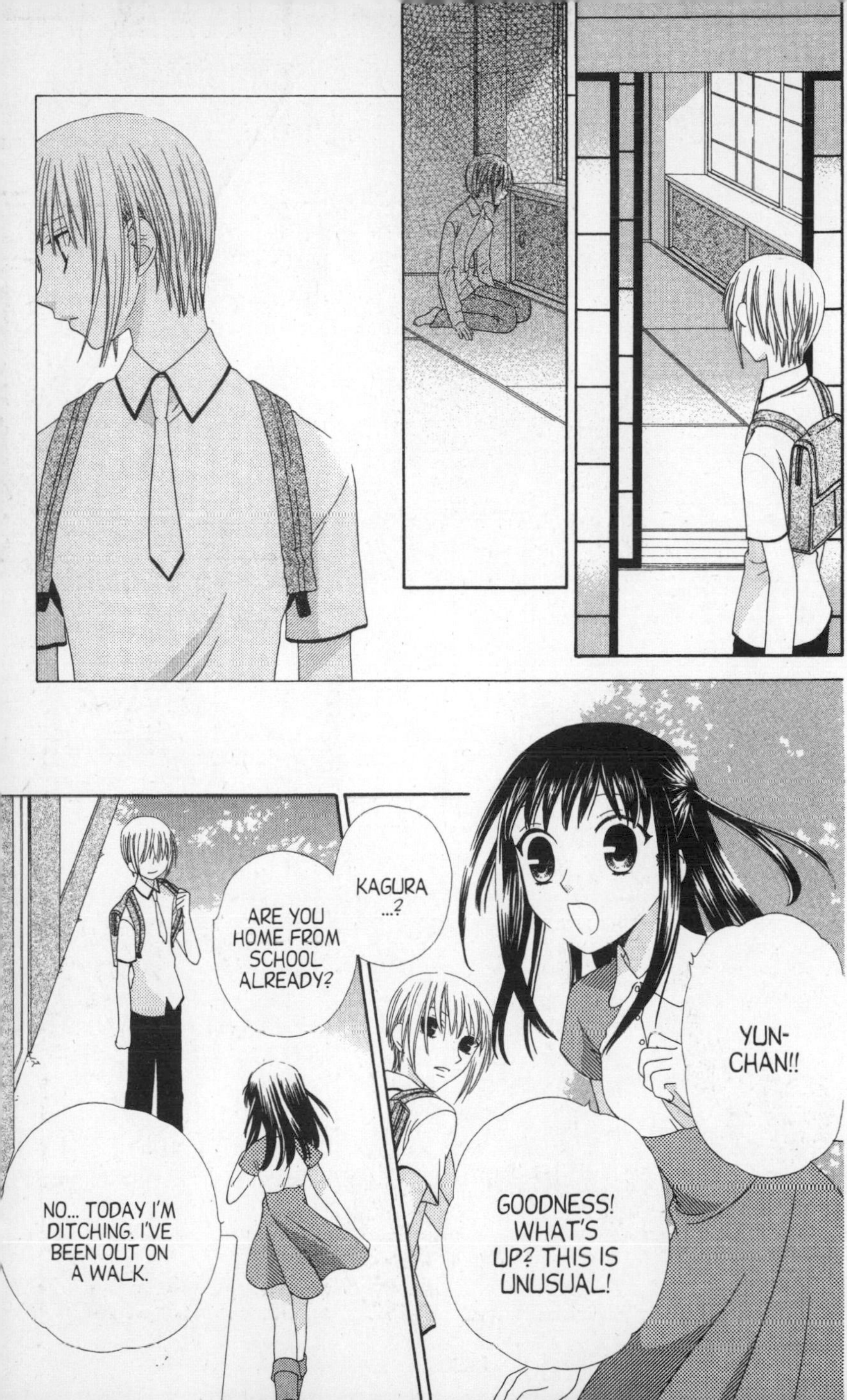
YUN-CHAN!!
KAGURA ...?
GOODNESS! WHAT'S UP? THIS IS UNUSUAL!
ARE YOU HOME FROM SCHOOL ALREADY?
NO... TODAY I'M DITCHING. I'VE BEEN OUT ON A WALK.

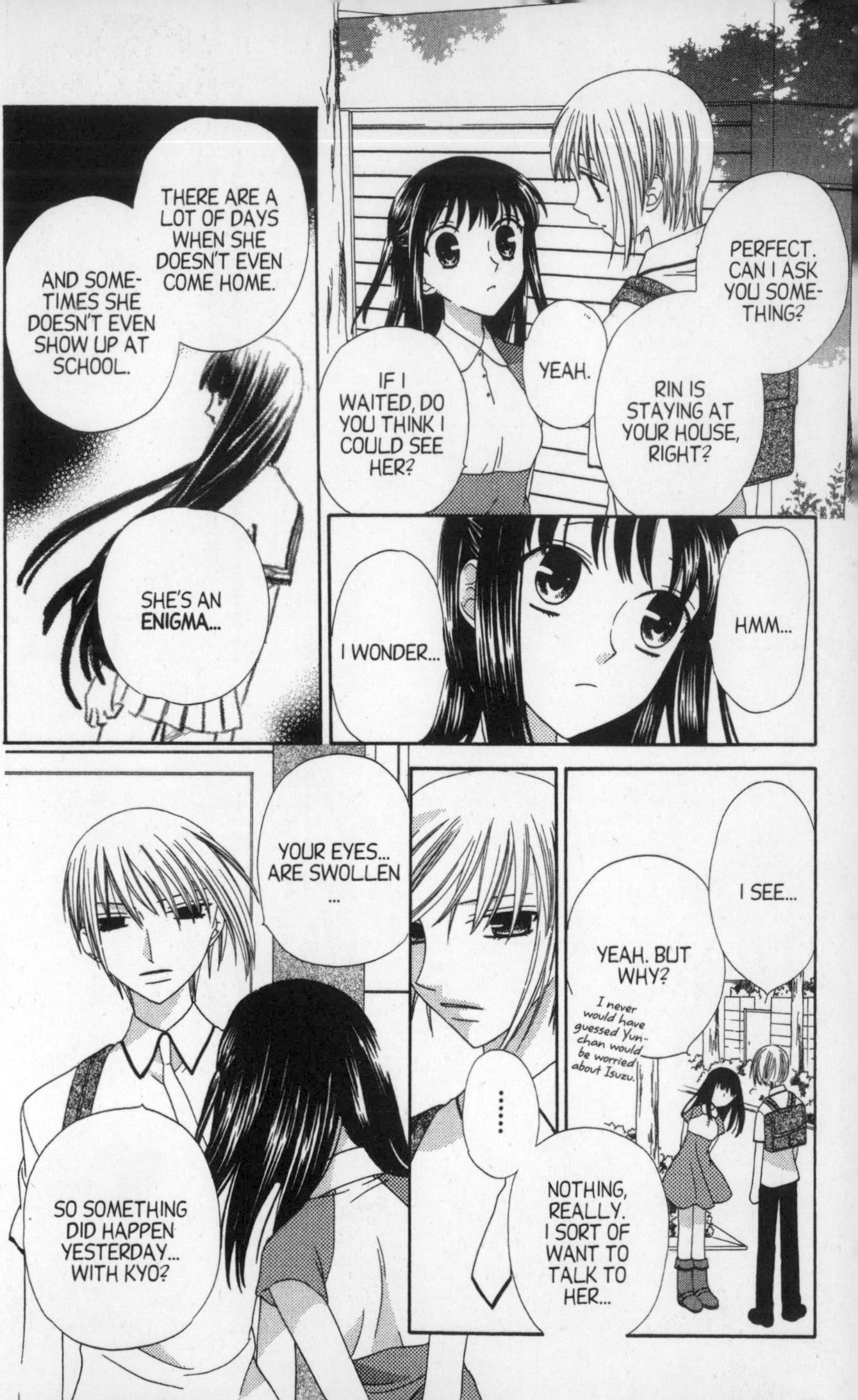
PERFECT. CAN I ASK YOU SOME-THING?
RIN IS STAYING AT YOUR HOUSE, RIGHT?
YEAH.
IF I WAITED, DO YOU THINK I COULD SEE HER?
HMM...
I WONDER...
THERE ARE A LOT OF DAYS WHEN SHE DOESN'T EVEN COME HOME.
AND SOME-TIMES SHE DOESN'T EVEN SHOW UP AT SCHOOL.
SHE'S AN ENIGMA...
I SEE...
YEAH. BUT WHY?
I never would have guessed Yun-chan would be worried about Isuzu.
NOTHING, REALLY. I SORT OF WANT TO TALK TO HER...
......
YOUR EYES... ARE SWOLLEN ...
SO SOMETHING DID HAPPEN YESTERDAY... WITH KYO?

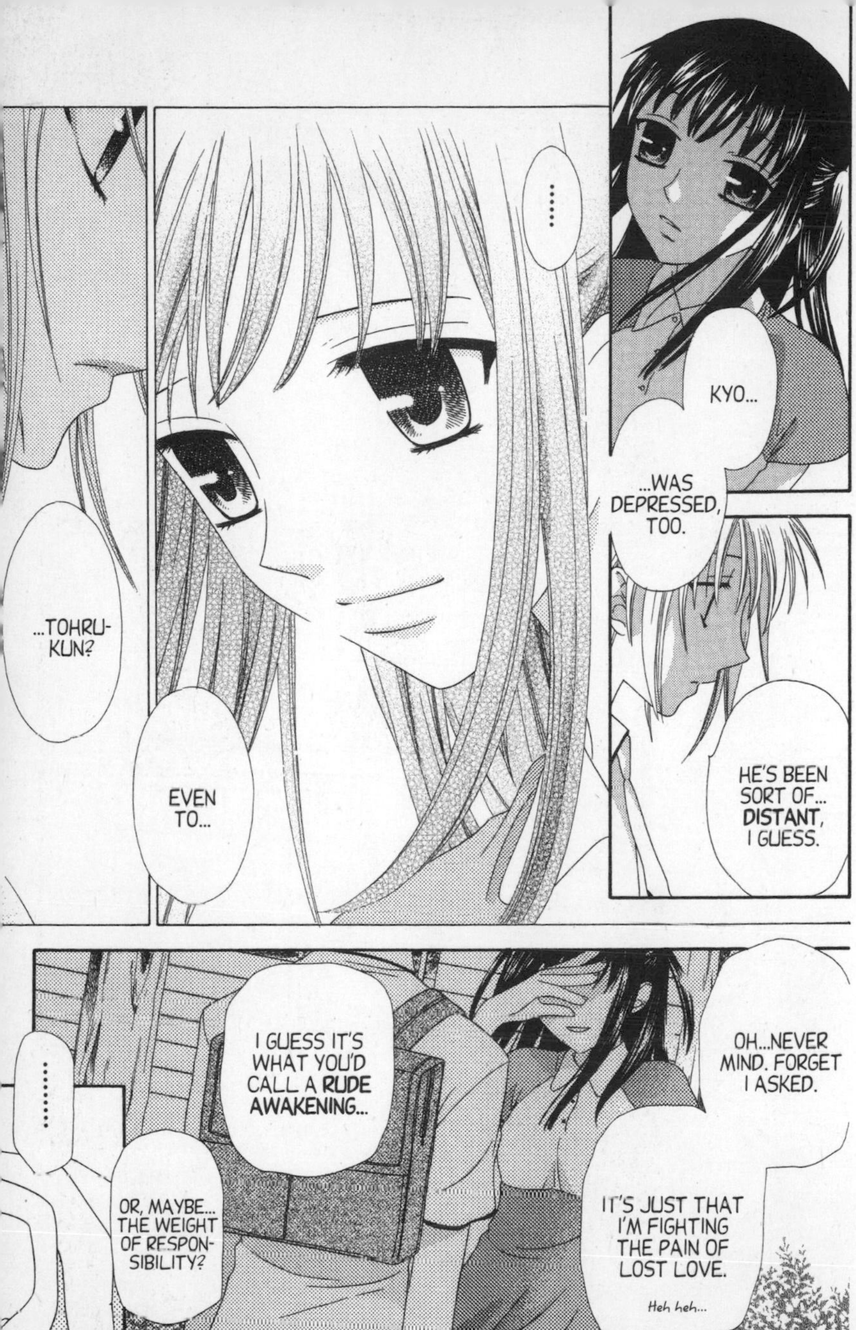
KYO...
...WAS DEPRESSED, TOO.
HE'S BEEN SORT OF... DISTANT, I GUESS.
......
EVEN TO...
...TOHRU-KUN?
OH...NEVER MIND. FORGET I ASKED.
IT'S JUST THAT I'M FIGHTING THE PAIN OF LOST LOVE.
Heh heh...
I GUESS IT'S WHAT YOU'D CALL A RUDE AWAKENING...
OR, MAYBE... THE WEIGHT OF RESPONSIBILITY?
......

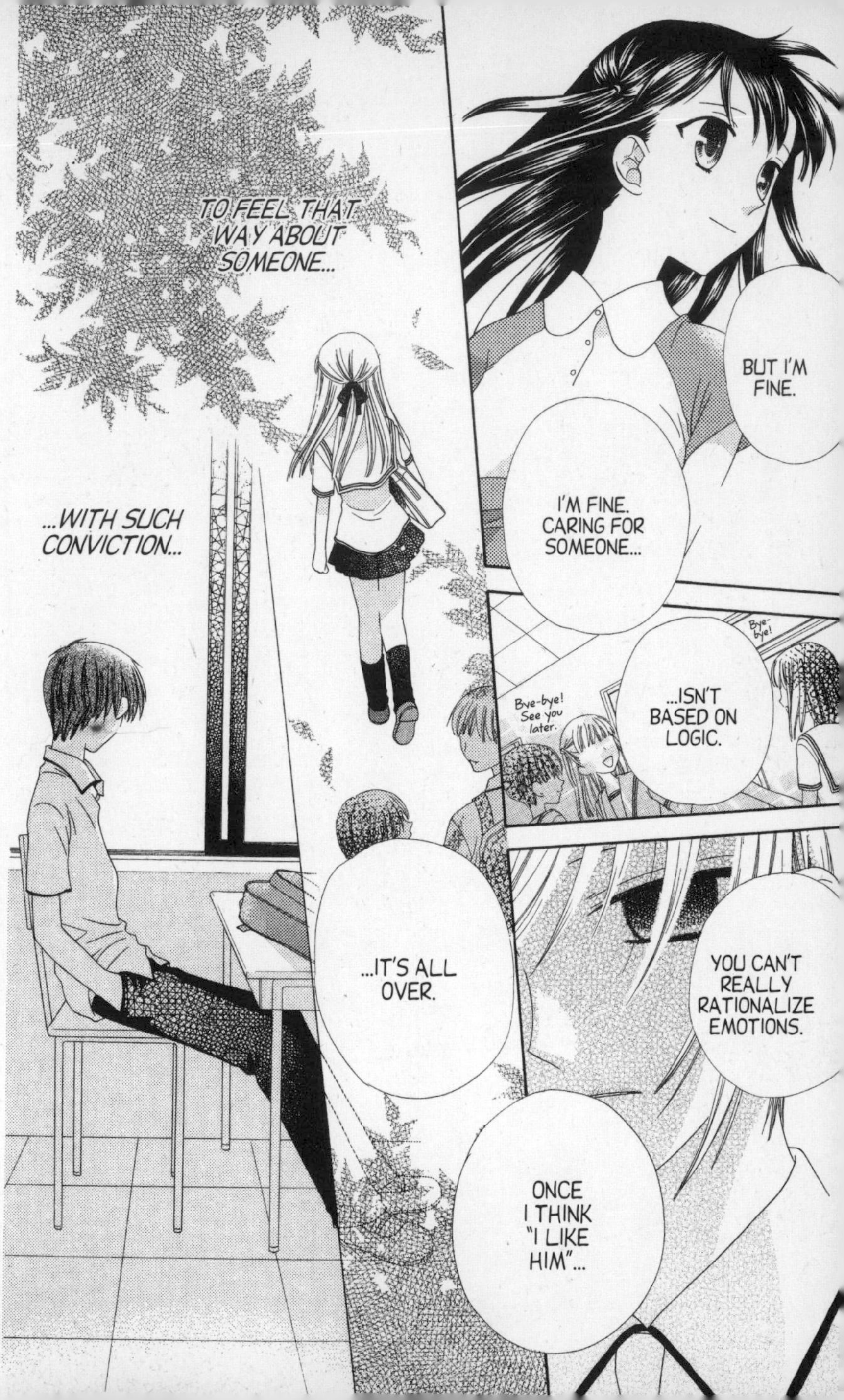
BUT I'M FINE.
I'M FINE. CARING FOR SOMEONE...
Bye-bye!
...ISN'T BASED ON LOGIC.
Bye-bye! See you later.
YOU CAN'T REALLY RATIONALIZE EMOTIONS.
ONCE I THINK "I LIKE HIM"...
...IT'S ALL OVER.
TO FEEL THAT WAY ABOUT SOMEONE...
...WITH SUCH CONVICTION...

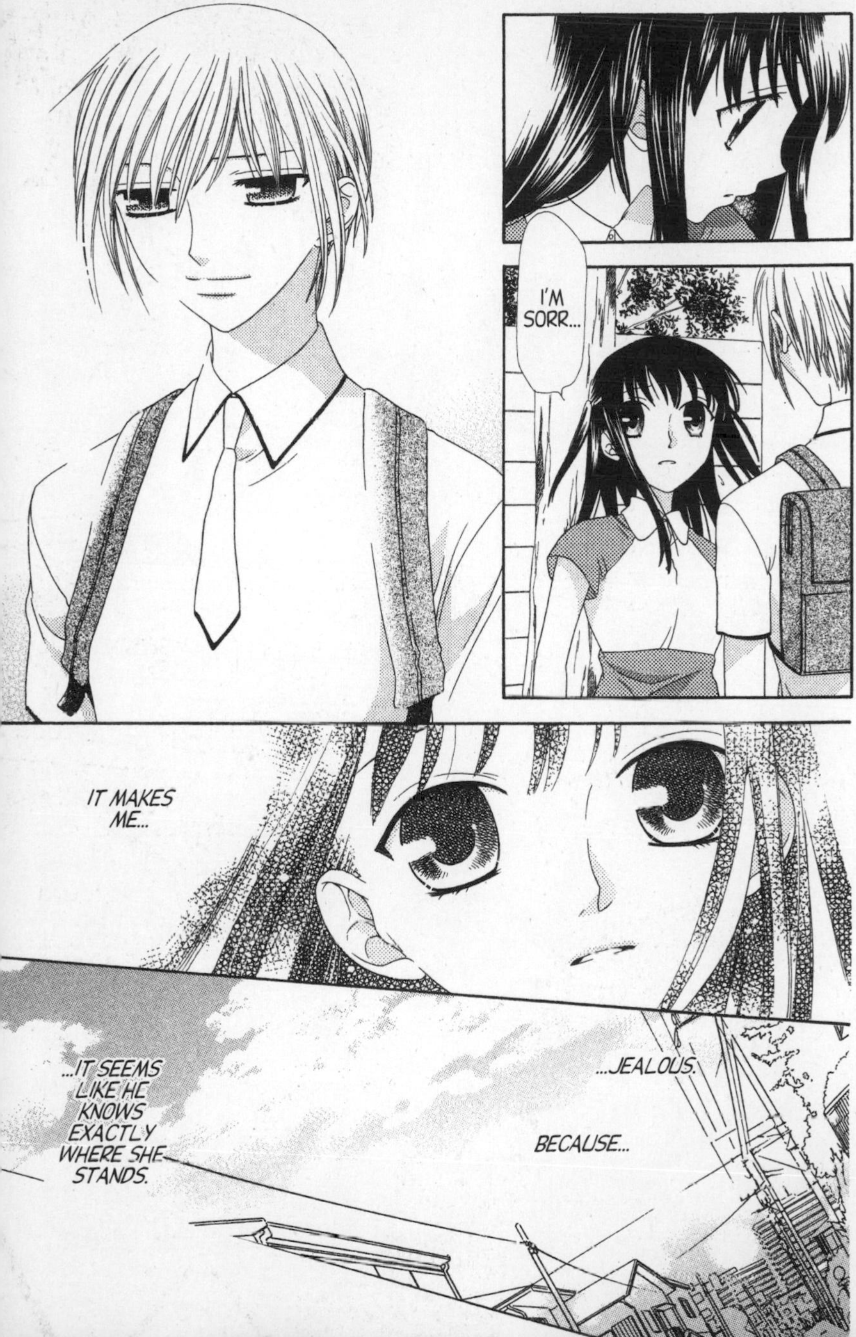
I'M SORR...
IT MAKES ME...
...JEALOUS.
BECAUSE...
...IT SEEMS LIKE HE KNOWS EXACTLY WHERE SHE STANDS.

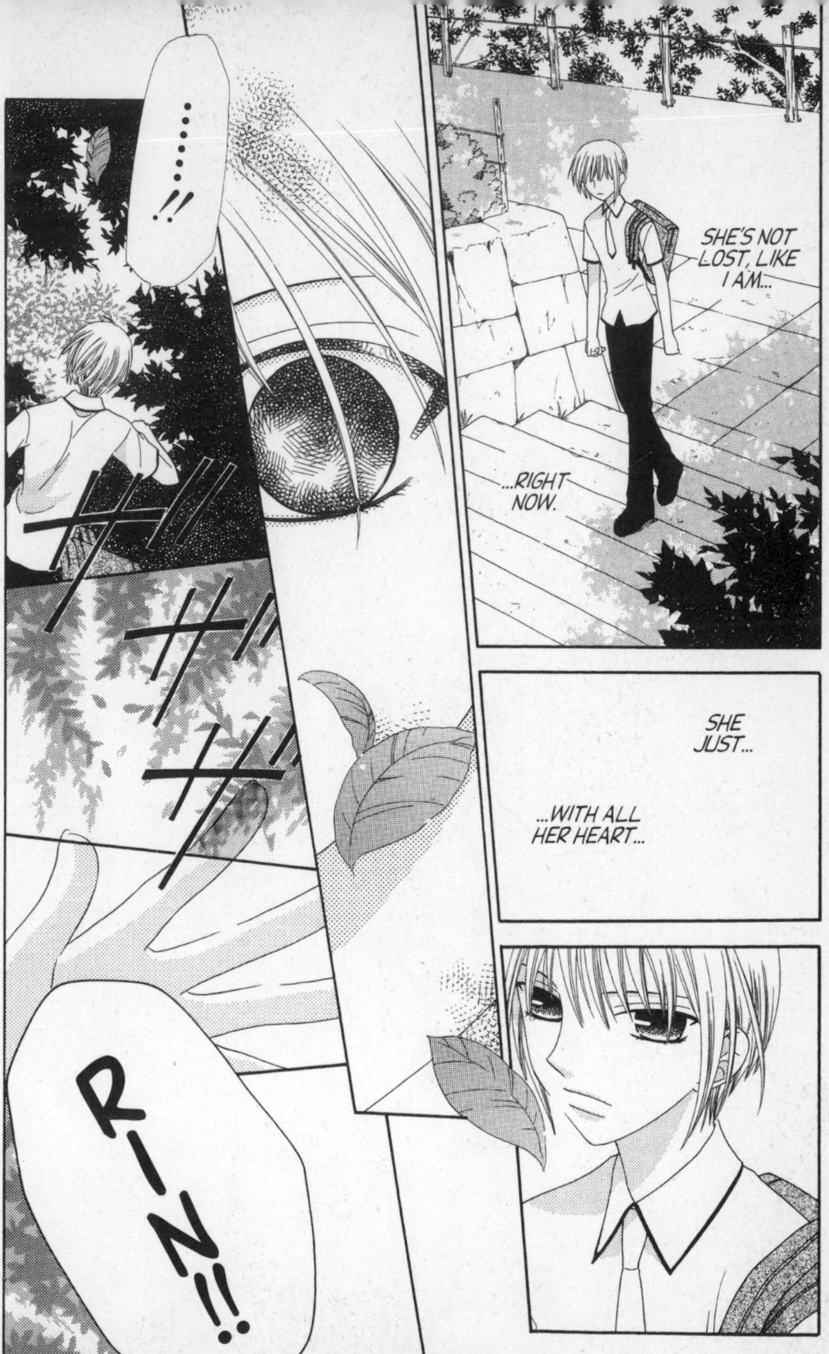
SHE'S NOT LOST, LIKE I AM...
...RIGHT NOW.
SHE JUST...
...WITH ALL HER HEART...
......!!
RIN!!

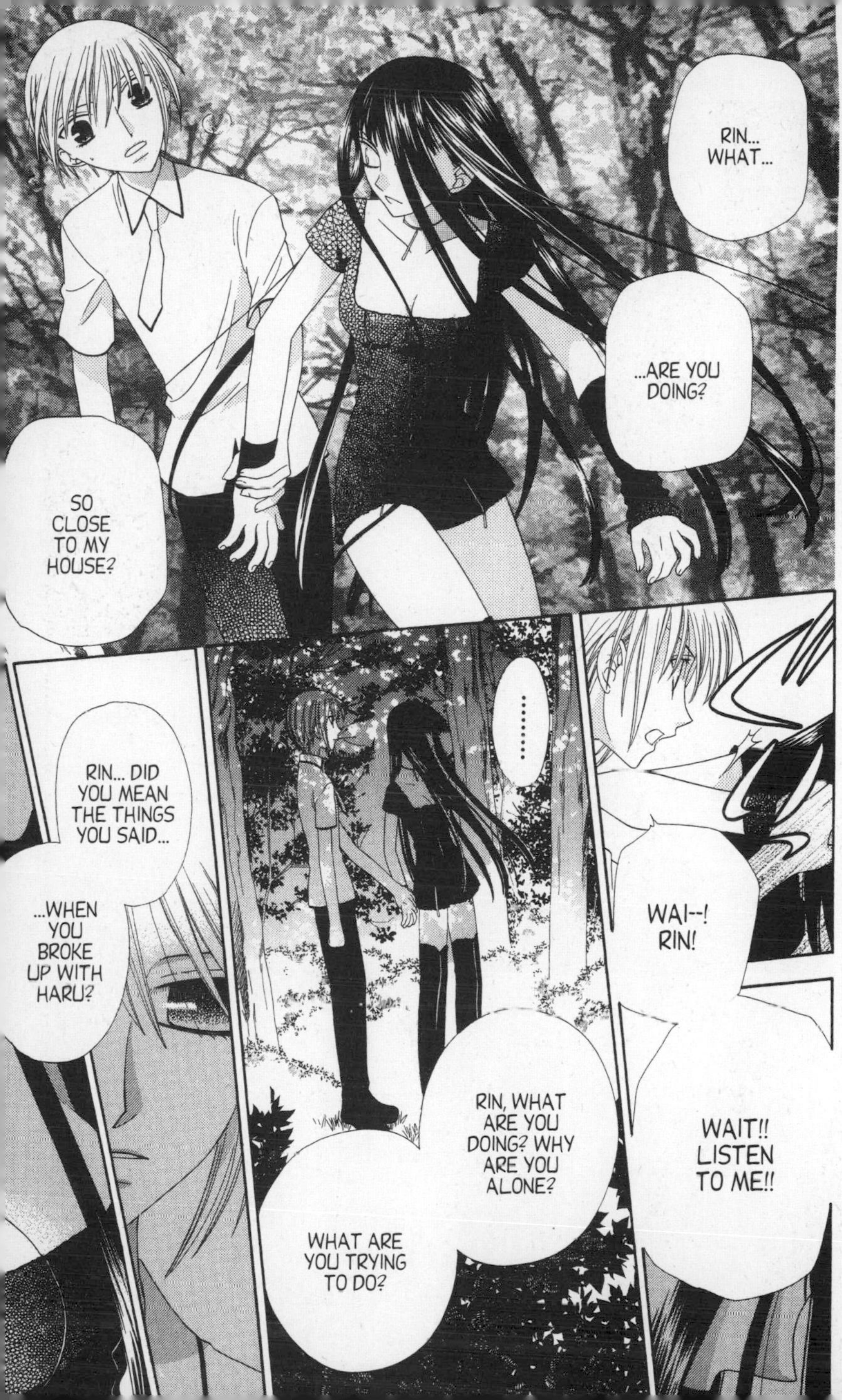
RIN... WHAT...
...ARE YOU DOING?
SO CLOSE TO MY HOUSE?
WAI--! RIN!
WAIT!! LISTEN TO ME!!
......
RIN, WHAT ARE YOU DOING? WHY ARE YOU ALONE?
WHAT ARE YOU TRYING TO DO?
RIN... DID YOU MEAN THE THINGS YOU SAID...
...WHEN YOU BROKE UP WITH HARU?

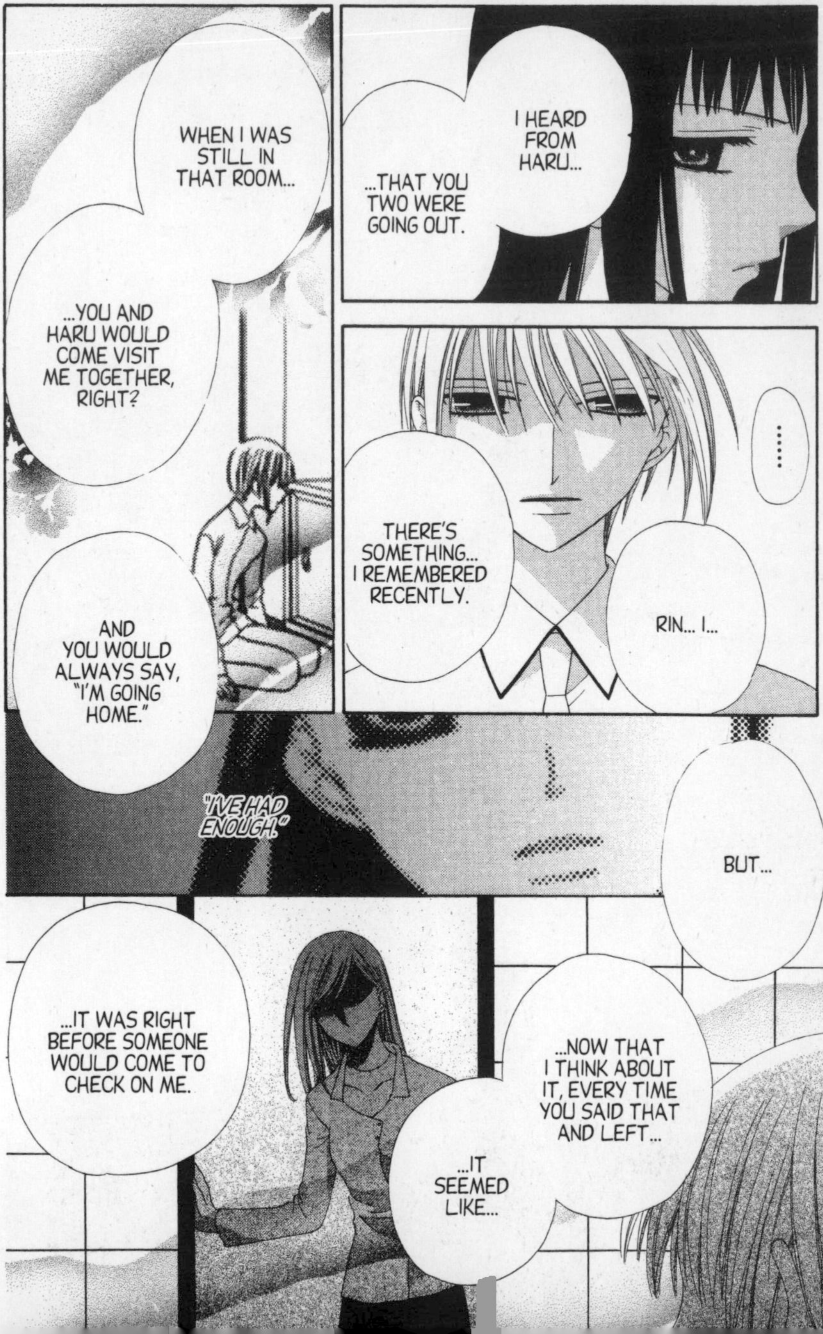
I HEARD FROM HARU...
...THAT YOU TWO WERE GOING OUT.
......
RIN... I...
THERE'S SOMETHING... I REMEMBERED RECENTLY.
WHEN I WAS STILL IN THAT ROOM...
...YOU AND HARU WOULD COME VISIT ME TOGETHER, RIGHT?
AND YOU WOULD ALWAYS SAY, "I'M GOING HOME."
BUT...
"I'VE HAD ENOUGH."
...NOW THAT I THINK ABOUT IT, EVERY TIME YOU SAID THAT AND LEFT...
...IT SEEMED LIKE...
...IT WAS RIGHT BEFORE SOMEONE WOULD COME TO CHECK ON ME.

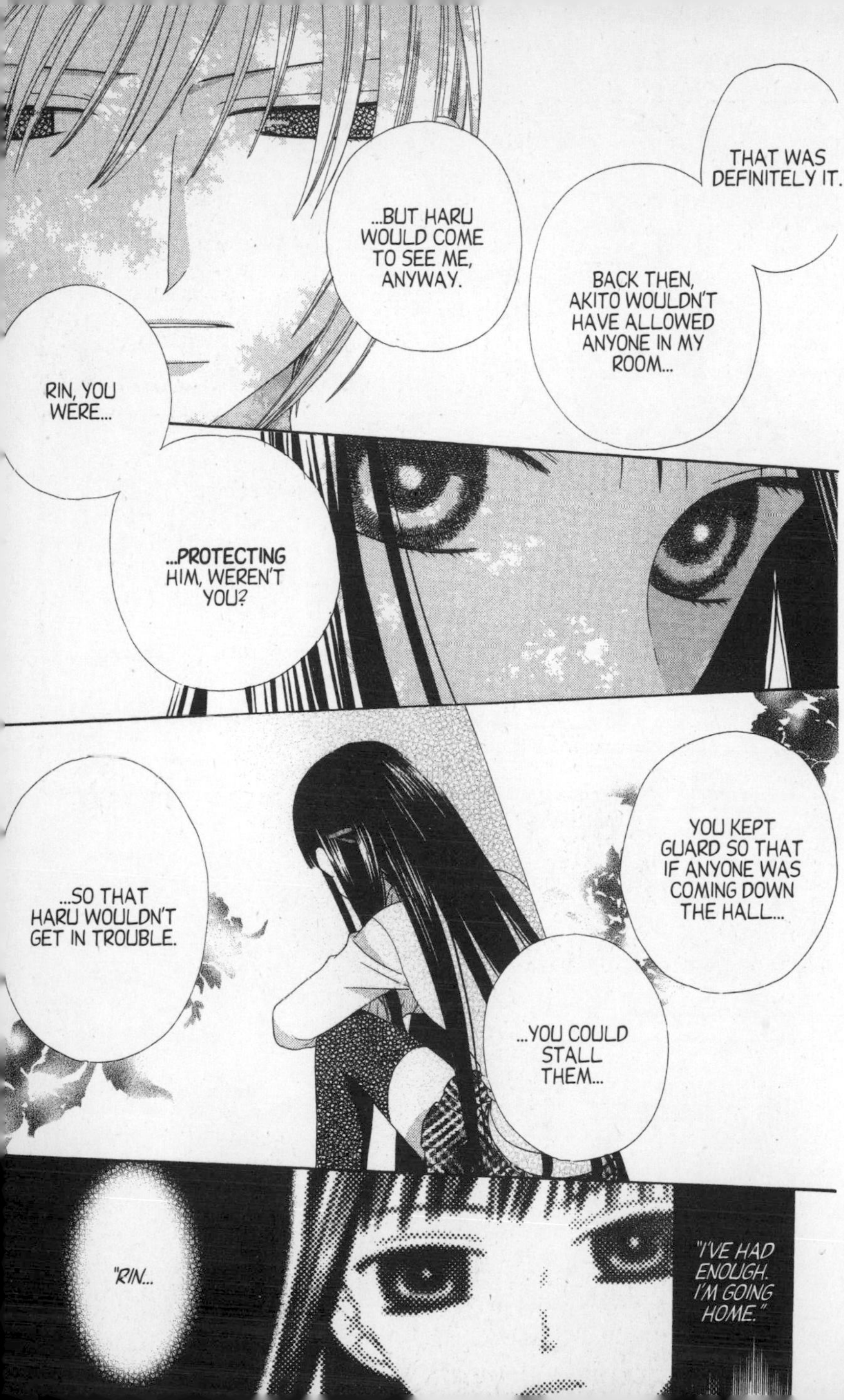
THAT WAS DEFINITELY IT.
BACK THEN, AKITO WOULDN'T HAVE ALLOWED ANYONE IN MY ROOM...
...BUT HARU WOULD COME TO SEE ME, ANYWAY.
RIN, YOU WERE...
...PROTECTING HIM, WEREN'T YOU?
YOU KEPT GUARD SO THAT IF ANYONE WAS COMING DOWN THE HALL...
...YOU COULD STALL THEM...
...SO THAT HARU WOULDN'T GET IN TROUBLE.
"I'VE HAD ENOUGH. I'M GOING HOME."
"RIN...

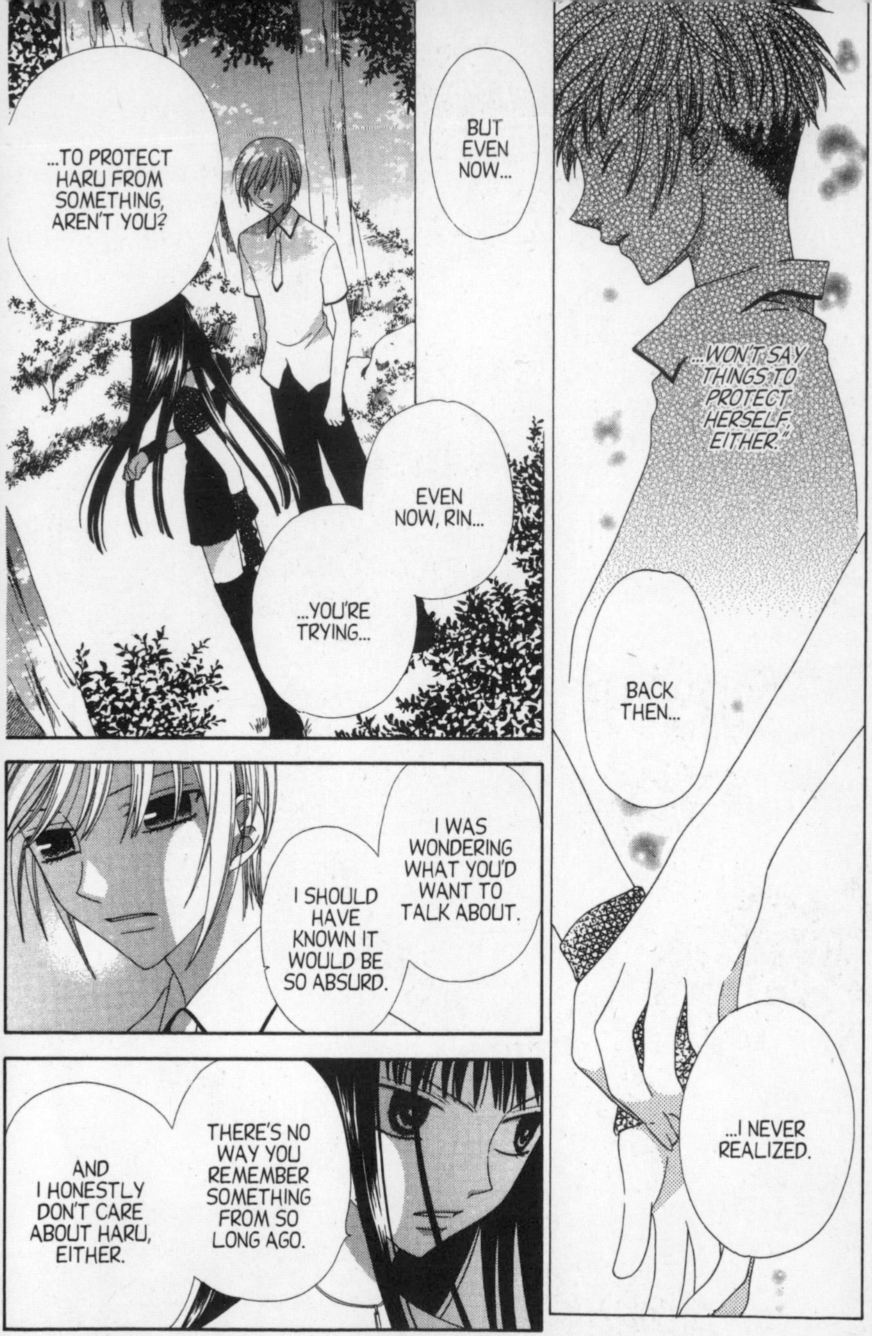

...WON'T SAY THINGS TO PROTECT HERSELF, EITHER."
BACK THEN...
...I NEVER REALIZED.
BUT EVEN NOW...
EVEN NOW, RIN...
...YOU'RE TRYING...
...TO PROTECT HARU FROM SOMETHING, AREN'T YOU?
I WAS WONDERING WHAT YOU'D WANT TO TALK ABOUT.
I SHOULD HAVE KNOWN IT WOULD BE SO ABSURD.
THERE'S NO WAY YOU REMEMBER SOMETHING FROM SO LONG AGO.
AND I HONESTLY DON'T CARE ABOUT HARU, EITHER.

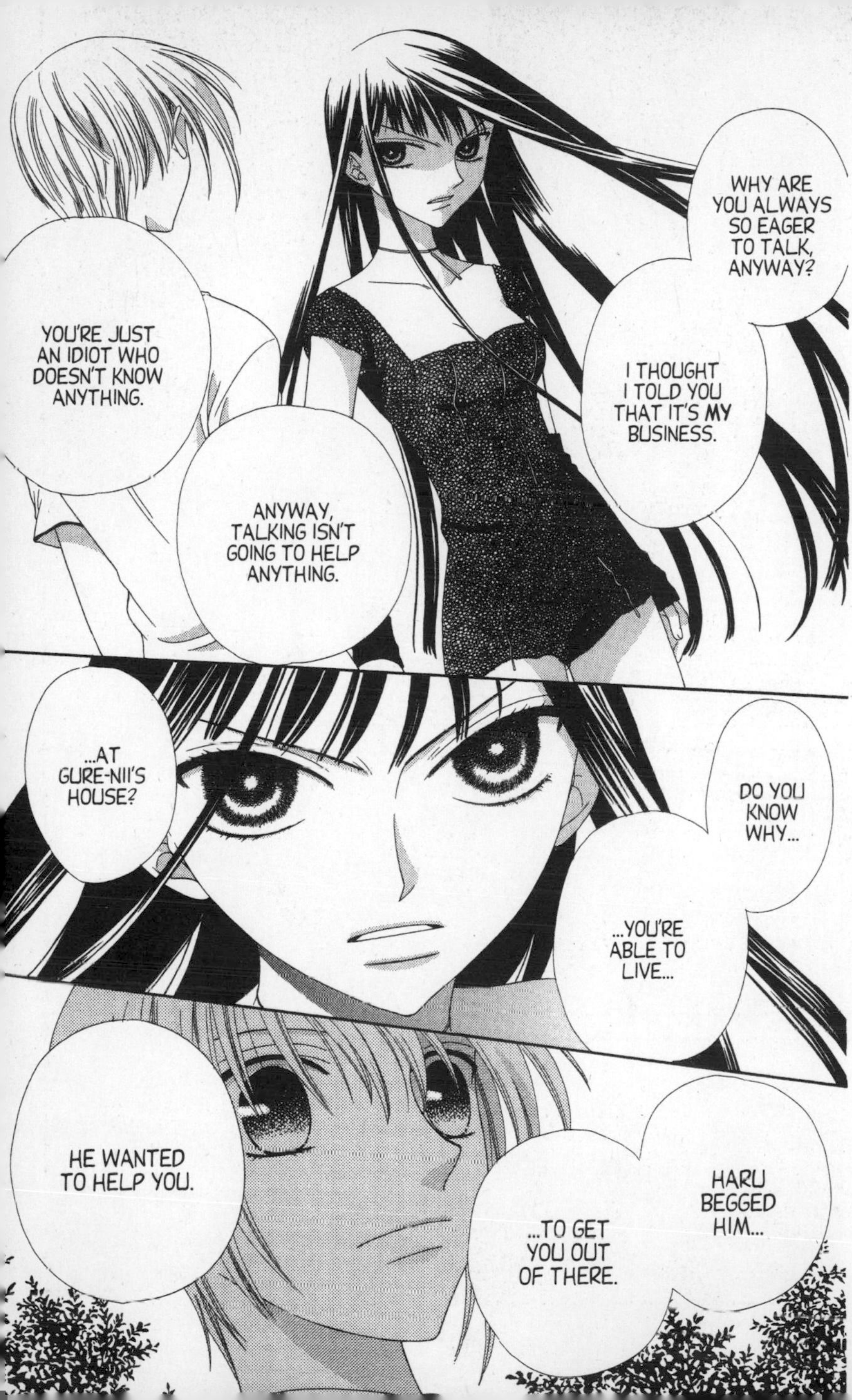
WHY ARE YOU ALWAYS SO EAGER TO TALK, ANYWAY?
I THOUGHT I TOLD YOU THAT IT'S MY BUSINESS.
YOU'RE JUST AN IDIOT WHO DOESN'T KNOW ANYTHING.
ANYWAY, TALKING ISN'T GOING TO HELP ANYTHING.
DO YOU KNOW WHY...
...YOU'RE ABLE TO LIVE...
...AT GURE-NII'S HOUSE?
HARU BEGGED HIM...
...TO GET YOU OUT OF THERE.
HE WANTED TO HELP YOU.

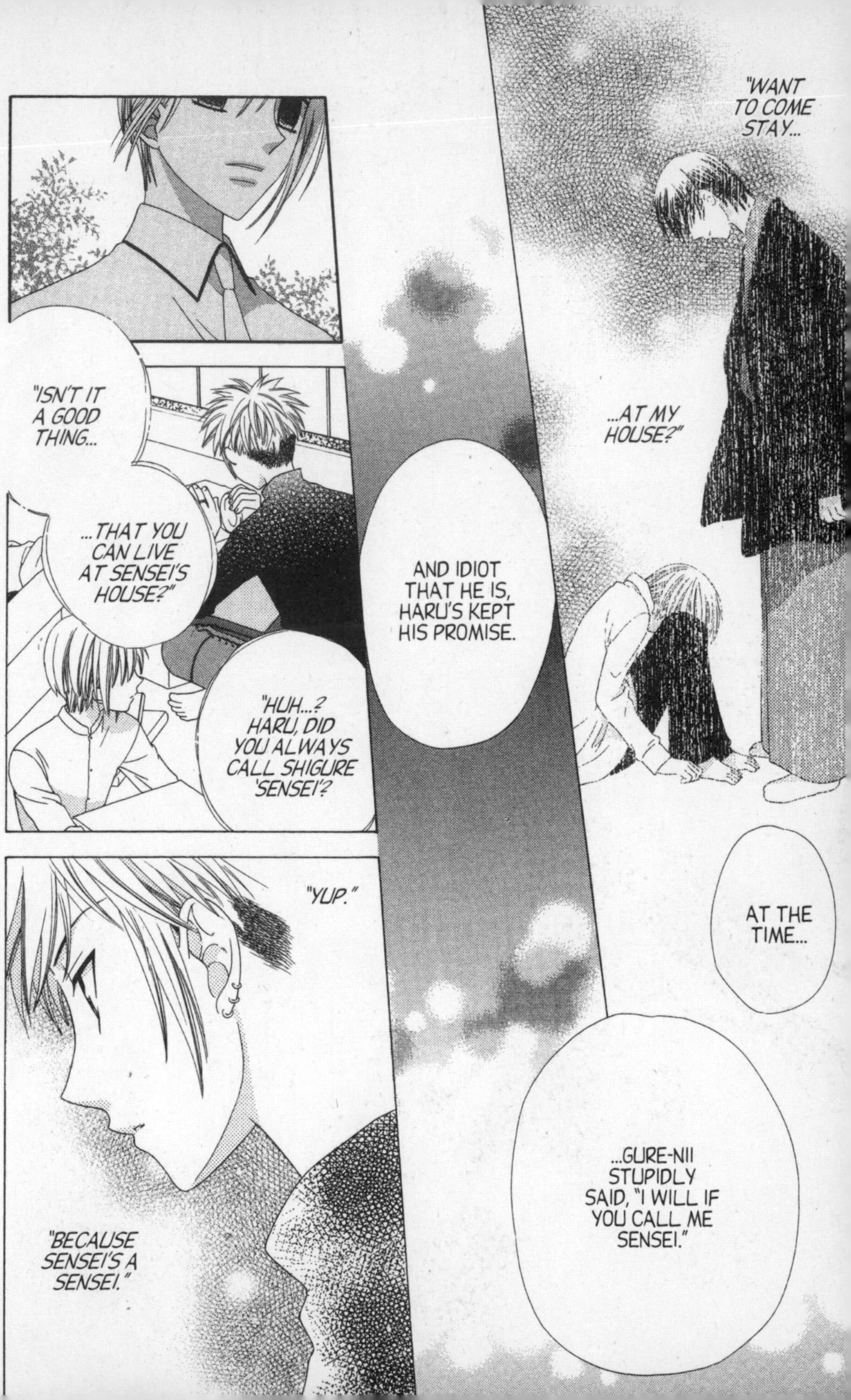
"WANT TO COME STAY...
...AT MY HOUSE?"
AT THE TIME...
...GURE-NII STUPIDLY SAID, "I WILL IF YOU CALL ME SENSEI."
AND IDIOT THAT HE IS, HARU'S KEPT HIS PROMISE.
"ISN'T IT A GOOD THING...
...THAT YOU CAN LIVE AT SENSEI'S HOUSE?"
"HUH...? HARU, DID YOU ALWAYS CALL SHIGURE 'SENSEI'?
"YUP."
"BECAUSE SENSEI'S A SENSEI."

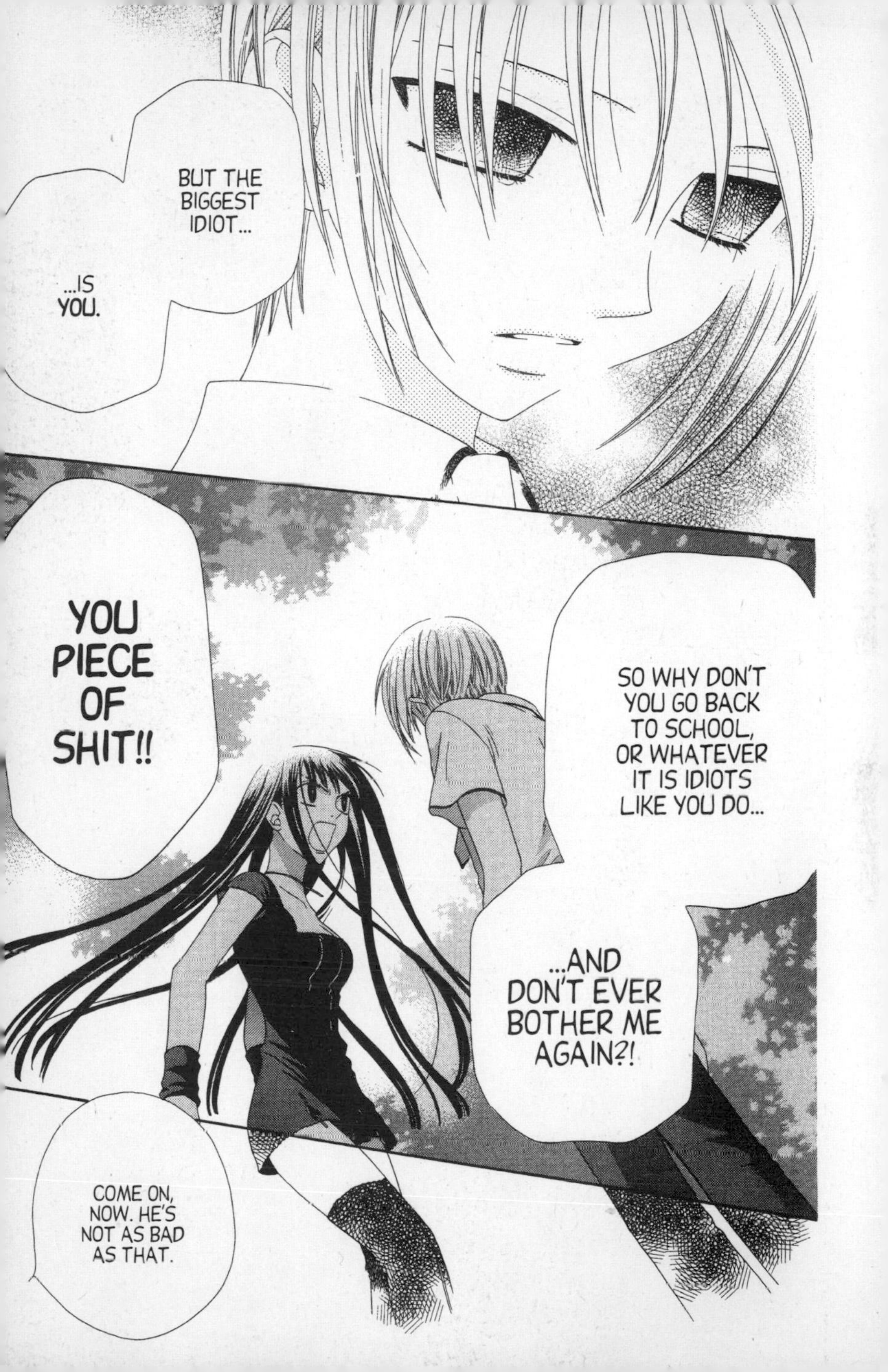
BUT THE BIGGEST IDIOT...
...IS YOU.
SO WHY DON'T YOU GO BACK TO SCHOOL, OR WHATEVER IT IS IDIOTS LIKE YOU DO...
...AND DON'T EVER BOTHER ME AGAIN?!
YOU PIECE OF SHIT!!
COME ON, NOW. HE'S NOT AS BAD AS THAT.

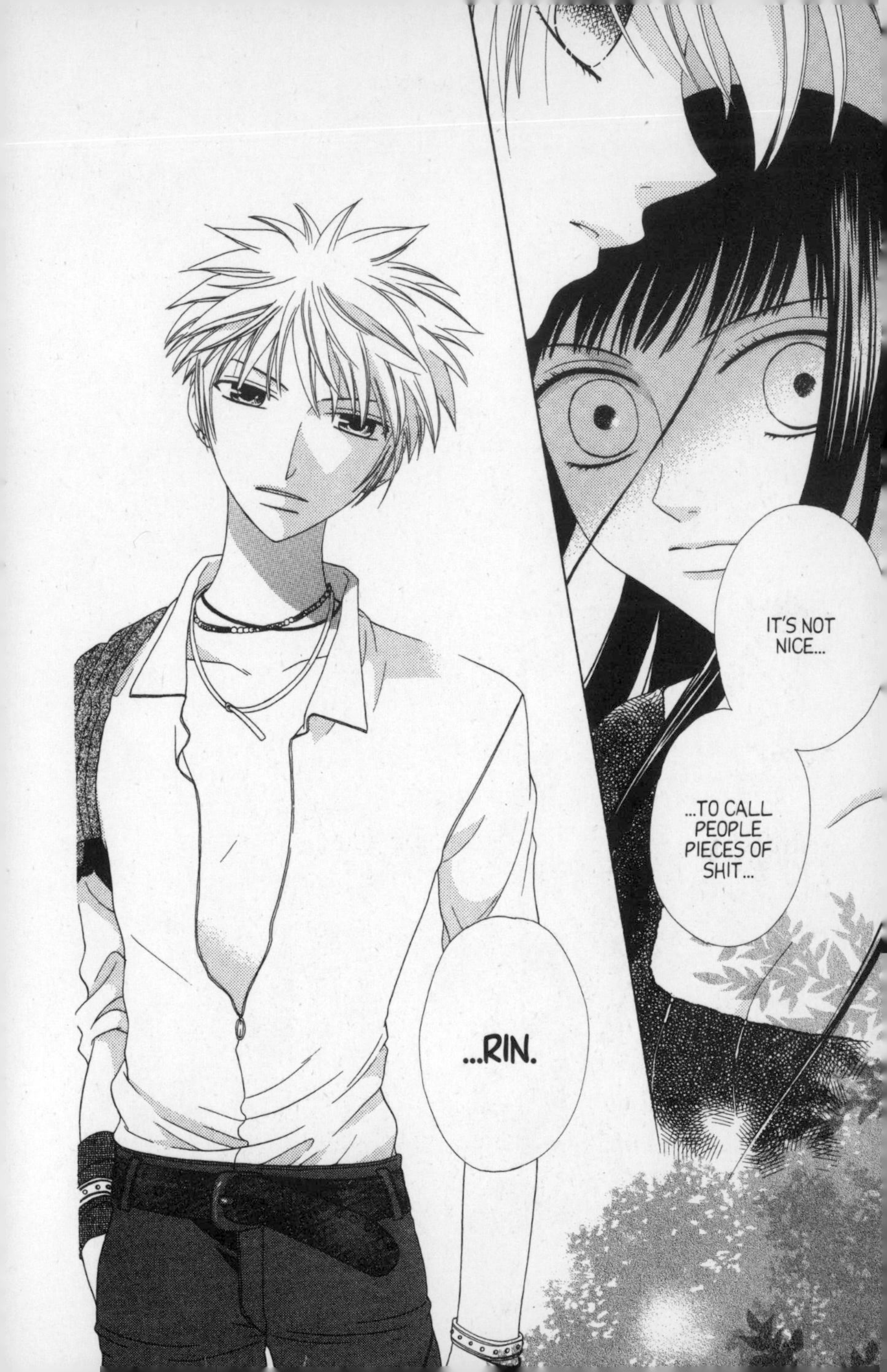
IT'S NOT NICE...
...TO CALL PEOPLE PIECES OF SHIT...
...RIN.

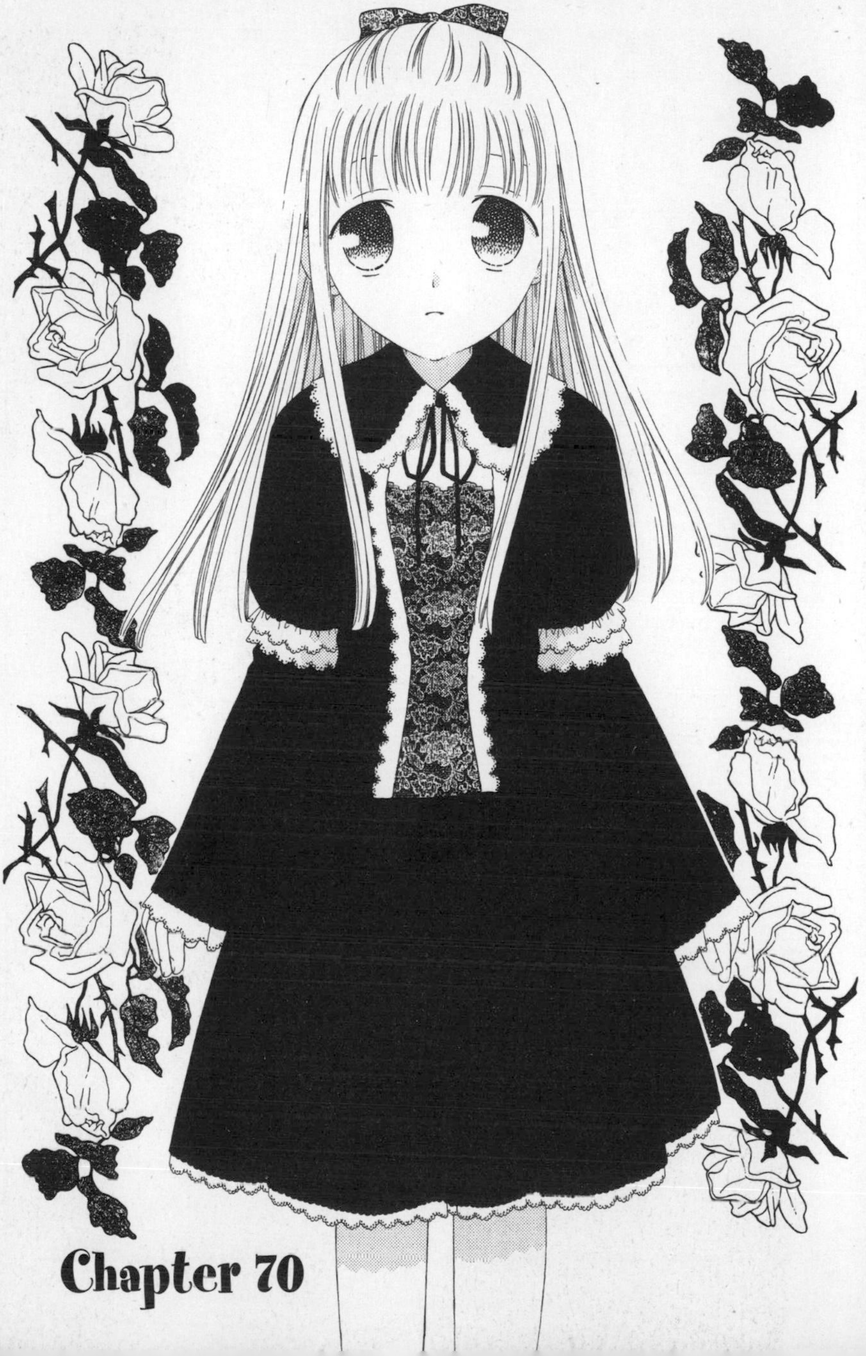

Chapter 70

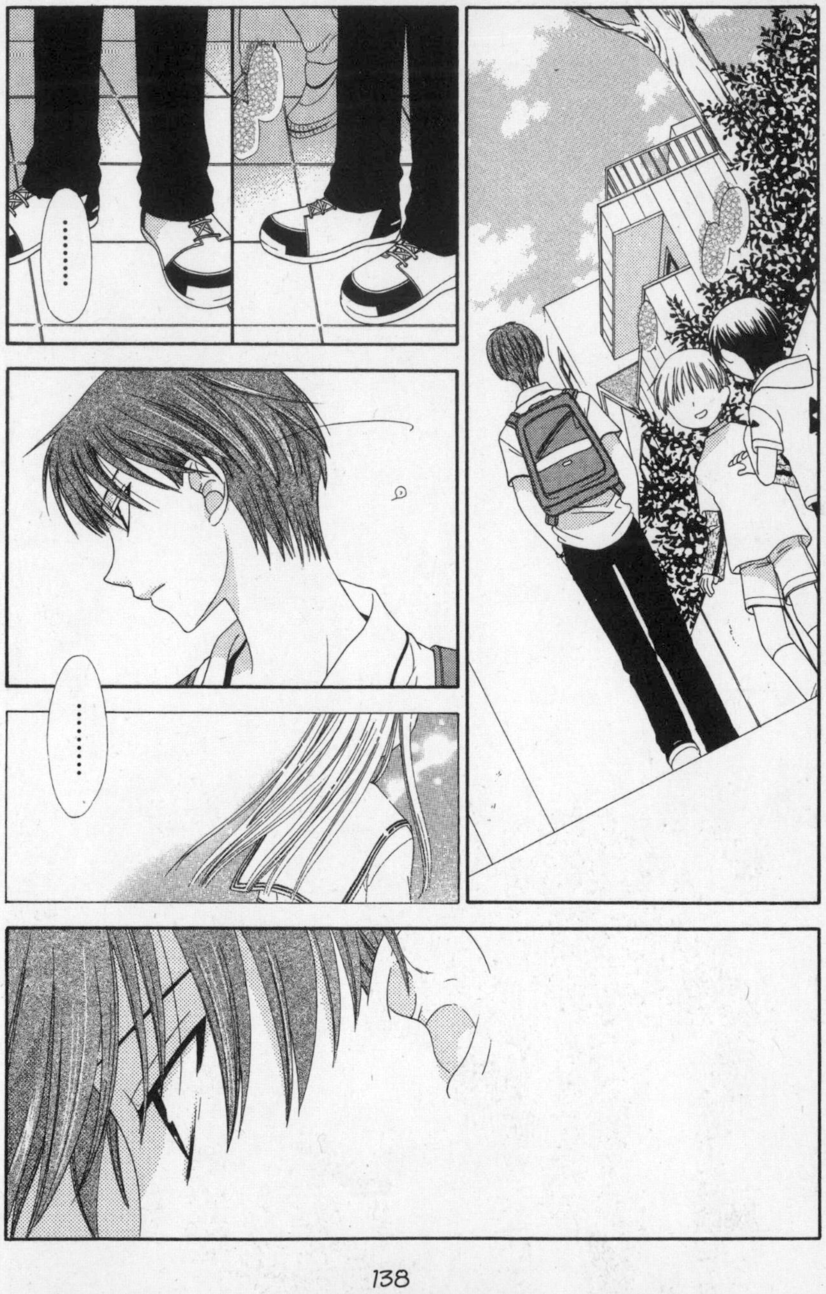
......
......

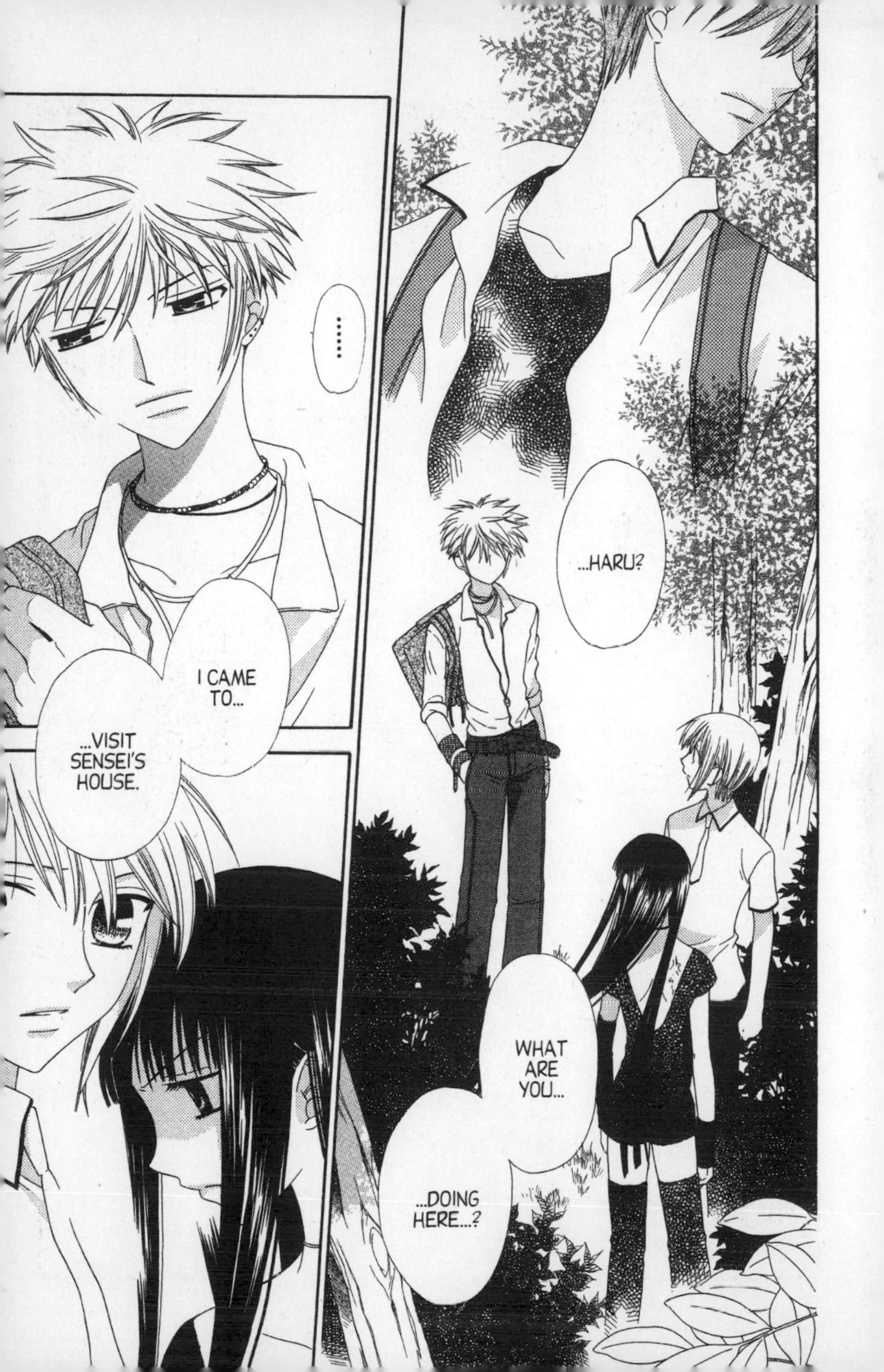
...HARU?
WHAT ARE YOU...
...DOING HERE...?
......
I CAME TO...
...VISIT SENSEI'S HOUSE.

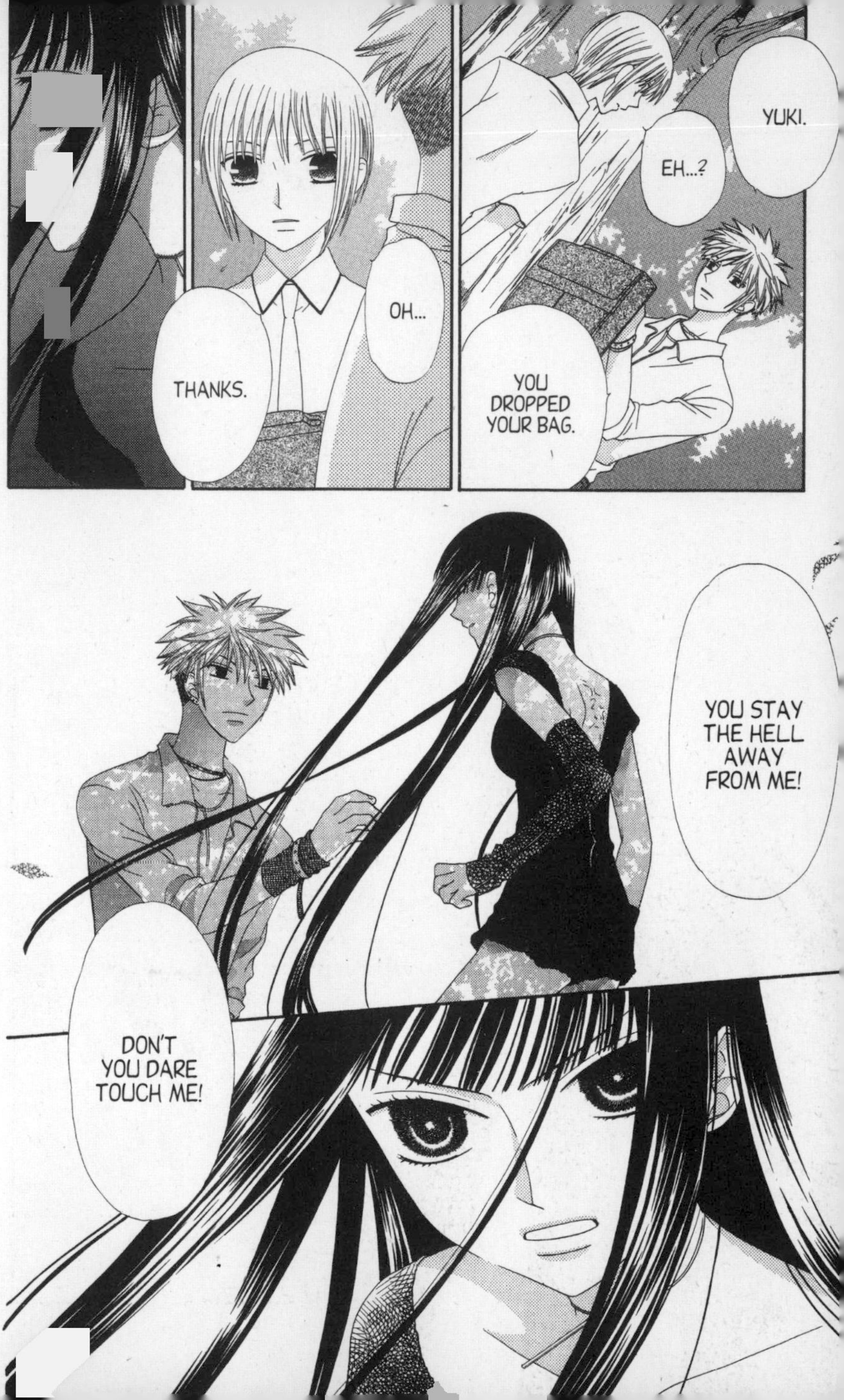
YUKI.
EH...?
YOU DROPPED YOUR BAG.
OH...
THANKS.
YOU STAY THE HELL AWAY FROM ME!
DON'T YOU DARE TOUCH ME!

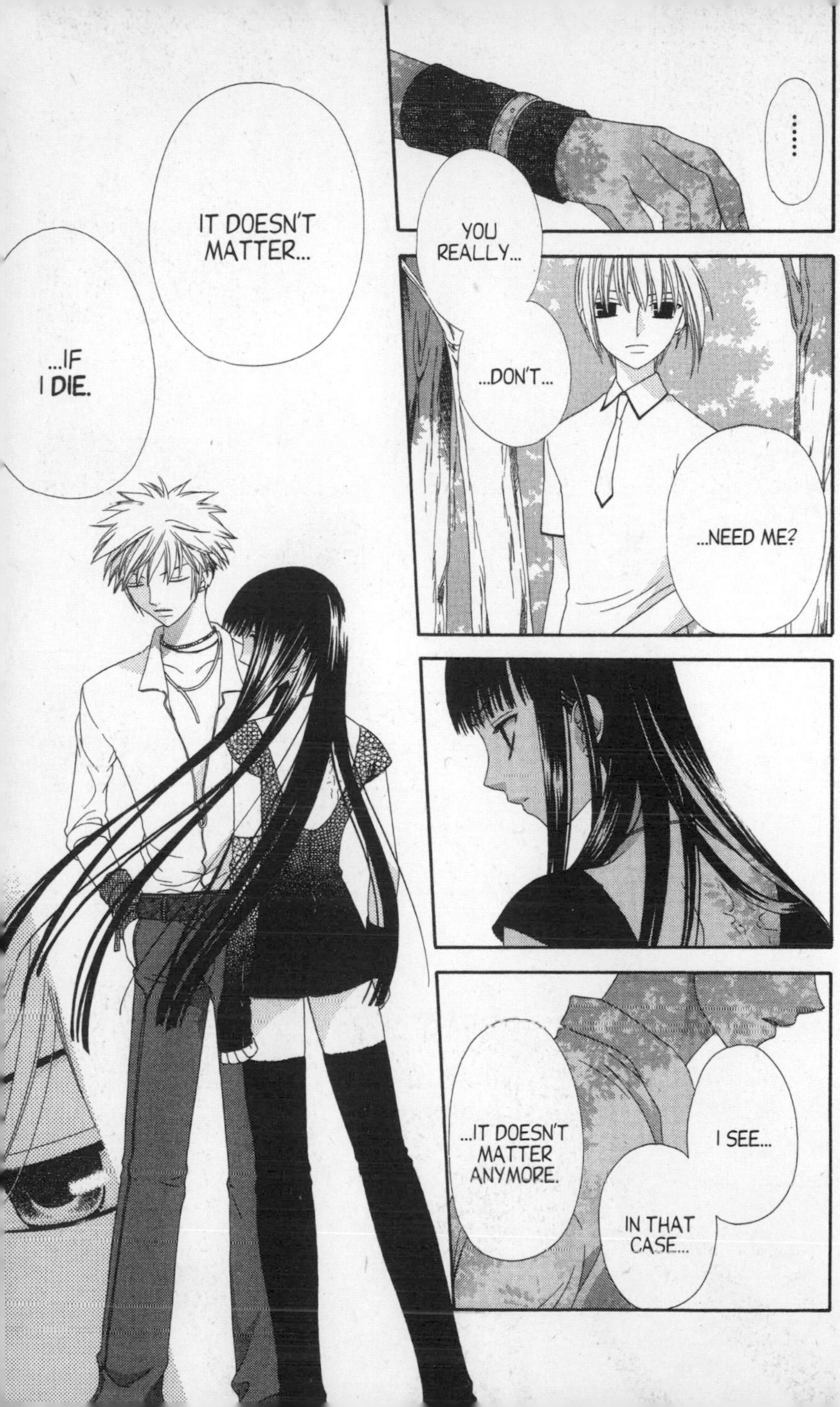
......
YOU REALLY...
...DON'T...
...NEED ME?
I SEE...
IN THAT CASE...
...IT DOESN'T MATTER ANYMORE.
IT DOESN'T MATTER...
...IF I DIE.

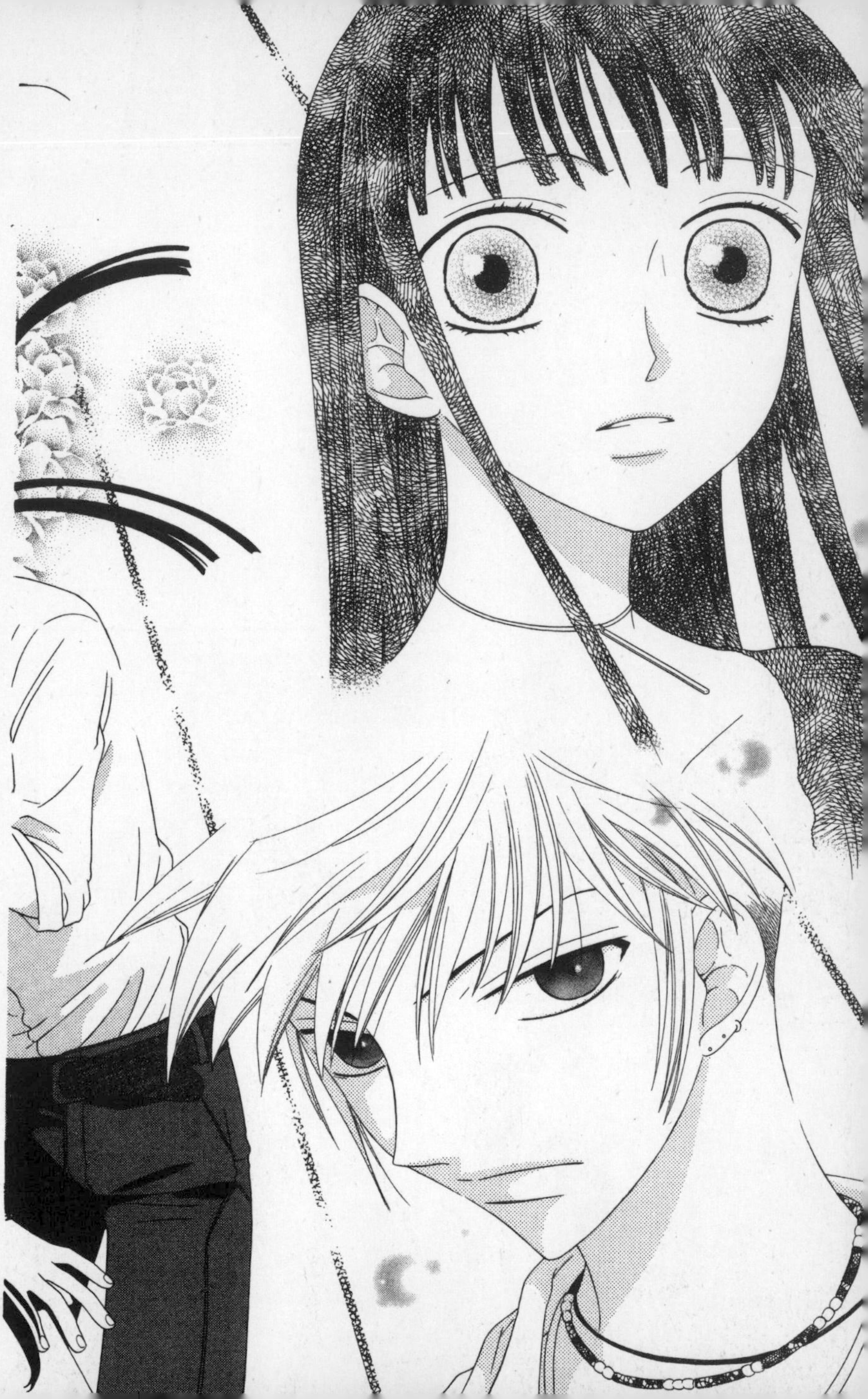

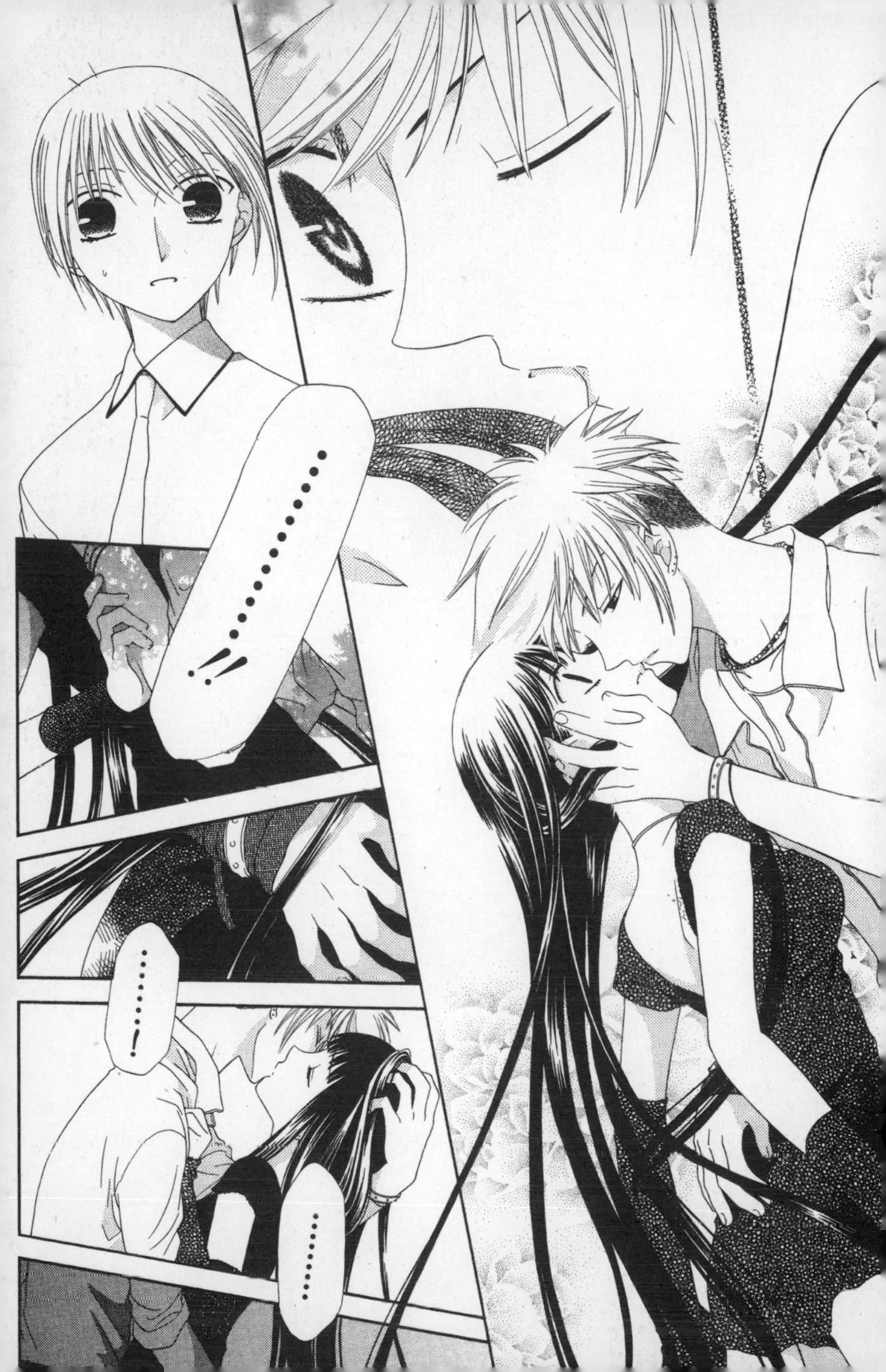
......!!
......!
......

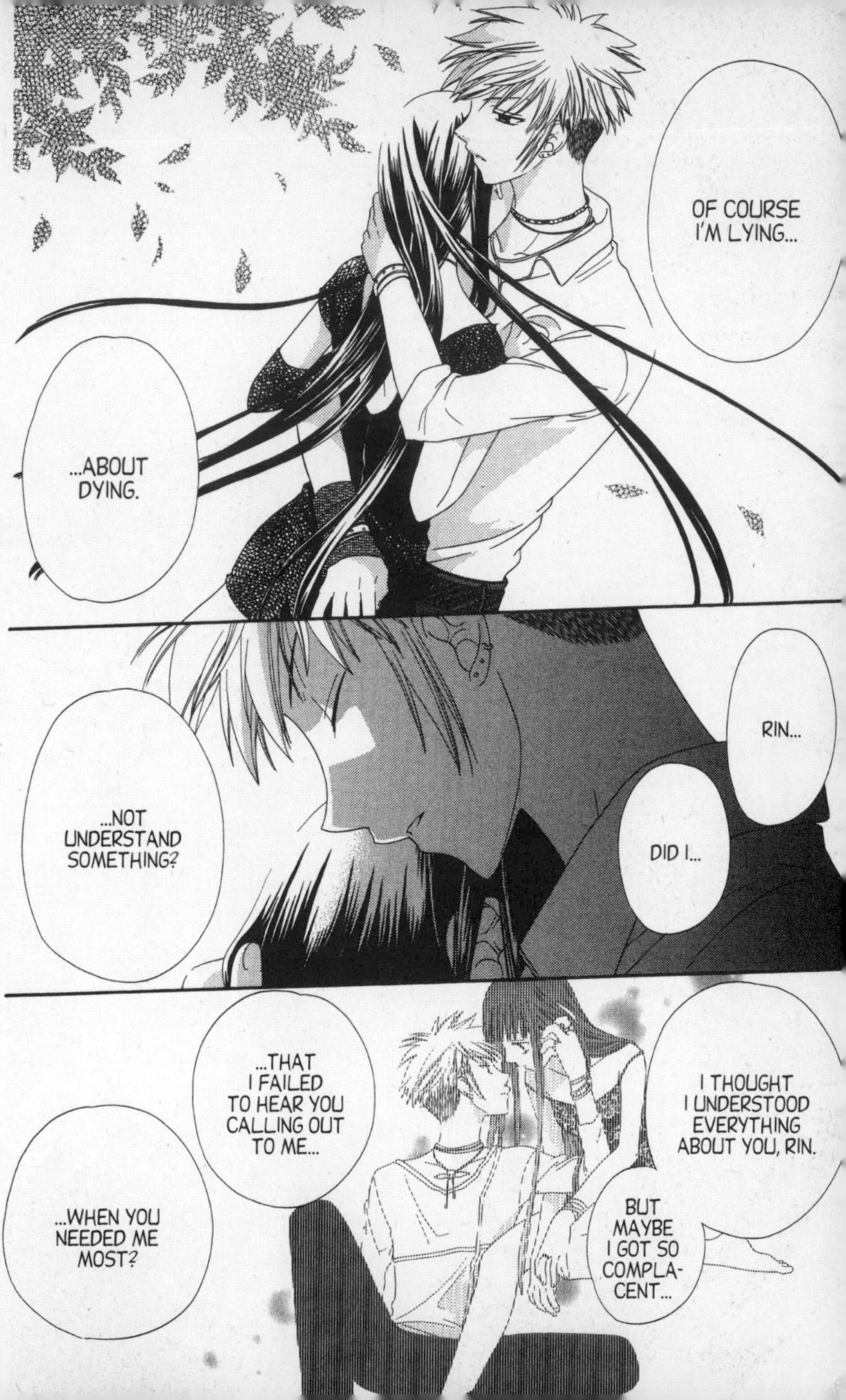
OF COURSE I'M LYING...
...ABOUT DYING.
RIN...
DID I...
...NOT UNDERSTAND SOMETHING?
I THOUGHT I UNDERSTOOD EVERYTHING ABOUT YOU, RIN.
BUT MAYBE I GOT SO COMPLA-CENT...
...THAT I FAILED TO HEAR YOU CALLING OUT TO ME...
...WHEN YOU NEEDED ME MOST?

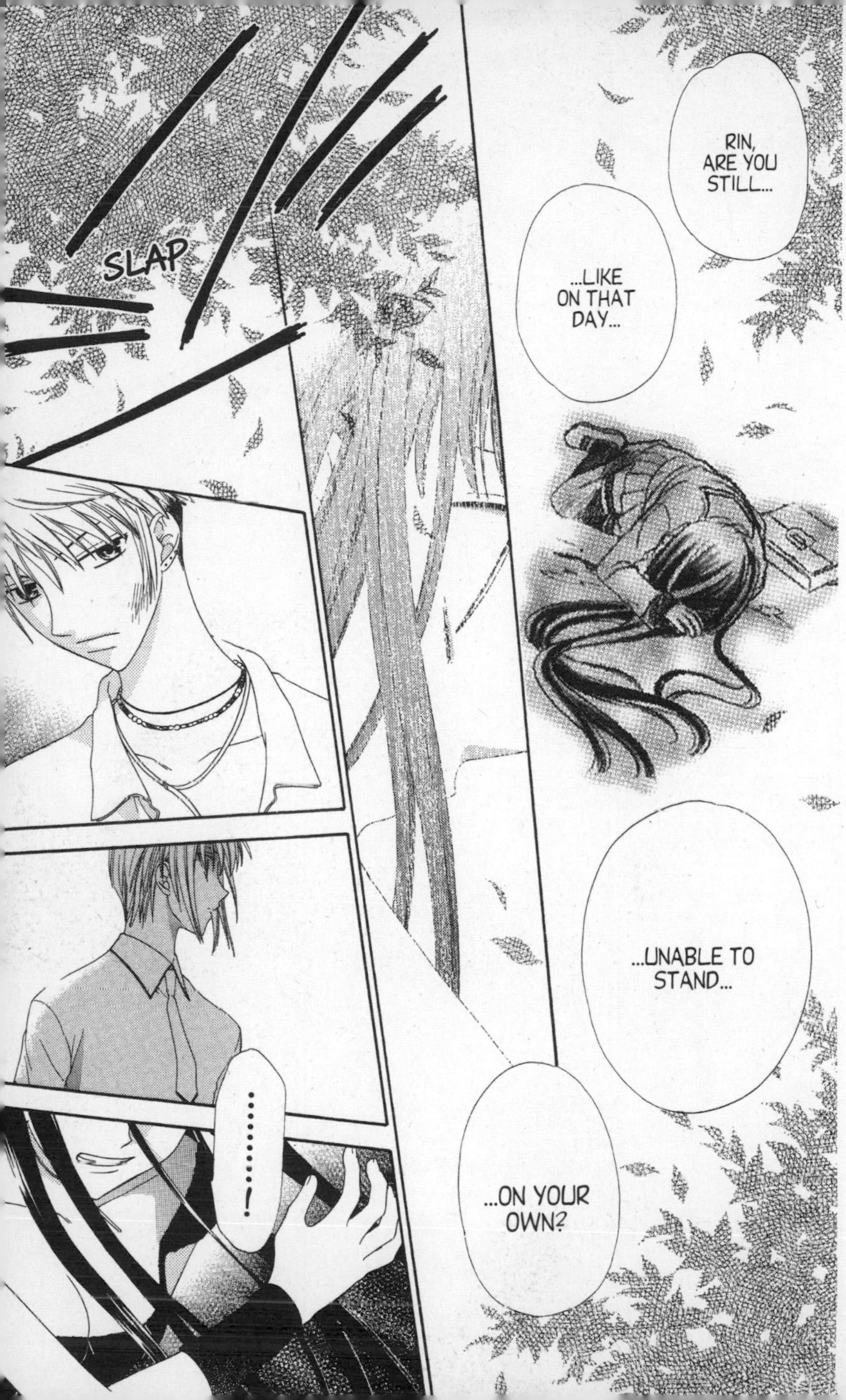
RIN, ARE YOU STILL...
...LIKE ON THAT DAY...
...UNABLE TO STAND...
...ON YOUR OWN?
SLAP
.........!

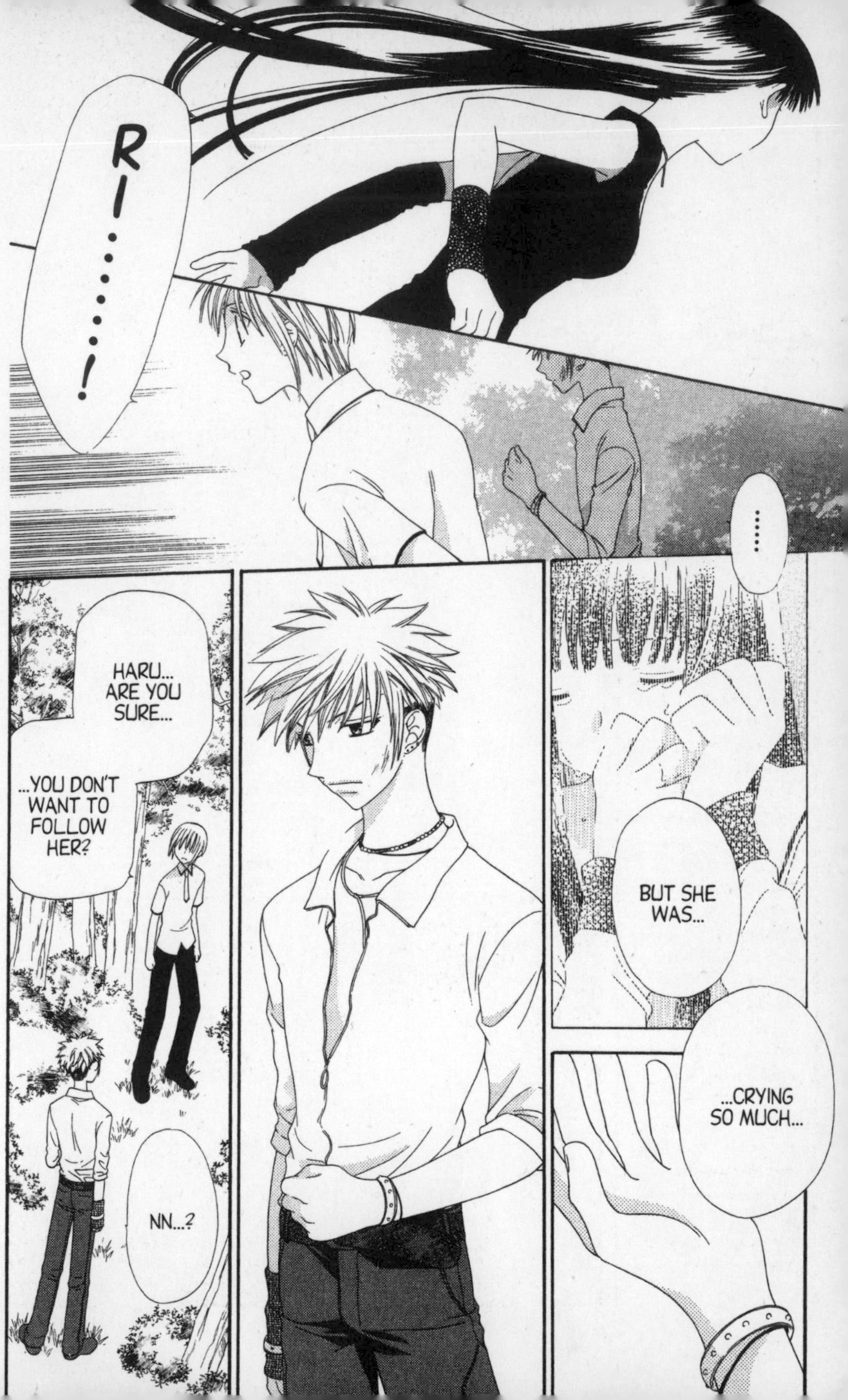
RI......!
......
BUT SHE WAS...
...CRYING SO MUCH...
HARU... ARE YOU SURE...
...YOU DON'T WANT TO FOLLOW HER?
NN...?

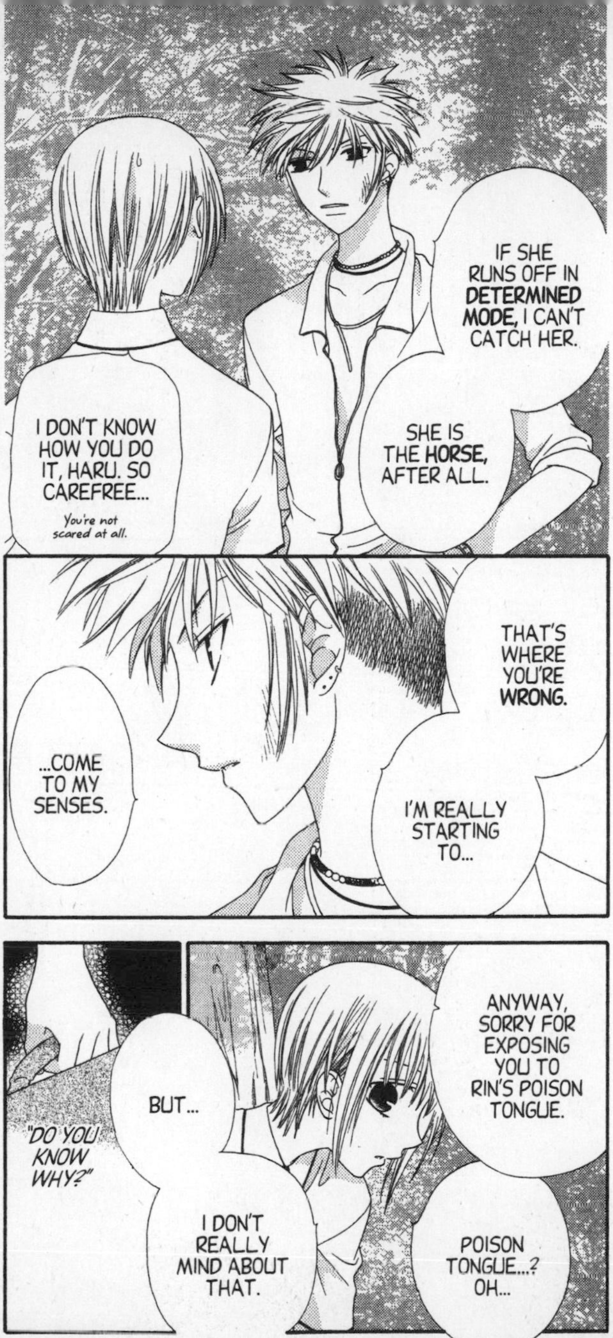
IF SHE RUNS OFF IN DETERMINED MODE, I CAN'T CATCH HER.
SHE IS THE HORSE, AFTER ALL.
I DON'T KNOW HOW YOU DO IT, HARU. SO CAREFREE...
You're not scared at all.
THAT'S WHERE YOU'RE WRONG.
I'M REALLY STARTING TO...
...COME TO MY SENSES.
ANYWAY, SORRY FOR EXPOSING YOU TO RIN'S POISON TONGUE.
POISON TONGUE...? OH...
BUT...
I DON'T REALLY MIND ABOUT THAT.
"DO YOU KNOW WHY?"

2-D iendfrays

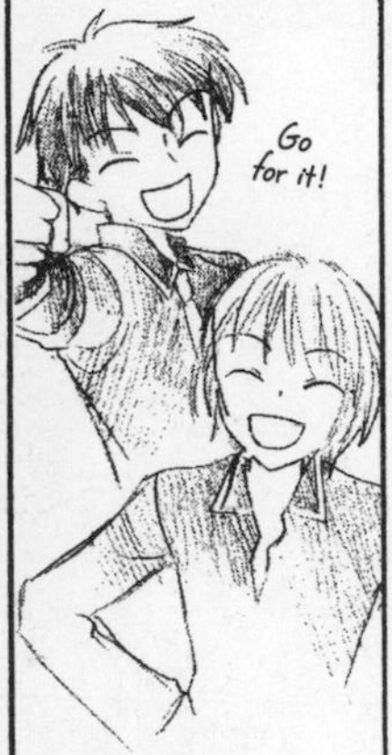
Go for it!

It sounds like a name for a comedy duo... When I started drawing students in the background of school scenes, before I knew it, this miracle pair became the main classmates. But they don't have names. (They're all like that.) I get a lot of letters saying, "Tohru's class really gets along," and I think, "Yup! They really do." If it's a classroom that seems to welcome people with open arms, it's not scary to enter it.

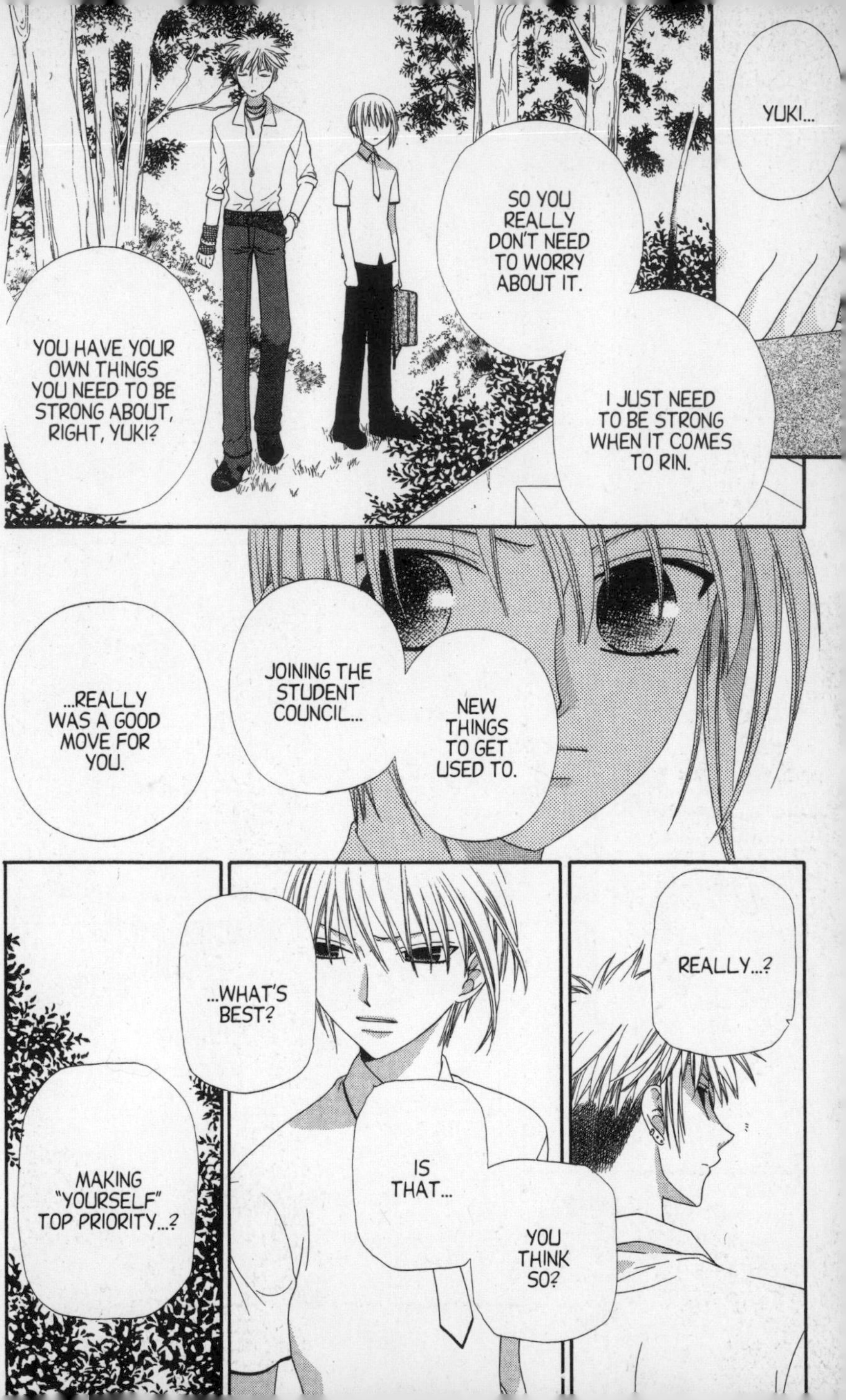
YUKI...
SO YOU REALLY DON'T NEED TO WORRY ABOUT IT.
I JUST NEED TO BE STRONG WHEN IT COMES TO RIN.
YOU HAVE YOUR OWN THINGS YOU NEED TO BE STRONG ABOUT, RIGHT, YUKI?
NEW THINGS TO GET USED TO.
JOINING THE STUDENT COUNCIL...
...REALLY WAS A GOOD MOVE FOR YOU.
REALLY...?
...WHAT'S BEST?
IS THAT...
YOU THINK SO?
MAKING "YOURSELF" TOP PRIORITY...?

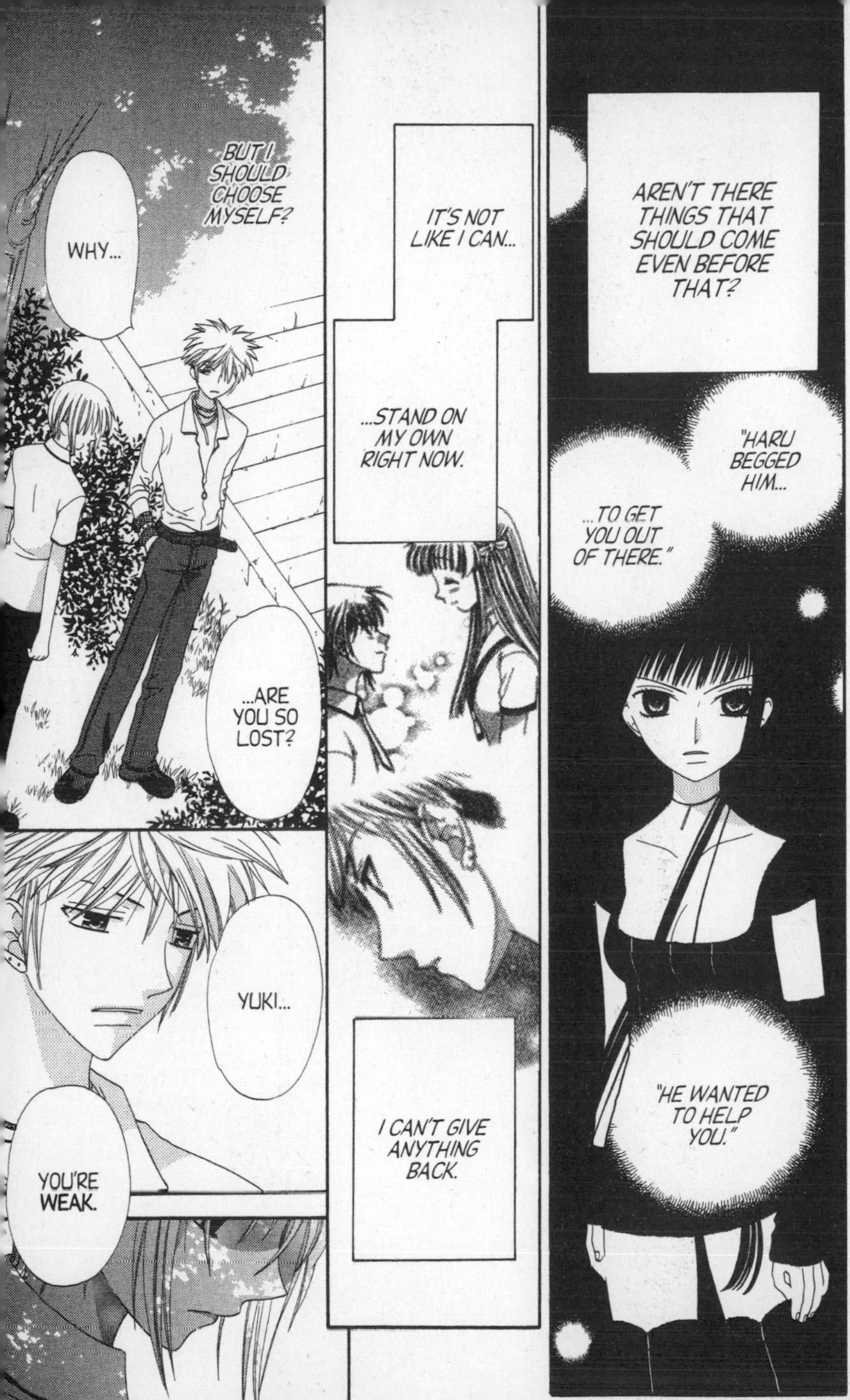
AREN'T THERE THINGS THAT SHOULD COME EVEN BEFORE THAT?
"HARU BEGGED HIM...
...TO GET YOU OUT OF THERE."
"HE WANTED TO HELP YOU."
IT'S NOT LIKE I CAN...
...STAND ON MY OWN RIGHT NOW.
I CAN'T GIVE ANYTHING BACK.
BUT I SHOULD CHOOSE MYSELF?
WHY...
...ARE YOU SO LOST?
YUKI...
YOU'RE WEAK.

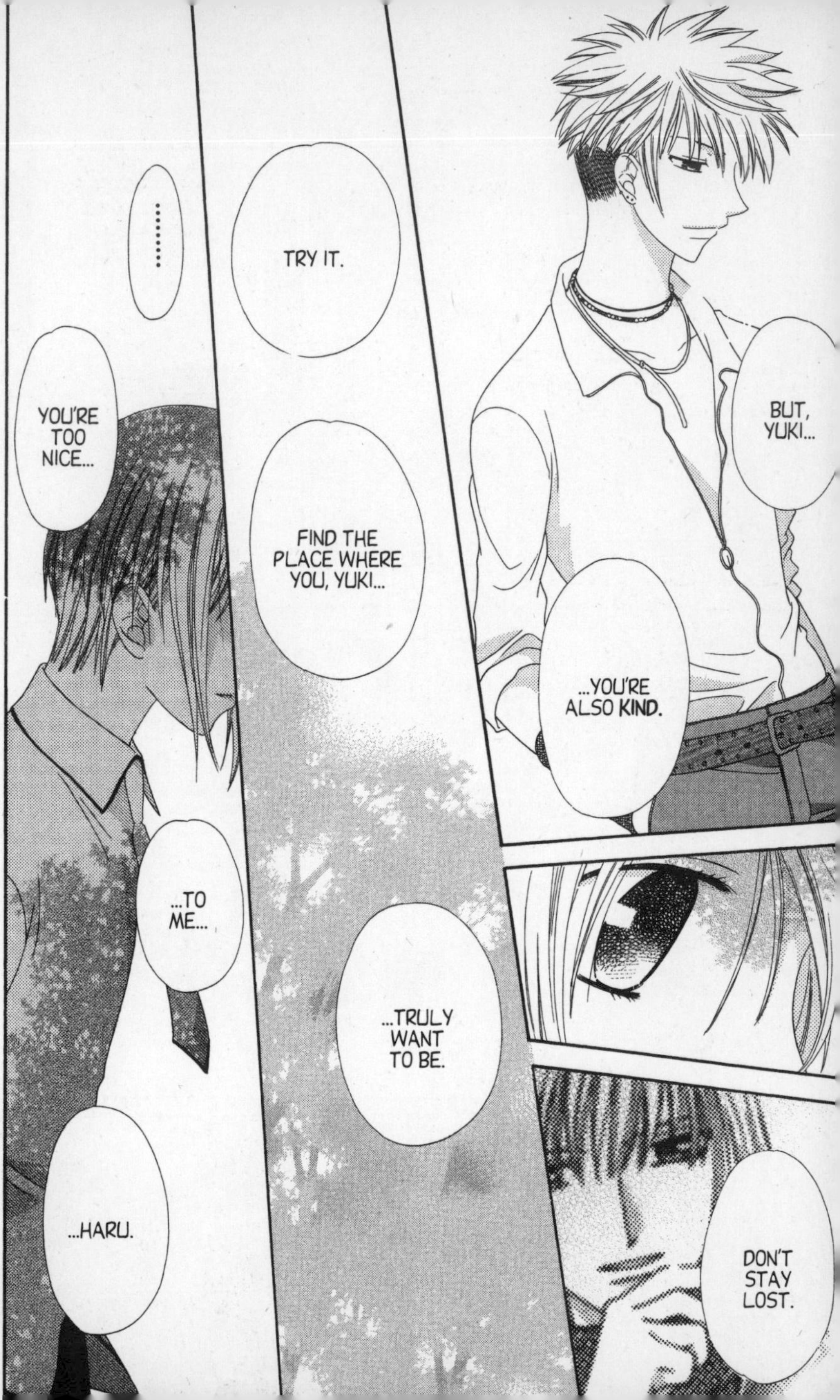

BUT, YUKI...
...YOU'RE ALSO KIND.
DON'T STAY LOST.
TRY IT.
FIND THE PLACE WHERE YOU, YUKI...
...TRULY WANT TO BE.
....
YOU'RE TOO NICE...
...TO ME...
...HARU.

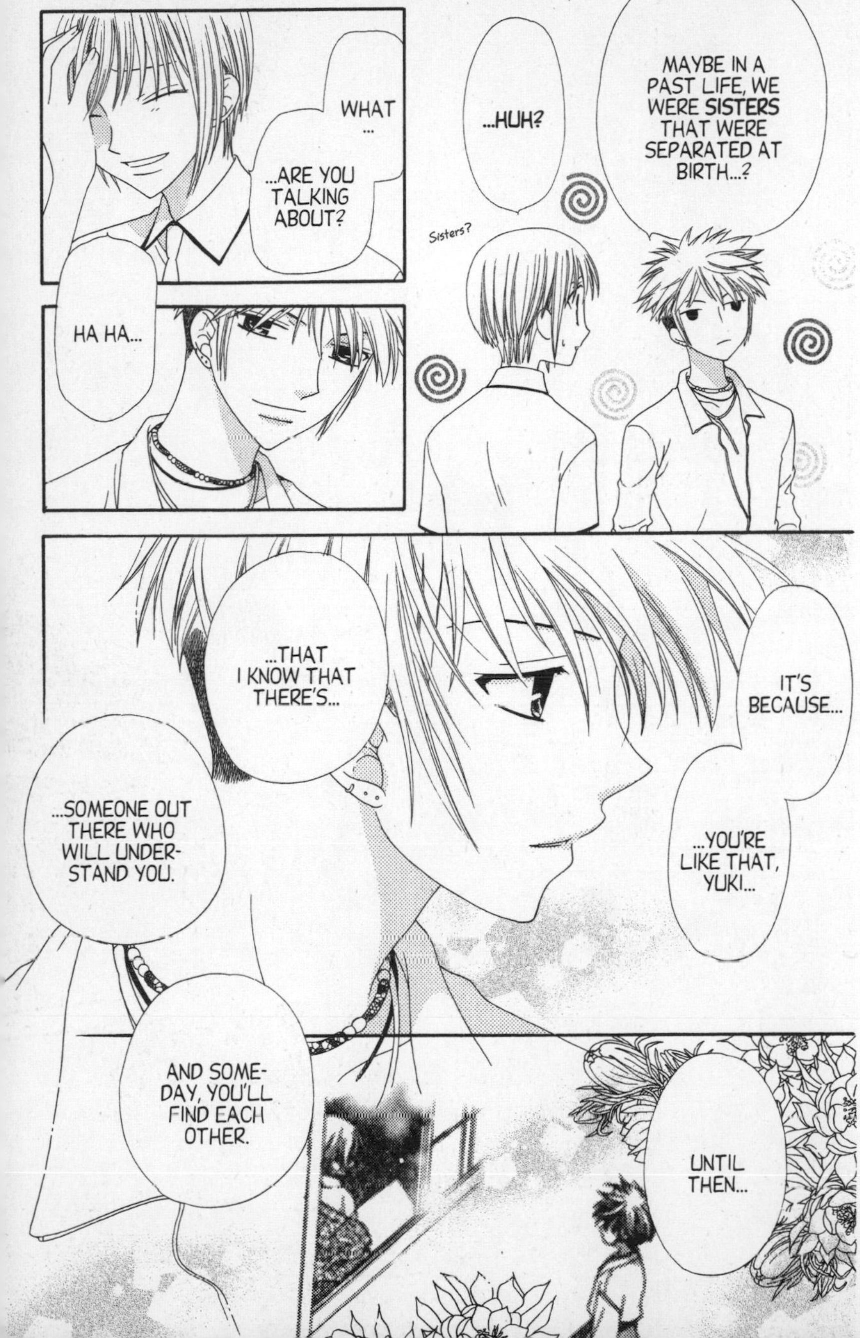
MAYBE IN A PAST LIFE, WE WERE SISTERS THAT WERE SEPARATED AT BIRTH...?
...HUH?
Sisters?
WHAT ... ...ARE YOU TALKING ABOUT?
HA HA...
IT'S BECAUSE...
...YOU'RE LIKE THAT, YUKI...
...THAT I KNOW THAT THERE'S...
...SOMEONE OUT THERE WHO WILL UNDER-STAND YOU.
AND SOME-DAY, YOU'LL FIND EACH OTHER.
UNTIL THEN...

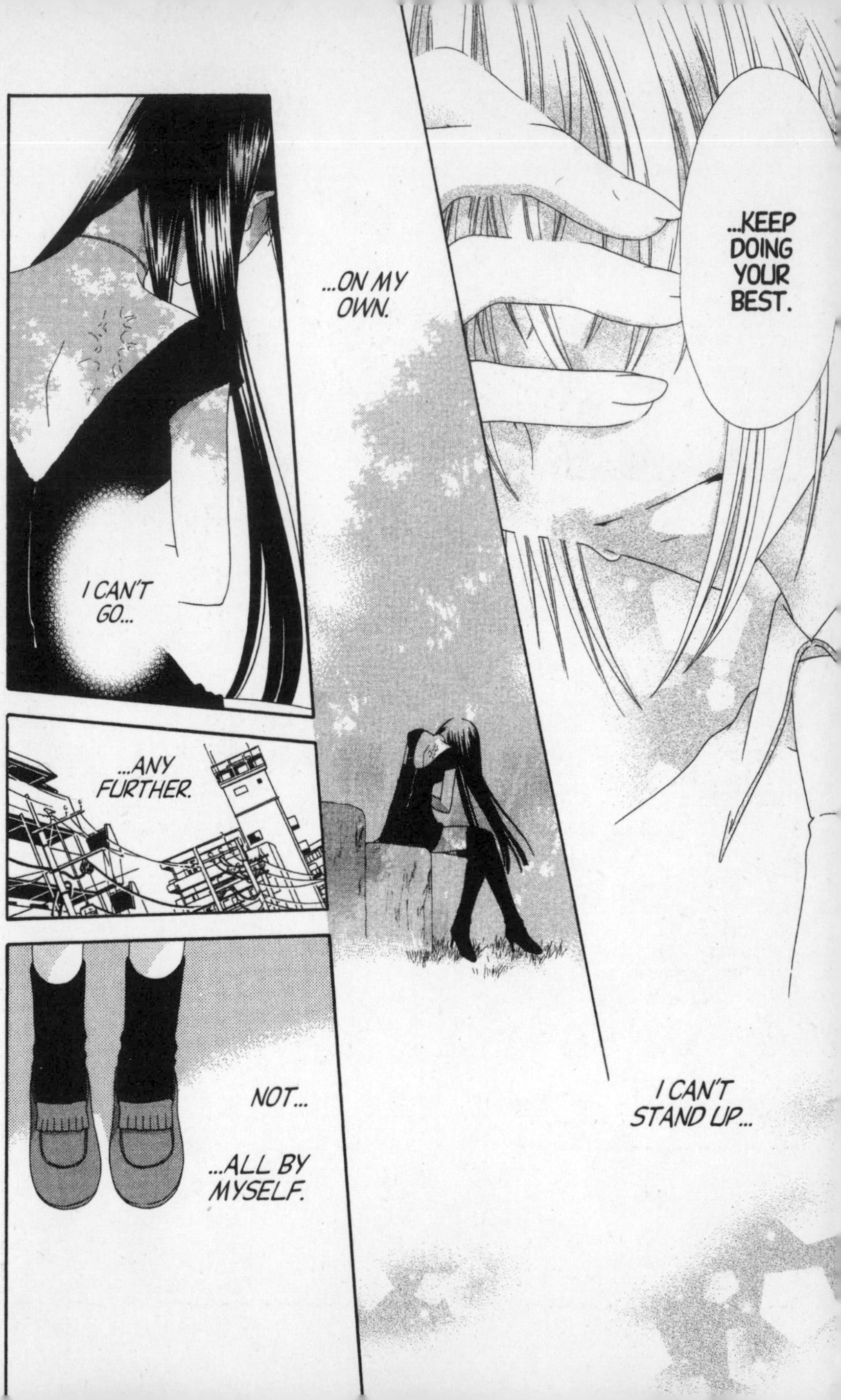
...KEEP DOING YOUR BEST.
I CAN'T STAND UP...
...ON MY OWN.
I CAN'T GO...
...ANY FURTHER.
NOT...
...ALL BY MYSELF.

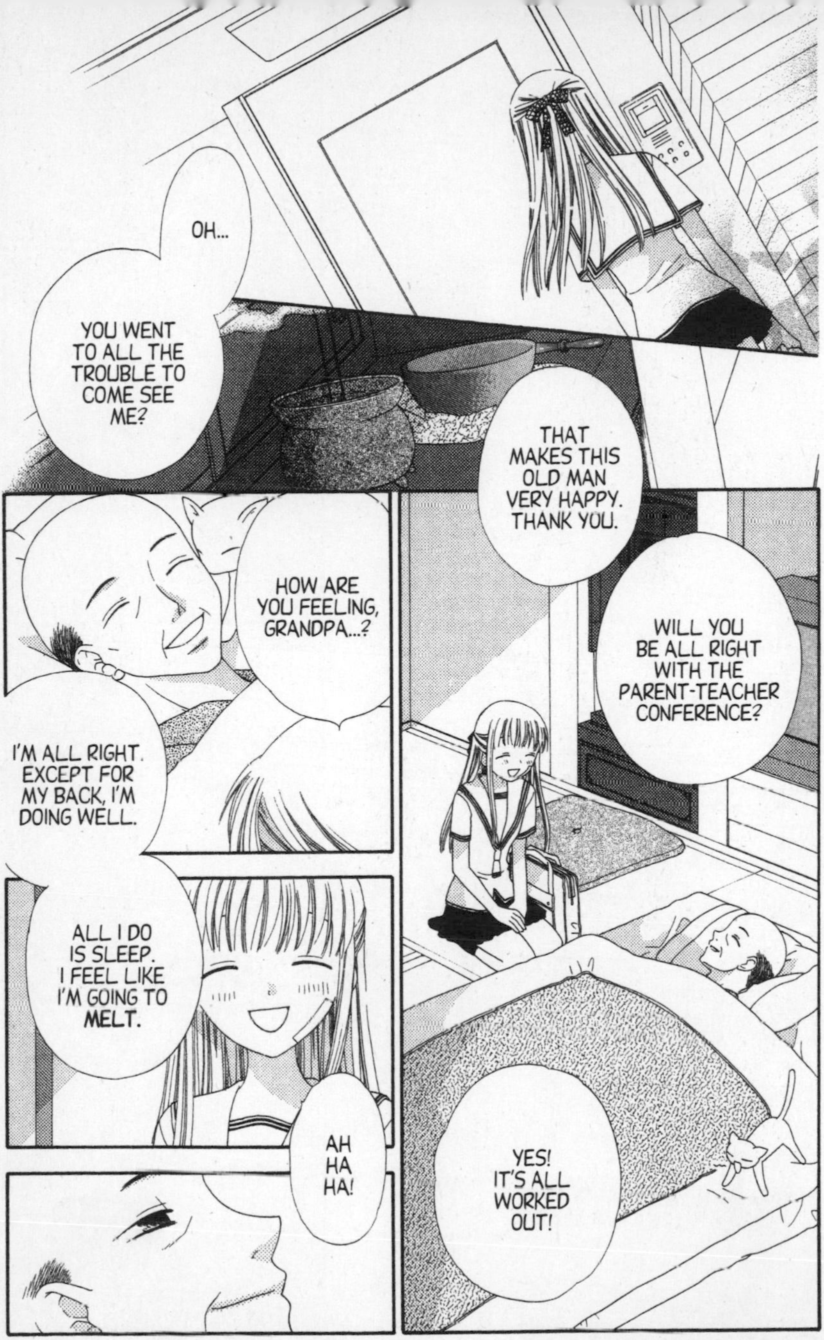
OH...
YOU WENT TO ALL THE TROUBLE TO COME SEE ME?
THAT MAKES THIS OLD MAN VERY HAPPY. THANK YOU.
WILL YOU BE ALL RIGHT WITH THE PARENT-TEACHER CONFERENCE?
YES! IT'S ALL WORKED OUT!
HOW ARE YOU FEELING, GRANDPA...?
I'M ALL RIGHT. EXCEPT FOR MY BACK, I'M DOING WELL.
ALL I DO IS SLEEP. I FEEL LIKE I'M GOING TO MELT.
AH HA HA!

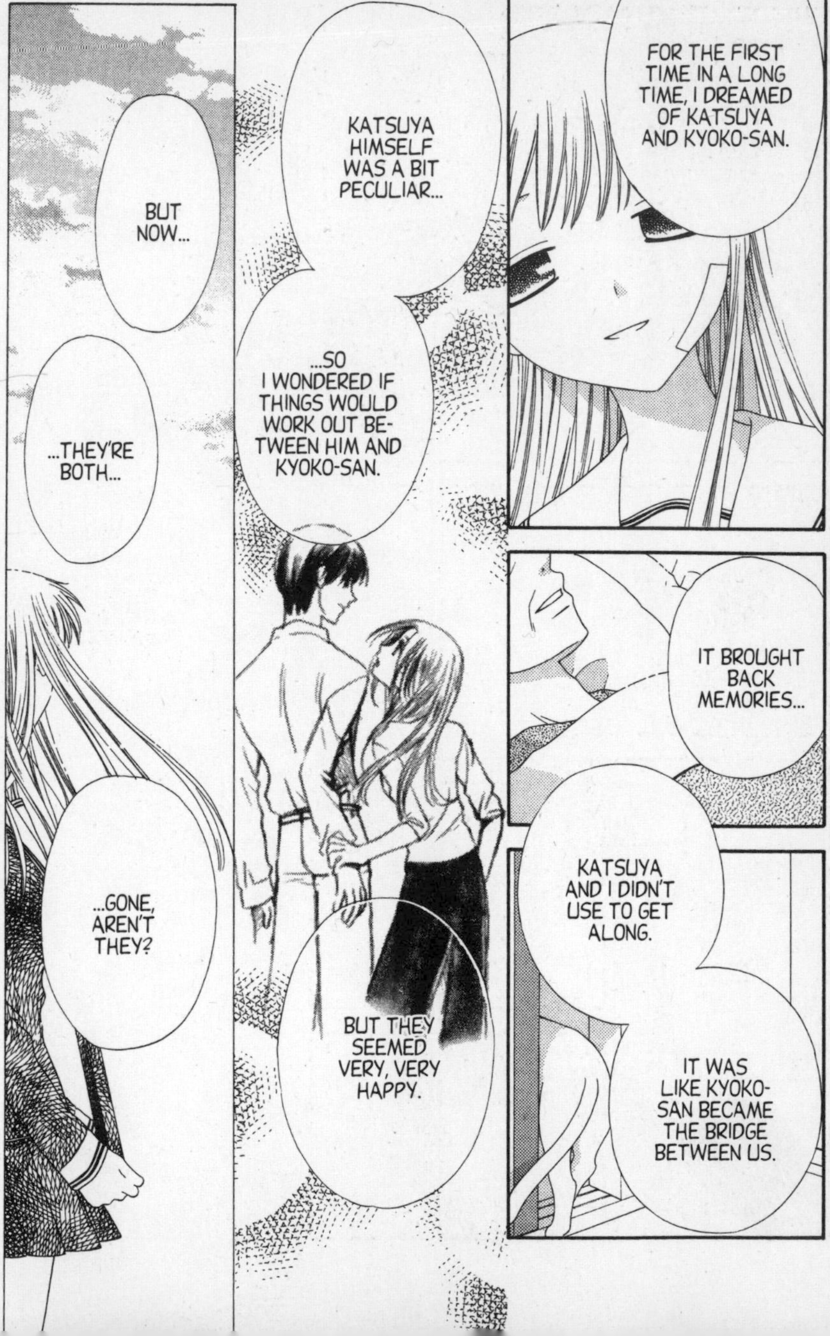
FOR THE FIRST TIME IN A LONG TIME, I DREAMED OF KATSUYA AND KYOKO-SAN.
IT BROUGHT BACK MEMORIES...
KATSUYA AND I DIDN'T USE TO GET ALONG.
IT WAS LIKE KYOKO-SAN BECAME THE BRIDGE BETWEEN US.
KATSUYA HIMSELF WAS A BIT PECULIAR...
...SO I WONDERED IF THINGS WOULD WORK OUT BETWEEN HIM AND KYOKO-SAN.
BUT THEY SEEMED VERY, VERY HAPPY.
BUT NOW...
...THEY'RE BOTH...
...GONE, AREN'T THEY?

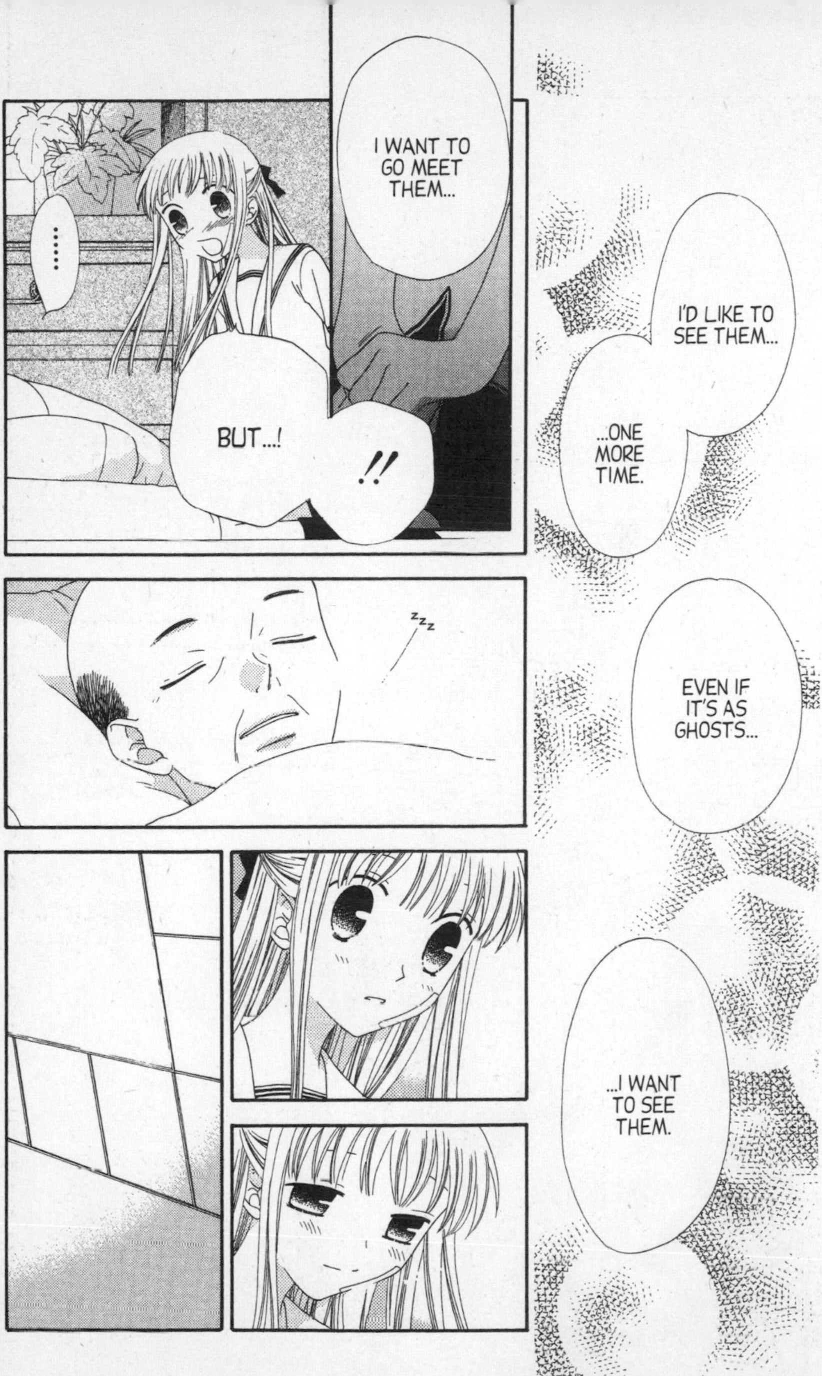

I WANT TO GO MEET THEM...
BUT...!
!!
......
zzz
I'D LIKE TO SEE THEM...
...ONE MORE TIME.
EVEN IF IT'S AS GHOSTS...
...I WANT TO SEE THEM.

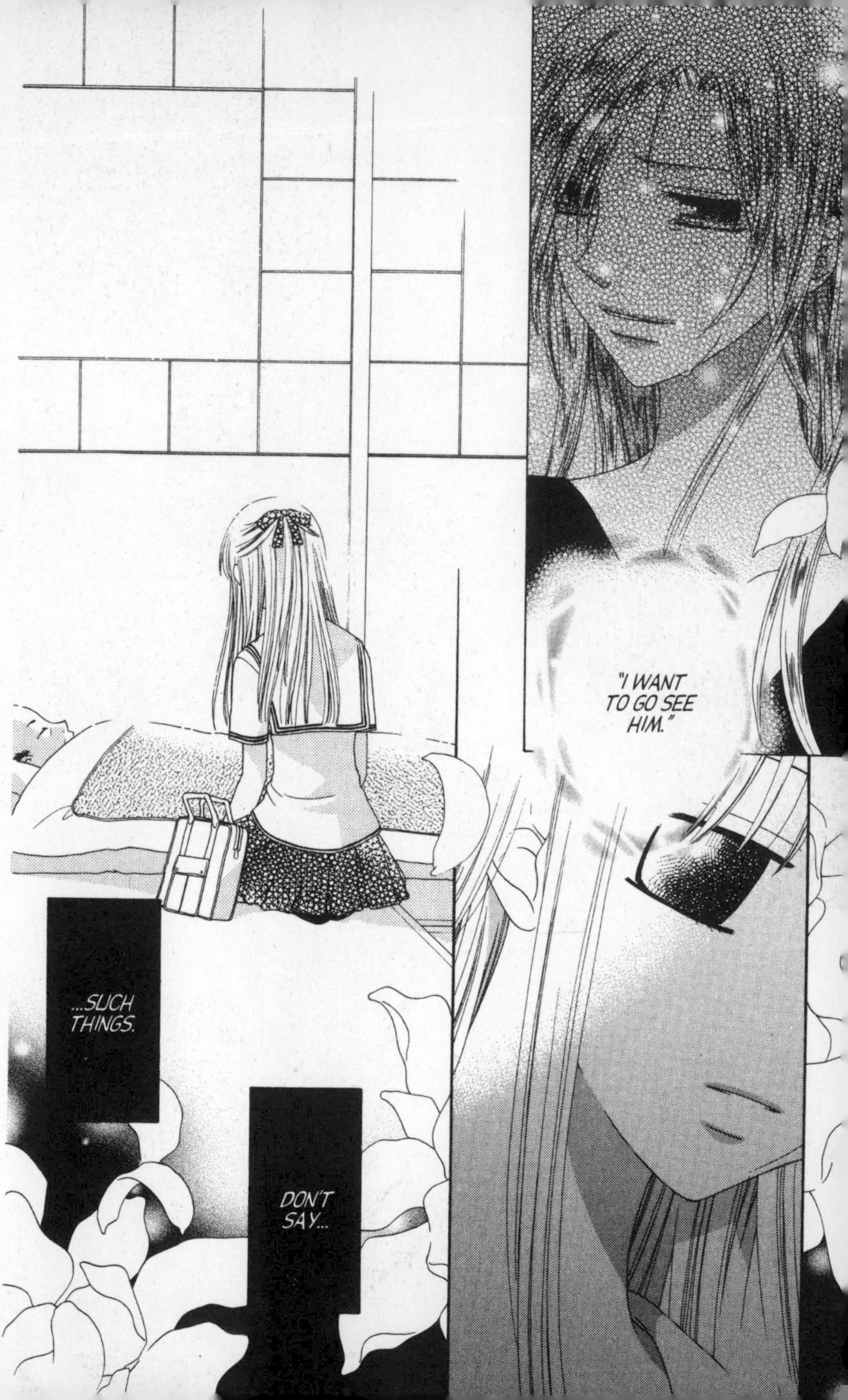
"I WANT TO GO SEE HIM."
DON'T SAY...
...SUCH THINGS.

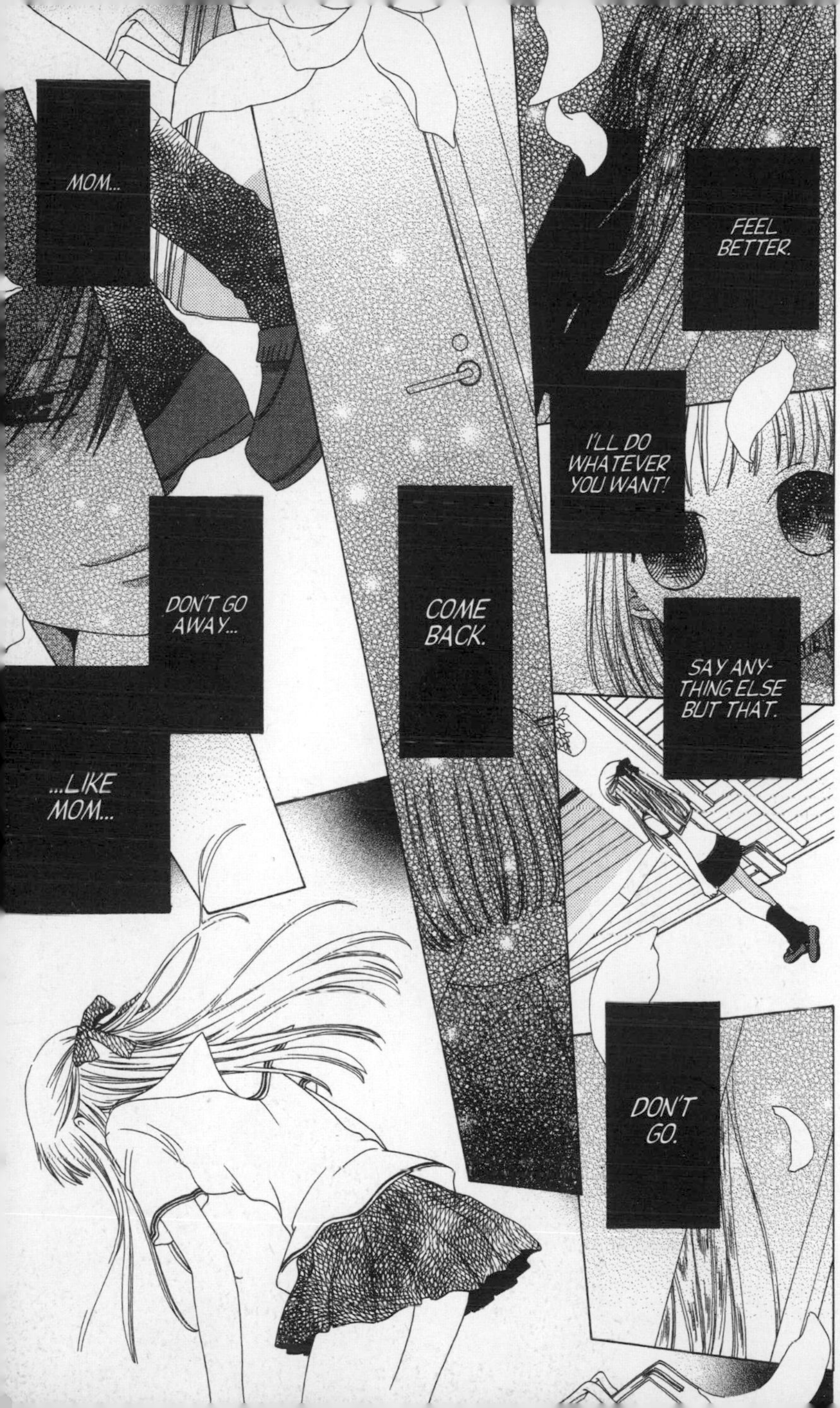

FEEL BETTER.
I'LL DO WHATEVER YOU WANT!
SAY ANYTHING ELSE BUT THAT.
DON'T GO.
COME BACK.
MOM...
DON'T GO AWAY...
...LIKE MOM...

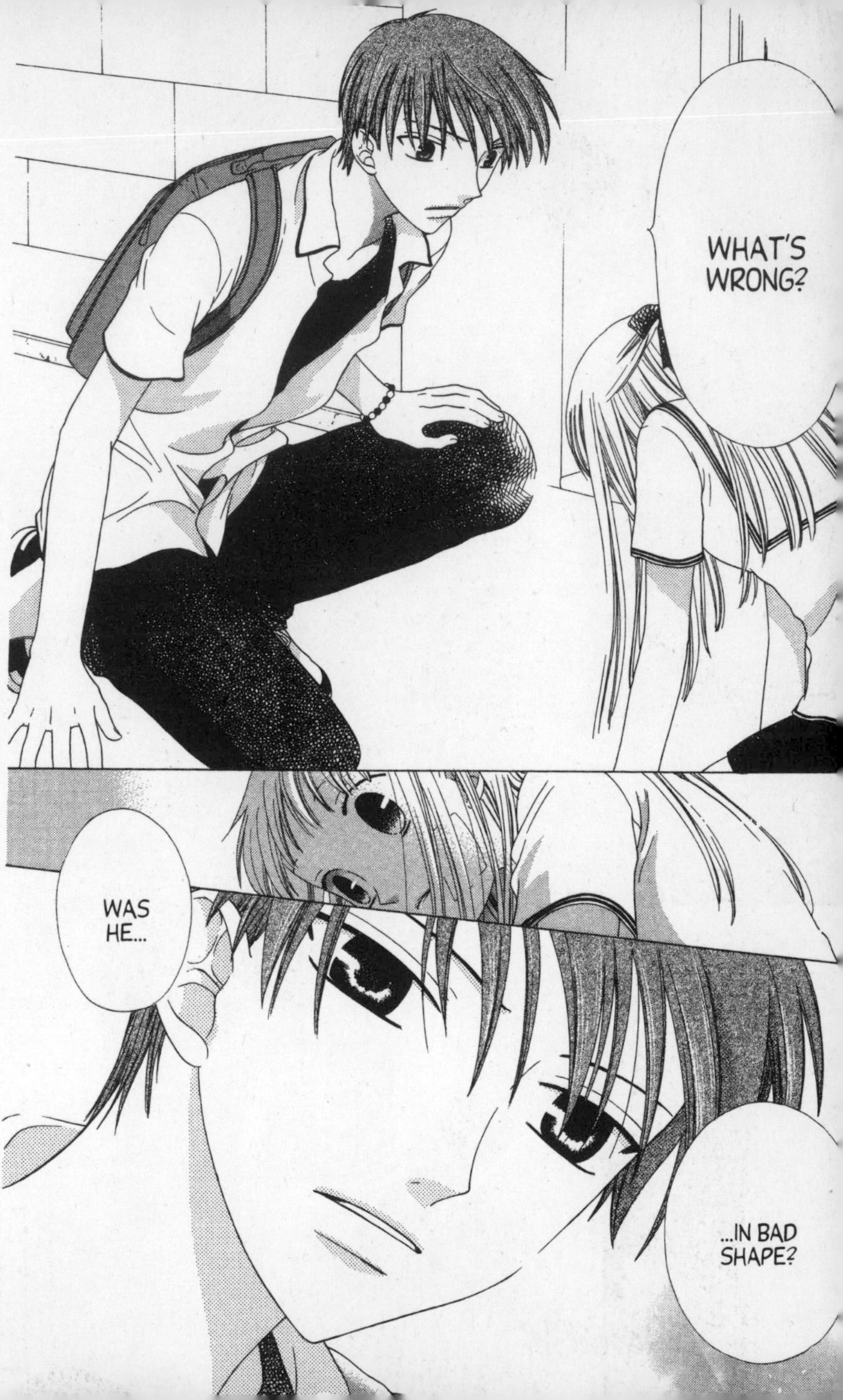
WHAT'S WRONG?
WAS HE...
...IN BAD SHAPE?

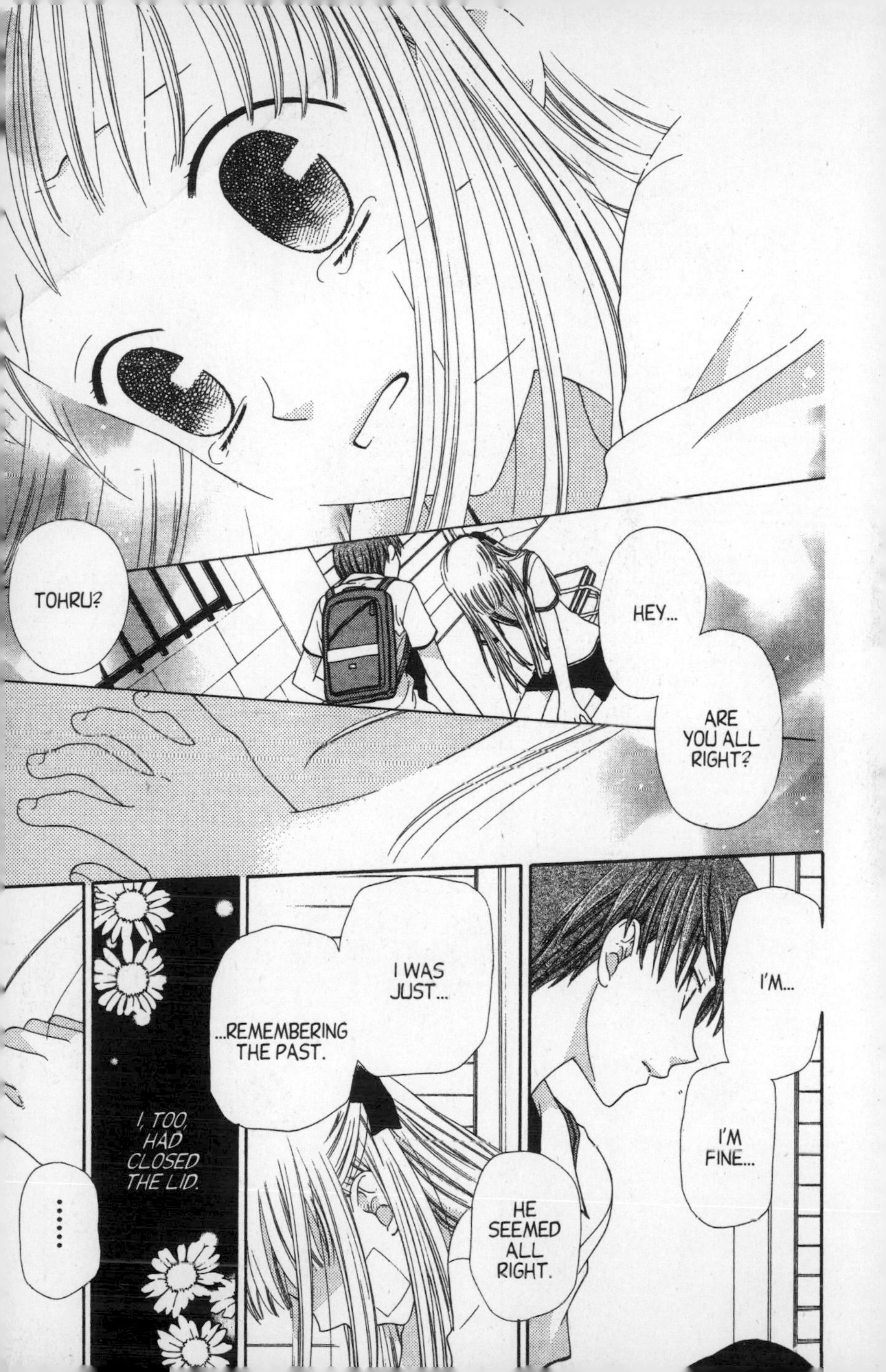
HEY...
ARE YOU ALL RIGHT?
TOHRU?
I'M...
I'M FINE...
I WAS JUST...
...REMEMBERING THE PAST.
HE SEEMED ALL RIGHT.
I, TOO, HAD CLOSED THE LID.
......

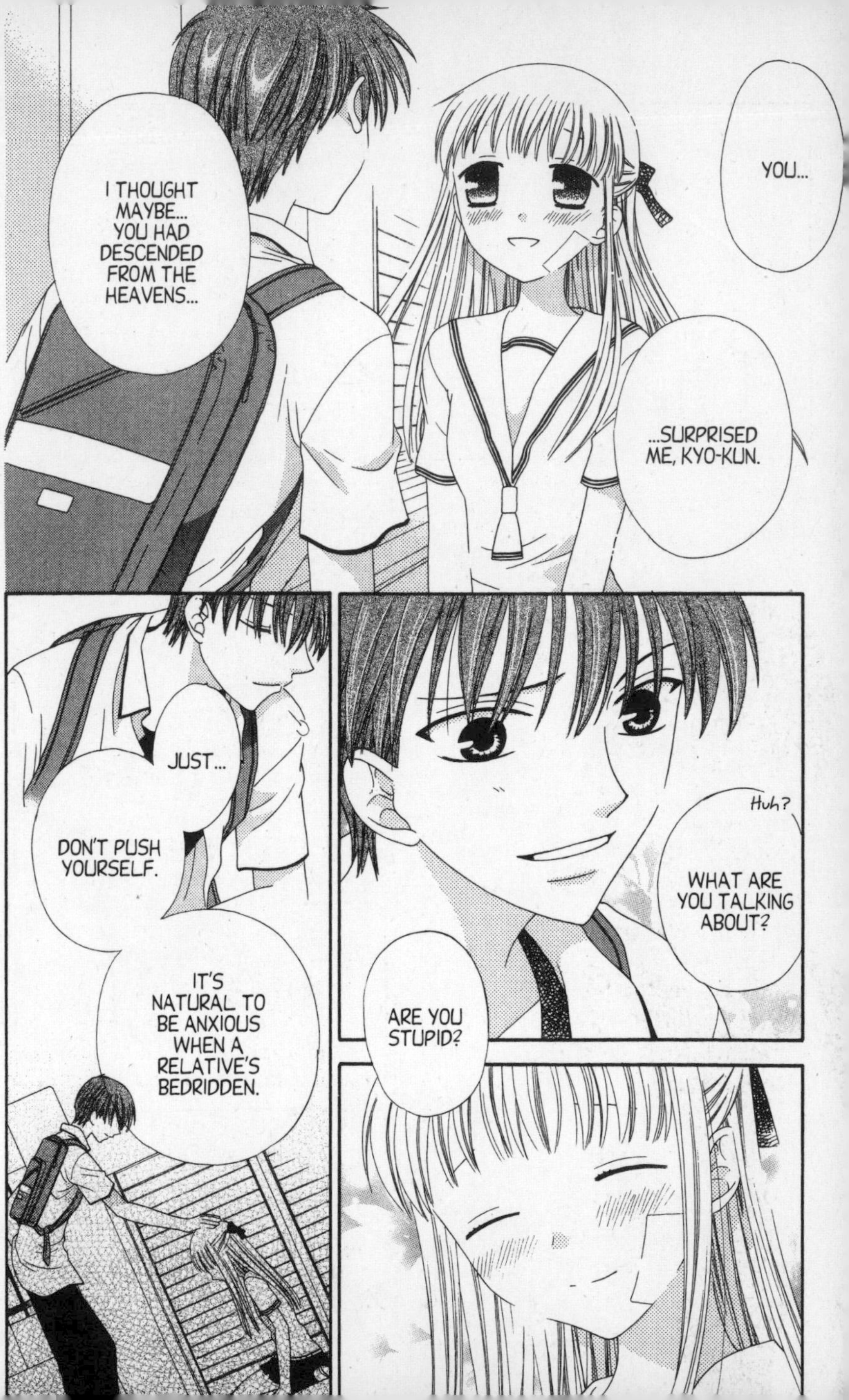
YOU...
...SURPRISED ME, KYO-KUN.
I THOUGHT MAYBE... YOU HAD DESCENDED FROM THE HEAVENS...
Huh?
WHAT ARE YOU TALKING ABOUT?
ARE YOU STUPID?
JUST...
DON'T PUSH YOURSELF.
IT'S NATURAL TO BE ANXIOUS WHEN A RELATIVE'S BEDRIDDEN.

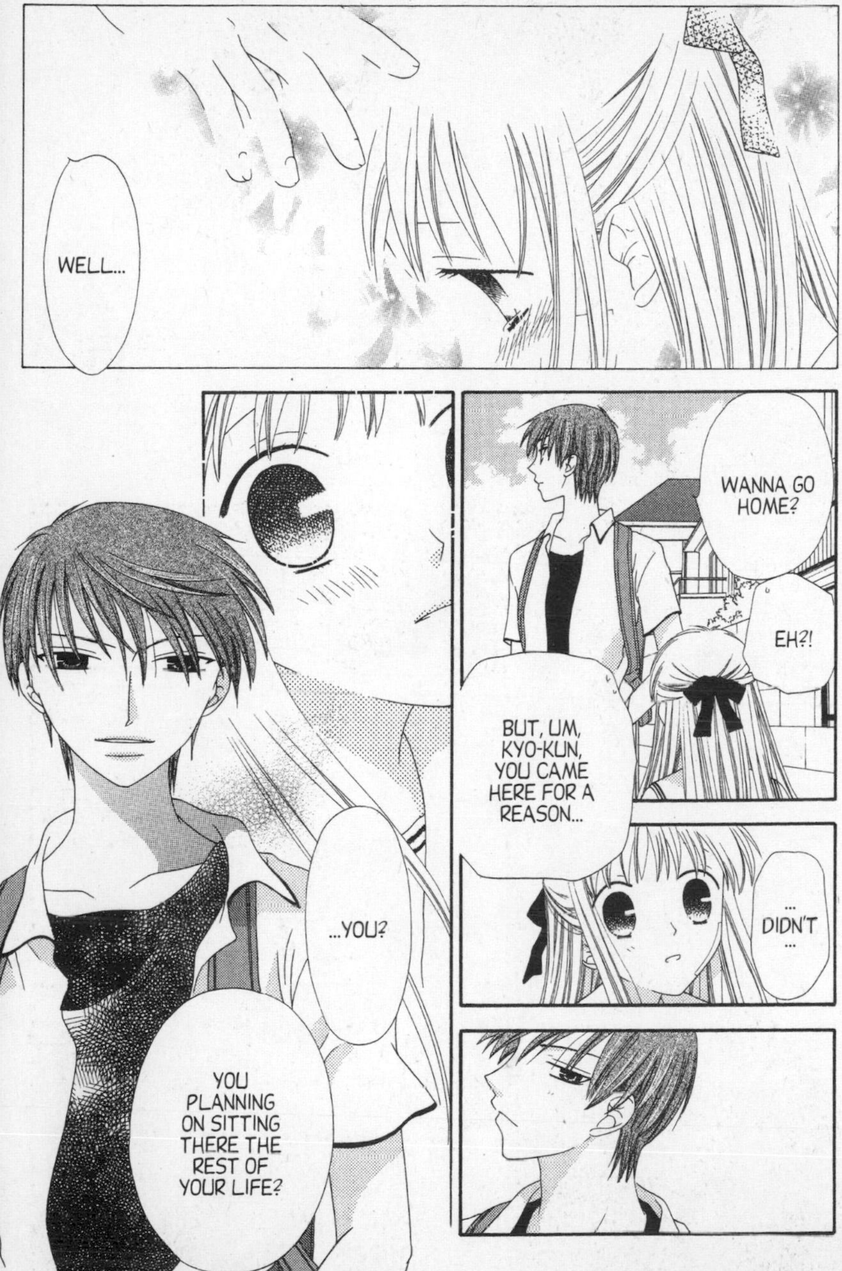
WELL...
WANNA GO HOME?
EH?!
BUT, UM, KYO-KUN, YOU CAME HERE FOR A REASON...
...DIDN'T...
...YOU?
YOU PLANNING ON SITTING THERE THE REST OF YOUR LIFE?

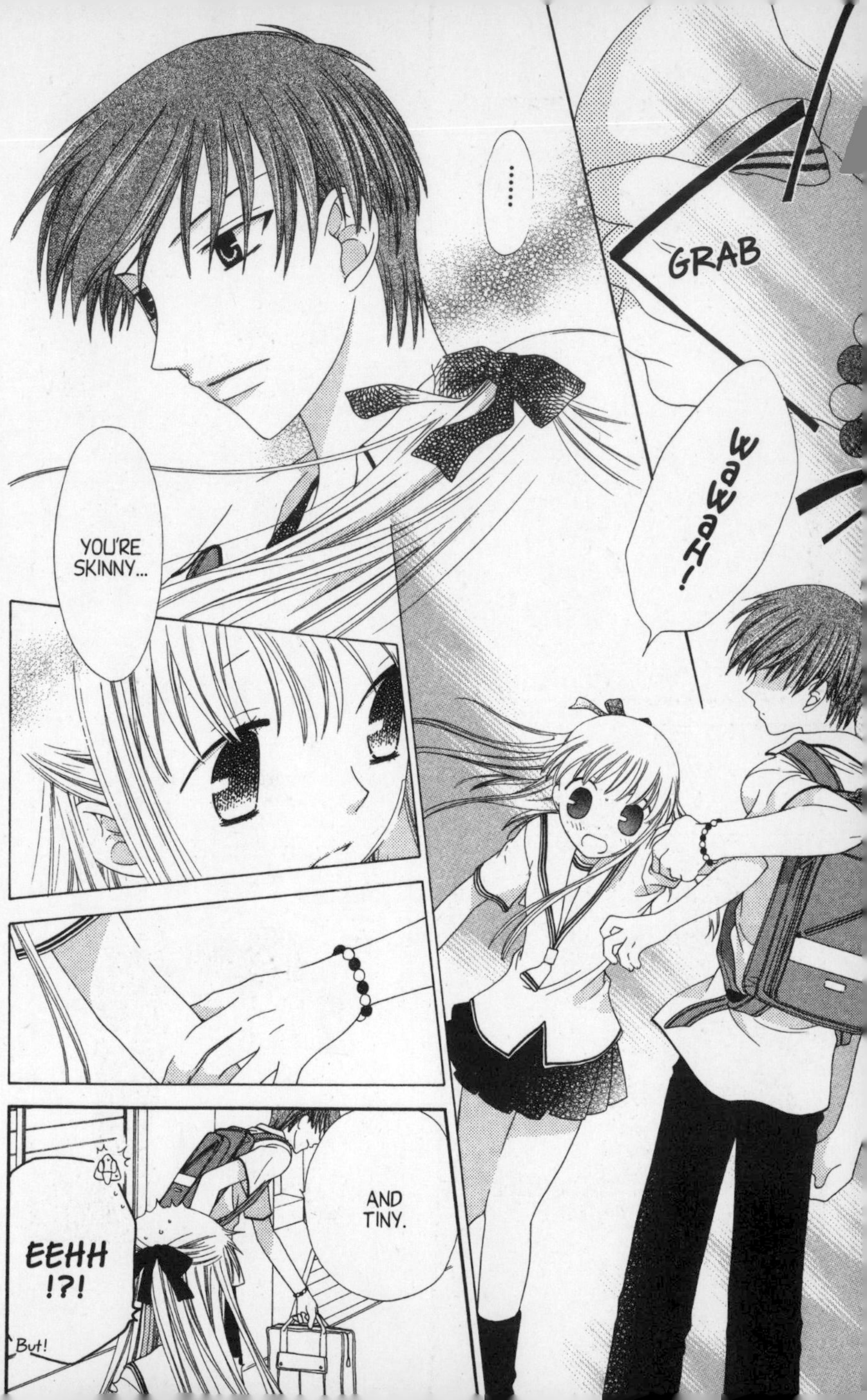
GRAB
WaWaH!
......
YOU'RE SKINNY...
AND TINY.
EEHH !?!
But!

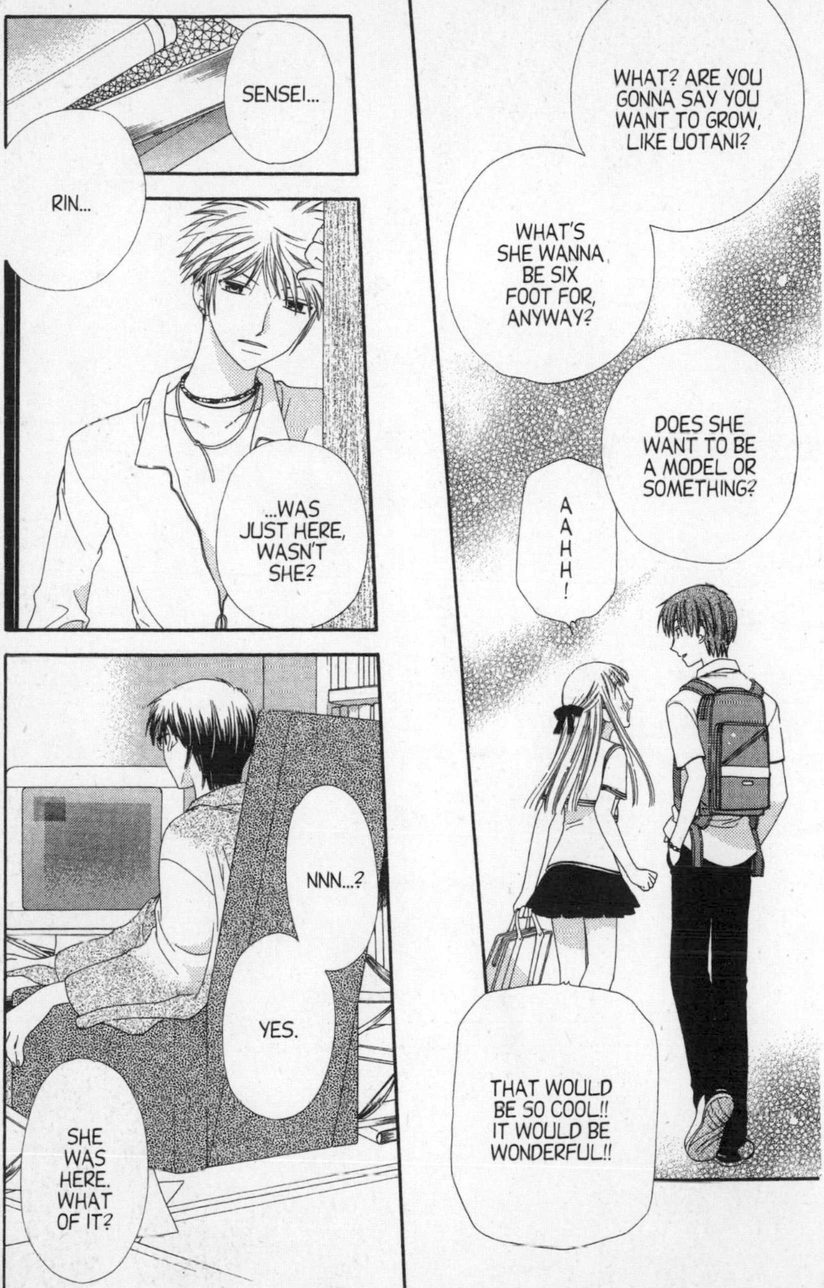
WHAT? ARE YOU GONNA SAY YOU WANT TO GROW, LIKE UOTANI?
WHAT'S SHE WANNA BE SIX FOOT FOR, ANYWAY?
DOES SHE WANT TO BE A MODEL OR SOMETHING?
AAHH!
THAT WOULD BE SO COOL!! IT WOULD BE WONDERFUL!!
SENSEI...
RIN...
...WAS JUST HERE, WASN'T SHE?
NNN...?
YES.
SHE WAS HERE. WHAT OF IT?

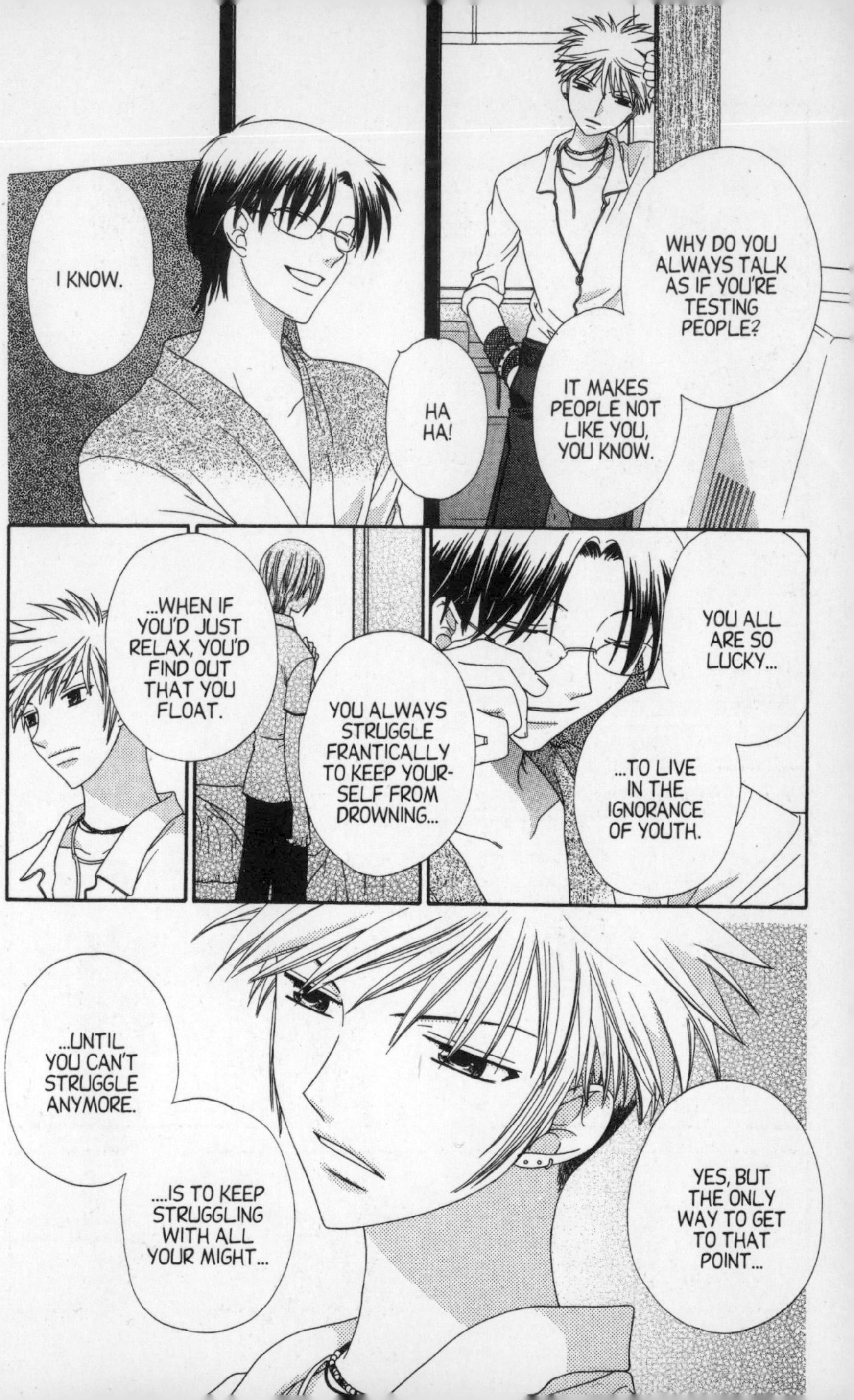
WHY DO YOU ALWAYS TALK AS IF YOU'RE TESTING PEOPLE?
IT MAKES PEOPLE NOT LIKE YOU, YOU KNOW.
HA HA!
I KNOW.
YOU ALL ARE SO LUCKY...
...TO LIVE IN THE IGNORANCE OF YOUTH.
YOU ALWAYS STRUGGLE FRANTICALLY TO KEEP YOUR-SELF FROM DROWNING...
...WHEN IF YOU'D JUST RELAX, YOU'D FIND OUT THAT YOU FLOAT.
YES, BUT THE ONLY WAY TO GET TO THAT POINT...
....IS TO KEEP STRUGGLING WITH ALL YOUR MIGHT...
...UNTIL YOU CAN'T STRUGGLE ANYMORE.

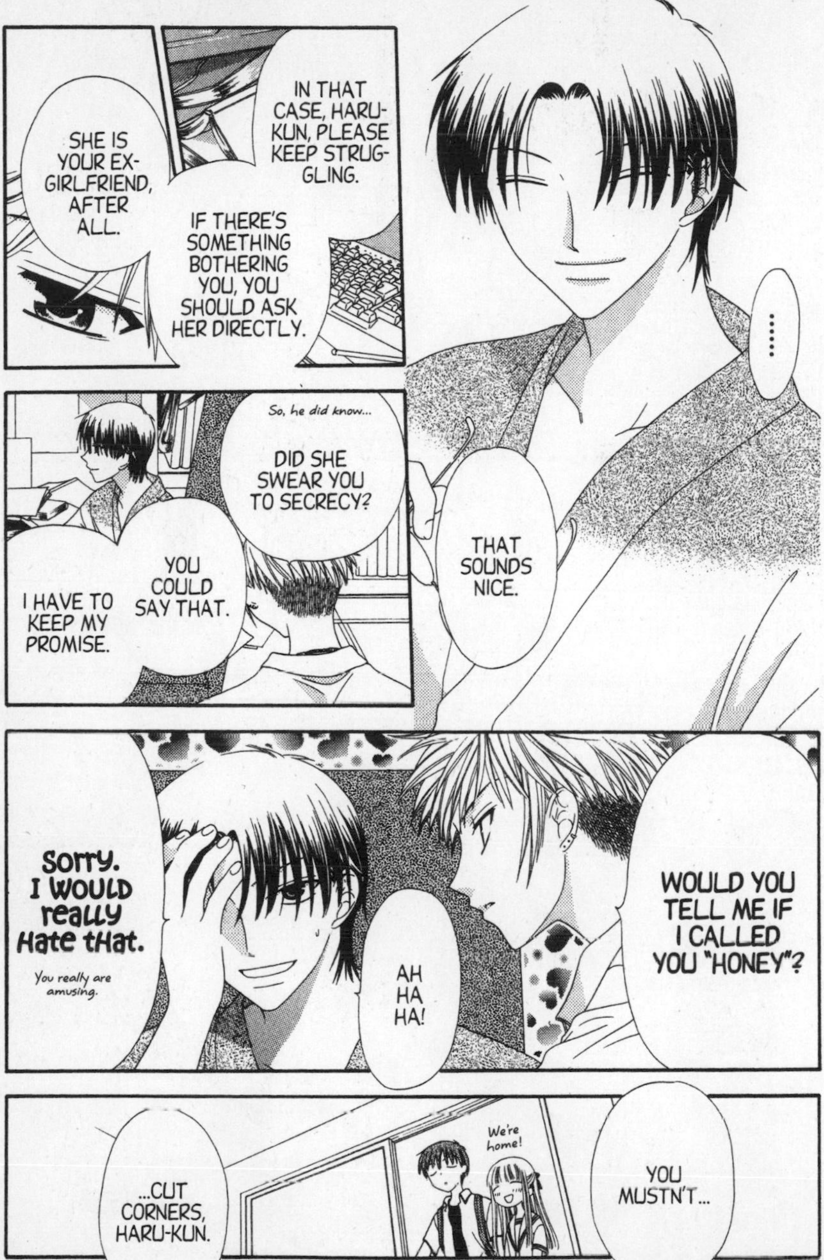

......
THAT SOUNDS NICE.
IN THAT CASE, HARU-KUN, PLEASE KEEP STRUGGLING.
IF THERE'S SOMETHING BOTHERING YOU, YOU SHOULD ASK HER DIRECTLY.
SHE IS YOUR EX-GIRLFRIEND, AFTER ALL.
So, he did know...
DID SHE SWEAR YOU TO SECRECY?
YOU COULD SAY THAT.
I HAVE TO KEEP MY PROMISE.
WOULD YOU TELL ME IF I CALLED YOU "HONEY"?
AH HA HA!
Sorry. I WOULD really Hate tHat.
You really are amusing.
YOU MUSTN'T...
We're home!
...CUT CORNERS, HARU-KUN.

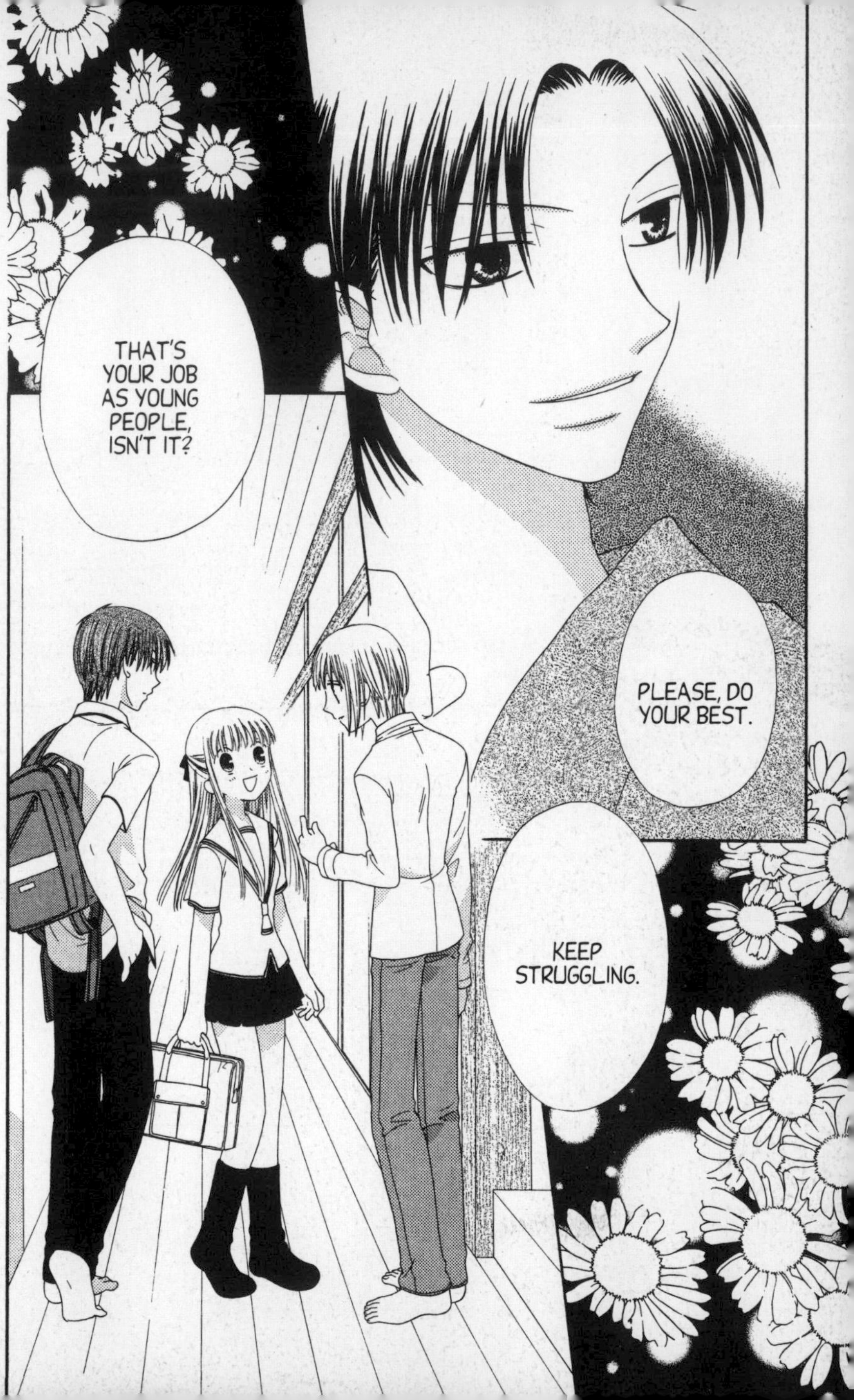
THAT'S YOUR JOB AS YOUNG PEOPLE, ISN'T IT?
PLEASE, DO YOUR BEST.
KEEP STRUGGLING.

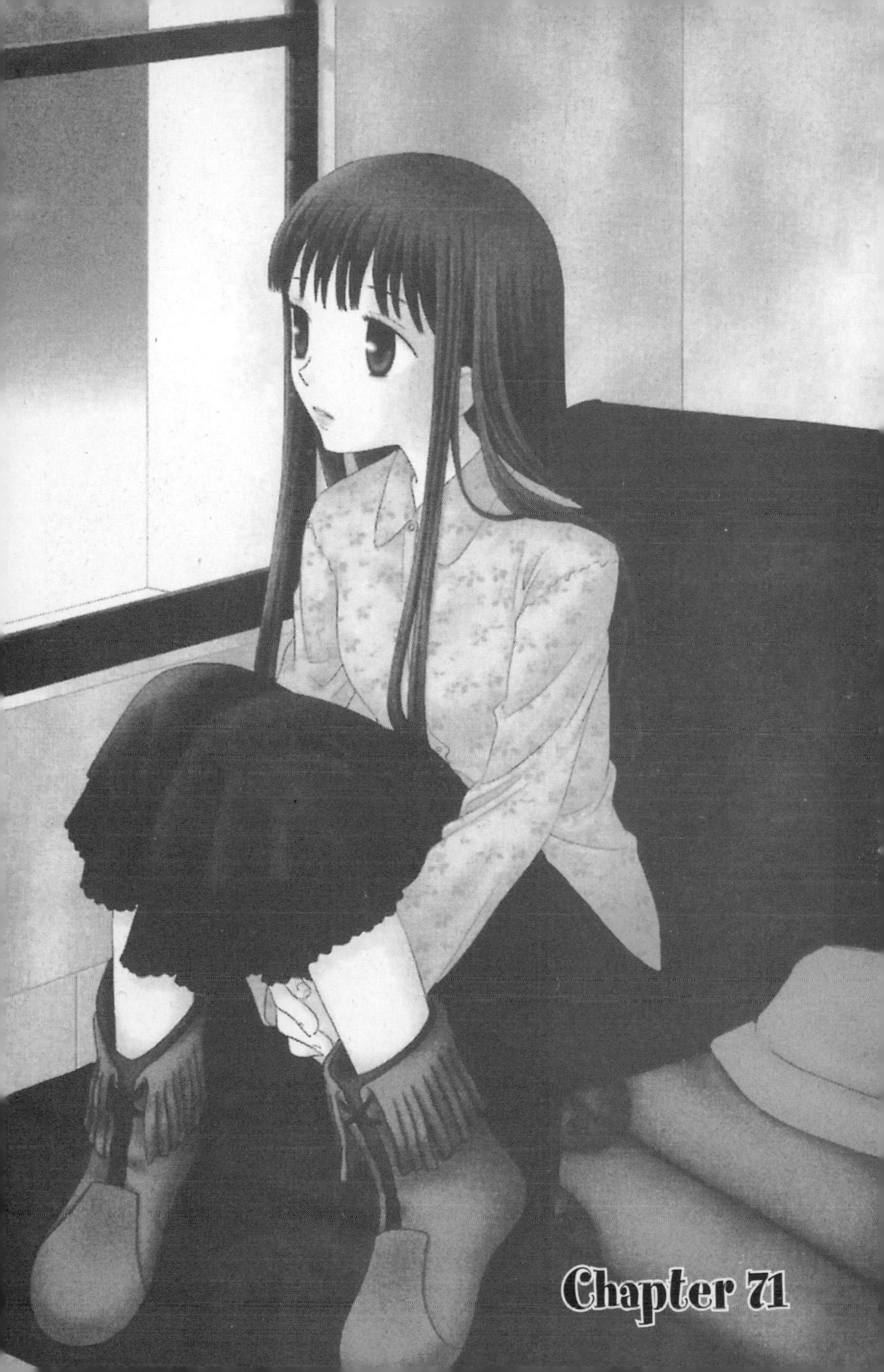
Chapter 71

I feel so grateful!

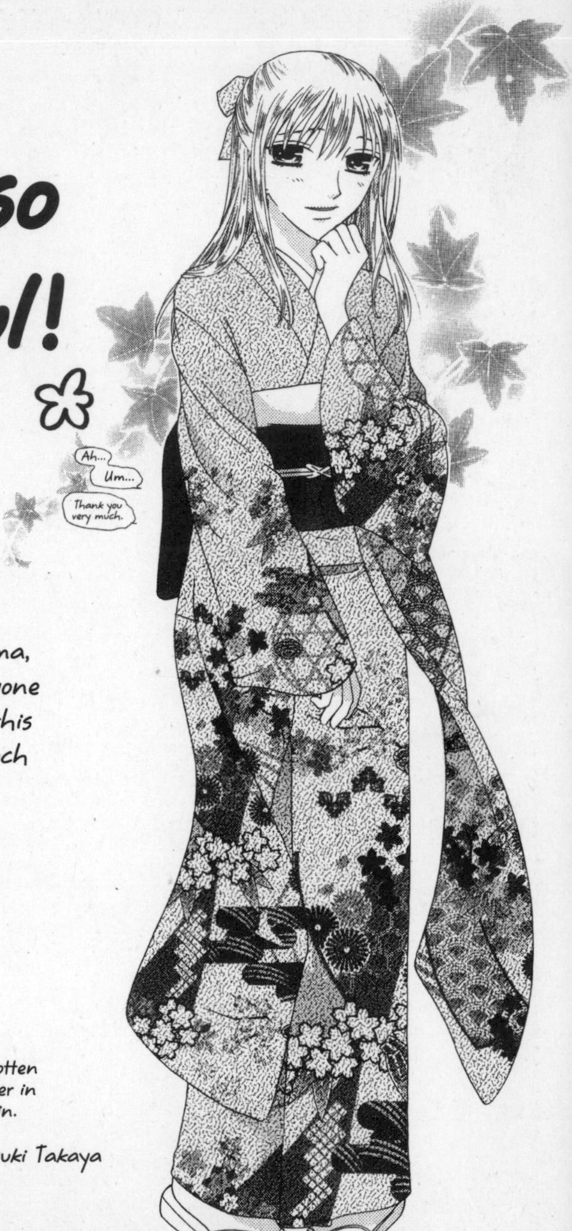
Ah...
Um...
Thank you very much.

Harada-sama, Araki-sama, Mother, Father and everyone who reads and supports this manga, thank you so much for your support!

Next is the one about whom I've gotten letters asking, "Is she the character in charge of sexiness?" Yup. It's Rin.

-Natsuki Takaya

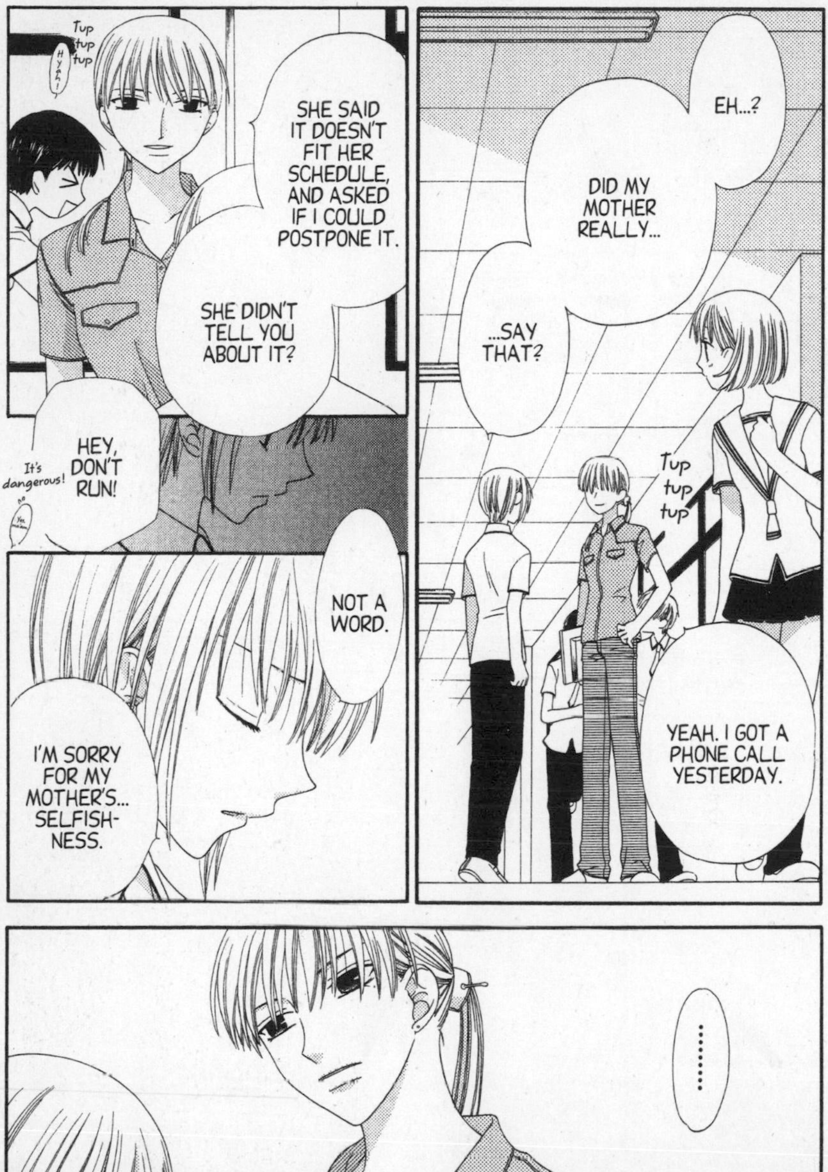
EH...?
DID MY MOTHER REALLY...
...SAY THAT?
Tup tup tup
YEAH. I GOT A PHONE CALL YESTERDAY.
Tup tup tup
Hyah!
SHE SAID IT DOESN'T FIT HER SCHEDULE, AND ASKED IF I COULD POSTPONE IT.
SHE DIDN'T TELL YOU ABOUT IT?
HEY, DON'T RUN!
It's dangerous!
NOT A WORD.
I'M SORRY FOR MY MOTHER'S... SELFISH-NESS.
....

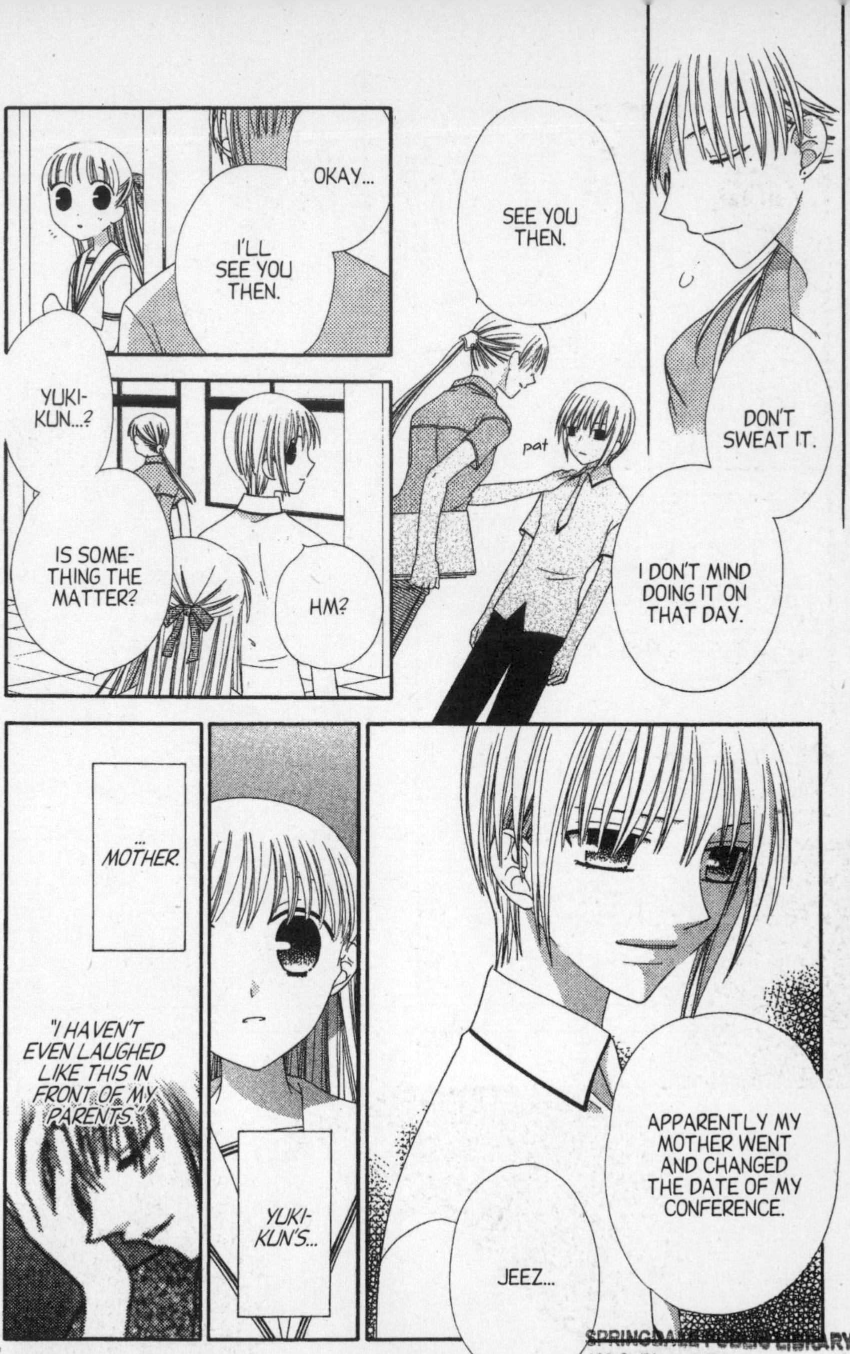

DON'T SWEAT IT.
I DON'T MIND DOING IT ON THAT DAY.
SEE YOU THEN.
pat
OKAY...
I'LL SEE YOU THEN.
YUKI-KUN...?
IS SOME-THING THE MATTER?
HM?
APPARENTLY MY MOTHER WENT AND CHANGED THE DATE OF MY CONFERENCE.
JEEZ...
YUKI-KUN'S...
...MOTHER.
"I HAVEN'T EVEN LAUGHED LIKE THIS IN FRONT OF MY PARENTS."

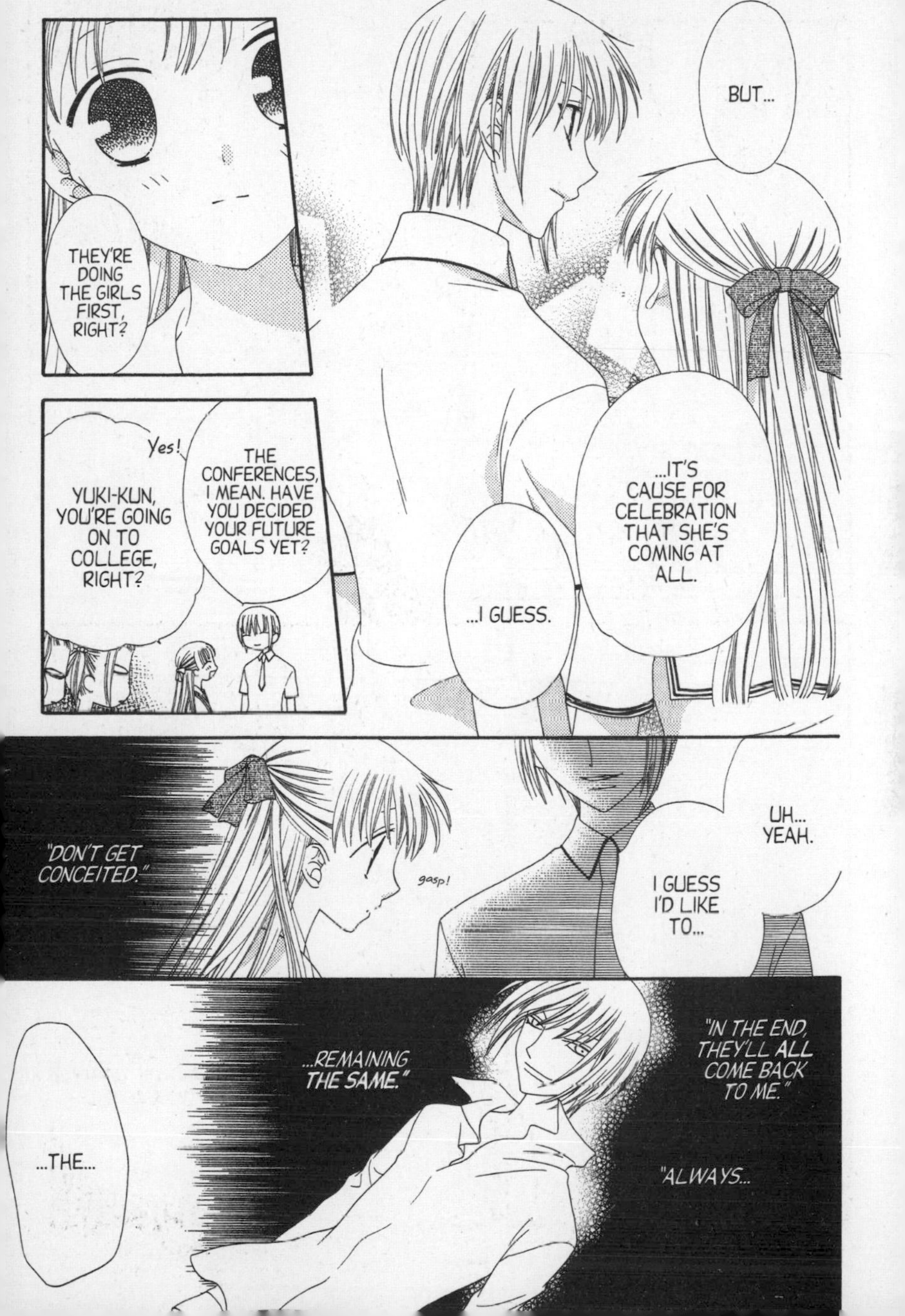
BUT...
...IT'S CAUSE FOR CELEBRATION THAT SHE'S COMING AT ALL.
...I GUESS.
THEY'RE DOING THE GIRLS FIRST, RIGHT?
THE CONFERENCES, I MEAN. HAVE YOU DECIDED YOUR FUTURE GOALS YET?
Yes!
YUKI-KUN, YOU'RE GOING ON TO COLLEGE, RIGHT?
UH... YEAH.
I GUESS I'D LIKE TO...
gasp!
"DON'T GET CONCEITED."
"IN THE END, THEY'LL ALL COME BACK TO ME."
"ALWAYS...
...REMAINING THE SAME."
...THE...

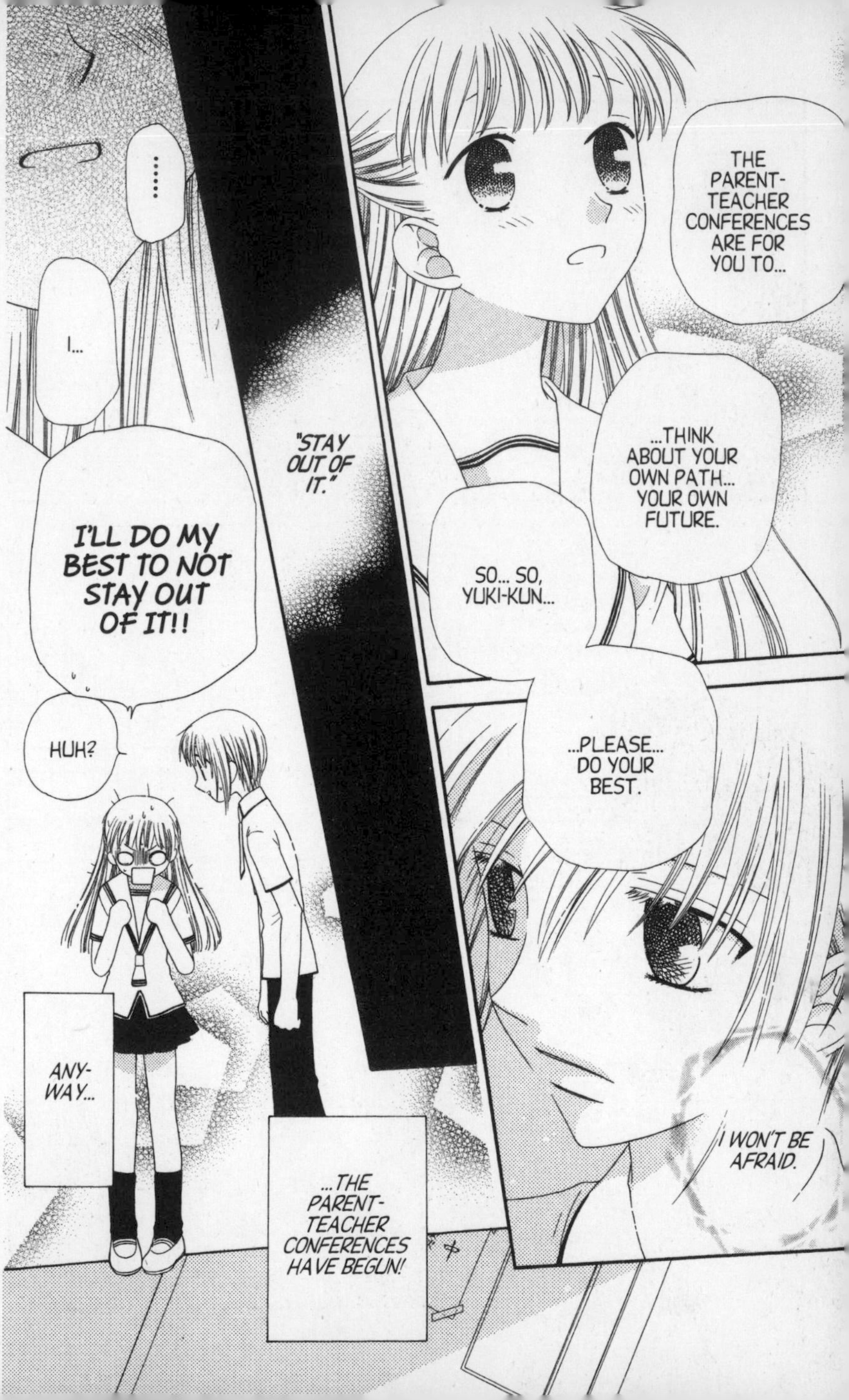
THE PARENT-TEACHER CONFERENCES ARE FOR YOU TO...
...THINK ABOUT YOUR OWN PATH... YOUR OWN FUTURE.
SO... SO, YUKI-KUN...
...PLEASE... DO YOUR BEST.
I WON'T BE AFRAID.
"STAY OUT OF IT."
......
I...
I'LL DO MY BEST TO NOT STAY OUT OF IT!!
HUH?
ANY-WAY...
...THE PARENT-TEACHER CONFERENCES HAVE BEGUN!

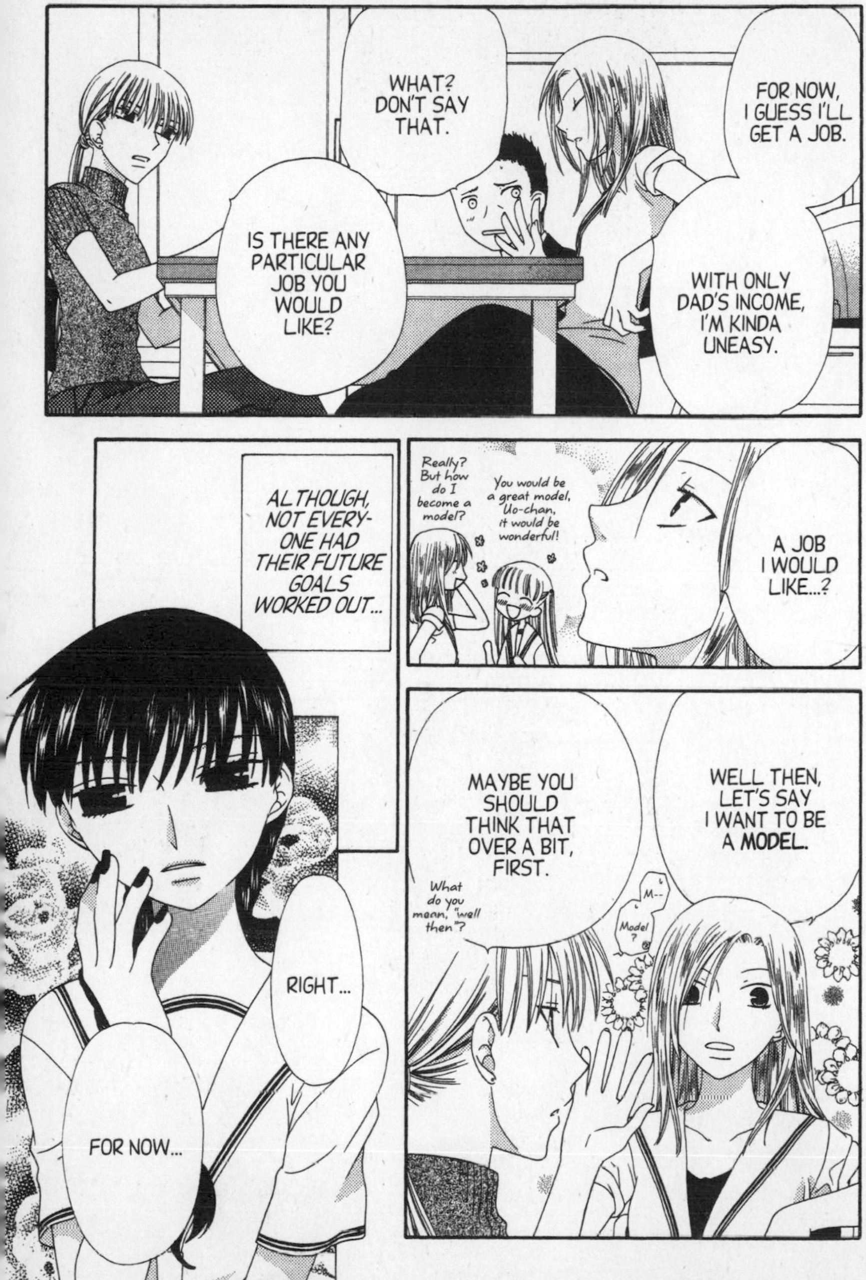
FOR NOW, I GUESS I'LL GET A JOB.
WITH ONLY DAD'S INCOME, I'M KINDA UNEASY.
WHAT? DON'T SAY THAT.
IS THERE ANY PARTICULAR JOB YOU WOULD LIKE?
A JOB I WOULD LIKE...?
You would be a great model, Uo-chan, it would be wonderful!
Really? But how do I become a model?
WELL THEN, LET'S SAY I WANT TO BE A **MODEL**.
M--
Model?
MAYBE YOU SHOULD THINK THAT OVER A BIT, FIRST.
What do you mean, "well then"?
ALTHOUGH, NOT EVERY-ONE HAD THEIR FUTURE GOALS WORKED OUT...
RIGHT...
FOR NOW...

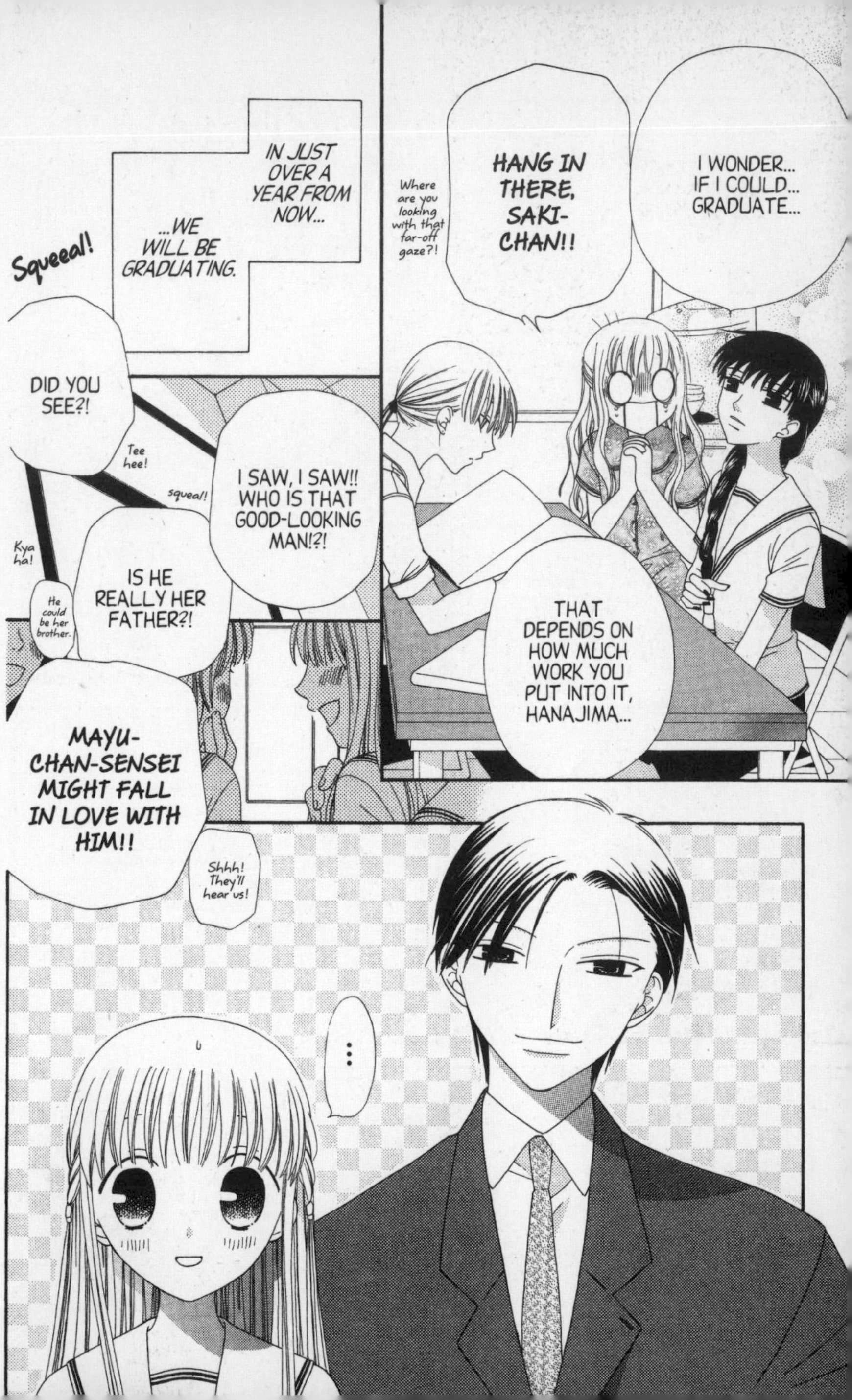
I WONDER... IF I COULD... GRADUATE...
HANG IN THERE, SAKI-CHAN!!
Where are you looking with that far-off gaze?!
THAT DEPENDS ON HOW MUCH WORK YOU PUT INTO IT, HANAJIMA...
IN JUST OVER A YEAR FROM NOW...
...WE WILL BE GRADUATING.
Squeeal!
I SAW, I SAW!! WHO IS THAT GOOD-LOOKING MAN!?!
DID YOU SEE?!
Tee hee!
squeal!
IS HE REALLY HER FATHER?!
Kya ha!
He could be her brother.
MAYU-CHAN-SENSEI MIGHT FALL IN LOVE WITH HIM!!
Shhh! They'll hear us!
...

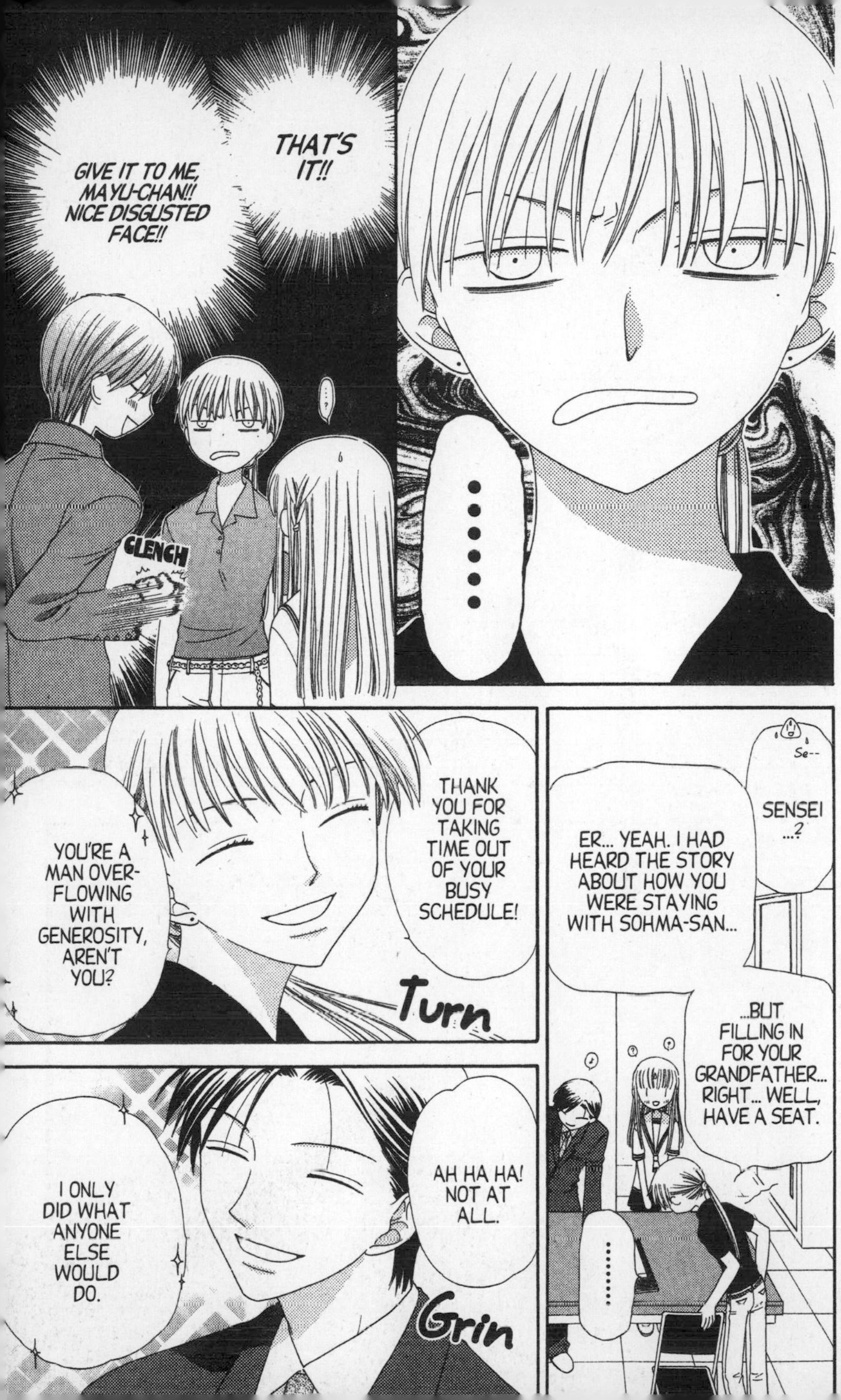
......
THAT'S IT!!
...?
GIVE IT TO ME, MAYU-CHAN!! NICE DISGUSTED FACE!!
CLENCH
Se--
SENSEI ...?
ER... YEAH. I HAD HEARD THE STORY ABOUT HOW YOU WERE STAYING WITH SOHMA-SAN...
...BUT FILLING IN FOR YOUR GRANDFATHER... RIGHT... WELL, HAVE A SEAT.
......
THANK YOU FOR TAKING TIME OUT OF YOUR BUSY SCHEDULE!
YOU'RE A MAN OVER-FLOWING WITH GENEROSITY, AREN'T YOU?
Turn
AH HA HA! NOT AT ALL.
I ONLY DID WHAT ANYONE ELSE WOULD DO.
Grin

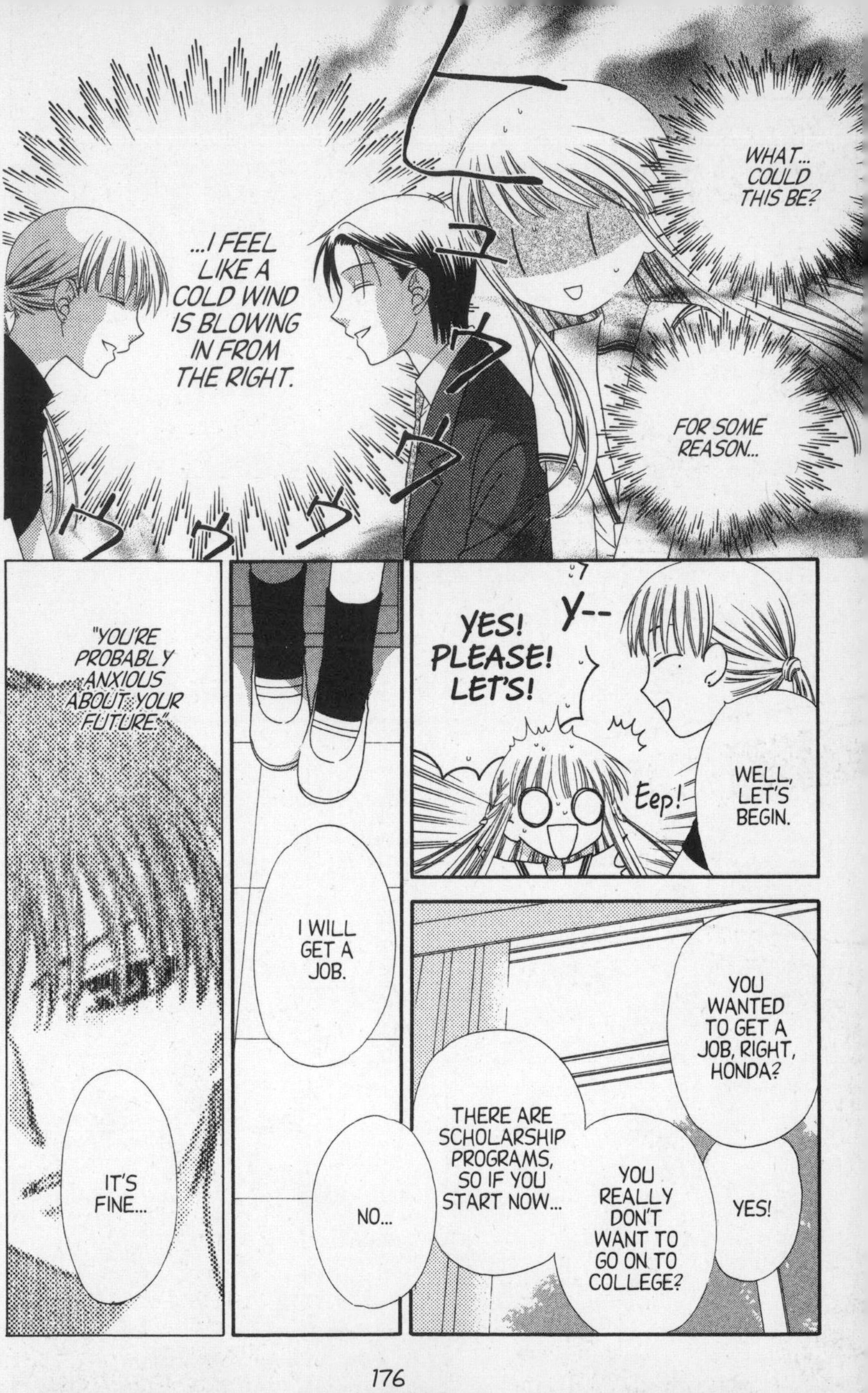

WHAT... COULD THIS BE?
FOR SOME REASON...
...I FEEL LIKE A COLD WIND IS BLOWING IN FROM THE RIGHT.
WELL, LET'S BEGIN.
Eep!
Y--
YES! PLEASE! LET'S!
YOU WANTED TO GET A JOB, RIGHT, HONDA?
YES!
YOU REALLY DON'T WANT TO GO ON TO COLLEGE?
THERE ARE SCHOLARSHIP PROGRAMS, SO IF YOU START NOW...
NO...
I WILL GET A JOB.
"YOU'RE PROBABLY ANXIOUS ABOUT YOUR FUTURE."
IT'S FINE...

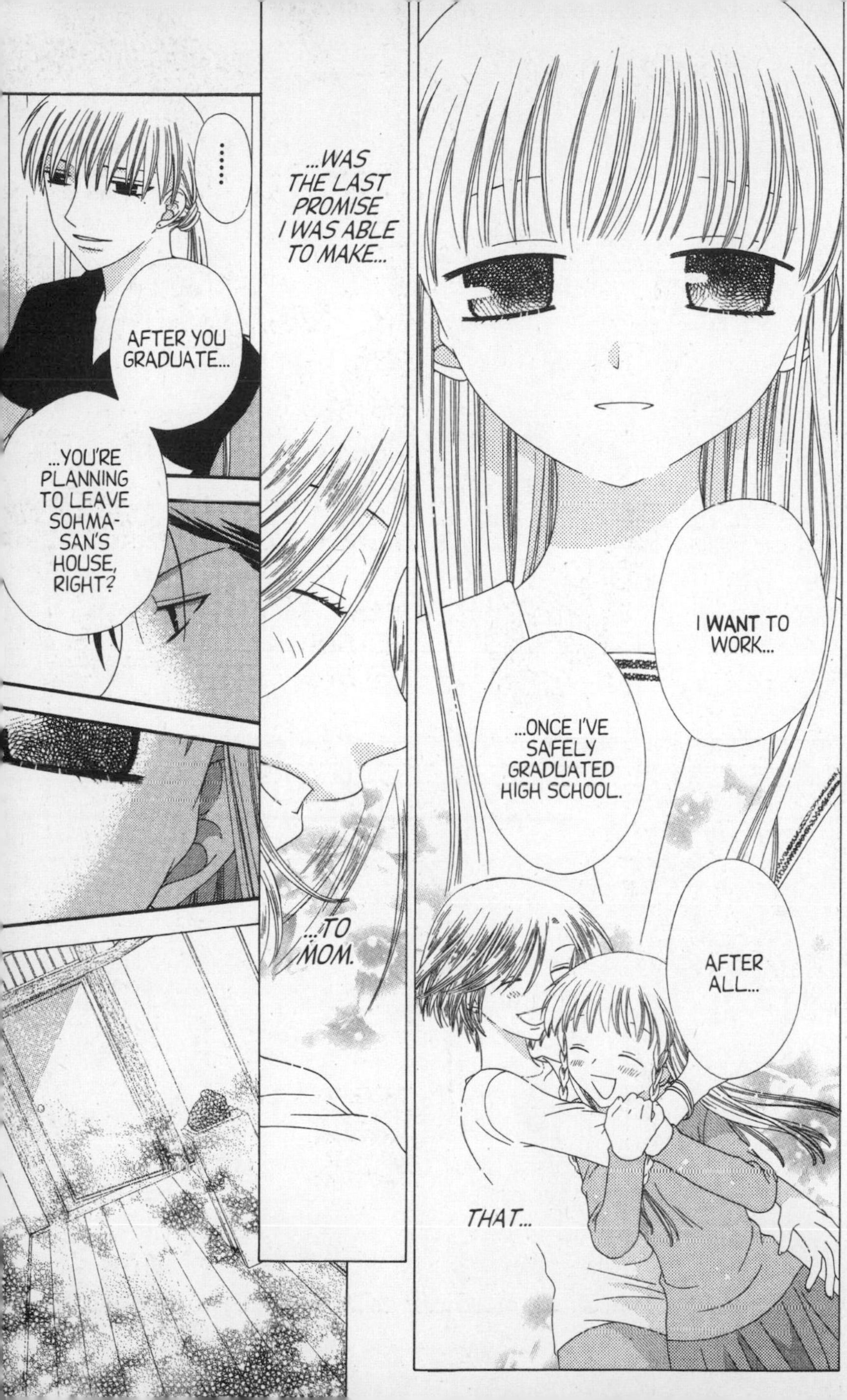
I WANT TO WORK...
...ONCE I'VE SAFELY GRADUATED HIGH SCHOOL.
AFTER ALL...
THAT...
...WAS THE LAST PROMISE I WAS ABLE TO MAKE...
...TO MOM.
......
AFTER YOU GRADUATE...
...YOU'RE PLANNING TO LEAVE SOHMA-SAN'S HOUSE, RIGHT?

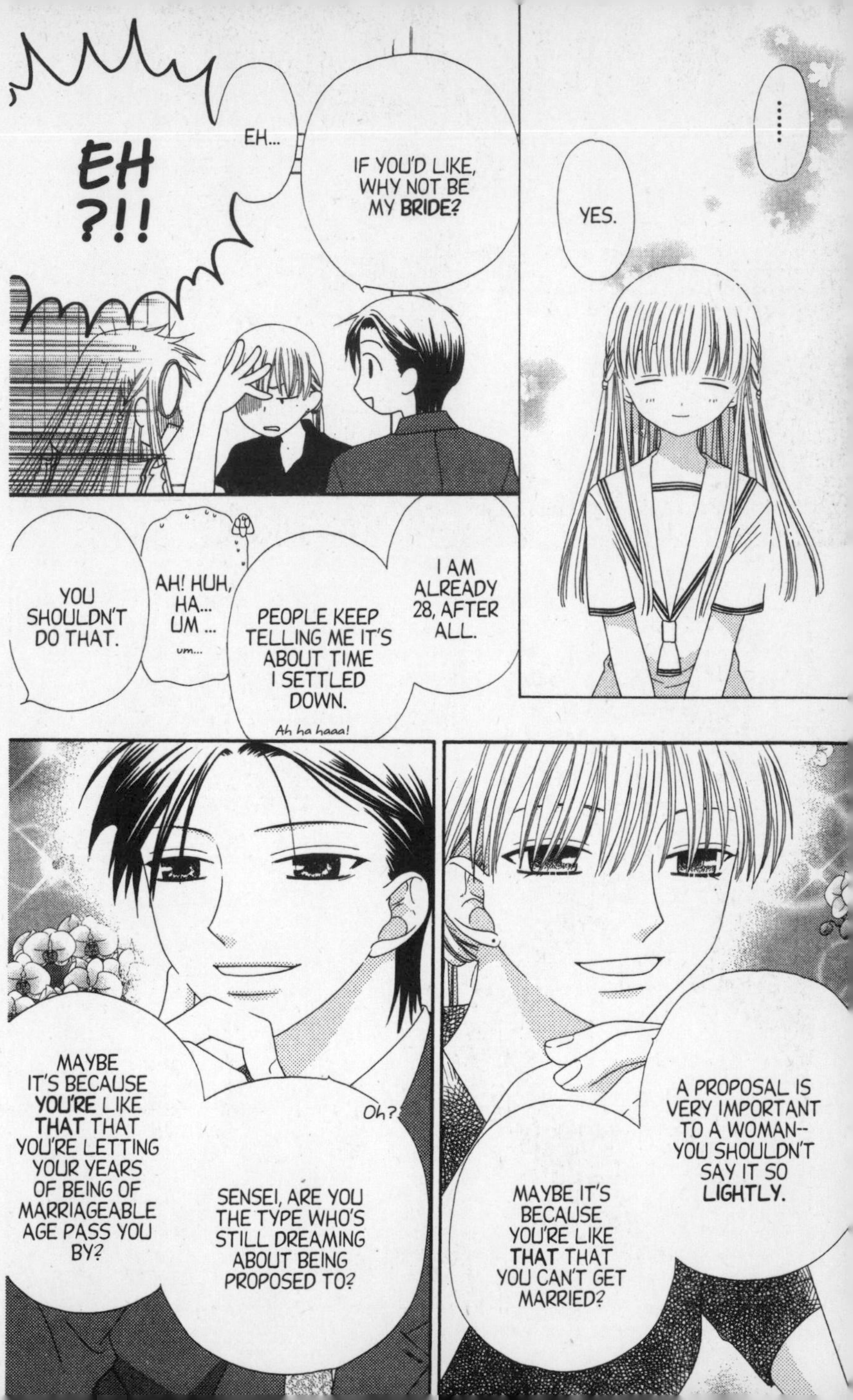
……
YES.
IF YOU'D LIKE, WHY NOT BE MY BRIDE?
EH...
EH ?!!
I AM ALREADY 28, AFTER ALL.
PEOPLE KEEP TELLING ME IT'S ABOUT TIME I SETTLED DOWN.
Ah ha haaa!
AH! HUH, HA... UM ...
um...
YOU SHOULDN'T DO THAT.
A PROPOSAL IS VERY IMPORTANT TO A WOMAN-- YOU SHOULDN'T SAY IT SO LIGHTLY.
MAYBE IT'S BECAUSE YOU'RE LIKE THAT THAT YOU CAN'T GET MARRIED?
Oh?
SENSEI, ARE YOU THE TYPE WHO'S STILL DREAMING ABOUT BEING PROPOSED TO?
MAYBE IT'S BECAUSE YOU'RE LIKE THAT THAT YOU'RE LETTING YOUR YEARS OF BEING OF MARRIAGEABLE AGE PASS YOU BY?

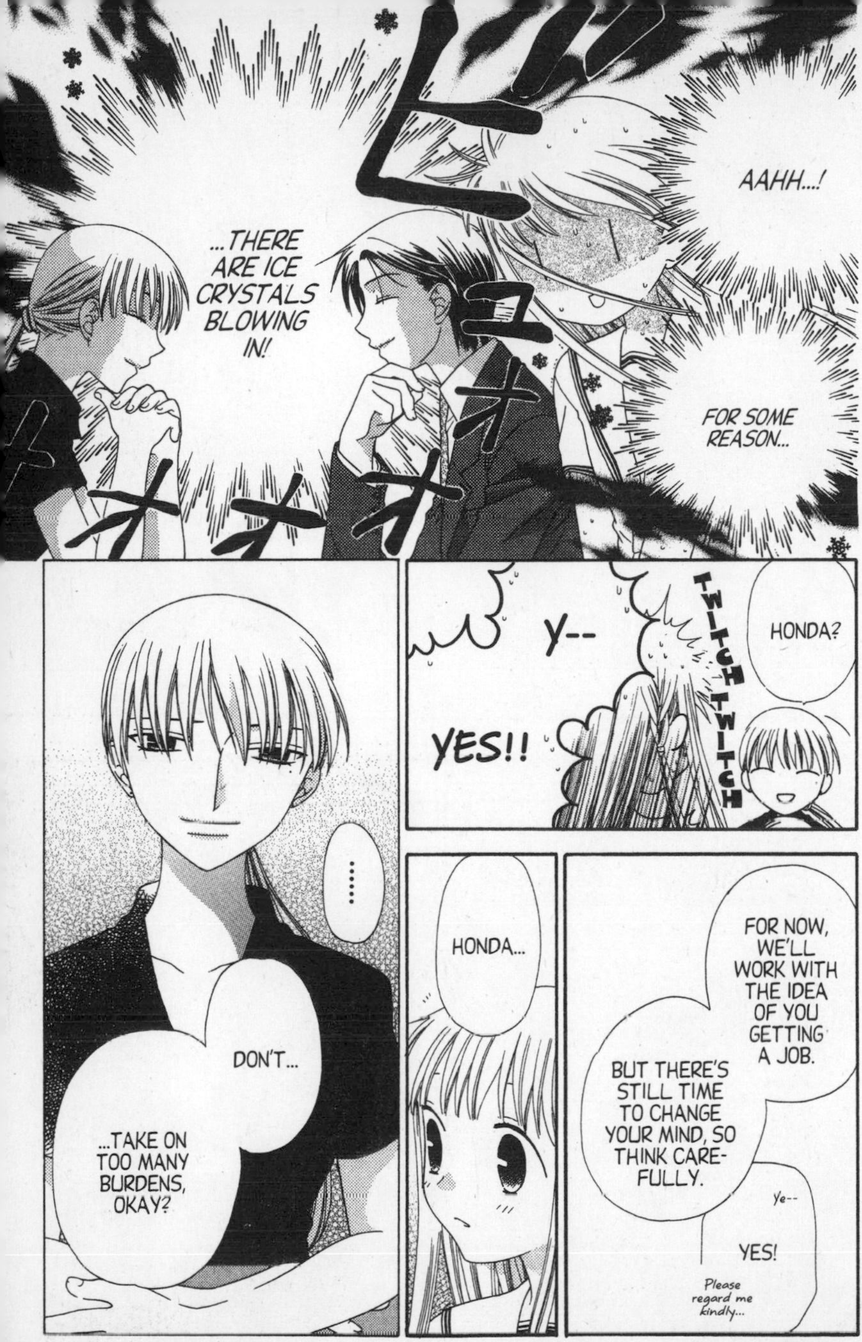
AAHH...!
FOR SOME REASON...
...THERE ARE ICE CRYSTALS BLOWING IN!
HONDA?
TWITCH TWITCH
Y-- YES!!
FOR NOW, WE'LL WORK WITH THE IDEA OF YOU GETTING A JOB.
BUT THERE'S STILL TIME TO CHANGE YOUR MIND, SO THINK CARE-FULLY.
Ye-- YES!
Please regard me kindly...
HONDA...
......
DON'T...
...TAKE ON TOO MANY BURDENS, OKAY?

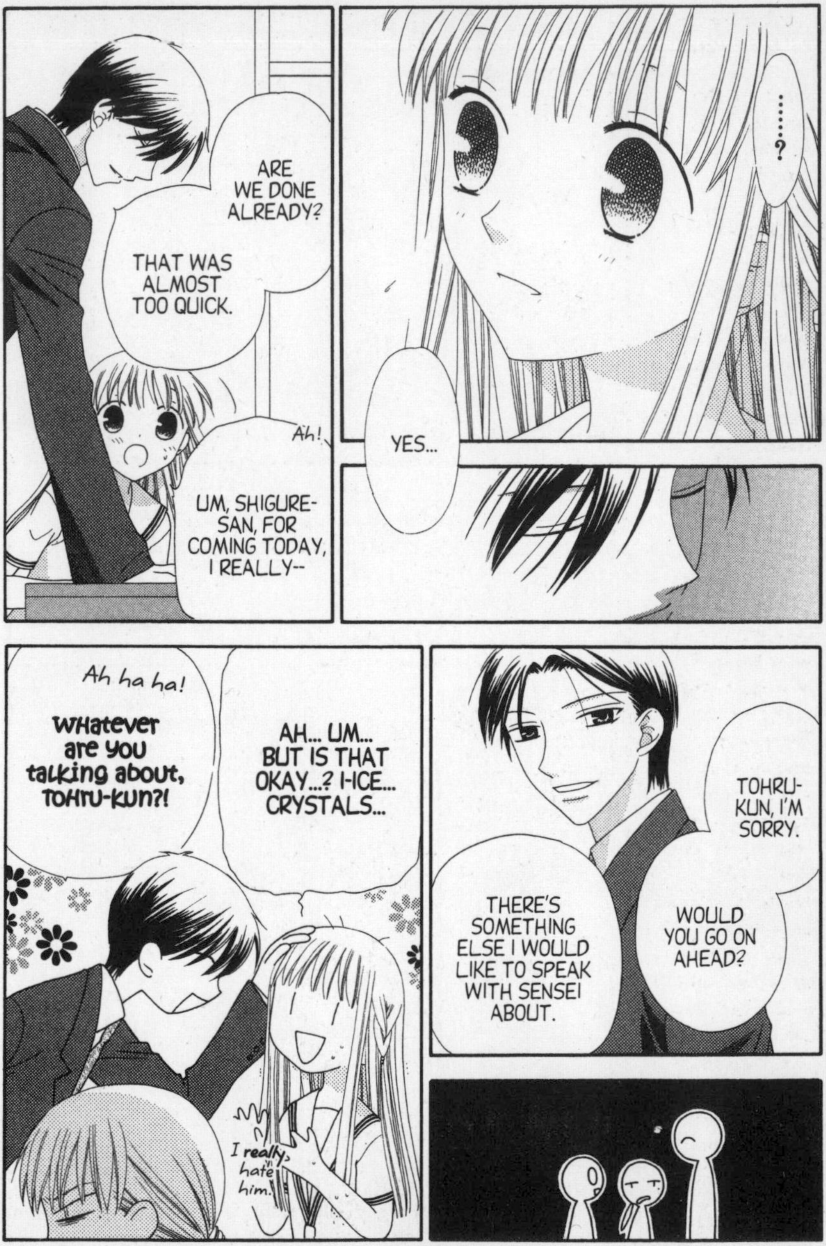
......?
YES...
ARE WE DONE ALREADY?
THAT WAS ALMOST TOO QUICK.
Ah!
UM, SHIGURE-SAN, FOR COMING TODAY, I REALLY--
TOHRU-KUN, I'M SORRY.
WOULD YOU GO ON AHEAD?
THERE'S SOMETHING ELSE I WOULD LIKE TO SPEAK WITH SENSEI ABOUT.
AH... UM... BUT IS THAT OKAY...? I-ICE... CRYSTALS...
Ah ha ha!
Whatever are you talking about, Tohru-kun?!
I really hate him.

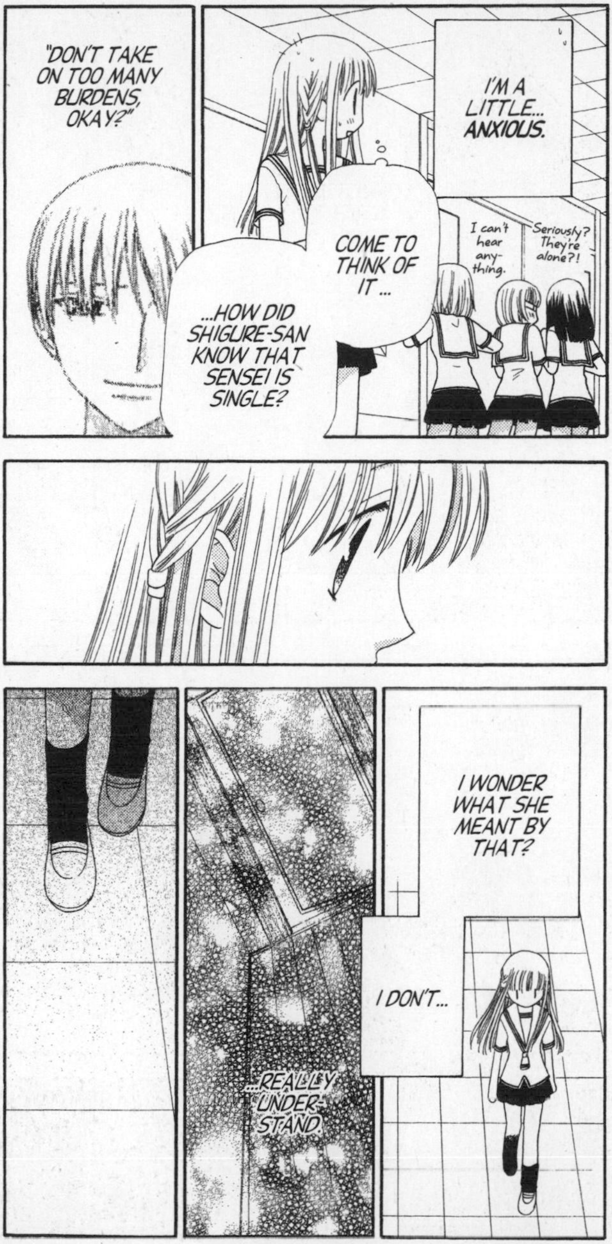
I'M A LITTLE... ANXIOUS.
Seriously? They're alone?!
I can't hear any-thing.
COME TO THINK OF IT ...
...HOW DID SHIGURE-SAN KNOW THAT SENSEI IS SINGLE?
"DON'T TAKE ON TOO MANY BURDENS, OKAY?"
I WONDER WHAT SHE MEANT BY THAT?
I DON'T...
...REALLY UNDER-STAND.

A story for here alone.

I got a letter saying, "We miss hearing about your life!"

So...a short return. I'm sorry, but really, not much has changed. I work, play video games, sometimes go to see plays or movies, get sick, go back to work... this is my life.

Oh yeah...When I was playing games earlier, and tried wearing headphones, I was really surprised. There were sounds I had never heard before! I guess my TV just has really bad speakers. I was so shocked that I dug out some of my old games and tried playing all of them again with headphones. There were so many sounds I didn't know about! (sob)

...Such is my life.

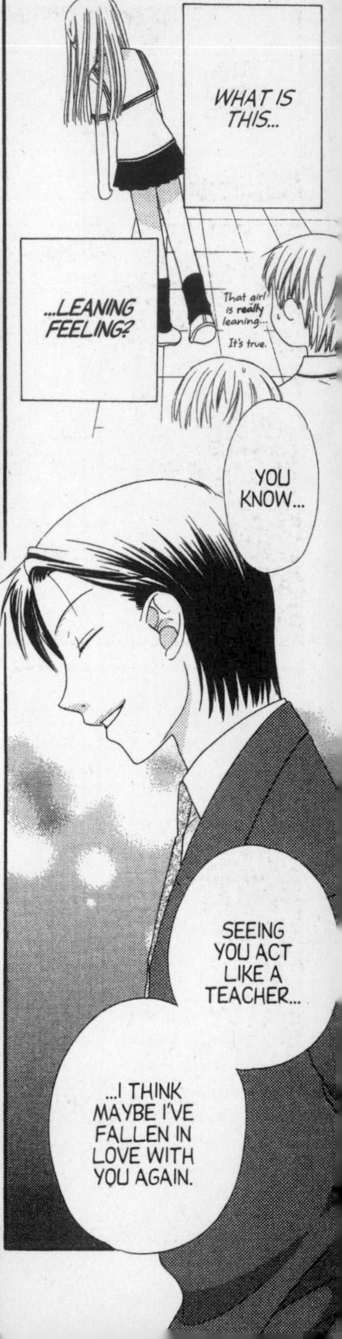
WHAT IS THIS...
...LEANING FEELING?
That girl is really leaning...
It's true.
YOU KNOW...
SEEING YOU ACT LIKE A TEACHER...
...I THINK MAYBE I'VE FALLEN IN LOVE WITH YOU AGAIN.
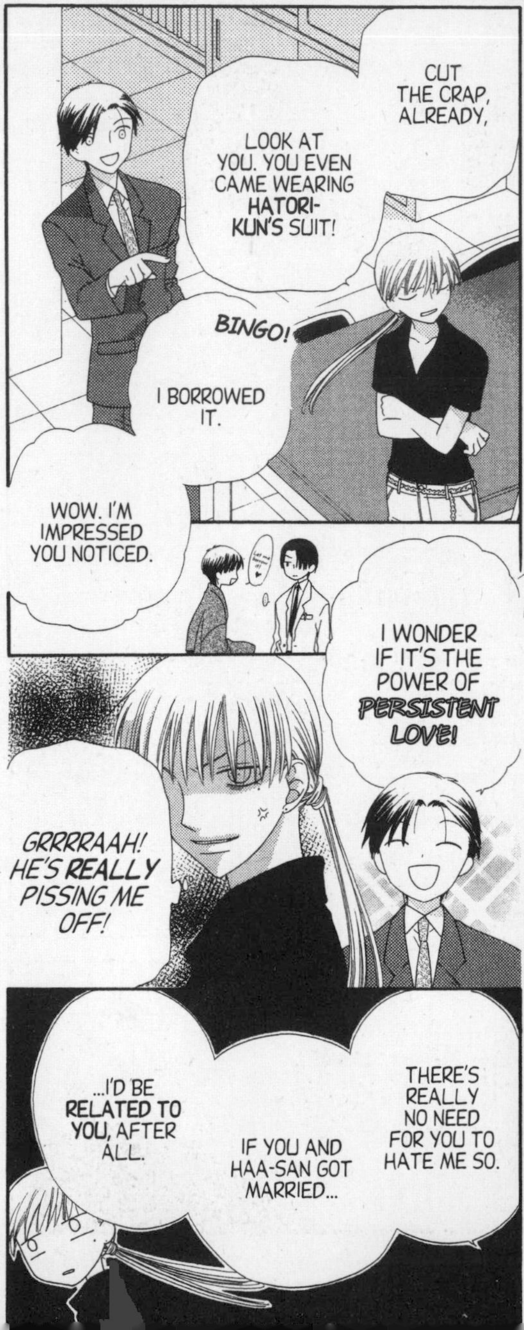
CUT THE CRAP, ALREADY,
LOOK AT YOU. YOU EVEN CAME WEARING **HATORI-KUN'S** SUIT!
BINGO!
I BORROWED IT.
WOW. I'M IMPRESSED YOU NOTICED.
I WONDER IF IT'S THE POWER OF ***PERSISTENT LOVE!***
*GRRRRAAH! HE'S **REALLY** PISSING ME OFF!*
THERE'S REALLY NO NEED FOR YOU TO HATE ME SO.
IF YOU AND HAA-SAN GOT MARRIED...
...I'D BE **RELATED TO YOU,** AFTER ALL.

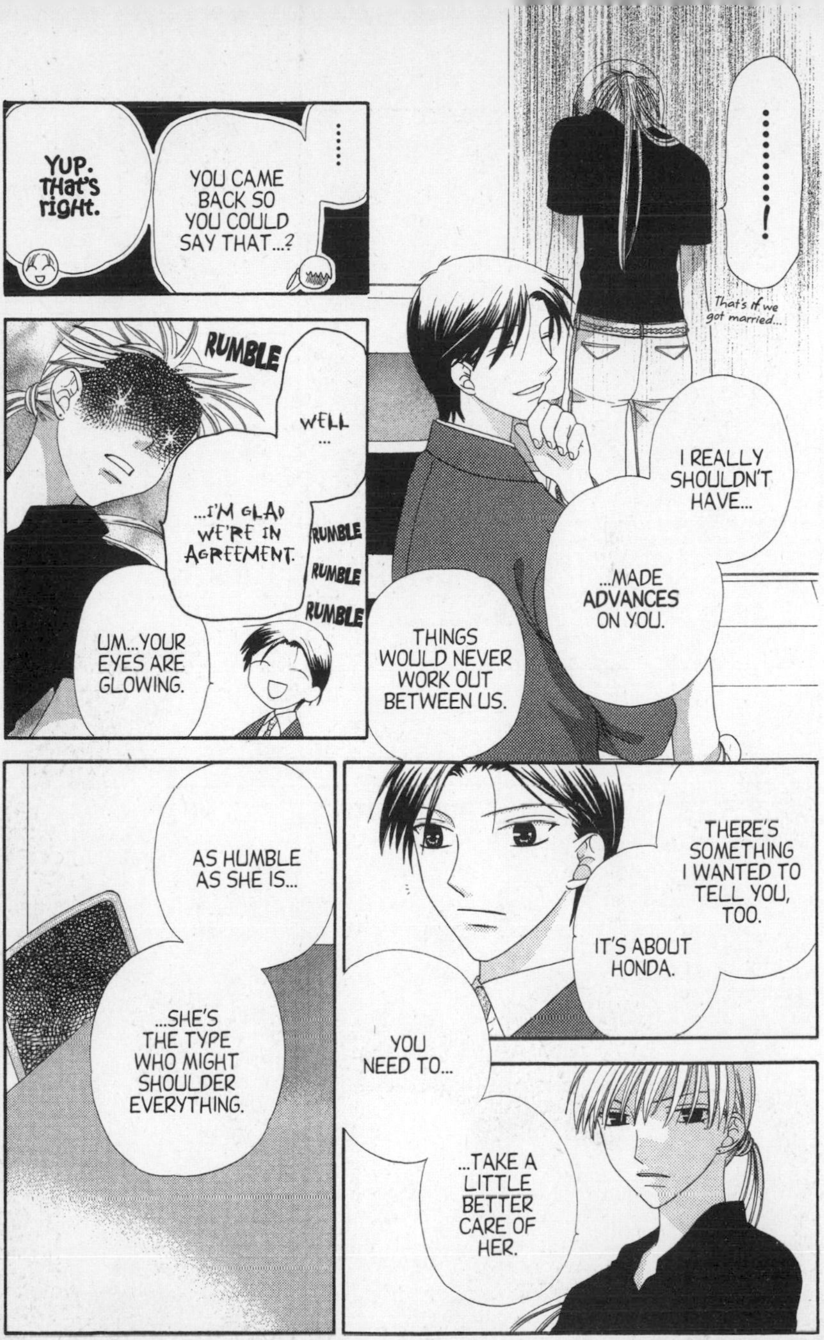
......!
That's if we got married...
I REALLY SHOULDN'T HAVE...
...MADE ADVANCES ON YOU.
THINGS WOULD NEVER WORK OUT BETWEEN US.
......
YOU CAME BACK SO YOU COULD SAY THAT...?
YUP. THAT'S RIGHT.
RUMBLE
WELL ...
...I'M GLAD WE'RE IN AGREEMENT.
RUMBLE
RUMBLE
RUMBLE
UM...YOUR EYES ARE GLOWING.
THERE'S SOMETHING I WANTED TO TELL YOU, TOO.
IT'S ABOUT HONDA.
YOU NEED TO...
...TAKE A LITTLE BETTER CARE OF HER.
AS HUMBLE AS SHE IS...
...SHE'S THE TYPE WHO MIGHT SHOULDER EVERYTHING.

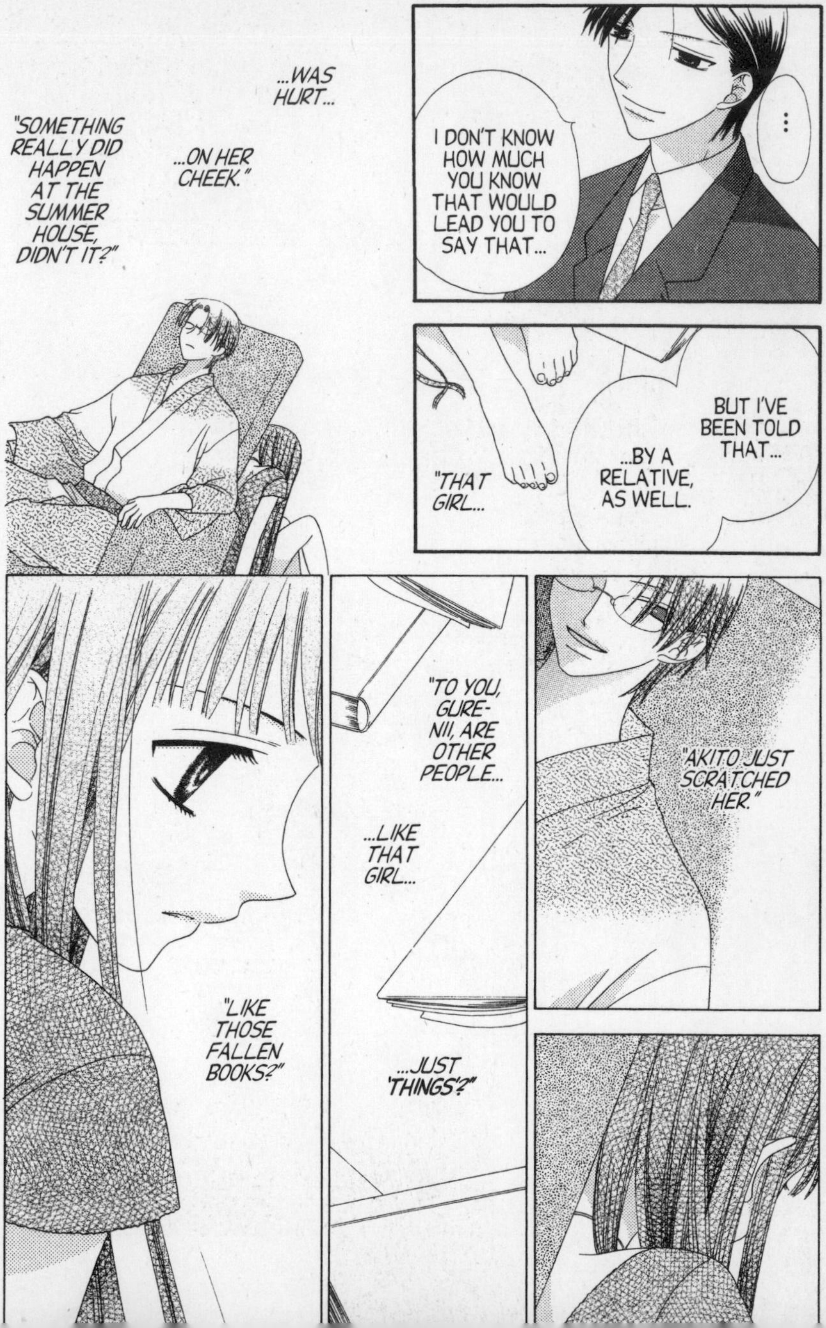
...
I DON'T KNOW HOW MUCH YOU KNOW THAT WOULD LEAD YOU TO SAY THAT...
BUT I'VE BEEN TOLD THAT...
...BY A RELATIVE, AS WELL.
"THAT GIRL...
...WAS HURT...
...ON HER CHEEK."
"SOMETHING REALLY DID HAPPEN AT THE SUMMER HOUSE, DIDN'T IT?"
"AKITO JUST SCRATCHED HER."
"TO YOU, GURE-NII, ARE OTHER PEOPLE...
...LIKE THAT GIRL...
...JUST 'THINGS'?"
"LIKE THOSE FALLEN BOOKS?"

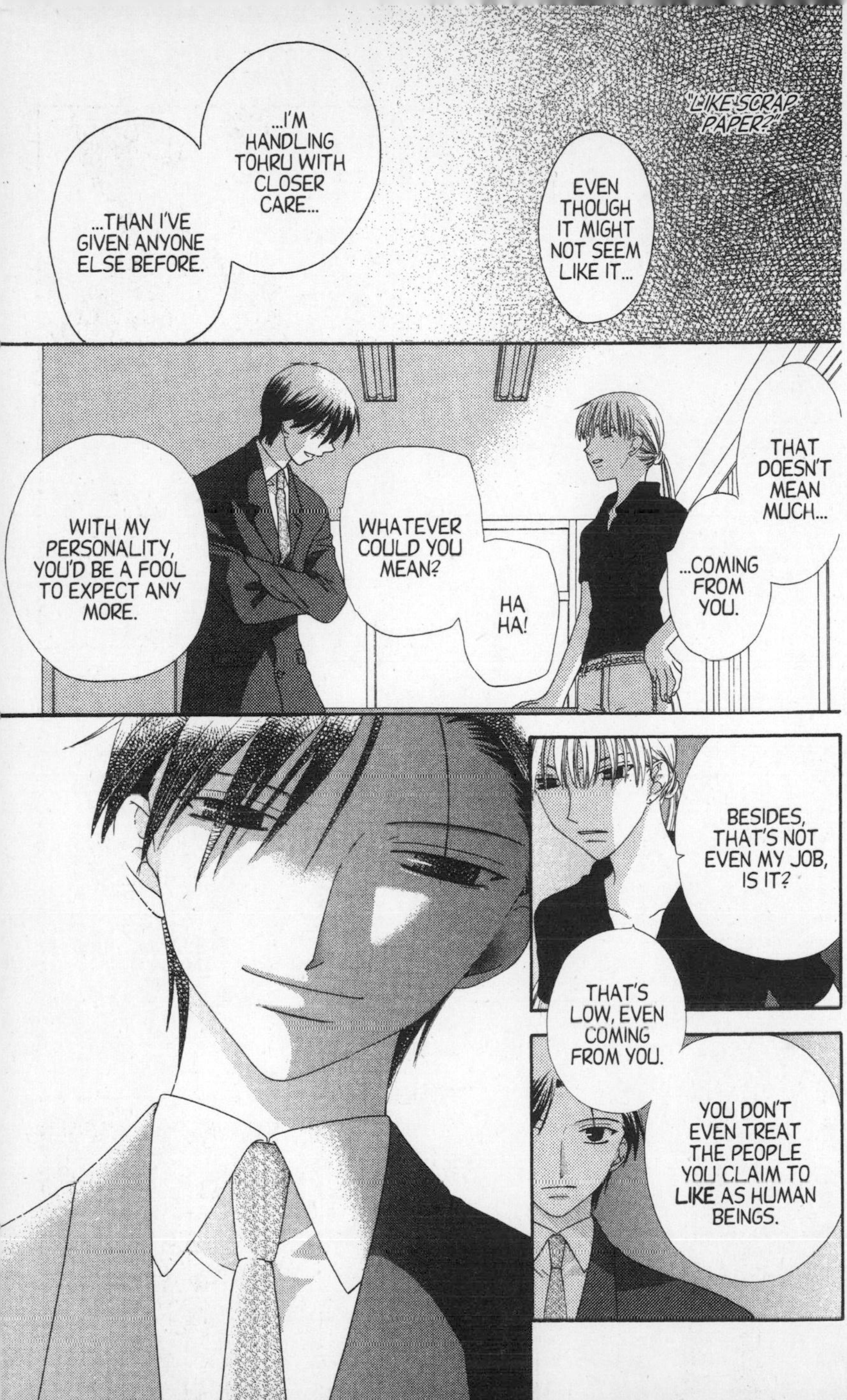
"LIKE SCRAP PAPER?"
EVEN THOUGH IT MIGHT NOT SEEM LIKE IT...
...I'M HANDLING TOHRU WITH CLOSER CARE...
...THAN I'VE GIVEN ANYONE ELSE BEFORE.
THAT DOESN'T MEAN MUCH...
...COMING FROM YOU.
WHATEVER COULD YOU MEAN?
HA HA!
WITH MY PERSONALITY, YOU'D BE A FOOL TO EXPECT ANY MORE.
BESIDES, THAT'S NOT EVEN MY JOB, IS IT?
THAT'S LOW, EVEN COMING FROM YOU.
YOU DON'T EVEN TREAT THE PEOPLE YOU CLAIM TO LIKE AS HUMAN BEINGS.

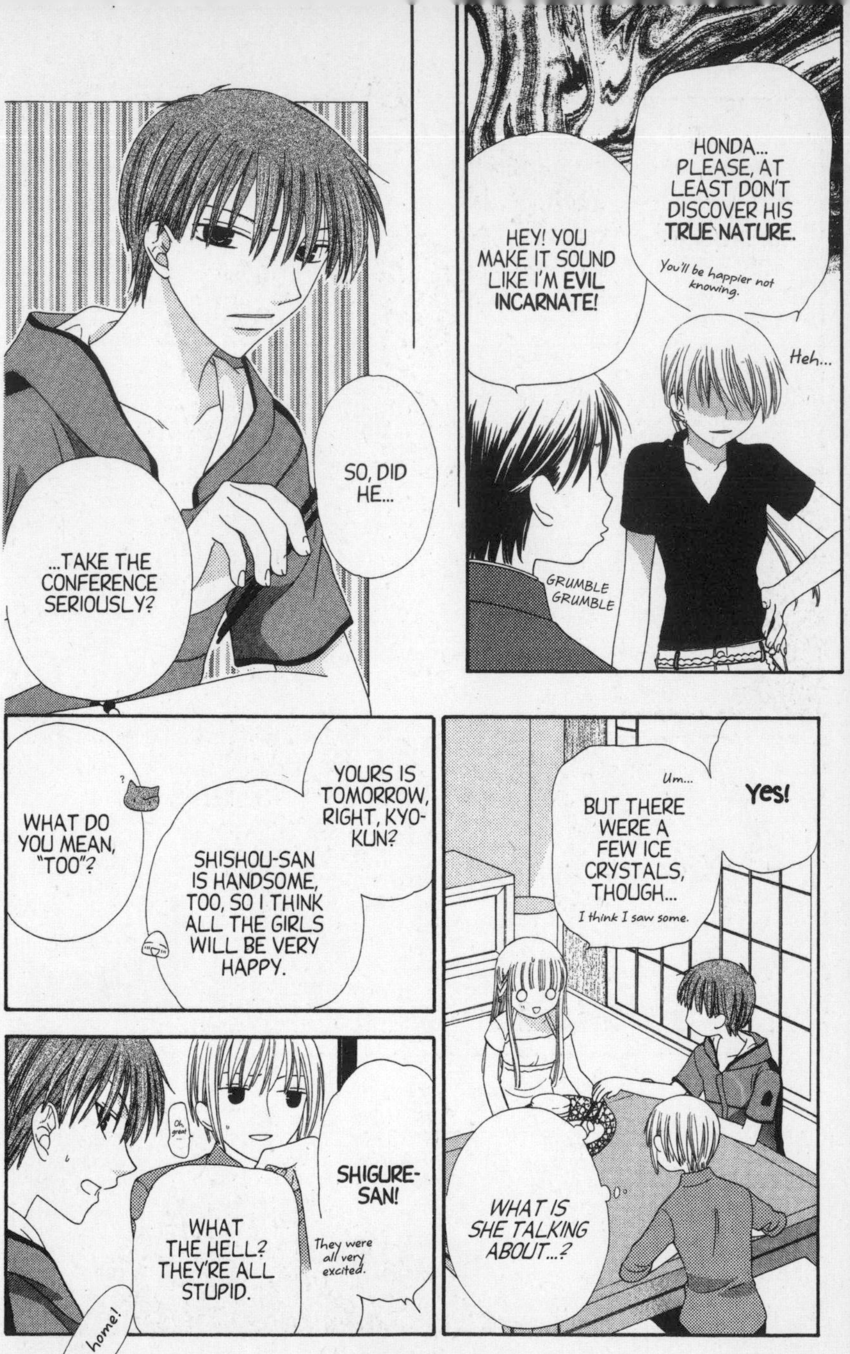
HONDA... PLEASE, AT LEAST DON'T DISCOVER HIS **TRUE NATURE.**
You'll be happier not knowing.
HEY! YOU MAKE IT SOUND LIKE I'M **EVIL INCARNATE!**
Heh...
GRUMBLE GRUMBLE
SO, DID HE...
...TAKE THE CONFERENCE SERIOUSLY?
YES!
Um...
BUT THERE WERE A FEW ICE CRYSTALS, THOUGH...
I think I saw some.
WHAT IS SHE TALKING ABOUT...?
YOURS IS TOMORROW, RIGHT, KYO-KUN?
SHISHOU-SAN IS HANDSOME, TOO, SO I THINK ALL THE GIRLS WILL BE VERY HAPPY.
WHAT DO YOU MEAN, "TOO"?
SHIGURE-SAN!
They were all very excited.
WHAT THE HELL? THEY'RE ALL STUPID.
Oh, great...
I'm home!

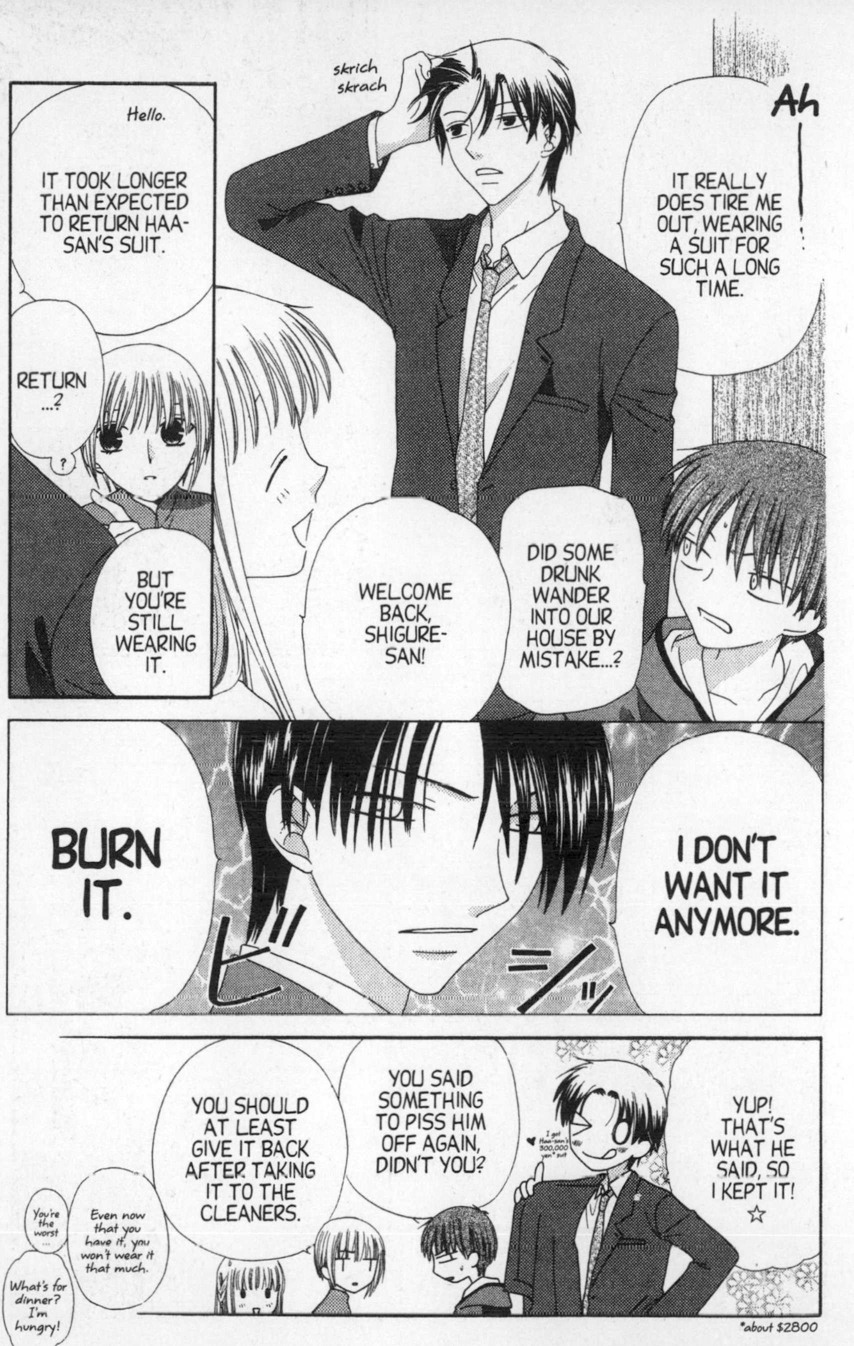
Ah
IT REALLY DOES TIRE ME OUT, WEARING A SUIT FOR SUCH A LONG TIME.
skrich skrach
DID SOME DRUNK WANDER INTO OUR HOUSE BY MISTAKE...?
WELCOME BACK, SHIGURE-SAN!
Hello.
IT TOOK LONGER THAN EXPECTED TO RETURN HAA-SAN'S SUIT.
RETURN ...?
?
BUT YOU'RE STILL WEARING IT.
I DON'T WANT IT ANYMORE.
BURN IT.
YUP! THAT'S WHAT HE SAID, SO I KEPT IT! ☆
I got Haa-san's 300,000 yen* suit
YOU SAID SOMETHING TO PISS HIM OFF AGAIN, DIDN'T YOU?
YOU SHOULD AT LEAST GIVE IT BACK AFTER TAKING IT TO THE CLEANERS.
Even now that you have it, you won't wear it that much.
You're the worst...
What's for dinner? I'm hungry!

*about $2800

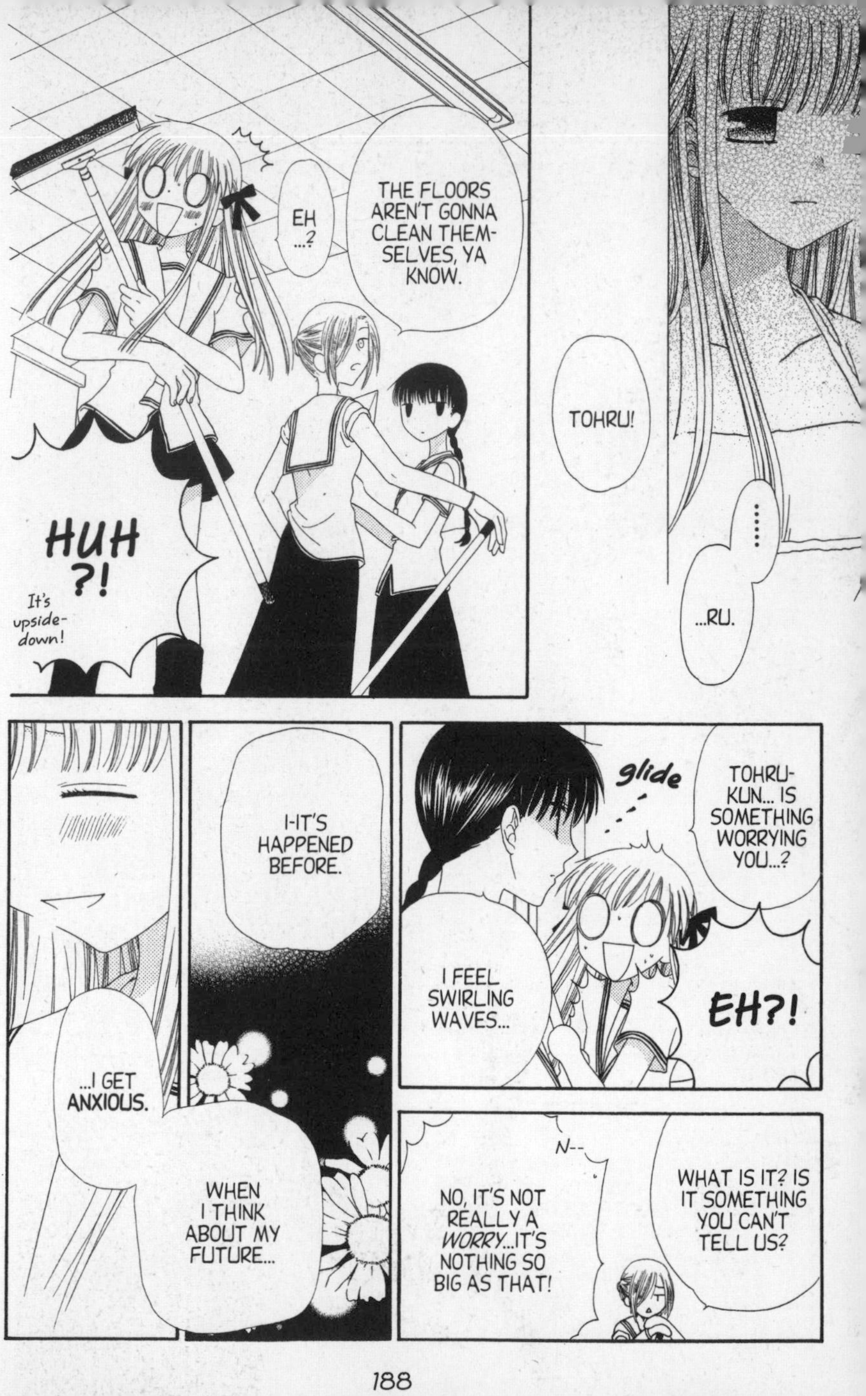
TOHRU!
......
...RU.
THE FLOORS AREN'T GONNA CLEAN THEMSELVES, YA KNOW.
EH ...?
HUH ?!
It's upside-down!
glide
TOHRU-KUN... IS SOMETHING WORRYING YOU...?
EH?!
I FEEL SWIRLING WAVES...
WHAT IS IT? IS IT SOMETHING YOU CAN'T TELL US?
N--
NO, IT'S NOT REALLY A *WORRY*...IT'S NOTHING SO BIG AS THAT!
I-IT'S HAPPENED BEFORE.
WHEN I THINK ABOUT MY FUTURE...
...I GET ANXIOUS.

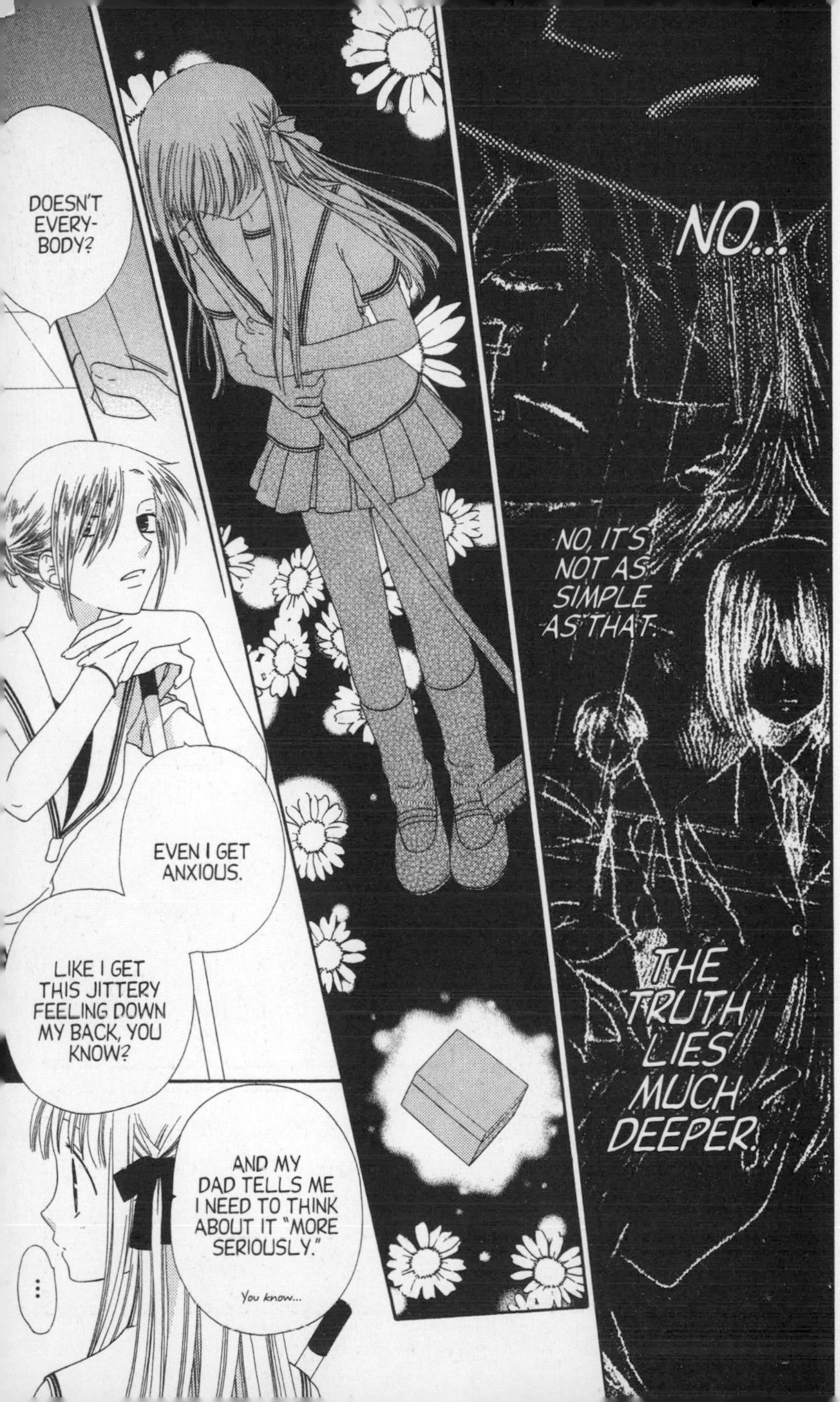
NO...
NO, IT'S NOT AS SIMPLE AS THAT.
THE TRUTH LIES MUCH DEEPER.
DOESN'T EVERY-BODY?
EVEN I GET ANXIOUS.
LIKE I GET THIS JITTERY FEELING DOWN MY BACK, YOU KNOW?
AND MY DAD TELLS ME I NEED TO THINK ABOUT IT "MORE SERIOUSLY."
You know...
...

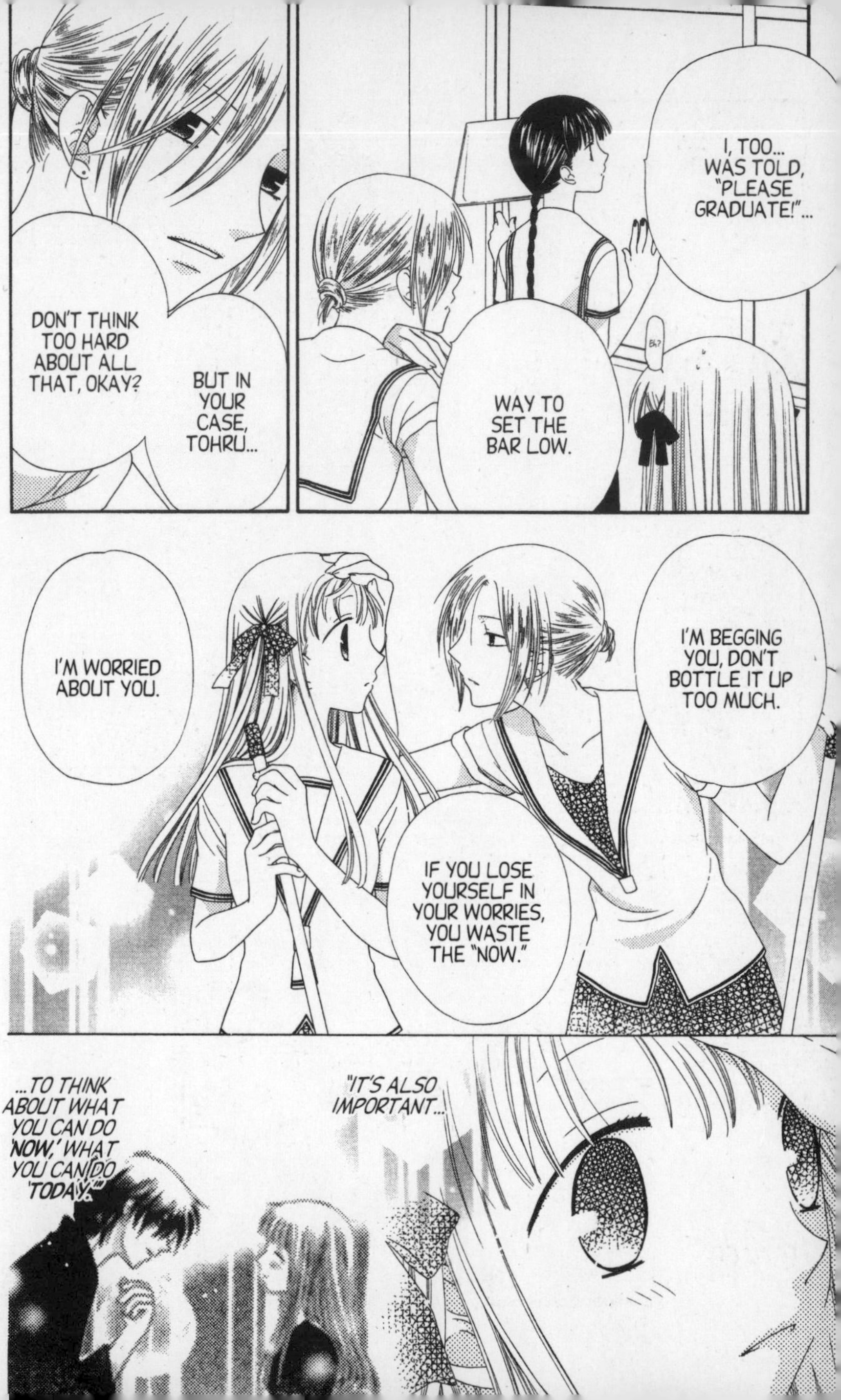
I, TOO... WAS TOLD, "PLEASE GRADUATE!"...
Eh?
WAY TO SET THE BAR LOW.
BUT IN YOUR CASE, TOHRU...
DON'T THINK TOO HARD ABOUT ALL THAT, OKAY?
I'M BEGGING YOU, DON'T BOTTLE IT UP TOO MUCH.
I'M WORRIED ABOUT YOU.
IF YOU LOSE YOURSELF IN YOUR WORRIES, YOU WASTE THE "NOW."
"IT'S ALSO IMPORTANT...
...TO THINK ABOUT WHAT YOU CAN DO 'NOW,' WHAT YOU CAN DO 'TODAY.'"

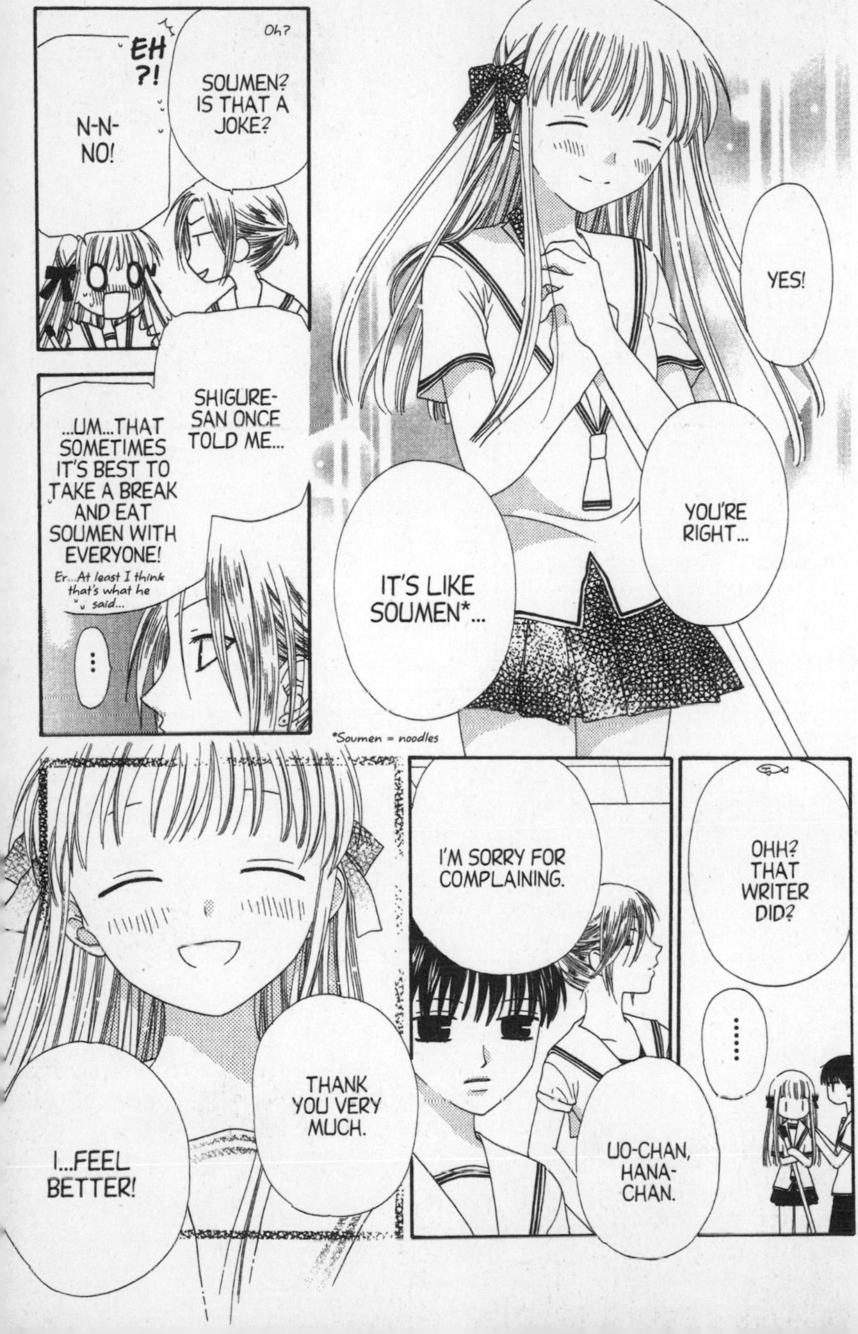
YES!
YOU'RE RIGHT...
IT'S LIKE SOUMEN*...
Oh?
SOUMEN? IS THAT A JOKE?
EH?!
N-N-NO!
SHIGURE-SAN ONCE TOLD ME...
...UM...THAT SOMETIMES IT'S BEST TO TAKE A BREAK AND EAT SOUMEN WITH EVERYONE!
Er...At least I think that's what he said...
...
OHH? THAT WRITER DID?
......
I'M SORRY FOR COMPLAINING.
UO-CHAN, HANA-CHAN.
THANK YOU VERY MUCH.
I...FEEL BETTER!

*Soumen = noodles

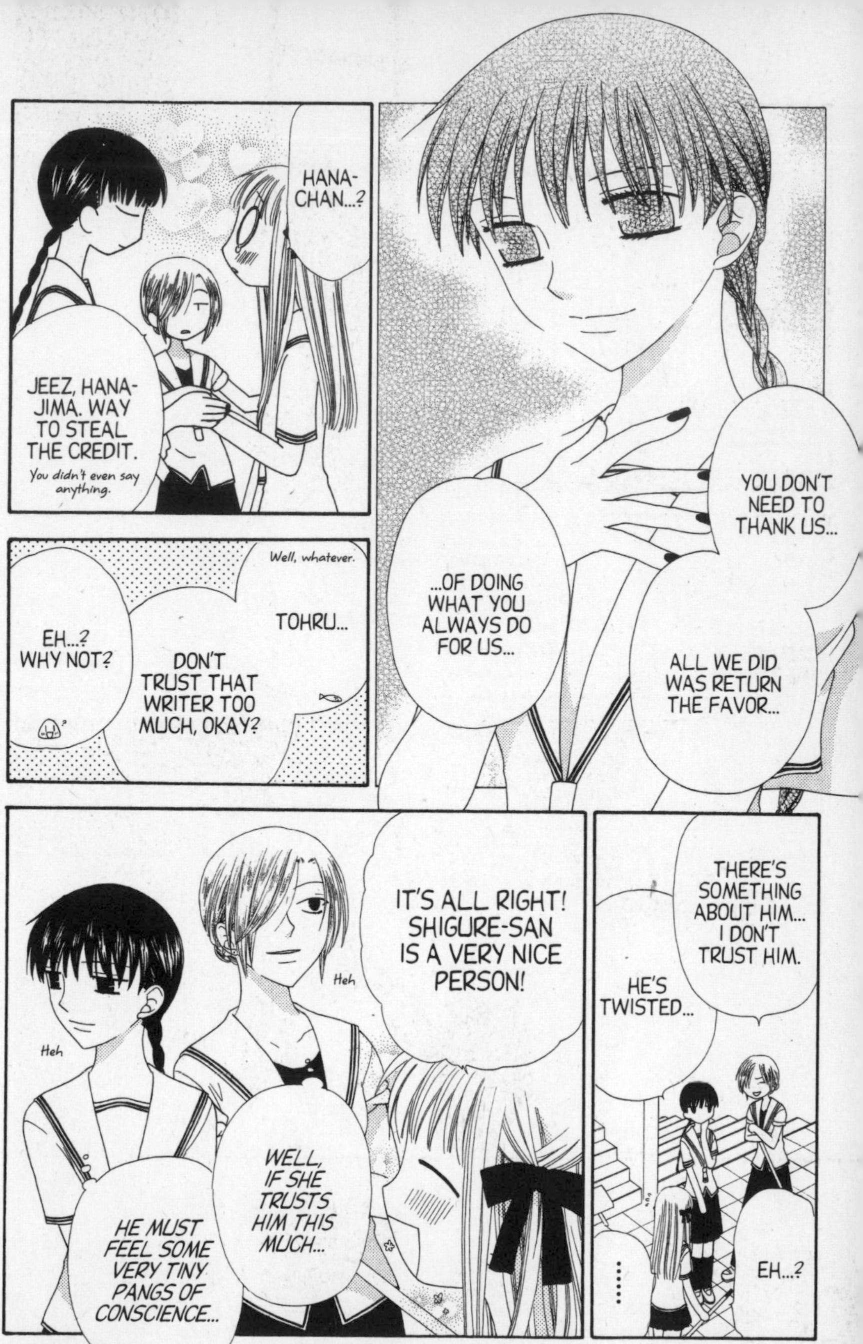
YOU DON'T NEED TO THANK US...
ALL WE DID WAS RETURN THE FAVOR...
...OF DOING WHAT YOU ALWAYS DO FOR US...
HANA-CHAN...?
JEEZ, HANAJIMA. WAY TO STEAL THE CREDIT.
You didn't even say anything.
Well, whatever.
TOHRU...
DON'T TRUST THAT WRITER TOO MUCH, OKAY?
EH...? WHY NOT?
THERE'S SOMETHING ABOUT HIM... I DON'T TRUST HIM.
HE'S TWISTED...
......
EH...?
IT'S ALL RIGHT! SHIGURE-SAN IS A VERY NICE PERSON!
Heh
WELL, IF SHE TRUSTS HIM THIS MUCH...
Heh
HE MUST FEEL SOME VERY TINY PANGS OF CONSCIENCE...

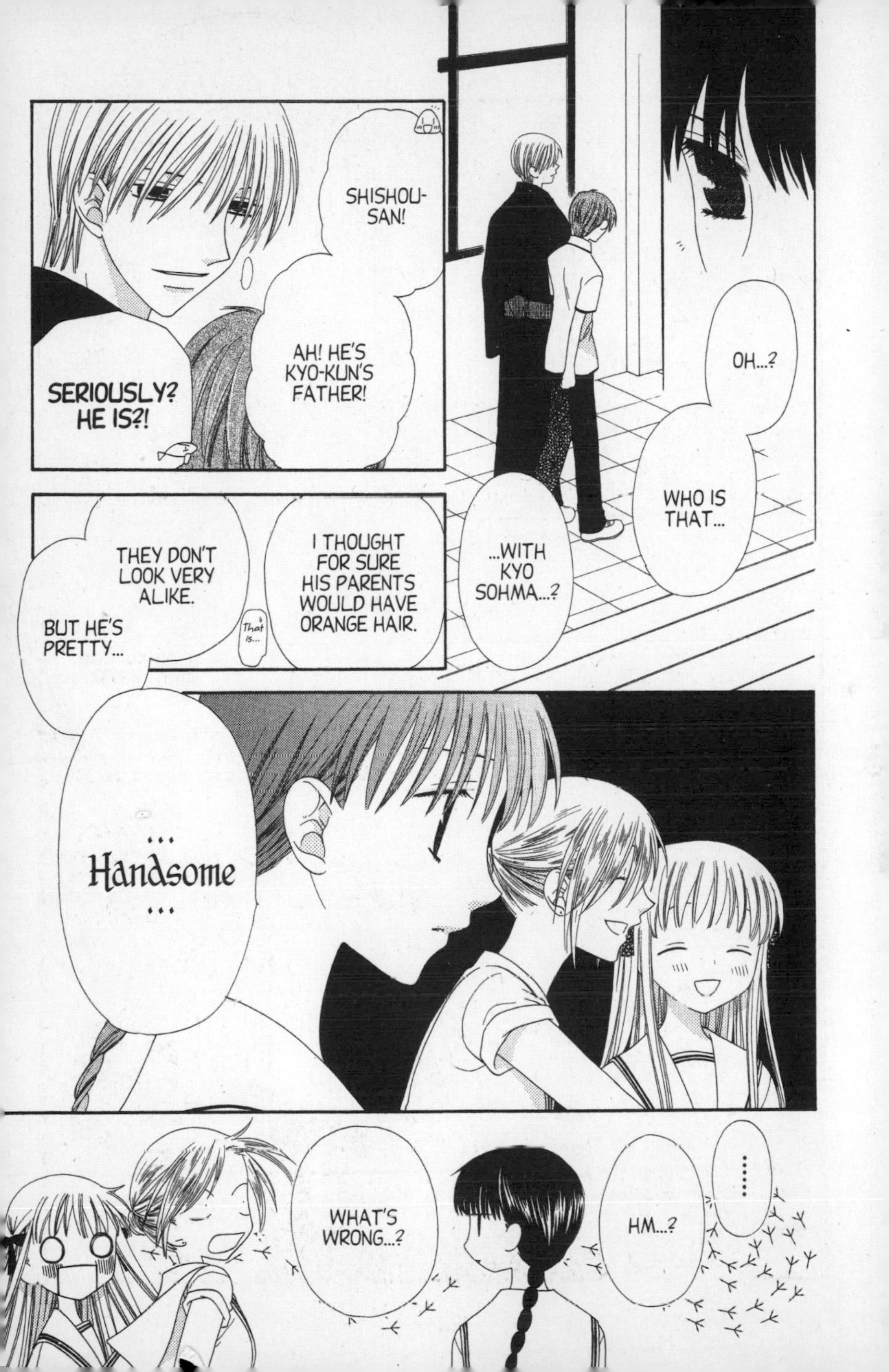
OH...?
WHO IS THAT...
...WITH KYO SOHMA...?
SHISHOU-SAN!
AH! HE'S KYO-KUN'S FATHER!
SERIOUSLY? HE IS?!
I THOUGHT FOR SURE HIS PARENTS WOULD HAVE ORANGE HAIR.
That is...
THEY DON'T LOOK VERY ALIKE.
BUT HE'S PRETTY...
... Handsome ...
......
HM...?
WHAT'S WRONG...?

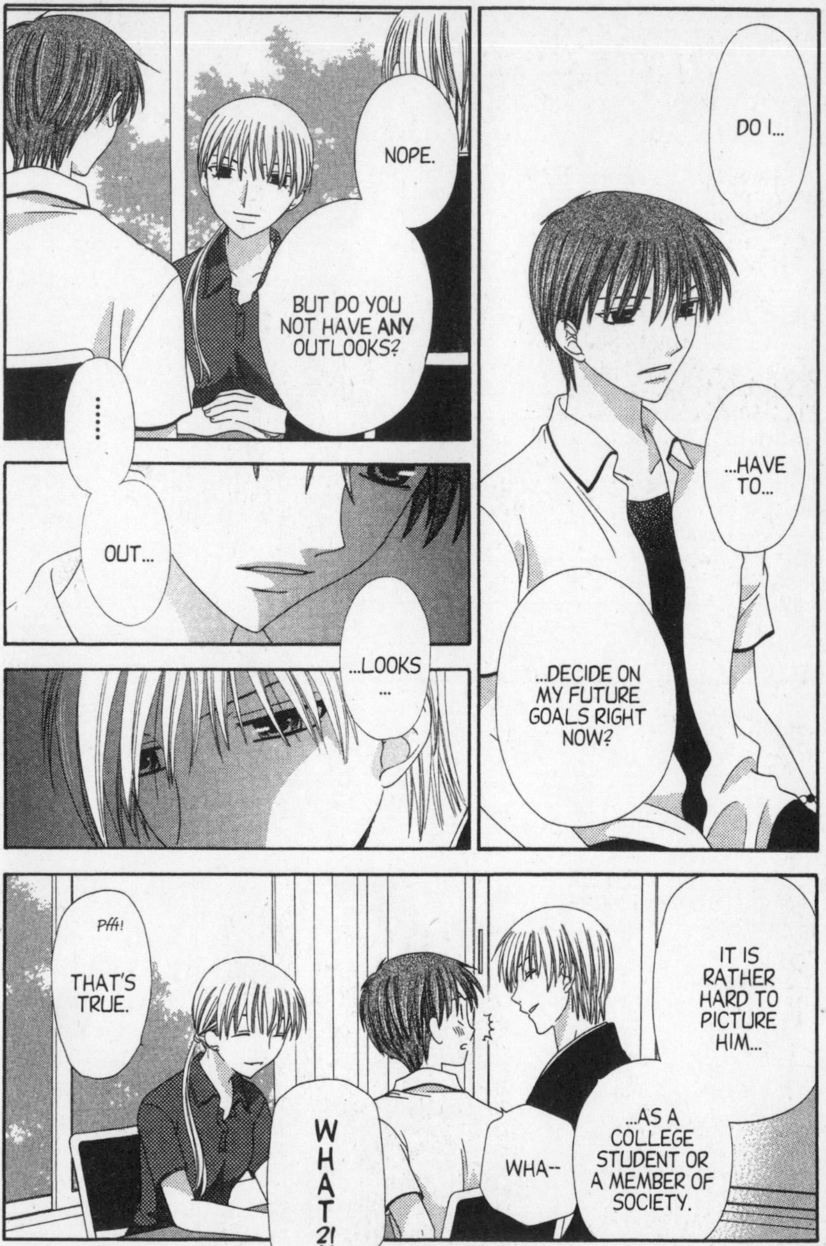
DO I...
...HAVE TO...
...DECIDE ON MY FUTURE GOALS RIGHT NOW?
NOPE.
BUT DO YOU NOT HAVE ANY OUTLOOKS?
......
OUT...
...LOOKS ...
IT IS RATHER HARD TO PICTURE HIM...
...AS A COLLEGE STUDENT OR A MEMBER OF SOCIETY.
WHA--
WHAT?!
Pff!
THAT'S TRUE.

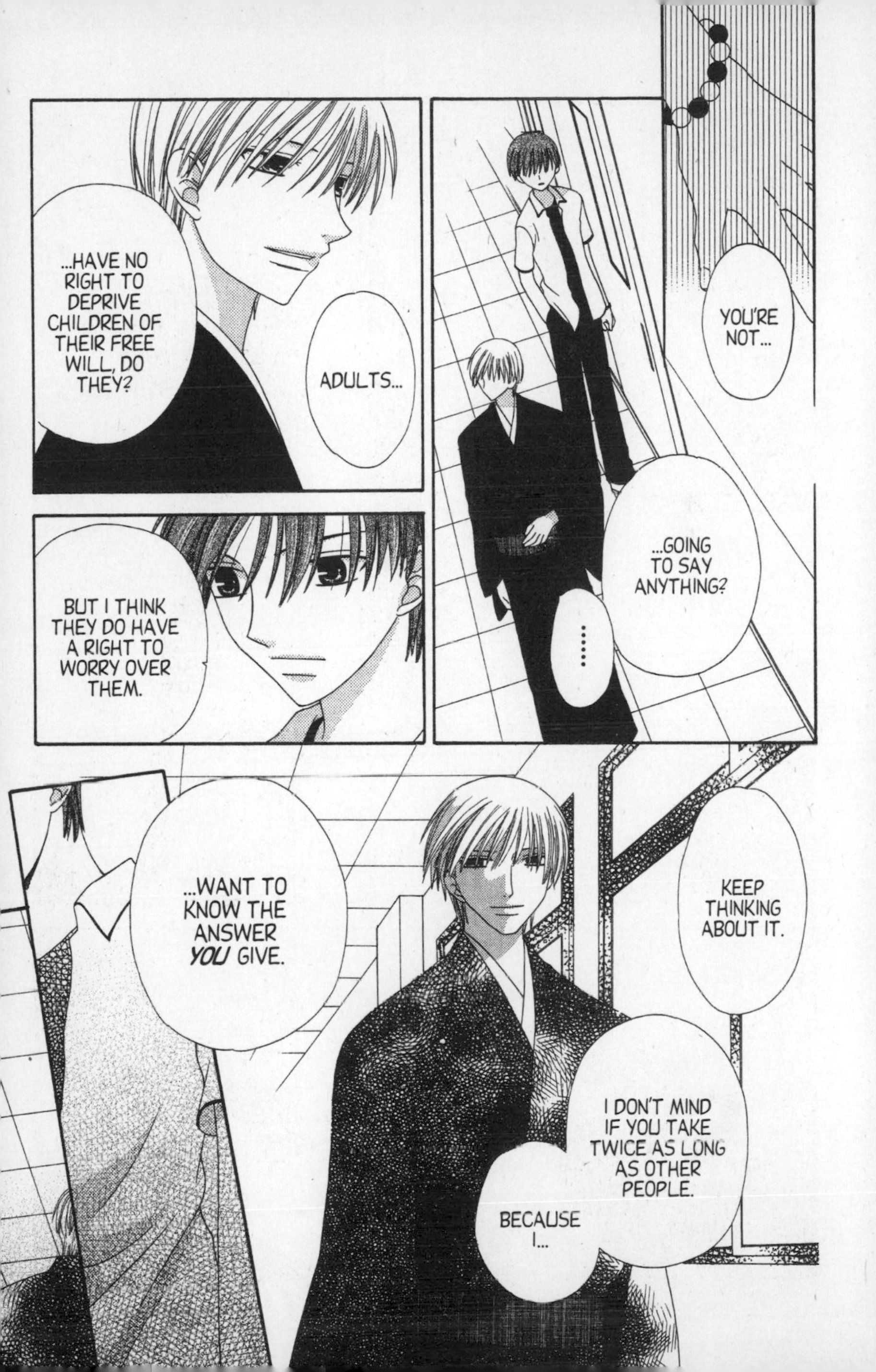
YOU'RE NOT...
...GOING TO SAY ANYTHING?
......
ADULTS...
...HAVE NO RIGHT TO DEPRIVE CHILDREN OF THEIR FREE WILL, DO THEY?
BUT I THINK THEY DO HAVE A RIGHT TO WORRY OVER THEM.
KEEP THINKING ABOUT IT.
I DON'T MIND IF YOU TAKE TWICE AS LONG AS OTHER PEOPLE.
BECAUSE I...
...WANT TO KNOW THE ANSWER *YOU* GIVE.

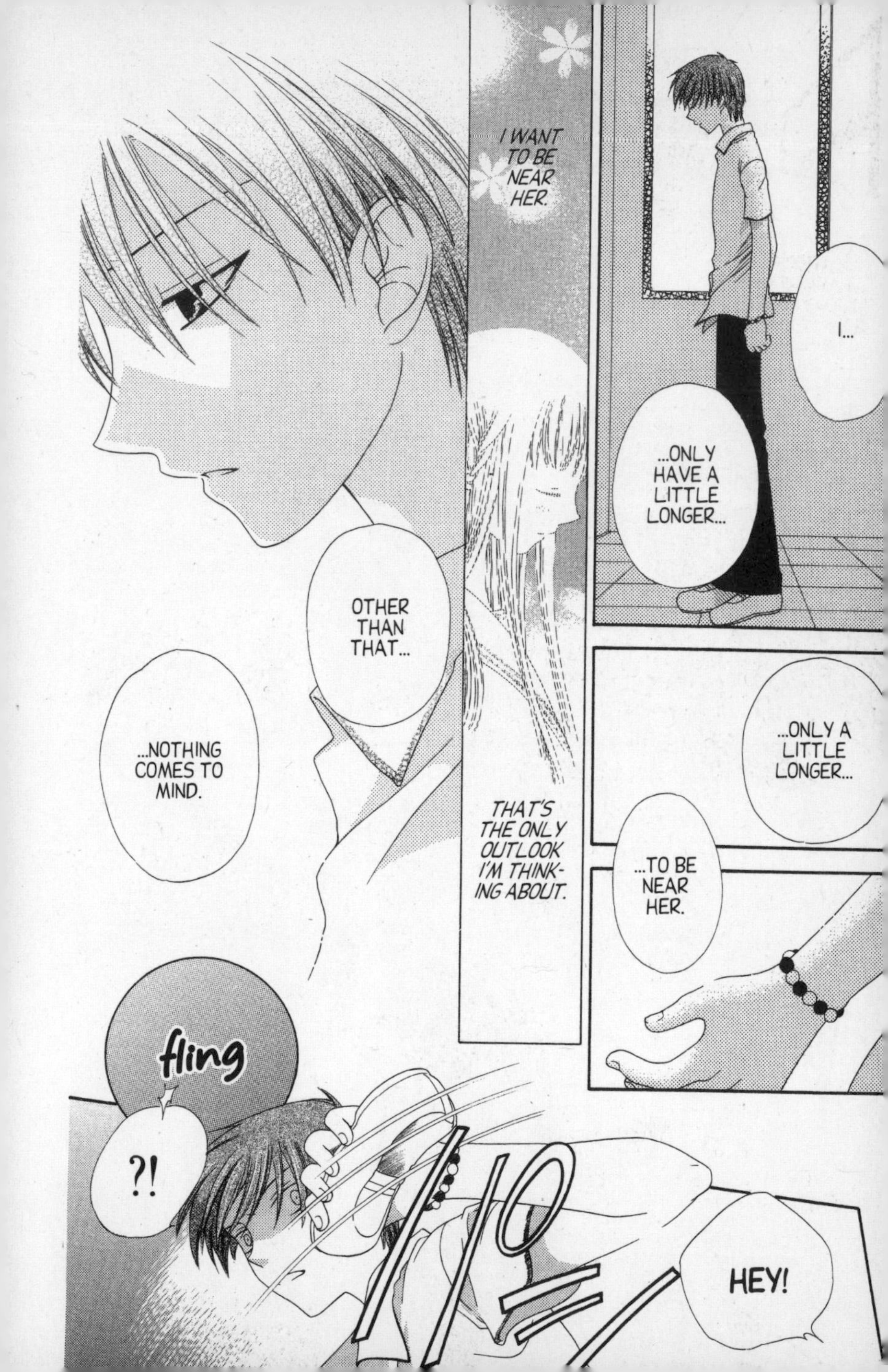
I...
...ONLY HAVE A LITTLE LONGER...
...ONLY A LITTLE LONGER...
...TO BE NEAR HER.
I WANT TO BE NEAR HER.
THAT'S THE ONLY OUTLOOK I'M THINKING ABOUT.
OTHER THAN THAT...
...NOTHING COMES TO MIND.
HEY!
fling
?!

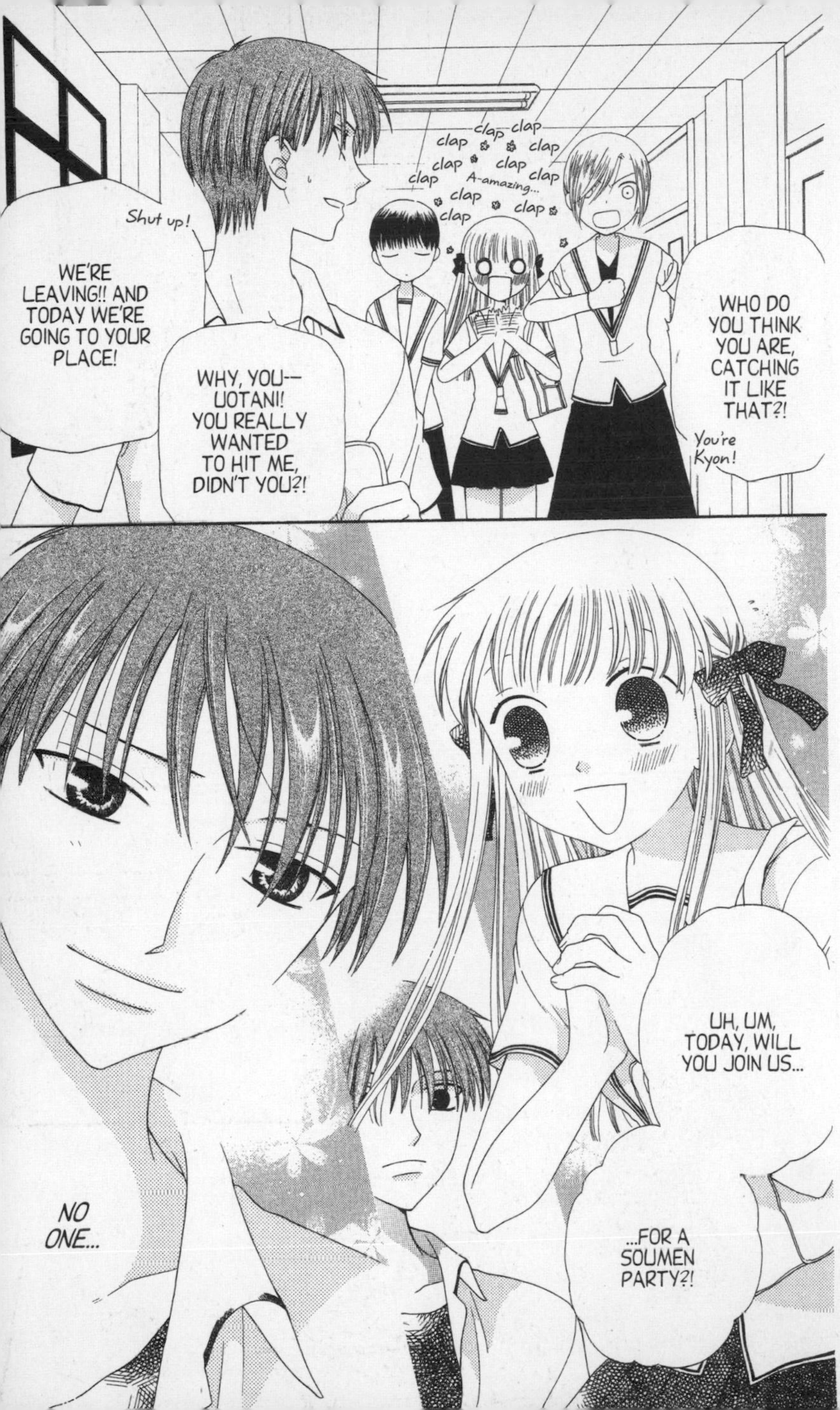
WHO DO YOU THINK YOU ARE, CATCHING IT LIKE THAT?!
You're Kyon!
clap clap clap clap clap clap clap clap clap clap clap
A-amazing...
WHY, YOU-- UOTANI! YOU REALLY WANTED TO HIT ME, DIDN'T YOU?!
Shut up!
WE'RE LEAVING!! AND TODAY WE'RE GOING TO YOUR PLACE!
UH, UM, TODAY, WILL YOU JOIN US...
...FOR A SOUMEN PARTY?!
NO ONE...

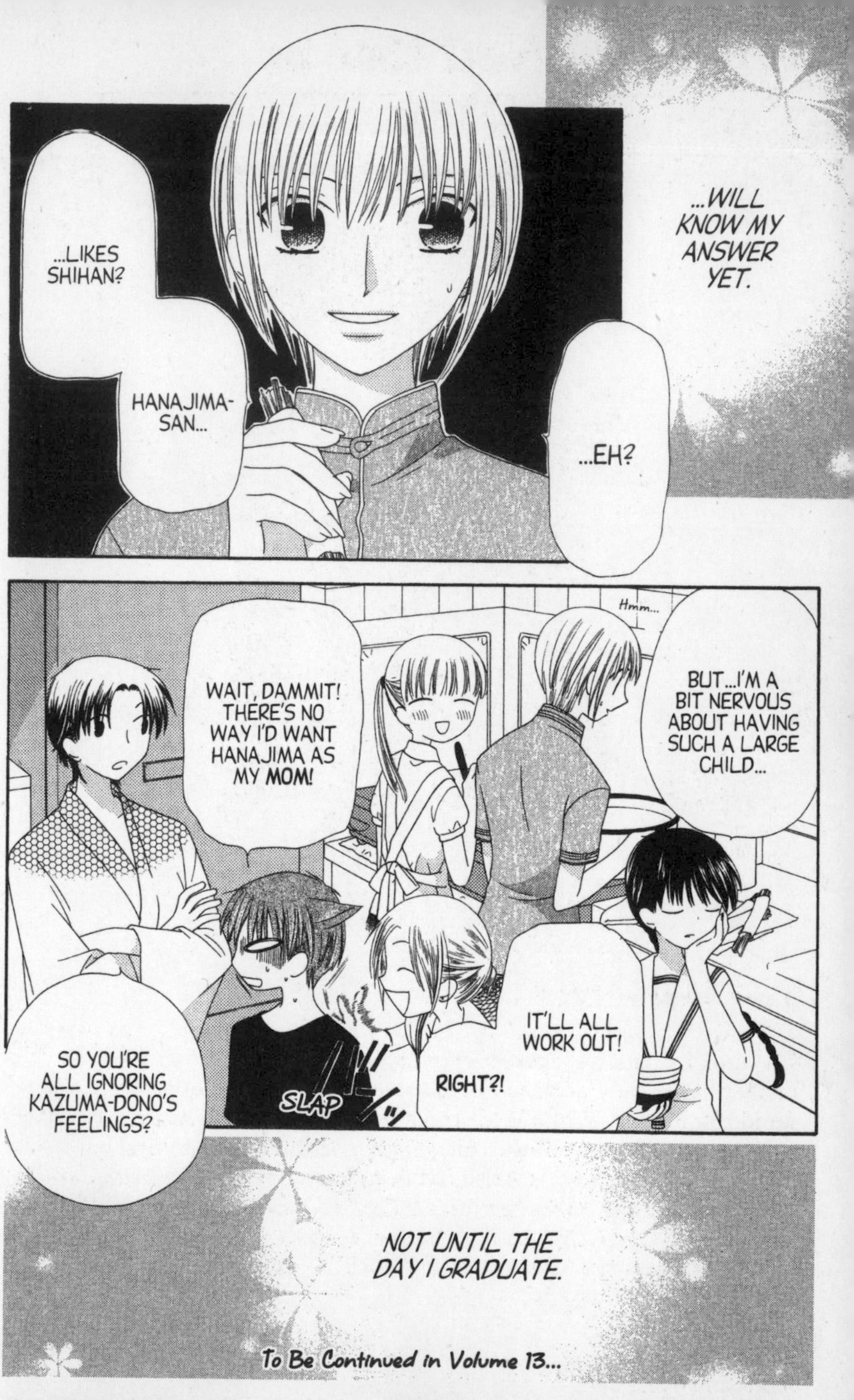

...WILL KNOW MY ANSWER YET.
HANAJIMA-SAN...
...LIKES SHIHAN?
...EH?
Hmm...
BUT...I'M A BIT NERVOUS ABOUT HAVING SUCH A LARGE CHILD...
WAIT, DAMMIT! THERE'S NO WAY I'D WANT HANAJIMA AS MY MOM!
IT'LL ALL WORK OUT!
RIGHT?!
SLAP
SO YOU'RE ALL IGNORING KAZUMA-DONO'S FEELINGS?
NOT UNTIL THE DAY I GRADUATE.
To Be Continued in Volume 13...

Next time in...

The #1 selling shojo manga in America!

Fruits Basket

TOKYOPOP

13

Natsuki Takaya

Yuki Takes a Stand...

The time for Yuki's parent-teacher conference has finally arrived, and Yuki's mother has already decided his future for him, because apparently Yuki can't decide for himself. While Yuki struggles to get a word in, Ayame shows up and ruffles many a feather. Meanwhile, Tohru goes on a quest to find out if Kureno Sohma is *the* Kureno that Arisa has been in love with all this time. Along the way, Tohru meets Momo--Momiji's little sister, who is tragically not allowed to talk with her big brother. Later, while on a class trip to Kyoto, a girl confesses to Kyo that she's in love with him! How will Kyo react? More importantly, how will Tohru feel about this?

Fruits Basket Volume 13
Available April 2006

Year of the Monkey: Chimps Ahoy!

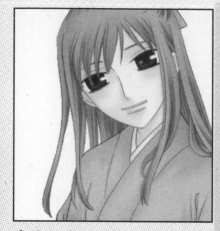

Monkey

Years*: 1944, 1956, 1968, 1980, 1992, 2004, 2016, 2028, 2040
Positive Qualities: Inventive, Entertaining, Opportunist, Popular, Versatile
Grievances: Distrusting, Easily Discouraged
Suitable Jobs: Financial Adviser, Banker, Actor, Comedian
Compatible With: Dragons, Rats
Must Avoid: Tigers
Ruling Hours: 3 PM to 5 PM
Season: Summer
Ruling Month: August
Sign Direction: West-Southwest
Fixed Element: Metal
Corresponding Western Sign: Leo

Whether swinging from trees or learning sign language, Monkeys are truly the unpredictable geniuses of the Chinese Zodiac. Given an infinite amount of Monkeys, mathematician Brett Watson and the late author Douglas Adams might just be right in assuming that Monkeys could bash out a script for Hamlet one of these days. Afterall, Monkeys do have an uncanny "Monkey see, Monkey do" ability whenever it comes to mimicking what humans do. For anyone born in the Year of the Monkey, the ninth cycle of the Chinese Zodiac, they will be blessed with the Monkey's undying curiosity and magnetic personality.

Clever to the core, Monkeys are quite intelligent and imaginative enough to come up with innovative new ways of doing daily tasks. Monkeys have an almost natural-born ability to see through difficult problems or even financial matters with relative ease. In fact, whenever money is concerned, Monkeys are perfectly suited to be stockbrokers, bankers and financial advisors. Unfortunately, the Monkey's easy success has its price; they tend to be easily confused and often become discouraged by the littlest hint of criticism--as in the case of Ritsu Sohma dressing like a girl.

Personality wise, Monkeys are very charming and energetic individuals that crave to be the center of attention. However, being an endless fun seeker has its drawbacks in that they are highly self-indulgent and often prone to temptation. Remaining vigilant and keeping the old saying "hear no evil, see no evil, speak no evil" in mind might just end up being a lifesaver.

Ladies born in this year tend to be very glamorous and enjoy keeping themselves neatly dressed. They are very particular about their hair, but can be excessive when it comes to cosmetics. Though easily agreeable and fun loving, ladies of this year are perfectionists and very vocal. They will never settle down with a partner unless they are evenly matched and challenged.

Celebrity Monkeys:
Gillian Anderson
Kim Cattrall
Geena Davis
Eliza Dushku
Carrie Fisher
Justin Timberlake
Naomi Watts
Elijah Wood

* Note: It is important to know what day Chinese New Year's was held on as that changes what Zodiac animal you are. Example: 1980 actually began on February 16 and anyone born before that date is actually a Sheep.

Fans Basket

Hello, faithful *Furuba* fans! Can you believe it's been *four months* since the last volume of *Fruits Basket* hit the bookstores? Since then, I've gotten more fan mail than ever! I may not have time to write everyone back, but I vow to read every letter and look at every piece of art that you dedicated fans send my way! You all make working on *Furuba* so much fun! Thank you!

- Paul Morrissey, Editor

Tohru & Kyo

When you've fallen in love
How do you escape
When all of your choices
Are made by fate
If you wait too long
The one you've been waiting for
Will be gone
So follow your heart
And try to say how you feel
Otherwise the one thing you dream
Will never be real

Kayla Marie Casper
Age 14
Prairieville, LA

Thanks, Kayla. I sure hope Tohru and Kyo follow the advice contained in your poem!

Phetmany Bounsana
Age 15
Wichita, KS

4.9.03

I love Tohru's dress, Phetmany. Her wings are a lovely touch, as well. Hmmm... Tohru *is* like an angel, isn't she? Nicely done! Good to know people are reading *Furuba* in Kansas, too!

Tori Schweyer
Age 14
Santa Cruz, CA

I really like this sketch of Kyo, Tori. It's full of attitude, and you've perfectly captured Kyo's cocky personality.

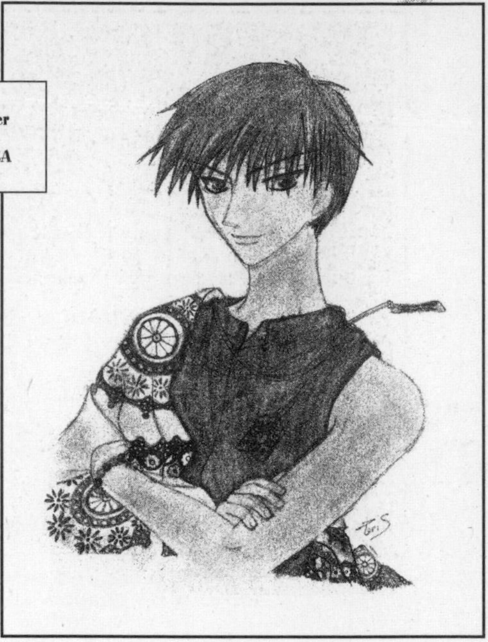

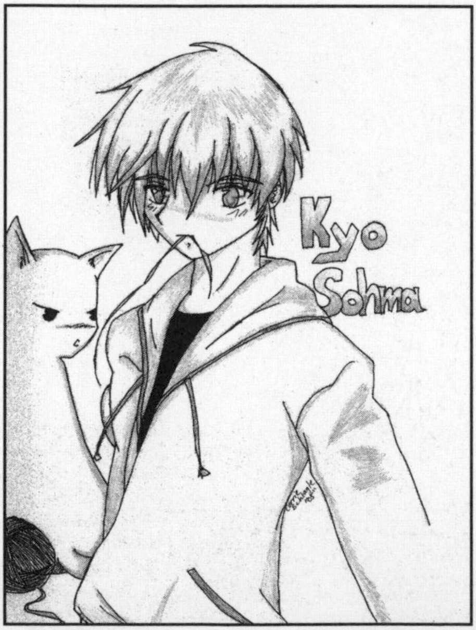
Kyo
Sohma

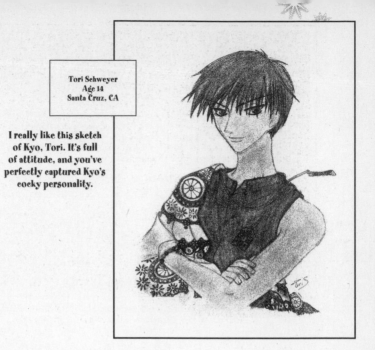

CJ Schlagle
Age 20
National Park, NJ

People really seem to be into Kyo these days. Personally, I'm probably more like Yuki, but I can understand why everyone loves Kyo. I love how he has a piece of yarn in his mouth. Nice touch, CJ!

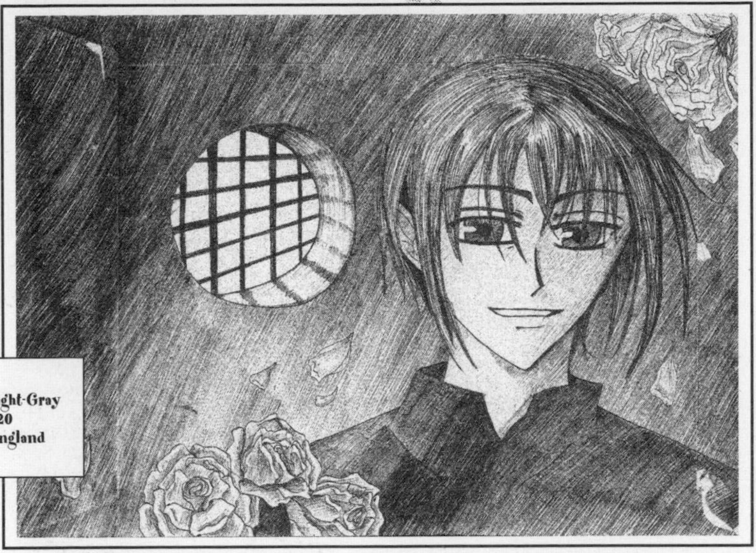

Rebecca Knight-Gray
Age 20
Surrey, England

Wow! Check this out! Believe it or not, this is the *envelope* in which Rebecca sent her fan art! All pen and ink. Amazing work, Rebecca.

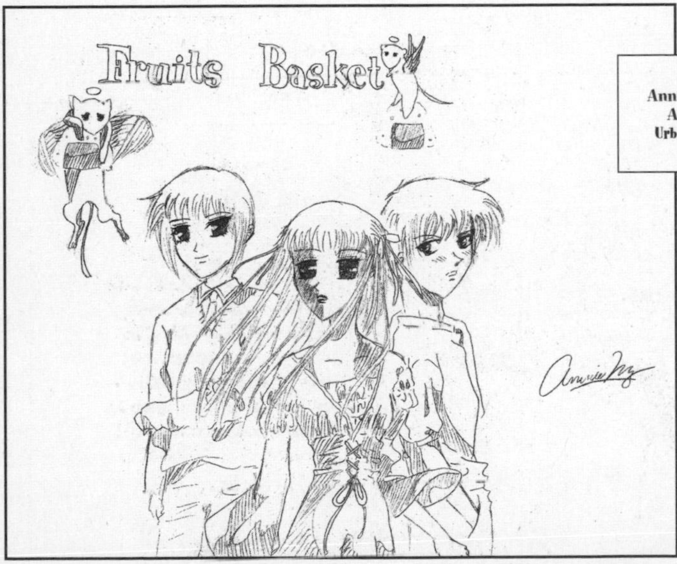
Fruits Basket

Annie Rong
Age 11
Urbana, IL

Awesome sketch, Annie. Everyone really seems to respond to the love triangle in *Fruits Basket*, and you're no exception. But why does poor Yuki have a halo and angel wings? Is that because, like Kyo, you want him dead? Hehe...

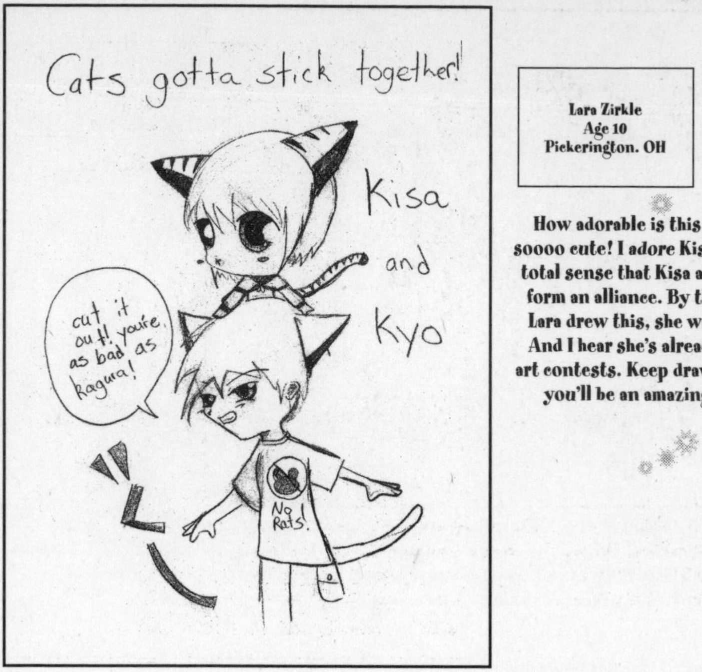
Cats gotta stick together!
Kisa and Kyo
cut it out!! you're as bad as kagura!
No Rats!

Lara Zirkle
Age 10
Pickerington. OH

How adorable is this picture? It's soooo cute! I adore Kisa, and it makes total sense that Kisa and Kyo would form an alliance. By the way, when Lara drew this, she was only nine! And I hear she's already won a few art contests. Keep drawing, Lara, and you'll be an amazing manga-ka!

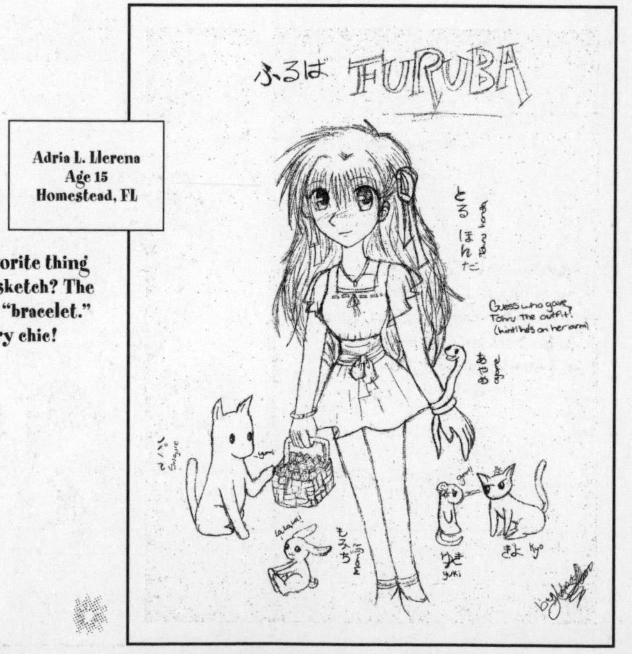
ふるば FURUBA
とおる ほんだ Tohru honda
Guess who gave Tohru the outfit! (hint: he's on her arm)
あやめ ayame
きよ Kyo

Adria L. Llerena
Age 15
Homestead, FL

My favorite thing in this sketch? The Ayame "bracelet." Very chic!

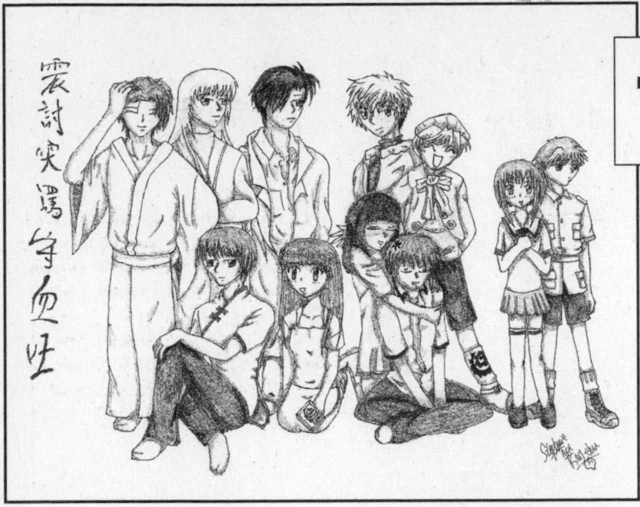

Kari-chan (aka Steph)
Age 18
Estancia, NM

Great job, Kari-chan! Here's Tohru and all of her friends. Speaking of friends, I particularly enjoyed reading what all of *your* friends wrote in your letter. They're very supportive of your art. That's cool. Thanks for making all of them *Furuba* fans, too!

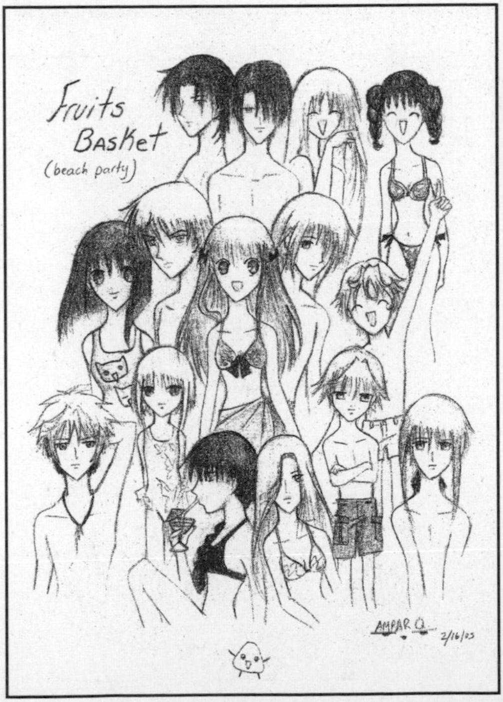
Fruits Basket
(beach party)
AMPARO
2/16/03

Ambar Quintero
Age 14
Somerton, AZ

Here's a great picture to keep you all warm during the winter month of December. Is that Ritsu in the bottom right corner? If so, I wonder why he didn't wear a bikini!

animetayl
Age 21
Calgary, Canada

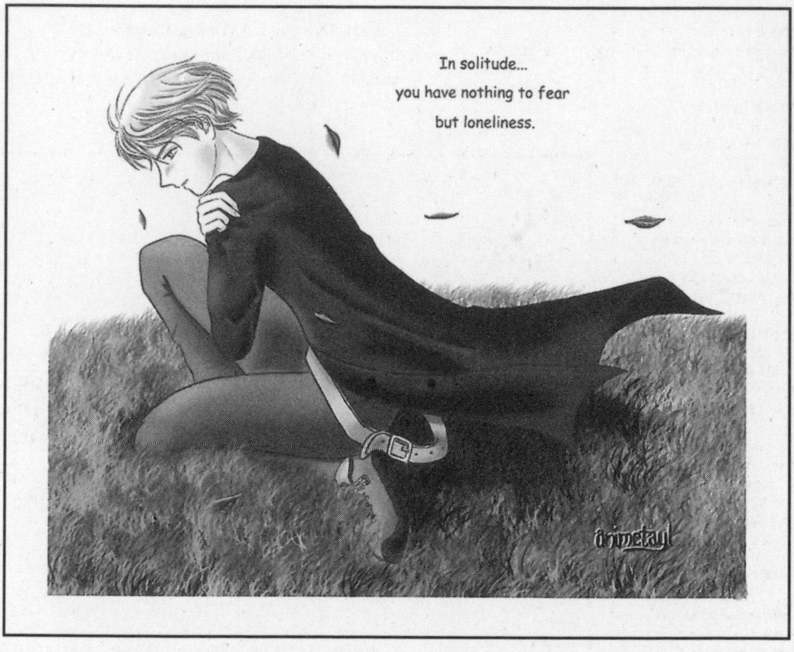
In solitude...
you have nothing to fear
but loneliness.
animetayl

Here's another piece featuring the moody and angsty Kyo. I love the grayscale "coloring," animetayl. And the accompanying haiku isn't too shabby, either!

Do you want to share your love for *Fruits Basket* with fans around the world? "Fans Basket" is taking submissions of fan art, poetry, cosplay photos, or any other Furuba fun you'd like to share!

How to submit:

1) Send your work via regular mail (NOT e-mail) to:

"Fans Basket"
c/o TOKYOPOP
5900 Wilshire Blvd.
Suite 2000
Los Angeles, CA 90036

2) All work should be in black-and-white and no larger than 8.5" x 11". (And try not to fold it too many times!)

3) Anything you send will not be returned. If you want to keep your original, it's fine to send us a copy.

4) Please include your full name, age, city and state for us to print with your work. If you'd rather us use a pen name, please include that, too.

5) IMPORTANT: If you're under the age of 18, you must have your parent's permission in order for us to print your work. Any submissions without a signed note of parental consent cannot be used.

6) For full details, please check out our website: http://www.tokyopop.com/aboutus/fanart.php

Disclaimer: Anything you send to us becomes the exclusive property of TOKYOPOP Inc. and, as we said before, will not be returned to you. We will have the right to print, reproduce, distribute, or modify the artwork for use in future volumes of Fruits Basket or on the web royalty-free.

Maggie Linehan
Age 13
Philadelphia, PA

Fantastic pen art, Maggie! You could use it to teach kids the sounds animals make! And Yuki *is* a "scuffling" kind of guy, isn't he?

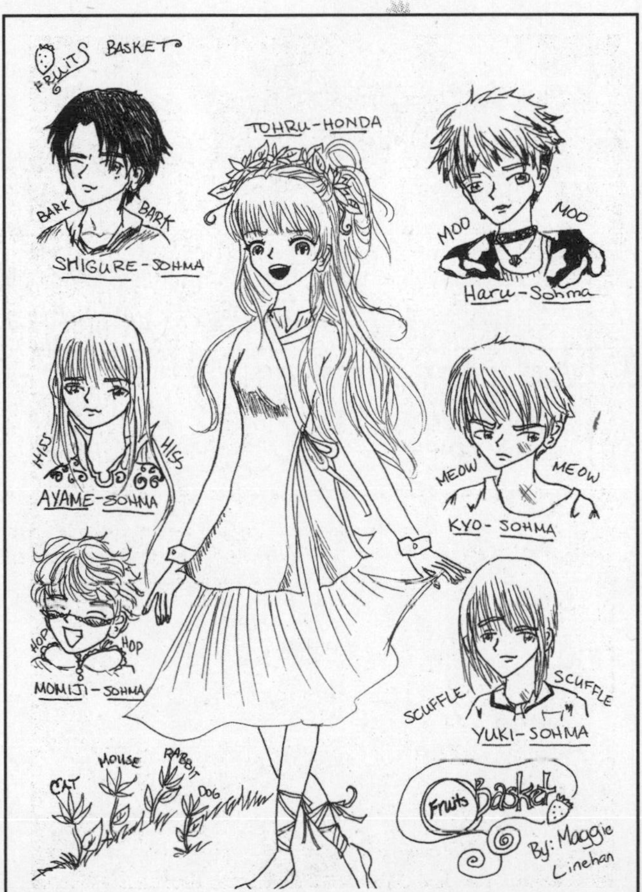

FRUITS BASKET
TOHRU-HONDA
BARK BARK
SHIGURE-SOHMA
MOO MOO
Haru-Sohma
HISS HISS
AYAME-SOHMA
MEOW MEOW
KYO-SOHMA
HOP HOP
MOMIJI-SOHMA
SCUFFLE SCUFFLE
YUKI-SOHMA
CAT
MOUSE
RABBIT
DOG
Fruits Basket
By: Maggie Linehan

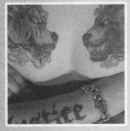

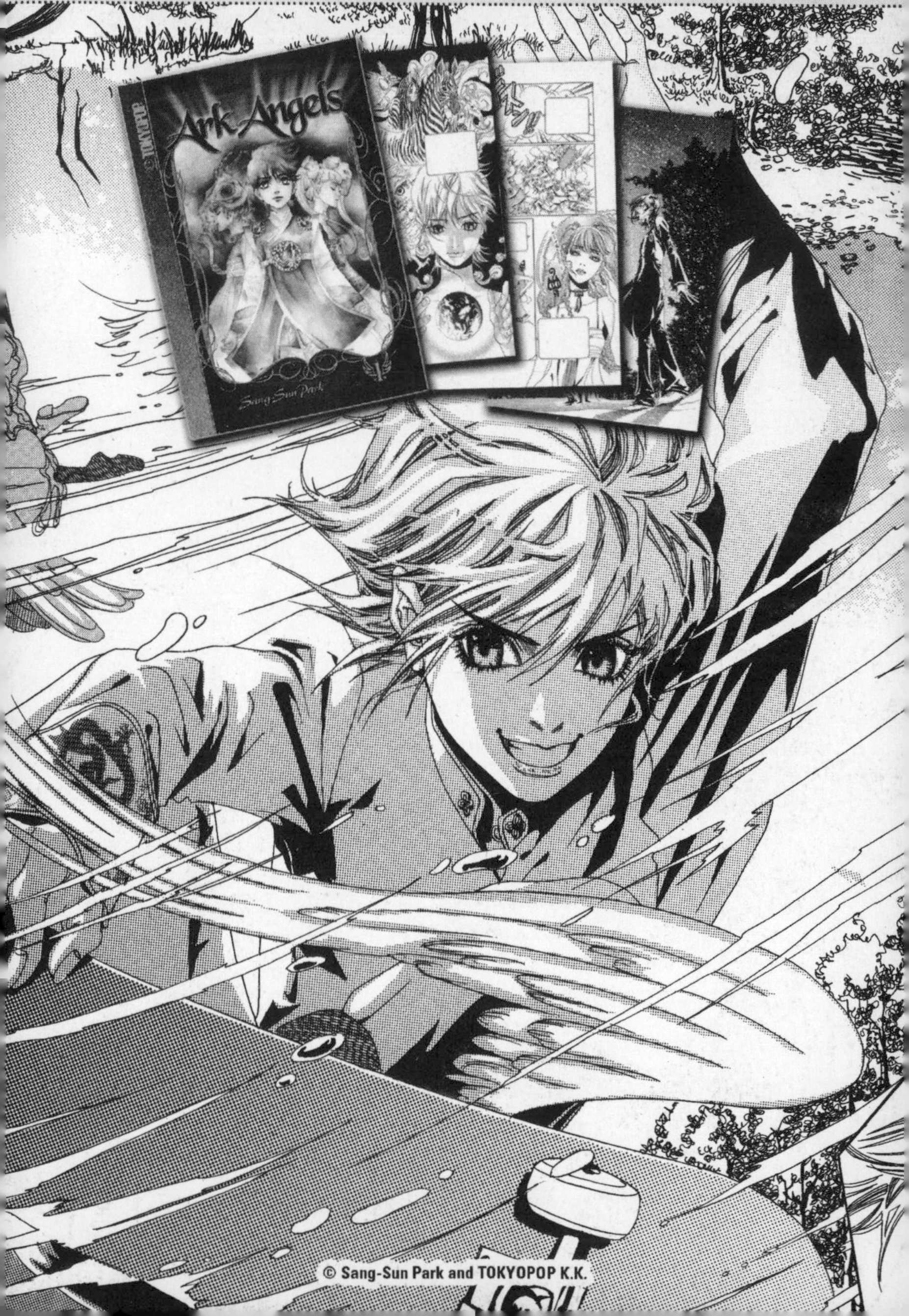
Ark Angels
Sang-Sun Park

Ark Angels

Girls just wanna have fun— while saving the world.

From a small lake nestled in a secluded forest far from the edge of town, something strange has emerged: Three young girls— Shem, Hamu and Japheth—who are sisters from another world. Equipped with magical powers, they are charged with saving all the creatures of Earth from extinction. However, there is someone or something sinister trying to stop them. And on top of trying to save our world, these sisters have to live like normal human girls: They go to school, work at a flower shop, hang out with friends and even fall in love!

FROM THE CREATOR OF THE TAROT CAFÉ!

T TEEN AGE 13+

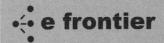

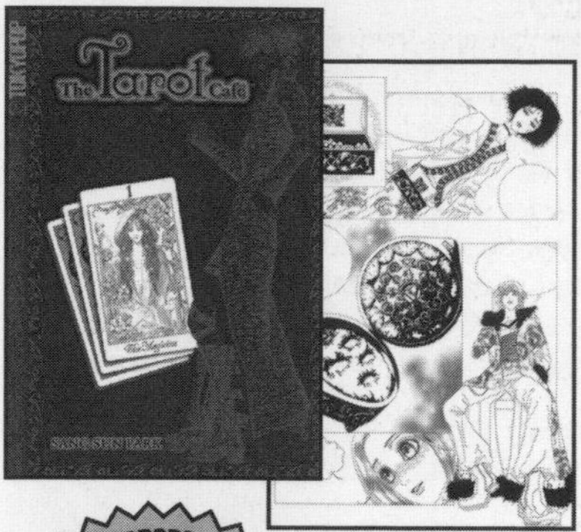
The Tarot Café
TOKYOPOP
SANG-SUN PARK

BY SANG-SUN PARK

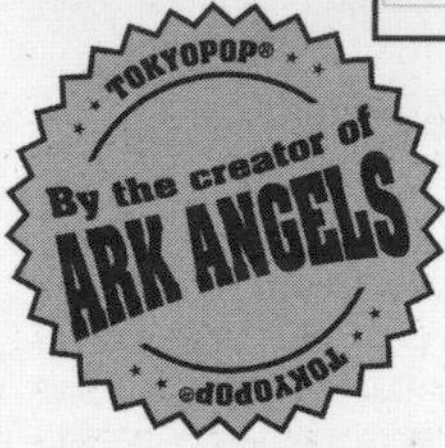
TOKYOPOP®
By the creator of
ARK ANGELS
TOKYOPOP®

THE TAROT CAFÉ

I was always kind of fond of *Petshop of Horrors,* and then along comes *The Tarot Café* and blows me away. It's like *Petshop,* but with a bishonen factor that goes through the roof and into the stratosphere! Sang-Sun Park's art is just unreal. It's beautifully detailed, all the characters are stunning and unique, and while at first the story seems to be yet another Gothy episodic piece of fluff, there is a dark side to Pamela and her powers that I can't wait to read more about. I'm a sucker for teenage werewolves, too.

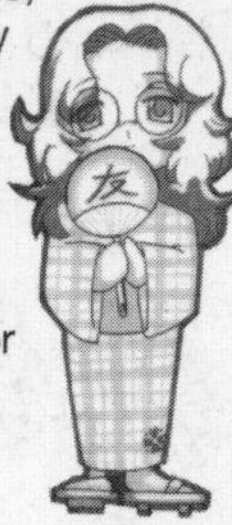

~Lillian Diaz-Pryzbyl, Editor

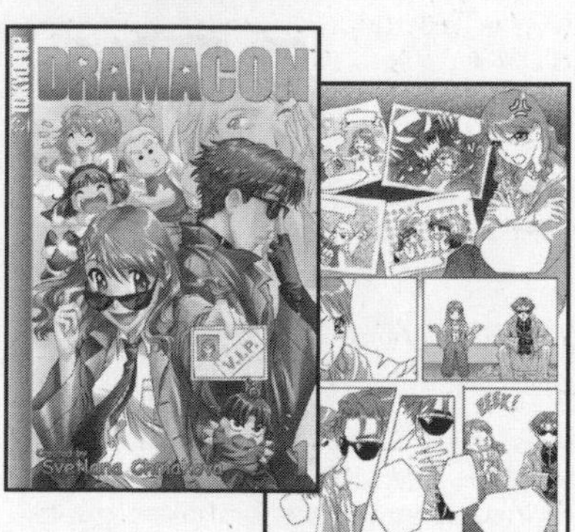
DRAMACON
TOKYOPOP
V.I.P.
Svetlana Chmakova
EEEK!

BY SVETLANA CHMAKOVA

DRAMACON

I love this manga! First of all, Svetlana is amazing. She's the artist who creates "The Adventures of CosmoGIRL!" manga feature in *CosmoGIRL!* magazine, and she totally rules. *Dramacon* is a juicy romance about a guy and a girl who meet up every year at a crazy anime convention. It grabbed me from the first panel and just wouldn't let go. If you love shojo as much as I do, this book will rock your world.

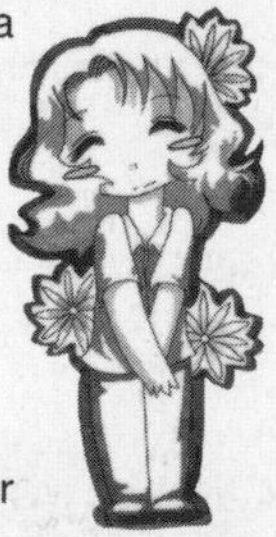

~Julie Taylor, Senior Editor

© Granger/Henderson/Salvaggio and TOKYOPOP Inc.

PSY-COMM
BY JASON HENDERSON, TONY SALVAGGIO AND SHANE GRANGER

In the not-too-distant future, war is entertainment—it is scheduled, televised and rated. It's the new opiate of the masses and its stars are the elite Psychic Commandos—Psy-Comms. Mark Leit, possibly the greatest Psy-Comm of all time, will have to face a tragedy from his past...and abandon everything his life has stood for.

War: The Ultimate Reality Show!

© Yasutaka Tsutsui, Sayaka Yamazaki

TELEPATHIC WANDERERS
BY SAYAKA YAMAZAKI AND YASUTAKA TSUTSUI

When Nanase, a beautiful young telepath, returns to her hometown, her life soon becomes more than unsettling. Using her telepathic powers, Nanase stumbles across others who possess similar abilities. On a train she meets Tsuneo, a man with psychic powers who predicts a dire future for the passengers! Will Nanase find her way to safety in time?

A sophisticated and sexy thriller from the guru of Japanese science fiction.

© Koge-Donbo

PITA-TEN OFFICIAL FAN BOOK
BY KOGE-DONBO

Koge-Donbo's lovable characters—Kotarou, Misha and Shia—are all here, illustrated in a unique, fresh style by the some of the biggest fans of the bestselling manga! Different manga-ka from Japan have added their personal touch to the romantic series. And, of course, there's a cool, original tale from Koge-Donbo, too!

Pita-Ten as you've never seen it before!

STOP!

This is the back of the book.
You wouldn't want to spoil a great ending!

This book is printed "manga-style," in the authentic Japanese right-to-left format. Since none of the artwork has been flipped or altered, readers get to experience the story just as the creator intended. You've been asking for it, so TOKYOPOP® delivered: authentic, hot-off-the-press, and far more fun!

DIRECTIONS

If this is your first time reading manga-style, here's a quick guide to help you understand how it works.

It's easy... just start in the top right panel and follow the numbers. Have fun, and look for more 100% authentic manga from TOKYOPOP®!

100% AUTHENTIC MANGA